Creating Games with Unity, Substance Painter, & Maya

Creating Games with Unity, Substance Painter, & Maya

Models, Textures, Animation, & Code

Jingtian Li, Adam Watkins,
Kassandra Arevalo, and
Matthew Tovar

CRC Press
Taylor & Francis Group
Boca Raton London New York

CRC Press is an imprint of the
Taylor & Francis Group, an **informa** business

first edition published 2021
by CRC Press
6000 Broken Sound Parkway NW, Suite 300, Boca Raton, FL
33487-2742

and by CRC Press
2 Park Square, Milton Park, Abingdon, Oxon, OX14 4RN

© 2021 Taylor & Francis Group, LLC

CRC Press is an imprint of Taylor & Francis Group, LLC

ISBN: 978-0-367-50603-2 (hbk)
ISBN: 978-0-367-50601-8 (pbk)
ISBN: 978-1-003-05049-0 (ebk)

Typeset in Myriad Pro
by codeMantra

To my parents, my sister Rui, my dog Walker,
and everyone who supported me!

– Jingtian Li

To Isaiah, Anaya, and (as always) my ravishingly beautiful
and stunningly intelligent wife, Kirsten.

– Adam Watkins

To my family and colleagues. Thank you for all the support.

– Kassandra Arevalo

Dedication to my parents, Alejandra & Manuel Tovar.

– Matthew Tovar

Contents

Acknowledgments xv
Authors xvii
Introduction xix

Chapter 1: Maya Modeling 1
    Basics of Navigation 1
    Rendering 2
    What is a 3D Model? 3
    Translation 3
    Anatomy of a Model 4
        Edge 4
        Vertex 4
        Face 4
        Object Mode 5
        Normal 5
    Modeling Rules 5
        Polycount 6
        Topology 6
        Size and Proportion 7
    Basics of Modeling 7
    Tutorial 1.1: Modeling a Security Camera 7
    Other Useful Commands 32
    Grow and Shrink Selection 32
    Extract Faces 33
    Combine and Separate 33
    Create Cables or Pipes 34
    Extrude Along a Curve 37
    Duplicate, Duplicate with Transform 38
    Duplicate Special 39
    Mirror 39
    Center Pivot 40
    Change Pivot 40
    Snapping 41
    Hide Model 41
    View Control 41
    Assignments 41
    Geometry Errors 42

Tutorial 1.2: Modular Set Pieces 43
Grid. 44
Create a Base Floor 44
Conclusion. 55

Chapter 2: Maya Set UV 57
The UV Editor 57
UV Points 59
UV Tiles 60
Cut UV 62
The Problem 62
UV the Floor 63
Texel Density. 71
Chose the Right Texel Density 72
UV the Pod. 74
Conclusion. 89

Chapter 3: Set Texturing 91
PBR 92
Baking 93
Tutorial 3.1: Texturing Modular Pieces 94
The Substance Painter UI 96
Navigation 97
Light Direction 97
Ambient Occlusion. 98
PBR Material Channels. 98
Generators. 100
Levels. 122
Assignment: Texturing the Rest of the
Models 129
Conclusion. 132

Chapter 4: Unity Asset Creation 133
Game Engines. 134
Unity 134
Tutorial 4.1: Installing Unity, Visual
Studio, and Starting a Project 136
A Bit about the Unity UI 140
Tutorial 4.2: Exporting Asset from Maya
and Substance Painter into Unity 144
Rebuilding Materials 150
Moving On…For Now 154

Tutorial 4.3: Creating Prefabs 155
A Bit about Colliders 156
Tutorial 4.4: A Bit of Material Adjustment. . . . 159
Conclusion. 169

Chapter 5: Unity Level Creation 171
A Quick Review on Snapping 172
The Long View 173
Tutorial 5.1: Level Layout. 173
Kitbashing 185
Tutorial Conclusion. 198
Tutorial 5.2: Walking Through. 199
Conclusion. 205
Post Script 206

Chapter 6: Lighting and Baking 209
What It Means for You? 211
Unity Lights. 212
Tutorial 6.1: Lighting the Scene 216
The Power of Prefabs. 219
Make Way for Cookies! 223
Baking 233
Camera Adjustments and Postprocessing. . . 236
Final Challenge 241
Conclusion. 242

Chapter 7: Character Modeling 243
Concept Art. 244
Style Sheets. 244
Workflow 245
Polycount. 245
Setting Up Image Plane in Maya 245
Eyeball. 247
Create the Eyelids 249
Create the Eye Socket 253
Forehead and Nose 256
Mouth 261
Rest of the Head 262
Ear. 264
Neck. 265
Internal Structures 267
Body. 268

Hands 274
Hairs 281
Weapon 292
Final Clean Up 295
Conclusion 297

Chapter 8: **UV Mapping.** 299
UV Mapping. 300
Tutorial 8.1: Character UV Mapping 300
Mesh Inspection and Cleanup. 300
Body UV. 302
Eye UV 308
Hair UV. 309
Garment UV 312
Conclusion 319

Chapter 9: **Character Texture Painting** 321
Skin Texturing 323
Hair 331
Eye. 333
Upper Body 340
Pants. 348
Belts, Straps, Pockets, Holster, and
Boots 353
Gloves. 354
Watch 361
Gun 363
Other Details 363
Export Textures. 365
Conclusion 367

Chapter 10: **Rigging** 369
Joint Behavior 370
Joint Placement – Hip, Spine, Neck,
and Head. 371
Tutorial 10.1: Create the Joint Chain for
Our Character 371
Joint Placement – Left Arm 374
Joint Setup – Right Arm. 382
Joint Setup – Legs 383
Foot Roll Rig. 387
Setting Up the Foot Hierarchy. 390

Tutorial 10.2: Bind and Paint Skin
Weighting 391
Painting Skin Weights 392
Mirroring the Skin Weights 397
Copying the Skin Weights 397
Tutorial 10.3: Set Up Arm Controls 400
Constrains 402
IK Arm Setup 403
Tutorial 10.4: Finger Controls 405
Tutorial 10.5: Clavicle and Body
Controls 406
Gun Joint 410
Final Hierarchy 410
Conclusion 410

Chapter 11: FPS Animation in Maya 413
FPS Animation Overview 413
Referencing the Character Rig 414
Save Files 415
Display Layers 415
Camera Configuration 418
Game Animations 420
Creating a Pose 421
Weapon Movement Simplified 422
Two-Handed Weapon Setup 424
Frame Rate 427
Idle Animation 427
Cleaning Up Odd Jitters 428
Ease-In's and Ease-Out's 429
Graph Editor 429
Keywords Aside 431
Attack Animation 431
Walk Animation 433
"Got Caught" Animation 434
Keywords Aside 436
Reload Animation 438
Considerations and Conclusion 440

Chapter 12: Auto Rigging 441
Mixamo 443
Tutorial 12.1: Mixamo-Based Auto
Rigging and MoCap 443

Substance Painter Output 450
Putting it All Together 451
Setting Up the Animator............... 454
Conclusion 464

Chapter 13: Introduction to C# 465
C#....................................... 466
C# in Unity and Visual Studio........... 470
Tutorial 13.1: Hello World! 472
Tutorial 13.2: Opening Doors........... 478
DOTween 486
Variables 489
A Final Note: Unity's API................ 498
Conclusion 500

Chapter 14: FPS Animations 501
Tutorial 14.1: First Person Animation in
Unity.................................... 502
Maya Animation Preparation............ 503
Baking Keys 503
Substance Painter Output 508
Putting It Together in Unity 510
Importing and Adjusting Animation
Rigs....................................513
Animations in Unity 514
Controlling Animations 516
Controlling Animator with Code 520
Tutorial Conclusion 531

Chapter 15: Raycasting and Render Textures 533
Tutorial 15.1: Animating the Camera..... 534
Tutorial Conclusion 544
Tutorial 15.2: Raycasting 544
Tutorial Conclusion 551
Tutorial 15.3: Camera Extras............ 553
Conclusion 560

Chapter 16: Weapons.......................... 561
Tutorial 16.1: Grenade Launcher........ 562
Making a "Smart" Grenade.............. 573
Tutorial Conclusion 581

Tutorial 16.2: Firing the Gun and
Introduction to Ammo................. 582
Tutorial Conclusion 593
Tutorial 16.3: Raycasting for Accuracy ... 593
Problem and Solution 597
Conclusion 601

Chapter 17: AI................................... 603
Tutorial 17.1: Creating an AI-Based
"Tic-Tac"............................... 605
Tutorial Conclusion 614
Tutorial 17.2: Using Animations
(Animator) with NavMesh.............. 615
Preparing FBX Animation Files 619
Placing Animations in the Animator..... 621
Changing the Triggers and Booleans
Via Script.............................. 626
Tutorial Conclusion 631
Tutorial 17.3: Animation Events and a
Working Weapon...................... 631
Creating the Function to Fire........... 632
Animation Events...................... 634
Awkward Implementation 635
Tutorial Conclusion 638
Tutorial 17.4: Assembling it all in
MainLevel............................. 639
Conclusion 642

Chapter 18: Health and Inventory 643
Tutorial 18.1: Player Health Script........ 644
Tutorial Conclusion 650
Tutorial 18.2: Building the AI Health
System 651
Tutorial Conclusion 659
Tutorial 18.3: Ammo 659
Reloading Ammo....................... 666
Conclusion 669

Chapter 19: UI................................... 671
Screen Space 672
Tutorial 19.1: Reticle, Ammo, and
Health UI.............................. 674

Health Indicator 681
Tutorial Conclusion 685
Tutorial 19.2: Using Code to Effect UI
Elements 686
Case Switches or Switch Statements. 688
Health UI 693
Tutorial Conclusion 695
Tutorial 19.3: Buttons and Moving
between Scenes. 696
Interactive Buttons 701
Tying Up Some Loose Ends 705
Conclusion 708

Chapter 20: Boss Battle. 709
Tutorial 20.1: Final Boss. 710
Boss Health Bar. 722
Final Theatrics. 725
Conclusion 731

Index 733

Acknowledgments

It takes the effort and support of many people to finish a book like this. We would like to say special thanks to everyone who contributed to this book.

The work of Matthew Tovar and Kassandra Arevalo and their careful additions to the rigging and animation chapters make this a better book. And, of course, the monumental undertaking of Jingtian Li and his indominable spirit in creating monster sections of this book is stunning to behold. If you're lucky, someday you'll work will colleagues as good as these.

Adam Watkins

Authors

Jingtian Li is a graduate of China's Central Academy of Fine Arts and New York's School of Visual Arts, where he earned an MFA in Computer Art. He currently is an Assistant Professor of 3D Animation & Game Design at the University of the Incarnate Word in San Antonio, Texas.

Adam Watkins is a 20-year veteran of 3D education. He holds an MFA in 3D Animation and a BFA in Theatre Arts from Utah State University. He currently is the Coordinator and Professor of the 3D Animation & Game Department at the University of the Incarnate Word in San Antonio, Texas.

Kassandra Arevalo is an instructor of 3D Animation & Game Design at the University of the Incarnate Word in San Antonio, Texas. She previously worked as an animator at Immersed Games.

Matthew Tovar is an industry veteran animator. He has worked at Naughty Dog, Infinity Ward, and Sony Interactive on such games as The Last of Us, Call of Duty: Modern Warfare, and, most recently, Marvel's Avengers with Crystal Dynamics. He is an Assistant Professor of 3D Animation at the University of the Incarnate Word in San Antonio, Texas.

Introduction

Making a game of their own is always the dream of many people since they are teenagers. As new technology emerges, that dream becomes more and more accessible each year. There is an exponential growth of game releases over the last decade. About 10,000 games were released on Steam in 2019, and around 1000 games per day were released on mobile devices.

One of the reasons that more games are coming out is because there are more and better tools to make them. To name a few, with the release of game engines like Unreal Engine, Unity, and many other free game engines, making games is within the reach of everyone. The competition between the game engine developers pushes them to implement new features every year, and we have seen a burst of improvements to the tools.

Outside of the game engines, new developments are happening in every corner of the game industry. Software like the Substance Suite solve the texturing process in innovative ways. Newer generations of hardware like Nvidia RTX and PlayStation 5 push real-time rendering to new heights. And new categories of devices like Oculus Rift, Steam VR, Microsoft Hololens are pioneering new user experiences. To add on top of that, services like Quixel Megascan and Adobe Mixamo are providing libraries of reusable assets that significantly improve productivity.

It is the best time than ever before for anyone who wants to dip into a game development journey. However, making a game is never an easy task. It requires all kinds of talents to put together a working game that has amazing visuals, engaging gameplay, immersive audio, and an overall well-balanced system. There are many sources you can learn different ingredients of game development, but fewer sources explain the whole recipe. This book is dedicated to cover the entire process of making a game, from making assets to programming, and all the way to package a complete game.

Who's It For?

This book is designed for beginners who want to start their game development journey and are unsure where to start and which direction to go. As the reader, you are going to jump into a well-organized learning track that guides you through all aspects of game development. It also shields you from noises and focuses on the fundamentals, which gives you a solid foundation and able to branch out to nitty-gritty details without losing the whole picture.

For any game enthusiasts and students, this book is a perfect fit to get started with game development. For teachers, this book offers a well-structured solution for your curriculum. For anyone who wants to utilize the game engine for interactive products, this book covers the skill you need extensively as well.

What Does this Book Cover?

This book covers all aspect of game development that includes but is not limited to the following.

Environment Modeling

Environment modeling is the process of making 3D models for environments. We are going to cover what is a 3D model, how to make them, and how to optimize them for your game.

Character Modeling

Character modeling is the process of making 3D characters. We will cover how to approach organic shapes with additional modeling methods.

UV Mapping

We are going to learn how to create a 2D coordinate of a 3D model to map textures to the model. The process is called UV Mapping.

Texturing

Texturing is the process of defining the color and all other aspects of the appearance of the model.

Rigging

Rigging is a technical skill to add skeleton and controllers to animate the character.

Character Animation

We are going to cover the techniques and theories to animate characters.

Game Engine Lighting and Baking

We are going to practice workflows on lighting an environment, which includes how lights work in the game engine, and technical details of baking the lighting.

Game Programming

We are going to cover programming languages, theory, and practices to create gameplay.

We will also explore audio and VFX solutions, and many other small details you need to know to create a game. At the end of this book, you should have everything you need under your belt to start making your next awesome game!

Final Notes

It is critical to point out that game development is time-consuming. Please dedicate your energy and time to the learning process, and don't easily give up on any obstacles. With the internet at your fingertip, you can find solutions for just about anything.

It is also important to acknowledge that tools change all the time, and you should always learn new stuff and explore new ideas. Please take away the theories we cover in this book but don't be religious of the tools we use.

The chapters are built so that the reader can jump into this book where they would like. Don't care about modeling? Don't do those chapters. Never want to code? Definitely steer clear of those. Notice that all the chapters will reference support files that can be downloaded to assist your work in the chapters. In many cases, just grab the support files from the chapter preceding the one you're about to start, and that's the perfect place to start the chapter at.

However, if you're tough…really tough. Start this book at the beginning and work your way all the way through and you will have created a game from beginning to end!

Alrighty, we know you are tired of reading introductions, and many people jump over it. It is time that we start this fantastic journey and start making some awesome games!

Adam Watkins and Jingtian Li
May 9, 2020
San Antonio, TX, USA

CHAPTER 1

Maya Modeling

We will jump into the production by discussing modeling. 3D models are the foundation of the graphics of modern games. They encompass the environment and characters you see on the screen. An eye-catching visual is one of the key components for a game to succeed. In this chapter, we will discuss in detail about how they are built.

Basics of Navigation

Autodesk Maya will be our tool of choice for modeling. It is not the best modeling tool on the market, but it is the most used over the entire production pipeline, especially

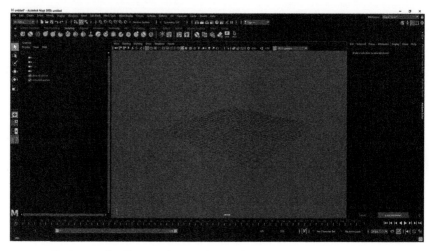

FIGURE 1.1 Maya's user interface. The origin is the area at the center of the grid.

for animation. So, let us get Maya up and running on your machine. The UI (user interface) will look like Figure 1.1. The large region in the middle of the UI is the viewport; this is where we see our models. It is currently empty, with just a grid in the middle to indicate the center of the world. The center of this grid is called the origin.

To Navigate around the viewport, hold down Alt key and drag the left-mouse button to look around the viewport. To zoom in and out, hold down the Alt key and drag the right-mouse button. To pan left and right, hold down the Alt key and drag the middle-mouse button.

A 3D space has width, height, and depth, each represented on three axes called the X, Y, and Z axes. The lower left corner of the viewport shows the directions of these axes.

Rendering

The shape is drawn by the Graphic API, but the lighting is calculated by the Fragment Shader written by the game engine programmer. It is a complicated process, and we do not have to understand the details and math behind it. It is enough to know that the *renderer* is the tool drawing whatever you see on screen. Maya's interactive renderer (that shows you what is currently in your scene) is called Viewport 2.0.

What is a 3D Model?

In the menus, go to Create->Polygon Primitives->Plane. This will create a shape in the middle of the viewport. On the right side of the UI, look for the Channel Box. This is a brief list of essential attributes we can tweak for the object. Under the INPUTS section, click on the polyPlane1 to open it and change the Subdivisions Width and Subdivisions Height to 1 to make the plane only one polygon (sometimes called a "face").

What we are seeing now is the building block of any model – a face with four corners that we typically call a rectangle in geometry classes; in 3D graphic terms, we call this a *quad*. Any complicated shape can be composed by assembling many quads together to create 3D forms.

Translation

On the right side of the UI, there is a column of manipulation tools. You can try and use the Q, W, E, and R buttons to switch between these tools: Q for the select tool, W for the move tool, E for the rotation tool, R for the scale tool.

To select the model, simply left-click on it or drag a selection box over it. To deselect the model, click in the empty space, or hold down Ctrl and click on the model, or drag a selection box over it.

To move the model, after selecting it, hit the W button. This will display new handles (called gizmos) that will allow you to move the object. Try dragging the various arrows to move it only along a particular axis. Look carefully at the gizmo, and you will see squares that can be dragged to move it along two axes at the same time; you can even drag the cyan square in the middle to move it freely along all axes in the 3D space.

To rotate the model, after selecting it, hit the E button, drag the circles on the gizmo to rotate it around different axes. You can also drag the yellow one on the outside to rotate it around a plane that is perpendicular to the angle of the viewport.

To scale the model, hit the R button, and drag the various boxes to scale it along their respective axes. You can also drag the various squares to scale it along two axes at the same time; you can even drag the yellow box in the middle to scale it up along all axes, essentially making it bigger.

There are more tricks about this sort of manipulation that we will cover later on when we jump into modeling.

Anatomy of a Model

Edge

Hold down the right mouse button on the model, and you will see a pop-up menu we call a *Marking Menu*. Here, we can see various parts of the form we can switch to. With the marking menu active, slide up and chose Edge; the four edges around the face now appear to be in a lighter blue color. You can click on any of the edges to select them. When an edge is selected, it will be highlighted with orange color. Once selected, you can change to the Move tool (hit W on the keyboard) and drag the three arrows to move the edge along the respective direction.

Vertex

You can also hold the right mouse button again and chose Vertex. Four purple points will show up on the corner of this face. These are the vertices where edges meet. You can click to select any of them and move them around just like how you can move an edge.

Face

Hold down the right mouse button again and chose Face; you can now select the face and move it around as well.

Edge, Vertex, and Face are the three important elements of any 3D form's polygons. We can add and tweak these elements to create any shape we want.

Object Mode

Hold down the right mouse button again. This time, we chose Object Mode. This will allow us to move the model altogether. Object, Vertex, Edge, and Face are the primary modes we keep switching between while making a model.

Normal

Use the alt-left, -middle, and/or -right mouse drag to rotate your camera to look at the bottom of the face. You can see it appears to be black. Any face in 3D has a front side and a back side. The front side will appear normal, while the back side will be black or invisible (depending on the rendering engine). Maya makes the back of the face black in the default setting. To view this, using the top menus find Display->Polygons->Face Normals.

Press the Q button to switch to the select mode to get rid of the Move tool handles. We can now see a green line sticking out from the front face of the model. In general, the front of the polygon should face outwards. It is possible though to render both sides of the face. Consider a situation like rendering a piece of paper. Here we would definitely want both sides of the polygons seen, but otherwise we want to avoid rendering both sides, if possible, to avoid performance overhead. Since games have to draw many frames each second, we want to always ensure that we aren't drawing anything we don't need to (Figure 1.2).

Modeling Rules

Before we start modeling anything, let's talk about a few important rules when modeling for games.

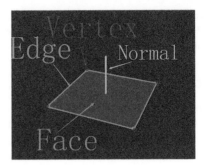

FIGURE 1.2 The elements and normal direction of the quad.

Polycount

Each of those four-sided faces we looked at earlier can be triangulated into two triangular polygons. We typically use the number of *triangles* of a model as the number for polycount, even we use quads to make a model. The reason we use the number of triangles instead of quads is because a triangle is guaranteed to be a flat surface, while this is not guaranteed for a geometric figure with more than three vertices. Thus, the rendering process uses triangles as the basic rendering unit. Fewer polygons means your game is easier to run (less data); so find the balance of including the needed number of polygons to describe a shape, but not extras.

Topology

Topology is how the faces are laid out on the model. Use quads if possible, because quads have a strong sense of directionality and are easy to represent shape evolution and deformation. We want the flow of the quads to represent the change of the surface. Figure 1.3 shows how topology is critical for deforming a face. The loops of faces around the orbicularis muscle, nasolabial fold, and orbicularis oris create an essential structure to support the facial expression. Long story short, topology is for the purpose of better representing the shape of the model and supporting the deformation for animation.

FIGURE 1.3 Effective topology (the flow of polygons) is critical to support the deformation that will come later in animation.

Size and Proportion

Size is a critical aspect in 3D modeling, no matter how detailed a model is. If the size or proportion is off, the model will never look right. In Maya, the default unit is a centimeter. This is the unit across many popular programs including Maya, Unreal Engine, Blender, etc. Other software, like Unity, use the meter as the default unit, but converting between the two scales is an easy math. One should always check sizes and dimensions to ensure things will work with physics simulation, rendering, and animation; for example, if you are modeling a staircase, then you have to know that the general height of a stair is around 18 cm and the depth is 28 cm. Converting to the right scale as you move assets from Maya to your game engine is trivial, but focus on building assets in Maya at the correct scale for its unit size (centimeters by default).

Basics of Modeling

We will jump into modeling right away and introduce various tools along the way. Keep in mind that the only way to improve is to practice; there is no shortcut to get better.

Tutorial 1.1: Modeling a Security Camera

> Step 1: Basic Shape. Choose Create->Polygon Primitives->Cube. This will create a cube at the origin. This cube is also referred to as box by 3D artists. In fact, what we are doing now has a nickname called box modeling.

Tips and Tricks

In Maya, with nothing selected, you can hold down the Shift+right mouse button to pull up a type of menu called a *marking menu*. If you do this in the Viewport where there is no other object, the marking menu that will show up allows for the creation of new object. You can use this to create a cube in the same way as Create->Polygon Primitives->Cube. Learning shortcuts like this will drastically improve your modeling speed.

Step 2: Dimension. With a bit of research, you will find that a common security camera is about 18 cm long, 10 cm high, and 10 cm wide. Make sure that the box is selected and look to the right side of the UI. In the Channel Box (Figure 1.4),

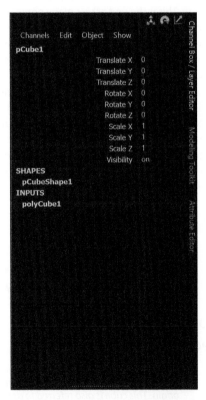

FIGURE 1.4 The Channel Box is at the top right of the Maya UI and allows you to change the position, rotation, and scale of a selected object.

change the Scale X and Scale Y to 10 and change the Scale Z to 18 (Figure 1.5).

Step 3: We are making a camera that looks like the one in Figure 1.6; one of the major differences between our box and the image is that the camera's corners are rounded.

Switch to edge mode (right-click and hold on the box, and choose Edge from the marking menu). Select the four edges across the length of the box (seen in Figure 1.7). Go to Edit Mesh->Bevel or press Ctrl + B to bevel these edges. This operation splits the edge you are selecting

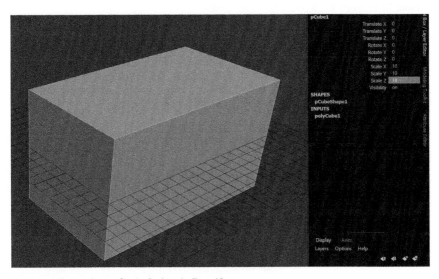

FIGURE 1.5 Adjusting the size of a cube (box) via the Channel Box.

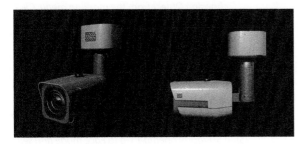

FIGURE 1.6 Our target camera.

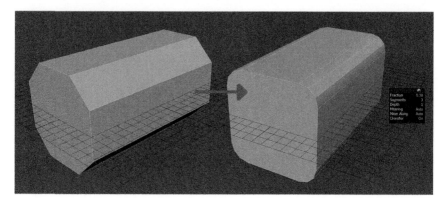

FIGURE 1.7 Using the bevel tool to round the edges of our cube.

to multiple ones. To round off these new edges, look for the pop-up menu (labeled polyBevel1) and change the Segments value to 3. Change the Fraction to 0.38 to shrink the distance between the newly beveled edges.

Tips and Tricks

To select the four edges, you can rotate the camera view to look at the side of the box, and then drag a section box over these four edges. Alternatively, you can select one of them, hold down the Shift button, and double-click the next one. Maya will select all edges that are between the same loop of faces; we call this selection of edges an edge ring.

Step 4: Soften edge. Swap out of Edge mode into Object mode by right-clicking (and hold) and choosing Object from the marking menu. Click in an empty space in the viewport to deselect the rounded cube. See a harsh line on the rounded-out corner? This is due to that edge being "hard." To soften it, swap to Edge mode and then select that edge and hold down the Shift button and double-click the next one to select the entire edge ring. Use Mesh Display->Soften Edge to make all the lines of this ring a soft edge (Figure 1.8).

Step 5: Frontal opening. Go to Face mode and select the front face of the camera. Go to Edit Mesh->

FIGURE 1.8 Softening the edges.

Extrude, or hold Ctrl + E to extrude the face.
This creates another segment right at the faces
we selected. Press the R button to switch to the
Scale tool. Drag the yellow box in the middle
of the Scale tool to scale the new face down to
make the thickness of the shell. Take a closer
look, and you can see the left and right contour
of the opening is rounded. With the Scale tool,
scale with just the red box handle (it will turn
yellow when you are using it) to scale the face
down across the X axis. Once done, we do
not need this in the middle anymore, so press
the delete button on the keyboard to delete it
(Figure 1.9).

Step 6: Add Curvature to the side edges. To round the
contour, we need more geometry. Go to Mesh
Tools->Multi Cut. Hold down Ctrl, and hover the
cursor on the side edge. Maya will give a preview
of the edges that will be created if you click the
mouse. Before clicking though, hold down the
Shift button, to snap where the previewed ring
will be created. This preview will snap every 10%
across the length of this edge. Move the cursor
until the preview lands at the middle of the edge,
and click to finish adding the new subdivisions

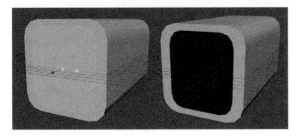

FIGURE 1.9 Using the Extrude tool to create an opening at the front of the camera.

(new edges). These edges have their tip and end connected. We call this kind of line an edge loop. Repeat and add the same edge loop on the other side (Figure 1.10).

Step 7: Turn on symmetry. Modeling is time-consuming, so we want to save time if possible. To do this, we can turn on symmetry, so we do not have to manually add the edge loop on the other side. The setting is located on the second row of buttons (Figure 1.11). By default, the setting is at Symmetry: Off. Click on the drop-down arrow on the right and choose Object X to toggle symmetry on across the X axis (Figure 1.11). After toggling symmetry on, selecting and performing commands on one side of the geometry will affect the other side.

Step 8: Add Curvature to the camera opening. Double-click on any edge of the edge loops we created in Step 6 to select the entire edge loop. Press Ctrl + B to bevel the edge loop and change the Segments to 2. Go to Vertex mode (right-click and hold on the shape, and choose Vertex from

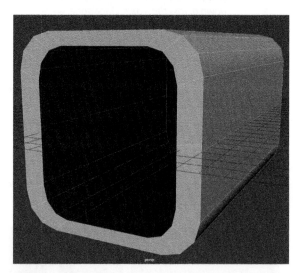

FIGURE 1.10 Added edge loops on either side of the camera chassis.

FIGURE 1.11 Turning symmetry on to allow us to mirror our modeling work.

the marking menu) and select the vertex in the middle on the edge of the hole. Use the Move tool (W) to drag it away from the center a little. Select the vertex above the middle vertex, hold down shift, and click on the vertex below the middle vertex to add it to the selection. Drag them also away from the center. Work your way around the opening and adjust the vertices until you get a proper curvature for the side (Figure 1.12).

Step 9: Extrude the inner face. Double-click on any edge of the hole to select the edge loop around the hole. Hold down shift and left-mouse-button and drag the loop inward a little; this is a quick shortcut to extrude a new ring of polygons. Select the edge ring along the newly extruded edge and hold down the Shift + right mouse button. In the resulting pop-up menu, select Soften/Harden Edges->Soften Edge; this will make the inner edges soft. This command is the same command in the Mesh Display-> Soften Edge. Hit the R button to switch to the Scale tool. Hold down Shift again and drag the yellow box in the middle to extrude a new small ring of polygons. Switch to Move tool, hold down shift and drag the new edge ring toward the back of the form to fill out the inside (Figure 1.13).

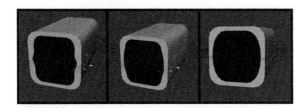

FIGURE 1.12 Using Vertex mode and symmetry to adjust the opening to create a round opening.

FIGURE 1.13 Using the Extrude tool (Shift–drag) to create polygons for the inside of the form.

Tips and Tricks

Shift + right mouse button is a very common shortcut. Basically, it will pull up tools or commands to the current element you have selected. If nothing is selected, doing this will pull up a wide selection of primitive polygons. Almost all commands we need can be found in this pop-up marking menu.

Step 10: Camera lens. Click in some empty area of the Viewport to deselect the camera body. With nothing selected, hold down the Shift + right mouse button and chose Cylinder. Go to the Channel box and set the Rotate X to 90. This will rotate the cylinder 90 degrees in X and lay the cylinder down. Scale and move the cylinder so that it is roughly the size of the lens of the Camera.

Step 11: Lens frontal rims. Switch to Vertex mode. Select the vertex at the center of the front faces, hold down the Ctrl + right-mouse button, and in the resulting pop-up marking menu, chose To Faces->To Faces. This will select all faces that share this vertex. Turn off the symmetry (remember up in the second row of the interface). Press R to go to the Scale tool and hold down the Shift button and drag the yellow box to extrude the face in. Using the Move tool, hold down the Shift button and drag the face back in; keep on extruding with Scale and Move tools to create all the rims of the lens (Figure 1.14).

Step 12: Bevel the rim. Select the harsh edge loops on the rims of the lens (remember, you can do this by double-clicking on an edge while in Edge mode) and press Ctrl + B to bevel them. Select all the edges in the front of the lens, do a Soften edge command to soften the edge of the lens (Figure 1.15).

Step 13: Curvature of the lens. Select the vertex at the center of the lens. Hold down Ctrl + right mouse button and chose To Faces->To Faces. Switch to the Scale tool and hold down the Shift button while you drag the yellow box to extrude the faces down to about half of the original size. Use the Move tool to drag the faces forward a little. Grab the vertex at the center again and move it forward a bit more. Select the edge loop around the center vertex and press Ctrl + B to bevel it. This will give us the curvature we need for the

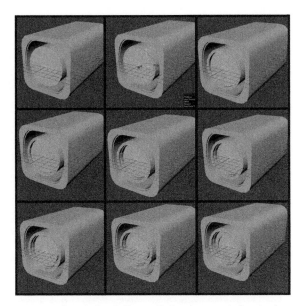

FIGURE 1.14 Using the Extrude, Move, and Scale tools to create the front rim of the lens.

FIGURE 1.15 Beveling and softening the edges to create the rim of the front lens.

lens. Finally, soften the edge loops we created to make the lens feel smooth (Figure 1.16).

Step 14: Clean up history. Maya remembers everything we've done and stores this in the Input stack under the Channel Box (Figure 1.17).

15

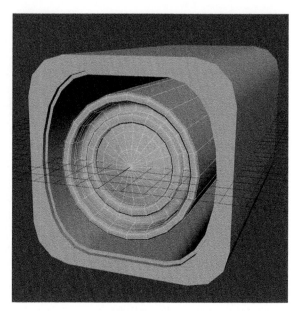

FIGURE 1.16 Finishing off the lens by adding curvature to the glass portion.

Go to Object mode and drag a big selection box to select both the shell and the lens of the camera. Go to Edit->Delete by Type->History to clean up the history. This will make all the construction history disappear (the shortcut for this operation is Alt + Shift + D). It is important to delete the history of the model regularly to ensure the model is stable and the scene is not getting heavier and heavier.

Step 15: Outer shell. Select the outer layer of faces of the lens that we made from a box. To do this, go to Face mode and grab one of the faces that goes across the depth of the model. Hold down Shift and double-click the next one to grab the whole loop across the depth of the model. Hold down Shift + right-mouse button and chose Duplicate Faces. Dragging the arrow that is facing away of the face that the arrows are sitting on, this Duplicate Faces command creates a new model from the faces selected. This allows you to shift the faces away so we can easily create a shell (Figure 1.18).

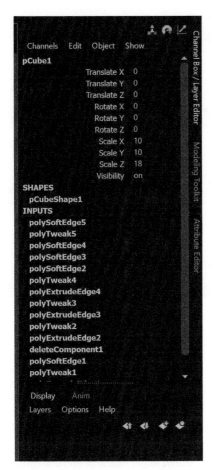

FIGURE 1.17 The Input stack of the Channel Box. This shows the History of steps created thus far.

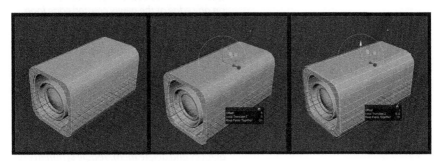

FIGURE 1.18 Creating a shell by duplicating faces.

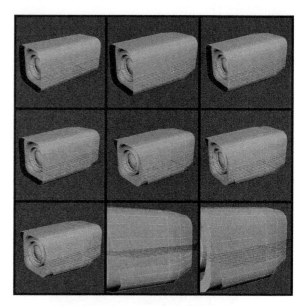

FIGURE 1.19 Try and follow this visual guide to tweak the shape to match the research.

Step 16: Tweak the shape. Figure 1.19 shows a sequence of steps using the techniques introduced in earlier steps. Try following the images to match the shape.

If you need help, the steps are: Grab the Outer shell we created in Step 15 and use the Scale tool to stretch it longer. Hold down Shift + right mouse button and chose Multi Cut. Hold down Ctrl and click to add an edge loop closer to the back end of the shell. Press Q to switch to selection tool and double-click on any edge of the newly created edge loop to select the whole loop. Scale this loop up and drag it slight down to create the wider portion of the shell. Add another loop closer to the front of the shell. With this loop still selected, press E to switch to the Rotate tool. Hold down Ctrl + Shift and rotate the loop to tilt it forward. (Note: you can see how the edge is constrained on the surface of the model when rotating, which is great to create the tilted frontal shape.) Select the front loop of faces and delete them. Toggle symmetry on and add edge loops to mark out the edge of the opening in the middle of the shell. Select the corresponding faces and delete them. Add an edge loop really close to the edge where the seam between the upper and lower shells is. Finally, delete the face loop in-between to open the seam.

Step 17: Upper shell hole. Add an edge loop at the center of the model. Then select the new loop, press Ctrl+B to bevel it and change the fraction to 0.32. Switch to Move tool and use the Ctrl+Shift trick to slide the edge in the center forward to mark the front edge of the opening. If you are not sure if the face is gone or not, you can go to Object mode and grab the shell and press Ctrl+1 to isolate it. You can press Ctrl+1 to toggle the isolation (Figure 1.20).

Step 18: Add thickness. Grab all the faces of the model (using Face mode and either double-clicking on any polygon or marquee-selecting). Press Ctrl+E and drag the arrow to extrude the faces out to add the thickness.

Step 19: Back arm. Create a cube. Move and scale it to create the basic shape of the back arm. Add an edge loop in the middle and bevel it to give it curvature. Don't forget to smooth the edges of the rounded back (Figure 1.21).

Step 20: Connect back arm. Grab the back arm and the inner shell of the camera. Go to Mesh->

FIGURE 1.20 Creating an upper shell hole, and finally isolating just the shell.

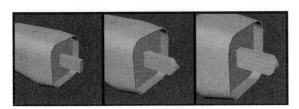

FIGURE 1.21 Creating the back arm by creating a simple cube, adding new edge loops, and tweaking those to create the desired shape.

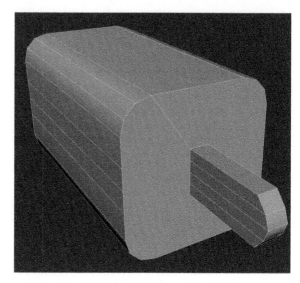

FIGURE 1.22 Using Booleans (Union) to merge two shapes together into one.

Booleans->Union. This will combine the selected meshes, blast out the overlapped part, and fuse the contact surface (Figure 1.22).

Step 21: Fix N-Gon. An N-Gon is any face with more than four edges. This can be a problem in 3D because it is unclear how the face should be divided into triangles for the rendering process. This can sometimes yield undesired output at the time of rendering. So it's best to rebuild N-Gons to either four-sided polygons (quads) or triangles. The big back face is a typical N-Gon. Switch to Multi Cut tool, and click and drag on one of the outer edges until it stops at one vertex. Click and drag on one of the inner edges until it hits another vertex. Maya will connect these two vertices with a new edge. Press the G button to commit the current operation and re-initiate the same tool again. Keep clicking and dragging to connect lines until there are no N-Gon anymore (Figure 1.23).

Why?

Notice that we had to end up with some triangles, and this is totally fine; otherwise, we need to add new edge loops

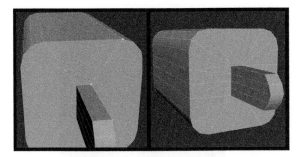

FIGURE 1.23 Using the Multi Cut tool to create new edges to rebuild the N-Gon into three- or four-sided polygons.

to the rest of the body, which takes more performance, and the render result will be the same.

Tips and Tricks

Click on the Modeling Toolkit button (Figure 1.24) on the right edge of the UI to switch to the Modeling Toolkit. Under the Tools section, you can also see Multi Cut. Click on it to toggle it on, and various settings of the tool will appear underneath. Scroll all the way down and open the Keyboard/Mouse Shortcuts section. You can see how versatile this tool is. Experiment with these different shortcuts to speed your workflow.

> Step 22: Base. Create a cube, set the Scale X and Scale Z of the box to 13, and set the Scale Y to 8. Grab the vertical edge of the cubes and press Ctrl + B to bevel them. Change the Fraction to 0.62 and Segments to 3. Move it to the back of the camera body and drag it higher (Figure 1.25).
>
> Step 23: Base bottom shell. Select the bottom face and extrude it down. Scale the new faces down to match Figure 1.26. Next, go to Multi Cut tool, and in the Modeling Toolkit, toggle on Edge flow under the Cut/Insert Edge Loop Tool section. Add an edge loop to the middle of the newly extruded segment. In Figure 1.26, you can see how edge flow automatically added the curvature.
>
> Step 24: Base bottom arm. Grab the bottom face again. Hold down the Shift + right mouse button and choose Circularize Components. This will round the shape up to a perfect circle.

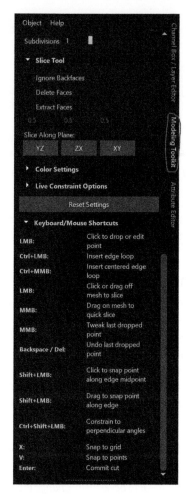

FIGURE 1.24 The Modeling Toolkit can provide faster ways to work with advanced modeling tools.

Unfortunately, it is tilted, but we can fix this by changing the Twist value to make it straight again. Extrude the face in the center down to create the length of the arm. Using the same technique used in Step 23, we can create a small rounded bottom for the arm. Finally, use the Multi Cut tool to fix the N-Gon (Figure 1.27).
Step 25: Create the arm bending socket edge. Select the edges across the bottom of the arm and press the R button to switch to Scale tool. This time,

FIGURE 1.25 Using the same techniques covered above to create the base of the camera.

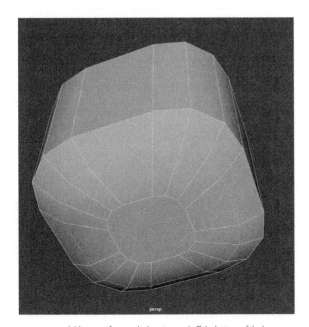

FIGURE 1.26 Adding new faces and edges to round off the bottom of the base.

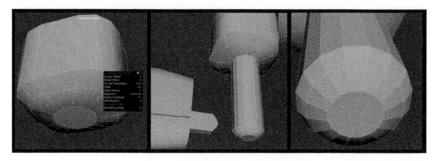

FIGURE 1.27 Creating the bottom arm and cleaning up the topology to eliminate N-Gons.

on the left side of the UI, look for the column of buttons we call the Toolbox. Try pressing Q, W, E, and R and you can see how to switch between these tools with the keyboard shortcuts. Double-click on the button that is highlighted when you press R to pull out the Scale tool settings. Check the Prevent Negative Scale option. Scale the lines on the X axis until they are flattened (they will not overshoot). Switch to Move tool and hold down the V button to turn on Vertex Snapping. While you are holding down the V button, drag the arrow of the move tool along the X axis (red-cone gizmo) and move your cursor to the point lying on the outer rim of the handle to snap the flattened line to that point only on the X axis. Do the same thing on the other side. Add another loop around the length of the handle to mark out the upper edge of the opening socket. What we are trying to achieve here is to mark the opening edge of the socket. The opening of the socket is highlighted in the last figure of Figure 1.28.

FIGURE 1.28 Building out the bottom of the arm using a few new tricks in each tool's options.

Tips and Tricks

Ctrl + Shift + right mouse button will also pull up the settings of the current tool. You can find the Prevent Negative Scale setting if you press R and then hold down the Ctrl + Shift + right mouse button. To quickly select part of a loop, select the beginning of the part of the loop and hold down Shift and double-click on the end of the part of the loop. This trick works on face loops, edge loops, and edge rings.

> *Step 26: Opening the socket. Delete the faces highlighted in the last figure of Figure 1.28. Grab the bottom edges and extrude them up. Scale them on the Y axis to flatten them. Switch to the Move tool and hold down V while dragging the edges up to snap the edges to the upper corner of the opening. Do not change the selection and hold down Shift + right mouse button and select the Bridge tool from the marking menu. This will bridge the two loops with faces. This command requires an equal number of polygons on the two loops (Figure 1.29).*
>
> *Step 27: Merge vertices. Select the edge on the upper corner of the opening and move it just a little bit in any direction. Notice that there are two vertices overlapping instead of one merged vertex (Figure 1.30); this creates a tear in the mesh.*
>
> *To fix it, we need to merge these vertices together. Press Ctrl + Z to undo the moving of the vertex. Then hold down Ctrl + Shift and drag over the two overlapping points to select both. Check to ensure that you are not*

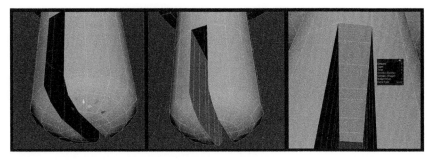

FIGURE 1.29 Creating the notch of the arm by deleting faces, extruding edges, and bridging.

FIGURE 1.30 Our previous steps have created a form with holes in the mesh.

selecting anything else on the back of the form. You can choose Edit Mesh->Merge to merge these two vertices to one single vertex. Alternatively, you can hold down Shift+right mouse button and select Merge Vertices, but this time, the Marking Menu will show a nested sub-menu. We just keep dragging up to select Merge Vertices to Center.

Step 28: Shrink and attach the camera to the base. Grab the faces of the back arm of the camera body and scale it up or down to make the size fit with the opening of the base. Move the base to attach the arm with the socket (Figure 1.31).

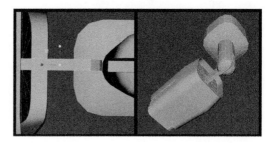

FIGURE 1.31 Scaling the faces of the back of the camera to fit the mounting base.

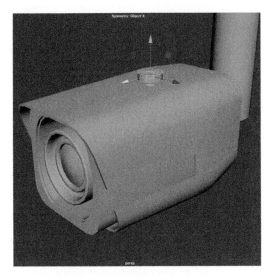

FIGURE 1.32 Roughing out the switch at the top using a cylinder.

> Step 29: Top switch. Create a cylinder (Create->
> Polygon Primitives->Cylinder). Move and scale
> it to the opening of the top shell of the camera.
> In the input section of the Channel box, click on
> the polyCylinder1 and change the Subdivision
> Axis to 12 (Figure 1.32).

Why?

We made the Subdivision Axis smaller to lower the
polycount of the little top switch. It is such a small part
that we do not need the same number of loops as the
lens. In games, polycount is important, and trimming
away those we don't need as we work will generate
cumulative benefits in the long run.

> Step 30: Reduce polycount. It is always possible to
> reduce polycount of a model to save a little bit of
> performance. Go to Display->Heads Up Display
> and check on Poly Count. You can see on the
> upper left corner of the viewport that we have
> 1736 Tris in total. There are two ways we can
> reduce polycount:
> 1. Delete edge loops that seems
>   unnecessary. Grab the outer shell of

the camera, select the edge loop in the middle, and hold down Shift+right mouse button and chose Delete Edge. Notice that there is no difference in the form after deleting it. Similar cleanups are shown in Figure 1.33.

2. If a loop cannot be completely deleted, triangulate parts of the loop. We clearly need no extra edge loop for the top flat surface of the outer shell, but we have two for the purpose of opening a hole on the top. To fix this, go to Object mode and hold down Shift+right mouse button and select Target Weld Tool. Click and drag the vertex in the middle area of the upper edge of the shell to the point next to it to weld it to that vertex. Using this technique, we can weld a lot of points without affecting the shape of the model. We may end up with some triangles, but it is totally fine for most non-deforming

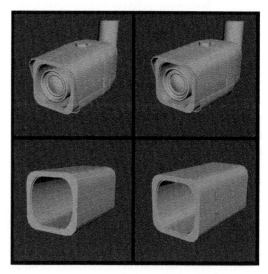

FIGURE 1.33 Strategically deleting unnecessary edges reduces our polycount without sacrificing form.

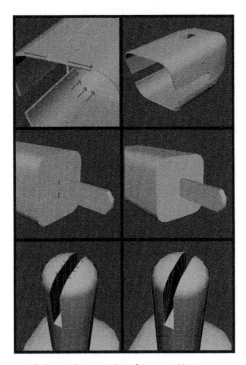

FIGURE 1.34 Reducing polycounts with careful vertex welding.

(not bending) forms, especially for a game model. Similar reducing results are shown in Figure 1.34.

Keep in mind that you still want to avoid too many triangles; triangles are harder to manage for the UV process (an important part of the texture process that we'll cover later), and they make it harder to do high-resolution sculpting (if you need to do so for complex forms including organic shapes). You can always consult the supervisors of your team to get their suggestions on the polycount if you do work for a studio. The final polycount after these optimizations is 1494 tris for our camera.

Tips and Tricks

The Delete Edge command should be what you use all the time to get rid of edges. The delete button on the keyboard does delete the edges but not delete the vertices on the edge, which means that when the renderer triangulates, it still produces the extra triangles from those left-over points.

> *Step 31: Clean up. On the top of the base, there is a big, flat N-Gon. Grab that top face and extrude it in. Hold down the Shift + right mouse button and select Merge Faces To Center. Select all models we created, press Alt + Shift + D to delete all the history. Finally, do a Modify->Freeze Transformation to clean up the transform.*

Why?

You may wonder what this Freezes Transformation does. Well, in Maya, a model has two primary components: transform and shape. Transform governs where the model is, how it is tilted, and how it is scaled; these are reflected in the translate, rotate, and scale values in the Channel Box. Shape governs the vertices, faces, and edges and how they are combined together to form the shape of the model; the final appearance of the model is the shape of the model moved, rotated, and scaled by the transform of the model. If you do recall, we have scaled the outer shell of the camera, and that scale value will appear in the Channel Box; freeze transform will clean that up and bake the scale we did to the transform of the model to the shape of the model. Many processes later (Rigging, UV Mapping) do require the transform of the model to be baked to the shape of the model through Freeze Transformation so that the final look of the model is the actual shape instead of a shape getting scaled, rotated, and moved by a transform.

> *Step 32: Naming and organization. On the left side of the UI, there is a pallet with a tab called Outliner; this is a list of the currently existing objects in the scene. Select anything in the*

viewport and you can also see it highlighted in the list of the Outliner. Alternatively, you can also select an object by clicking its name in the outliner. In the Outliner, you can hold down Shift to select multiple objects or hold down Ctrl to deselect.

Tips and Tricks

If you cannot see the Outliner, go to the column of buttons where we have the Move, Rotate, and Scale tools; the last button in that column is the toggle to show or hide the Outliner.

Select everything in the viewport in Object mode and press Ctrl+G to place them into a group. Something called group1 will appear in the outliner. This is a group (really a parent object). You can press the plus sign in front of it to open the group and see the children models inside of it. Double-click to rename any object there. For now, rename the group to security_cam_geo_grp. Spend some time renaming all other objects; the final naming is shown in Figure 1.35.

security_cam_switch_geo	
security_cam_outer_shell_geo	
security_cam_inner_shell_geo	
security_cam_len_geo	
security_cam_base_geo	

FIGURE 1.35 Names to use in naming the shapes build so far.

Tips and Tricks

Anything inside of a group will follow the group. You can now grab the group in the outliner and move the whole collection of shapes. You can put any object or objects under a group by grabbing the objects first and selecting the group last and pressing the P button on the keyboard. This is also something we call parenting. If you select something inside of a group and press Shift+P, this will get the object or objects out of the group (called unparenting). You can also parent one object to another object instead of a group. In the outliner, you can click the middle mouse button to drag anything around or drag one object to another to parent one object under another.

> *Step 33: Clean up the outliner. We do not need any other objects in the scene; there could be other empty groups in the outliner due to some operations we did to the model. We can grab anything outside of security_cam_geo_grp and delete them. Alternatively, we can go to File->Optimize Scene Size and let Maya clean these up for us.*
>
> *Step 34: Save the file. Go to File->Save Scene, in the pop-up Save window, change the File name to game_set_models, navigate to a folder that is safe and easy to find, and press the Save button to save it.*

Other Useful Commands

We have introduced some of the most important commands for modeling. Let's start a new scene and go over a few more before we do some assignments.

Grow and Shrink Selection

Create a sphere (Create->Polygon Primitives->Sphere) and select the top vertex. Hold down Ctrl+right mouse button and choose To Faces->To Faces to select the top faces. Hold down Ctrl+right mouse button again and chose Grow Selection->Grow to select all the direct neighbor faces. Press the G button three times to redo Grow Selection three more times. You can also find Shrink Selection in the Ctrl+right mouse button marking menu.

Extract Faces

With the top four rows of faces selected, hold down Shift+right mouse button, and choose Extract Faces. Drag the blue arrow to shift the face away; you can now see how Maya separated the model into two objects. Notice that in the outliner, you can see the pSphere1 becomes a group, and there are two objects inside of it. That transform1 is the remaining construction history that you can use Delete History to get rid of.

Combine and Separate

Some commands, like Bridge, can only be used for component on the same object. So to bridge the upper shell with the lower shell (Figure 1.36), you have

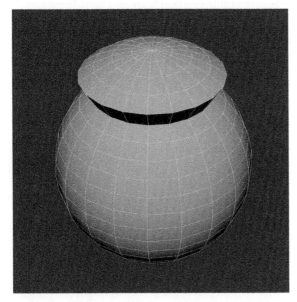

FIGURE 1.36 In order to bridge collections of polygons like this, you first must ensure that the polygons are parts of the same single object.

to combine the models together into one object. To combine models, grab all models you want to combine and use Mesh->Combine. By the way, you can also see the Separate command right below Combine. Separate will separate the model into multiple ones based on their connectivity.

Create Cables or Pipes

From time to time, we may want to create a cable or a pipe. Go to Create->Curve Tools->CV Curve Tool, and click and drag in the viewport to drop down a CV point. Click and drag again to add a new one; keep doing this and you will see a curve getting created. You can hit backspace to roll back and drag the middle mouse button to refine a placed CV point. When you are happy with the shape, hit Enter to finish the creation (Figure 1.37).

CV stands for Control Vertices. Maya will interpolate between the vertices to form a curve. This type of model is called NURBS, which uses mathematical interpolations between control vertices to create a form. These are fundamentally different from the camera model (polygon) we created earlier.

After creating the curve, you can still edit it by holding the right mouse button on it and choosing Control Vertex. Then you can move the CV to refine the shape as desired. The curve will be created on the grid by default. You can go to the front, top, or side view to create your curve

FIGURE 1.37 Using the CV Curve Tool to create a series of CVs that define a curve.

so that the curve snaps to the grid of that view. Go to Create->NURBS Primitives->Circle to create a circle. Grab the circle and the curve created previously, and go to Surfaces->Extrude☐ (be sure to click the square to pull up the Extrude Options window). There, change the Result position setting to "At path" and change the Pivot setting to "Component". Press the Extrude button, and you will see that a tube is created (Figure 1.38). This Extrude is not the same Extrude we did with polygons; it basically places the circle along the curve to create a frame and then interpolate a shape out of it.

You can scale the nurbsCricle1 to change the radius of the tube, and you can still tweak the shape of curve1 to change the shape of the tube (Figure 1.39).

However, this tube is not a polygon or polygon-based (which we will need for games). So to convert it into a polygon-based form, go to Modify->Convert->NURBS to Polygons☐. Change the tessellation method to "Control points". Press the Tessellate button to convert the tube to a polygon (Figure 1.40).

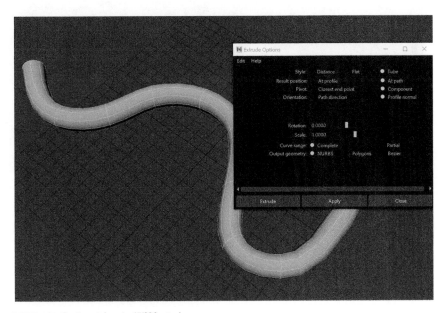

FIGURE 1.38 Creating a tube using NURBS extrude.

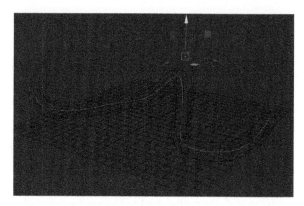

FIGURE 1.39 Once a NURBS form is created, the form can be adjusted by editing the curves used to create it.

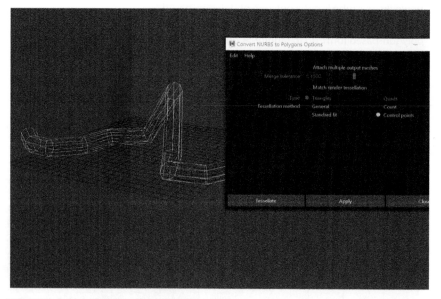

FIGURE 1.40 Tessellated NURBS form that is now a polygonal object.

Until now, you can still tweak the curves to change the radius and the shape of the curve. When you are happy with the form, select the polygonal shape and delete the history and delete all curves and the original NURBS surface as they're no longer needed.

Tips and Tricks

If, at any time, the tube model appears black, you can rotate the circle on the X axis until it flips back to normal. NURBS curves and surfaces are a different type of model that are mathematically interpolated between the control points we created. They are primarily used for architectural or industrial design. Most times, we don't use this type of model in game scenarios. However, they can be very useful to construct a form originally (that we then convert into polygons).

Extrude Along a Curve

Another variant of creating a tube is to create a curve in front of a face and then extrude that face along the curve. To do this, select both the face and the curve (Figure 1.41), and press Ctrl + E.

In the pop-up dialog boxes, increase the number of the Divisions setting to create a smooth extrusion along the curve (Figure 1.42). If the extrusion is backwards, you can grab the curve, do a Curves->Reverse Direction to fix it.

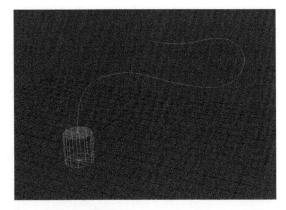

FIGURE 1.41 Extruding along a curve.

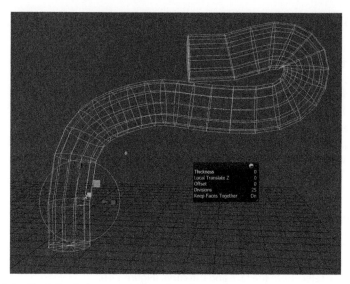

FIGURE 1.42 Tweaking the Extrude along curve options to get the resolution you desire.

Duplicate, Duplicate with Transform

You can grab any model and press Ctrl+D to duplicate it. The duplicated model will be at the same location as the original (although you'll see the name of the new form in the Outliner). Right after duplicating, you can use the Move tool to move the new duplicate away (Figure 1.43).

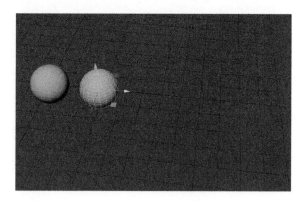

FIGURE 1.43 Duplicate allows for a quick copy of an original.

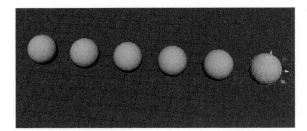

FIGURE 1.44 Duplicate with Transform (Shift + D) duplicates and transforms (moves) the object in the same command.

If you want to create another duplicate and have it move the same distance (or rotate the same amount), you can press Shift + D. You can keep pressing Shift + D to have multiple duplications, each offset the same amount as last time (Figure 1.44).

Duplicate Special

From time to time, we may want to create multiple duplications but as *instances*. An instance is a copy that keeps the link of the shapes between the original and the copy; we can adjust any one of the duplications to update the shape of all others (but not transform). Grab your model and go to Edit->Duplicate Special□. Change the Geometry type to "Instance". Change the first number of the Translate to 2 (the X axis), and the Number of copies to "10". Finally, press the Duplicate Special button, and you will see ten duplications of your model, each two units away from each other, and more importantly, editing any one of them will affect all others (Figure 1.45).

Mirror

Anytime you forget to have symmetry on and want to make the model symmetrical again, you can select the model in Object mode and do a Mesh->Mirror. Try different axes and directions to make sure you got the correct side mirrored. The merge threshold should be as low as 0.001 if you wish to only have the vertex in the center mirrored. You can also change the Border setting

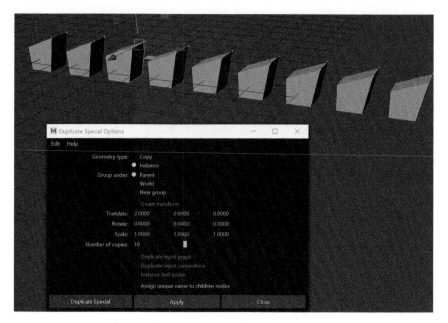

FIGURE 1.45 Using instances (as opposed to copies) to make copies of an object that will change when the original is manipulated.

to bridge or do not merge the geometry along the axis of symmetry to have a different result.

Center Pivot

You can grab any model in Object mode and do a Modify->Center Pivot; this will move the pivot of the model to the center of its bounding box. The Pivot is the location where the object is rotating around. It is needed whenever you want to be able to rotate or scale a model from its geometrical center.

Change Pivot

In any mode, you can hold down the D button on the keyboard and drag the gizmo to adjust the location or orientation of your pivot; you can also click on any elements on the model to snap your pivot to that element.

A good example that we want to do this is to change the pivot of the body of the camera to the hinge of the arm so that we can rotate it around the hinge.

Snapping

When moving an object or its various elements, you can hold down the X button to snap to the grid and V button to snap to vertices. The snapping toggles are on the Status line, which is the row of buttons under the main menu. The snap toggles are the six buttons with a magnet in their icon. Try these toggles and see what they do.

Hide Model

You can grab any model or its other elements and press Ctrl+H to hide them. To unhide, press Ctrl+Shift+H; this will only unhide the object you are selecting (probably in the Outliner) if you have something selected. It will unhide everything if you have nothing selected. After making a model, name it properly, freeze transformation, and hide it so you can move on to the next one without the other models blocking your view.

View Control

At any time, if your cursor is in the Viewport, you can press the spacebar to go to the Four View layout, and this will show you the Top, Perspective, Front, and Side views; you can then move the cursor to any view, and press the spacebar to maximize that view. However, we recommend to just hold down space and drag up, down, left, and right to go to these views.

Assignments

We have covered enough commands that you are now able to create models of your own; go ahead and start modeling some of your own models in Maya,

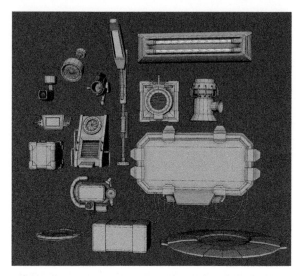

FIGURE 1.46 A selection of props that can be built using the techniques covered in this chapter.

and make sure you find references and get the correct measurement. Figure 1.46 shows a few examples of what we are looking for.

Geometry Errors

Sometimes in the modeling process, some errors can emerge. These errors might not even be readily visible in your model, but without fixing them, you can run into some serious problems later in a game engine. While these can be pretty technical, and the hard-core specifics are a bit outside the scope of this book, it's worthwhile to talk about them for a minute and – more importantly – evaluate how to fix them. Here are some typical geometry errors that we can now check on your model:

> **Non-Manifold Geometry**. *This geometry cannot be unfolded and flattened to a 2D surface. Typically, there is an edge shared by more than two faces or inconsistent normal directions. This type of model will confuse the renderer on which side is the outside of the geometry.*

Lamina Faces. *Two faces that share all of their edges. Typically, this is caused by duplicating and combining meshes that have the same faces.*
Zero Length Edge. *A self-descriptive situation in which an edge has no length.*
N-Gon. *We have covered N-Gon already; any face with more than four sides is a N-Gon.*

Luckily, even though the theory behind these errors is abstract, fixing them is usually pretty easy. To clean up the models, go to Mesh->Cleanup□. Under the Fix by Tessellation section, check on "Faces with more than 4 sides". Under Remove Geometry, check on "Lamina faces and Nonmanifold geometry". Press the Cleanup button; this will, in theory, clean up all the errors. Maya may choose to delete some of the faces because they are error geometries; make sure you check around the model and recreate any missing models.

Tutorial 1.2: Modular Set Pieces

Making a compelling and complex environment is a daunting task. To ease the pain, we are going to adapt to a modular workflow. This means we will make reusable pieces that are easy to combine with each other, like a system like Lego building blocks. The props we have made previously as assignments are already designed for that purpose, but to make the foundation of our game level, we need a more unified system. This means we need to have a chart of sizes that our models will have to exactly match, so they can be assembled seamlessly.

There are two size systems we can use: decimal and binary.

> *For decimal, we will have sizes like 10, 20, 30, 50, 100…*
> *For binary, we will have sizes like 16, 32, 64, 128, 256, 512… (both in cm)*

Both systems are popular, and we are going to follow the binary system. The author has found that it is easier to combine modules seamlessly and easier to match with textures sizes, which is also binary.

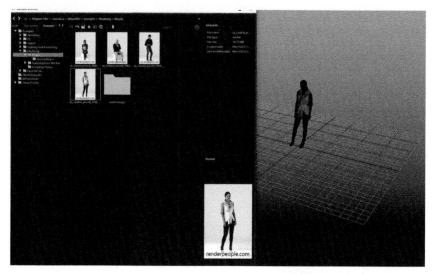

FIGURE 1.47 Setting up our grid to build modularly. The person acts as a size and scale reference.

Grid

Go to Display->Grid☐. Set the Length and width to 256, and set the Grid lines to 64 and Subdivisions to 4. Drag the slider of Grid lines and numbers to make it a blue color and press Apply and Close. This will create a grid that has its edge 256 cm away from the center and a blue grid line every 64 cm with four extra divisions in-between every blue grid line, which makes every grid 16 cm long.

To verify our sizes, go to Windows->General Editors-> Content Brower. Under the examples category on the left side of the window, choose Modeling->People. Drag a standing character to the viewport to import the human model; the height of the model should be slightly shorter than half of the grid length (Figure 1.47). If your character appears gray, hit 6 on your keyboard to have Maya show the materials as well.

Create a Base Floor

Step 1: Base floor dimension. Let's hide our other models, so we can start our new model with nothing else visible. Create a cube, set its

FIGURE 1.48 Creating and snapping the first-floor module to our grid.

Translate Y to −8, set its Scale X and Scale Z to 256, and set its Scale Y to 16. Switch to the Move tool and hold down both D and V buttons, and drag the pivot of the box to the upper corner on the negative X and Z quadrant. Release all the buttons. Now, hold down X button and drag the center of the gizmo to snap the model to the positive X and Z quadrant (Figure 1.48).

Why?

We want the model to be easily snapped together. Positioning the pivot to the corner of the box is extremely helpful for the snapping. We also want the pivot to be at the center of the world to avoid any offset.

Step 2: Floor edge trim. To help in adding trims to the side of the floor, grab the top face, and press Ctrl + E. Set the Offset setting to 16. This will give us a rim on the outside of the floor (Figure 1.49). Name this model floor_01 and hide it.

We are now done with this module. Every time we finish a module model, we can name it, hide it, and move on to the next one. This way, all of our models are created in one Maya file for easy access. This also allows us to maintain the scale of our game. We are not planning on making a whole lot of models for our environment, so keeping them all in one scene file is manageable. But if you'd rather, you are more than welcome to create new files for extra models instead. But be sure you

FIGURE 1.49 Creating the base trim of the module using Extrude.

maintain consistent Grid settings across the various scenes if you do so.

Step 3: Base wall dimension. Create a cube and set its Scale X to 256, Scale Y to 512, and Scale Z to 32. Snap its pivot to the lower back corner and then move it to the center of the grid (Figure 1.50).

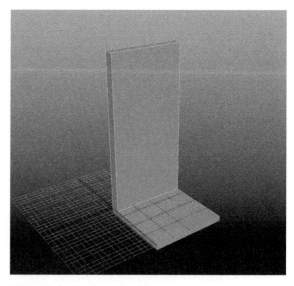

FIGURE 1.50 Creating a base wall module.

Step 4: Add bottom trim. Add an edge loop toward the bottom of the wall module. Extrude out the bottom face and move the top edge of the extruded face down to create a bottom trim (Figure 1.51); name this model wall_01.

Step 5: Arch wall. Follow the steps of Figure 1.52. Create a pipe (Create->Polygon Primitive->Pipe). Under the Input section of the Channel Box, click on polyPipe1 and set the Radius to 128, Height to 512, and Thickness to 32. Set the Rotate Z of the model to −90. Delete the frontal and bottom

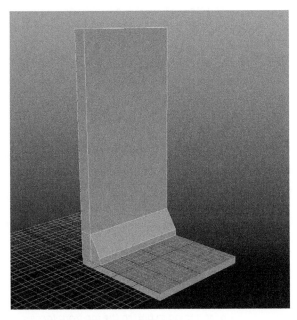

FIGURE 1.51 Creating trim for our wall_01.

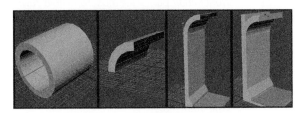

FIGURE 1.52 Creating the arched top of the wall by combining a pipe segment.

quarters of the pipe. Next, hold down D and V, and snap the pivot of the pipe to its back side corner. Hold down V and snap the pipe to the top of the wall we created in the previous two steps. Duplicate the wall and delete its top face. Combine it with the pipe by selecting both the wall and pipe and choosing Mesh->Combine. Grab the vertices of the pipe and the top of the wall and while holding down X drag them down until the top of the pipe is the same height as the height of the original wall. You can go to the side view to check out the alignment. Grab all the vertices and hold down Shift + right mouse button, go up and up again (or choose Edit Mesh->Merge). This will merge the vertices between the top of the wall and the bottom of the pipe. Double-click on one of the edges of the hole in front of the pipe and hold down Shift + right mouse button. Choose "Fill hole". Name this model wall_02.

Tips and Tricks

Step 5 has many steps, but the idea is simple. We want an arch on the top of the wall. Whenever we need something complex, we can break it up to smaller primitives. When we create these primitives, we can snap them together, combine them, and merge the vertices.

Step 6: Wall frame. Copy the arch wall we created and move its pivot to the origin. Change its Scale X to 0.25. Grab the front faces and press Ctrl + E. Change the Local Translate Z of the extrude to 16. Extrude the same amount again, but this time, scale the faces in on the X axis to create a little taper. Use scale or snapping to flatten the top front faces (Figure 1.53).

Step 7: Wall frame detail. Grab the faces in the front middle part of the model and hold down Shift + right mouse button and chose Duplicate Faces. Set the Local Translate Z to 16. Grab the bottom vertices and drag them up. Bridge the bottom edges and bevel the primary turning edges. This will give us extra volume; you can create additional ones to make the model more complex (Figure 1.54). Name this model wall_frame_01.

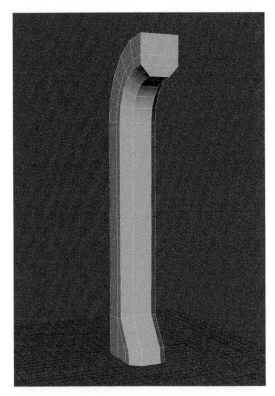

FIGURE 1.53 Creating a tapered wall section.

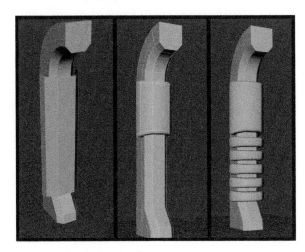

FIGURE 1.54 Extra detail on the walls.

Tips and Tricks

Always name and clean up your models when you have finished them. Your future self will thank you for making everything clean and tidy.

Step 8: Wall corner. We can create rounded corners for our rounded walls for when walls meet as we assemble them. Duplicate and snap our modules like the first figure in Figure 1.55. You can hold down the J button while rotating to snap your rotation for every 5 degrees. It is important that the modules are snapped to each other exactly. Have one blue (64 units) grid gap between the two hallways or corridors and the turning portion of the floor. This is to ensure that there is space for the rounded transition part.

Moving on to the second figure of Figure 1.55, select these two walls of the turning point, duplicate (Ctrl+D) them, and combine (Mesh->Combine) them. Grab the two columns of the faces that will connect to the turning portion. Hold down Shift+right mouse button and chose Bridge Faces. The result may look messy, so change the division to 7, and Curve type to Blend. The resulting middle part is going to be our turning module; delete the extra ones on the side and bridge the holes on the side to finish it. The outer corner is done the same way.

Step 9: Floor variations. Create a few varying sizes for the floor, like the gap we need to fill for

FIGURE 1.55 Creating a transition part for an outer corner.

the turning of the corridor we did for Step 4 (Figure 1.56). The sizes we choose to use are: 256×256×32, 256×128×32, 256×64×32.

Step 10: Stair frame. Create a cube and set the Scale X, Y and Z to 256. Snap its pivot to the back lower left corner and snap the cube to sit at the positive quadrant. Move (and snap) its bottom and top row of vertices to make a tilted frame for the stairs. Its bounding box length is 6×64 units (six blue grids). The footing of the shaft is 64 units, and the thickness of the shaft is 16 units (one gray grid). The results look like Figure 1.57.

Step 11: Stairs. Duplicate the stair frame to create the other side. Snap the duplication so that their whole width together is 256 units. Create a box, make its Scale X 32, Scale Y 8, and Scale Z 200. Move it to the first stairs location. It should be around 18 units high. Bevel all the edges of the box, and extrude from the two side faces to make the connection to the frame. Bevel the bottom edge of the frame to add a little detail. Fix the N-Gon after the bevel. Finally, bevel the edges of the frame (Figure 1.58).

Step 12: Stair handrail. Go to Create->Curve Tools-> CV Curve Tool; we have covered this tool

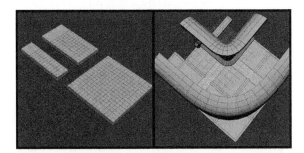

FIGURE 1.56 Creating other modular parts for floors.

FIGURE 1.57 Building the stairs. Note that for modularity to work, the exact positions of the snapped vertices are important.

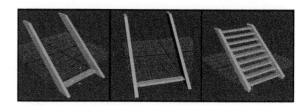

FIGURE 1.58 Creating the stair steps.

previously in the part about extruding along a curve. Use the Curve tool to create the profile of the handrail. Take care to make sure you have enough points on the arcing part; the amount of points you place will determine how many segments you will have on the final polygon shape. Use Extrude along curve techniques to create the handrail. Addition columns can be created using cylinders (Figure 1.59). Remember: be sure to covert the NURBS form into polygons.

Step 13: Other modular pieces. Other modular pieces are made with the same techniques covered previously; here is a list of all the pieces modeled:

Walls *– There are three walls, five wall frames, and some random small blocks. The size of the tall ones is 256×512 with a thickness of 32 (Figure 1.60).*

Arcs *– These arcs are having a radius of 256 units and a thickness of 32; an outside arc,*

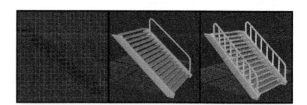

FIGURE 1.59 Creating the handrail using NURBS techniques.

FIGURE 1.60 Completed wall modules.

a wall, and a wall bottom trim are also built
(Figure 1.61).

Floor – Floors with 256×256×32, 256×128×32,
256×64×32 are built to create hallways with
different sizes. Two grid modules are also built
(Figure 1.62).

Pipes – Pipes came with three sizes, each with
a radius of 16, 8, and 4. Be sure to build some
turning structures to support complicated
combination (Figure 1.63).

Stairs – We have two stairs, a higher one with
a 256 units elevation and a lower one with a
64 units elevation. Handrails were also built
to support variations (Figure 1.64).

Windows – Window came in four sizes:
256×128×32, 128×128×32, 512×512×256,
96×64×160 (Figure 1.65).

There are 57 modular pieces. It is hard to
determine how many are needed, so it is wise
to build less and try creating a hallway or a
room and see if more modules are needed.

FIGURE 1.61 Completed arc modules.

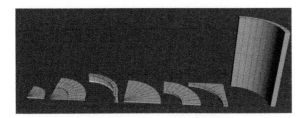

FIGURE 1.62 Completed floor modules.

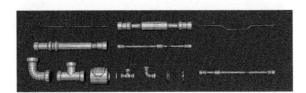

FIGURE 1.63 Collection of completed pipe modules.

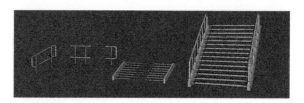

FIGURE 1.64 Stair modules.

FIGURE 1.65 A variety of finished window modules.

Step 14: Hero assets. Hero assets are the assets that we only use a few times and so might need a bit of extra care and detail. We will create two hero assets for the final scene; the creation process of these hero assets is tedious, expect to spend a lot of time on them and have a higher polycount on these assets. But even though the fidelity might be higher for these assets, the tools and commands used to create them are no more than what we have covered (Figure 1.66).

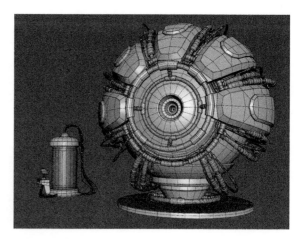

FIGURE 1.66 Hero assets.

Conclusion

We have finished the environment modeling part of our games. Well, of course, we've only created the individualized separated pieces; currently they aren't a level...yet. However, we will move them to the game engine and assemble them into our awesome level later. However, before we do that, we still need to go through UV mapping and Texturing so that our models are not white ghosts.

If you are able to complete these forms in this chapter, you're in good shape. If it is overwhelming and you'd rather move onto other stages, these completed models are available on the support website.

We will move on to the UV Mapping of our assets in the next chapter.

CHAPTER 2

Maya Set UV

UV Mapping is a pretty tricky concept for beginners but quite straightforward after you grasp the essence. It is a 2D coordinate to map a 2D image to the surface of the 3D model. Let us start with creating UVs for our first and simplest modular asset, the 256×256 floor piece (Figure 2.1).

The UV Editor

Go to the Workspace at the top right corner of the UI, and in the drop-down list, choose UV Editing; the viewport now splits into two windows. The UV Editor on the right is

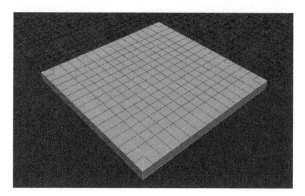

FIGURE 2.1 The 256 by 256 floor piece.

the place we edit our UVs. You can hold down Alt + middle mouse button to pan the view and Alt + right mouse button to zoom in or out. On the right of that window, we can also see a UV Toolkit panel, which contains many useful tools and commands to edit UV.

Select our floor piece; inside the UV Editor, you can see a blue shell that looks like an inverted T, this is the default UV of a cube. If you do recall, we started with a cube (if it is not blue, move the cursor to the UV Editor and press the number 5 button). Click on the checker icon at the row of buttons on top of the UI in the UV Editor. You can now see a checker texture getting displayed in both the UV Editor and on our model in the viewport (Figure 2.2).

Select the top face of the floor, and you can see how a face in the UV Editor is also highlighted. That face in the UV Editor is the UV of the top face of our 3D model. Go to the UV editor, press W to switch to move tool, and move this face in the UV editor to the U letter on the checker texture. You should also see the U letter appearing on the 3D model (Figure 2.3).

This face-to-face match is how UV works. UV is a 2D representation of the 3D model; it defines how an image can be mapped to the surface of the model. UV is also like a flattened shell of the 3D model if you will. This checker is a convenient way to preview how our UV maps texture on our model.

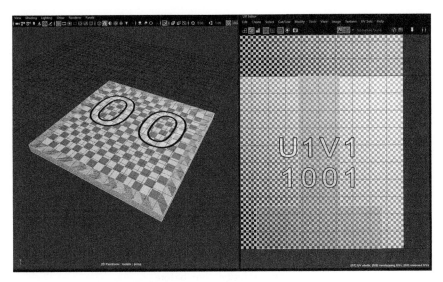

FIGURE 2.2 Check the UVs with the checker texture.

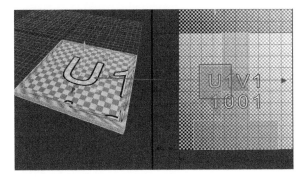

FIGURE 2.3 Make the letter U appear on the model by moving the UV.

UV Points

Other than edge, face, and vertex, there is a fourth
element called UV points. These UV points are a reference
to a vertex in 3D in the UV space, and they are the building
blocks of the UV of the model. Go to the UV Editor, hold
down the right mouse button, and chose UV. You can
now select UV points, and you can move, scale, and
rotate them around just like vertices in the UV Editor.

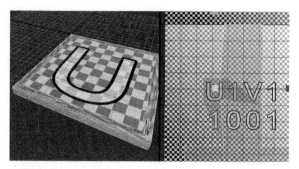

FIGURE 2.4 Scale the UV down to make the letter U look bigger than before.

Moving UV points affects the shape of the UV and affects the mapping of the textures. Figure 2.4 shows how scaling down the UVs of the top face down makes the letter U appear bigger than before.

UV Tiles

The checker texture has U1V1 1001 written on it, and this is the UV tile name. Pan the UV editor up, and you can see U1V2 1011 above U1V1 1001. This U1V2 1011 square area is just another UV tile. Hold down the right mouse button in the UV Editor and chose UV; drag a big selection box to select all the UV points. Press the W button to switch to the Move tool, and drag the UVs to the positive, X direction. You can see now Maya places more checker textures to the tiles your UV is overlapping with (Figure 2.5).

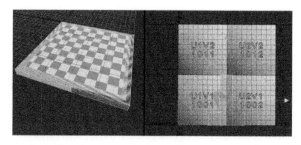

FIGURE 2.5 Maya places more checker textures to the tiles your UV is overlapping.

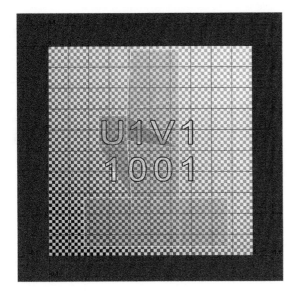

FIGURE 2.6 Maya shows only U1V1 1001 if all UVs are inside of the U1V1 tile.

In many modern renderers like Redshift, Octane, Arnold, or V-Ray, UV tiles can be used to apply multiple textures to one model. Every tile can receive a unique texture, but for our game engines, this feature is not supported. We have to ensure that all of our UVs are placed inside the U1V1 tile. You can grab all the UVs again and move them back and scale them down. You know they are all inside of U1V1 when Maya only shows one checker with U1V1 1001 on it (Figure 2.6).

Tips and Tricks

You are probably wondering what "U1V1, U2V2..." and "1001, 1002..." mean; they are essentially different UV tile naming conventions that different texturing software adapt. U1V1 is a system ZBrush uses. ZBrush is a sculpting software that allows artists to sculpt more detail on the surface of the model. 1001 is first used by Mari, a super-high-end texture software designed to create textures for movies. The texturing software we are going to use later is Substance Painter, which also adapts the 1001 system.

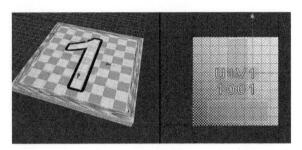

FIGURE 2.7 Cutting edges of the UV detach the face from the rest of the UV.

Cut UV

Select all the edges of the top face and go to the UV Editor. Hold down Shift + right mouse button (Remember that in the previous chapter, we talked about how this short cut will bring up the commands suited for the elements we are selecting), and chose Cut. You can now see these edges appearing thicker; switch to face mode and select the top face. Move the face around in the UV Editor. You can see how it is detached from the rest of the UV. You can now move it freely without affecting the UVs of other faces (Figure 2.7).

Try to select one of the edges of the detached UV and move it in the UV Editor; you can see how another edge also moves. This is because they are the same edge on the actual 3D model. In other words, they are two references of the same edge. UV points are also references of vertices, and sometimes they reference the same vertex.

The Problem

Looking at the checker texture mapped to our model, you can immediately see the outer frame of our model has a super-stretched texture. This stretching effect is due to the UV of these faces not being laid out correctly. We want all UVs of all faces to be flattened with the correct proportion and not overlapping with each other. We often don't rely on the default UV. Now, let's start creating the UV of our floor from scratch.

UV the Floor

Step 1: Project the UV. Select the floor piece in object mode, and freeze its transformation. Navigate the viewport so we are looking at the model at a non-straight angle. Go to UV->Planar☐. In the pop-up Planar Mapping Options window, go to the Project from section, and chose Camera. Check on keep image width/height ratio and hit the Project button. You can now see a projected figure of our model in the UV Editor. This planar projection projects our model form our viewing angle in 3D to UVs in the UV Editor, or to the UV space (Figure 2.8).

Step 2: Cut the UV Open. The projection will only project the model but will not be making a cut. Imagine you got a box package delivered to you. Without cutting the plastic tape open, there is no way you can flatten it to a 2D surface without faces overlapping each other. Let's check off the checker texture, so it is easier to see the edges.

Select all the edges of the bottom face, go to the UV Editor, hold down Shift+right mouse button, and chose Cut to cut them

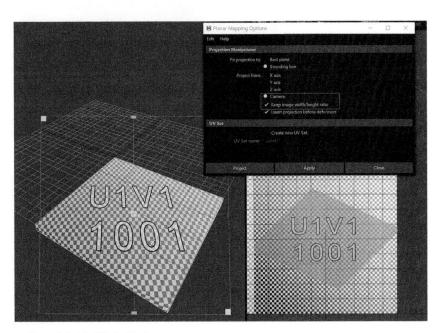

FIGURE 2.8 Project the UV to the UV editor.

open. Hold down the right mouse button in the UV Editor and chose UV Shell. UV shell is a shell of UV that all faces of it are connected. Click on the top face of the model in the UV Editor; all UVs that are connected to the top face (or not cut out from it) should all be selected. Use the Move tool to move it away. Grab the four edges of the top part and four vertical edges of the floor and cut them also. The edges we cut should appear thicker (Figure 2.9).

Step 3: Unfold. Select all the UVs in the UV Editor, hold down Shift + right mouse button, chose Unfold->Unfold. Maya automatically tries its best to unfold the UVs to the same 3D shape and with the same proportion for each face (Figure 2.10).

Step 4: Orient UV. Currently, all the UVs are tilted. To fix the orientation, go to the menus of the UV Editor, chose Modify->Orient Shells. Maya tries its best to make them straight. You can now grab any UV shell and rotate them while holding down the J button to adjust their rotation (Figure 2.11).

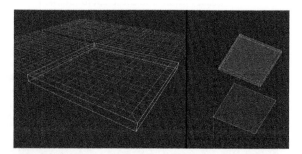

FIGURE 2.9 Cut the UVs of the floor.

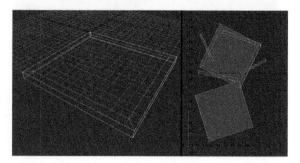

FIGURE 2.10 Unfold the UVs.

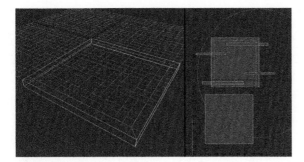

FIGURE 2.11 Orient the UVs.

Tips and Tricks

There is no telling how a UV should be oriented, and sometimes it doesn't make a huge difference, but we want similar UV shells oriented the same way most of the time.

> *Step 5: Layout the UV. Grab all the UVs, hold down the Shift and right mouse button, and chose Layout->Layout UV. The UV shells are now automatically rearranged into the U1V1 space. There is a small problem with this default behavior: there is no gap between the UV shells; there is also no gap between the edge of the U1V1 tile and the UV shells.*
>
> > *Many texture software bleed the color out of the UV shell a little to avoid the seam reading the background. Go to the Layout command again, but this time, click on the box icon of the command to pull out the Layout UVs Options window. Under the Layout Settings, change the Shell Padding and Tile padding to 10. This setting ensures that all UV shells are at least 10 pixels away from each other, and it also ensures they are 10 units away from the edge of the UV tile. Press the Layout UVs button, and you can see the difference this time in Figure 2.12.*

Tips and Tricks

Pixels are the smallest unit of a picture. If you zoom in close enough to any picture on a computer, you can see small, square, solid colors arranged in rows and columns.

Warning: A small step value will significa

Layout Settings

Texture Map Size: 1024
Padding Units: ● Pixels ○ UV
Shell Padding: 10.0000
Tile Padding: 10.0000
Shell Distribution: Distribute
Tiles U: 1   V: 1
Packing Region: Full square
U: 0.0000   1.0000
V: 0.0000   1.0000
Scale Mode: Uniform

Layout UVs   Apply

FIGURE 2.12 Add shell padding and tile padding in the layout settings.

All digital pictures are put together this way. When we are talking about the resolution of a computer screen, like a 4K monitor, the 4K means there are around 4000 pixels across its width. The exact number of pixels a 4K screen has is 3840 pixels on its width and 2160 pixels on its height.

Steps 1 to –5 can be used for almost all UVs, even for a complicated character model. Do a planar projection to project our model to UV space, cut the seams we think are needed to flatten it, and then Unfold, Orient, and Layout.

There is no universal rule on how UV should be cut and arranged. However, it is essential to know that if you don't cut enough, your UV is destined to be stretched. If you cut too much, it's hard to arrange. For every cut you do, there is a potential to see discontinued texture patterns on that edge, and we call this a seam artifact. Seam artifacts become less of a problem with modern texturing software. One last important note: you want to cut any edge that is a hard edge. We are going to explain why later.

Let's do the UV of our security camera.

We have updated the security camera and separated the vertical arm from the base (Figure 2.13).

We need the separation to rotate the camera on the Y-axis. Changes like this happen all the time, especially when the

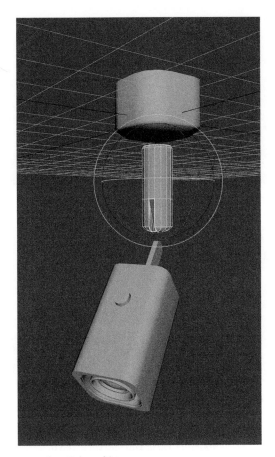

FIGURE 2.13 Separated arm of the camera.

mechanic of the object (arm rotation in this case) was not taken into consideration.

Step 6: Project the UV. Select all the models of the security camera, do a planar projection the same way we did in Step 1 (Figure 2.14).

Step 7: Cut the outer shell. Select the outer shell of the security camera, press Ctrl+1 to isolate it (Ctrl+1 is the toggle for isolating the current selection). Set symmetry to Object X (This could be easily Object Z if your model is rotated differently). Go to UV->3D Cut and Sew UV tool, in our 3D viewport, click and drag on the outer and inner edge loops of the thickness of the shells to cut them open. You can also double-click to cut an entire edge loop. Holding down Ctrl while

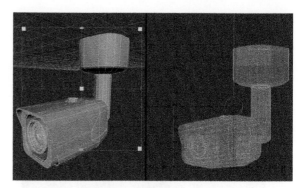

FIGURE 2.14 Project the UV of the camera.

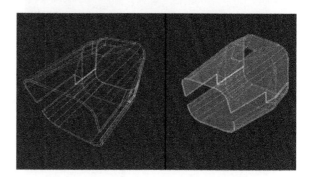

FIGURE 2.15 Cut the edges using 3D Cut and Sew UV tool.

dragging or double-clicking sews the edges back together. Go ahead and cut edges at the primary turnings of the faces along the thickness of the model (Figure 2.15). The 3D Cut and Sew UV tool adds color codding to shells once they are cut off.

Tips and Tricks

Cutting using the 3D Cut and Sew UV tool is no different than selecting the edges and cutting them in the UV Editor. Sometimes one method is easier than the other, and there are always multiple ways to achieve the same thing. Experience can help you to decide which way is faster.

Step 8: Unfold. Grab all UVs in the UV Editor, go to the UV Toolkit, under the Unfold section, click the Unfold button. This one is also no different than using the unfold command in the Shift + right mouse button marking menu. The author prefers the marking menu because one fast drag invokes the Unfold command right away (Figure 2.16).

Step 9: Optimize. With all the UV selected, go to the Modify menu under the UV Editor. Click on the square icon on the right side of the Optimize command to pull up the Optimize UVs Options window. Set the Iterations under the Optimize Options section to 100; to repeat it 100 times, click Apply and Close. You can see the UV has slightly changed; what Maya does here is to move UV points around to reduce stretching. In case you haven't tried, you can also find the Optimize command in the Shift + right mouse button marking menu and the UV Toolkit.

Step 10: Orient and Layout. Do an orient shell and layout exactly like in Steps 4 and 5 (Figure 2.17).

Step 11: Do the UV of the inner shell. Go ahead and create the UV of the inner shell the same way; the cut and result are shown in Figure 2.18.

Step 12: Do the other UVs. You can also create the other UVs the same way. Figure 2.19 shows all the cutting choices of the rest of the pieces.

Step 13: Combine UVs. Select all the models of the security camera, go to the UV Editor, grab all the UVs, do a Layout UV command (Figure 2.20).

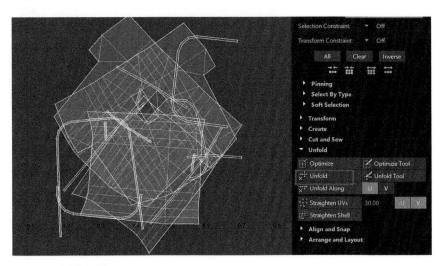

FIGURE 2.16 Unfold the UVs.

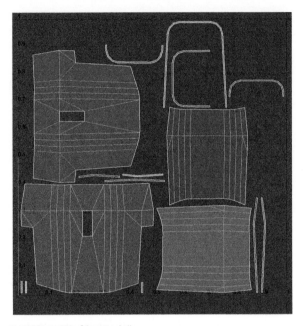

FIGURE 2.17 UVs of the outer shell.

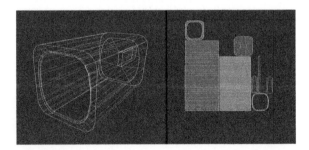

FIGURE 2.18 UVs of the inner shell.

Why?

We put all the UVs of all security camera models in one UV tile. By doing so, we can create one texture for the entire camera and save performance for our game. It is essential to pack UVs together in a uniform and organized way.

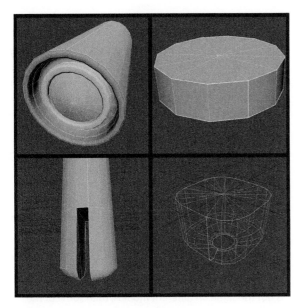

FIGURE 2.19 Cutting choices for the rest of the pieces.

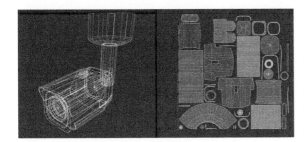

FIGURE 2.20 Layout the UVs of the entire camera.

Texel Density

Now we have two models UV mapped, so let's talk about texel density. Grab all your UVs of the camera, and go to the UV Toolkit. At the bottom of the Transform section, you will see a Texel Density (px/unit) part. Click on the Get button and you can see a value calculated; in our particular case, it is 3.1016. This value means there are 3.1 pixels per unit (cm) if you are using a texture of 512×512 resolution, which is defined in the Map Size section. Select the floor and press the Get button, and the value we get is 0.97. These two values indicate that the Camera is having 3×3 times, which is nine times the resolution of the floor. You can also visualize the difference in the viewport with the checker texture turned on. You can see how the edge length of the square on the camera is roughly three times smaller than the floor.

You may wonder what is so important about this. Through the experience we have gathered while developing games, consistency of the texel density helps a great deal in maintaining assets, saving performance, and having a consistent graphic. Ideally, 1 pixel of the texture on your model gets rendered as 1 pixel on your screen. A texture that has a higher resolution than that wastes performance. A texture that has a much lower resolution causes a pixelated or blurry result. If your texel density is not the same on different models, then some of the texture may feel more detailed than others, which causes inconsistency.

Chose the Right Texel Density

How high the texel density is depends on the camera view of your game. For third-person or first-person games, we can get to an object closer, and so we need more texel density. A top–down viewing angle requires lesser texel density. Strictly speaking, we also want the models closer to our player to have higher texel density, while things further away can have lower texel density.

Some games have two or three levels of texel densities. The assets to which the players can get as close as they want (characters, walls, weapons) have the highest texel density. Assets that are farther away that the player cannot reach but not very far (high ceiling, building, or trees outside of the window) have medium-level texel densities. Background assets (mountains, sky, the bird in the sky) have the lowest texel density.

Luckily for us, we are making an interior in which the player can pretty much get close to anything; so we are going for one consistent texel density. There are plenty of guidelines on exactly what the texel density is for various games. In our case, we aim for a medium- to high-quality texel density, like Uncharted 4. Our textures are going to range from 512×512 pixels to 4k (4096×4096 pixels), and the texel density is going to be around 5.12 pixels per centimeter or 512 per meter.

It is worth noting that we are not aiming for a fixed number for every asset. The texel density is allowed to vary a little; the only way to judge if something is too far off is by actually looking at it in the game engine.

> Step 14: Assign material and mark resolution. Go to our security camera, set the Map Size of the Texel Density section in the UV Toolkit to 1024, and press the Get button. We can see we are getting a texel density of 6.2, and we will settle with this for our camera. Select our camera models, hold down the right mouse button, chose assign new material, and select Blinn as the material. Hold down the right mouse button again on any of the models and chose Material Attribute to pull out the attribute editor on the right side of the UI. In the first text field of the settings, change the name of the material to SecurityCamera_1k. Naming the materials like this helps us remember the texture resolution we intend to use for our models.
>
> Step 15: Packing Floor. Go ahead and UV map all of our floor modules: there are five of them. Grab all of them, go to the UV Editor and select all the UVs. Go to the Layout UV option, Change the Packing Resolution under the Pack Settings section to 4096. Set the Texture Map Size under Layout Settings to 4096, set Shell Padding and Tile Padding to 10, and press the Layout UVs button. Maya should now pack all the UVs in to the U1V1 space.
>
> Go to the Texel Density section under the Transform section of the UV Toolkit and set the Map Size to 4096. Press the Get button; we get a resulting value of 4.2146, which is close enough to our goal of 5.12 pixels per unit (Figure 2.21).

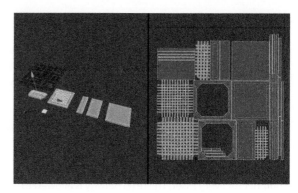

FIGURE 2.21 Packing the floor.

Why?

We packed all of our floors into one UV shell and used a 4k (4096×4096) texture for them with a resulting texel density of 4.2146 pixels per unit. Packing similar assets is a common practice; we pack models together to have a big texture for all of them, and this kind of texture is called an atlas. By using atlases, we are reducing draw calls from the game engine. 4K, of course, is a bigger texture and takes longer to load and needs more space in the memory. However, in many cases, the bottleneck is not how much memory is used, but rather how often you are reading and freeing memories. The standard may also vary from studio to studio; consult with your technical guides to determine the best practice for your platform and engine.

UV the Pod

One of the props we did for the environment was the pod (Figure 2.22).

The pod is the place where genetically engineered soldiers are created. It has a console, a tank, cables, and keyboards. Notice that we have two models for the pod, the glass and the rest of the pod. We do this because the glass is fundamentally different material wise. It is safe to separate these special types of materials, which makes it easier to work with later on in the game engines.

FIGURE 2.22 The pod model.

The glasses of the windows of our modular pieces are also separated the same way. Let's move on to the UV of the pod and introduce some more tricks of UV Mapping.

> *Step 16: Grab all the models of the pod, do a planar project like before.*
>
> *Step 17: Cut the cylindrical tank glass of the pod. Got to the back of the pod, select the vertical edge loop at the center of the glass of the tank, go to the UV Editor, and do a Cut command. Select all the UVs of the glass of the tank and do an Unfold, and an Optimize command (Figure 2.23).*
>
> *Step 18: Console monitor. Select the faces that belong to the display of the console. In the UV Editor, switch to face mode, hold down Shift + right mouse button, chose Create UV Shell. Switch to the Move tool and move the shell away from its original position. You can see how the outer edges are now cut; use Create UV Shell is a different way to separate UVs. Do an Unfold and Optimize command on the UVs of the display (Figure 2.24).*
>
> *Step 19: Keyboard UV Mapping. Select all the faces of the keyboard, and press Ctrl + 1 to isolate them. Select the back faces and do a Create UV Shell.*

FIGURE 2.23 Cutting the tank of the pod.

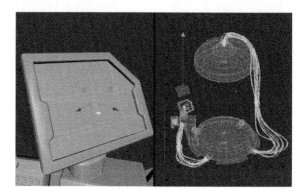

FIGURE 2.24 UV the monitor of the console by using the Created UV shell command.

Apply an Unfold and Optimize command, and move the shells out. Notice that the Create UV Shell command also switches the selection mode to Shell. We can use this to select all the keyboard buttons quickly, move them out, unfold, and optimize them (Figure 2.25).

Tips and Tricks

At the stage of cutting and unfolding UVs, we just do not worry about their arrangement. That's why we are moving them around freely. We can easily pack them back to the U1V1 space with the Layout UV command.

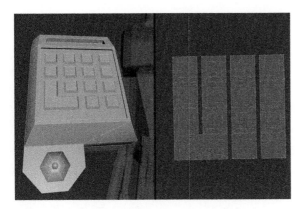

FIGURE 2.25 Create the UVs for the keys.

Step 20: Separate other parts of the keyboard.
Select the face loop across the thickness of
the keyboard, and select the face loop that
represents the depth of the small monitor at
the top of the console. Add select the loop that
represents the depth of the depression of the
area of the keys as well. Do a Create UV Shell
command and move the separated shell out
(Figure 2.26); you can see how easily we can
separate UVs with this create UV shell trick.
Step 21: Cut and unfold other parts of the keyboard.
Select the edges highlighted in Figure 2.27 and
cut them, grab all the UVs of the keyboard,
unfold, and optimize them.

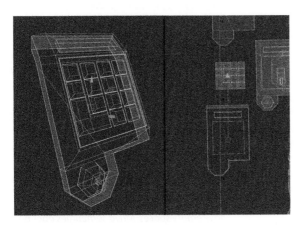

FIGURE 2.26 Separate other parts of the keyboard.

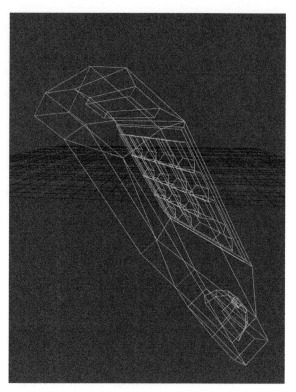

FIGURE 2.27 Edges to cut for the keyboard.

Step 22: UV Mapping the Cables. We have meticulously placed the cables for this model to give the model a sense of complexity and functionality. As complicated as they appear, the UV part is not as hard as you think. All we have to do is select an edge loop across the length of every individual cable, do a Cut, and then unfold and optimize (Figure 2.28).

Step 23: Other parts of the console. Other parts of the console should be straightforward; go ahead, and cut and unfold the rest of the console part.

Step 24: Packing. Grab all UVs of the pod, do a Modify->Orient Shells. Grab them again and do a Layout UV command, and make sure you have shell and tile padding set to 10 units in the Layout UV Options. Figure 2.29 shows the UV of our pod after layout. Notice that both UV sets have empty spaces. Maya sometimes does not do a good job using all the UV spaces.

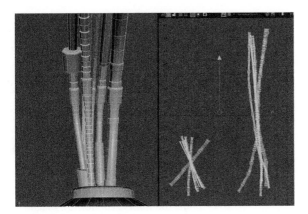

FIGURE 2.28 Create UV for the cables.

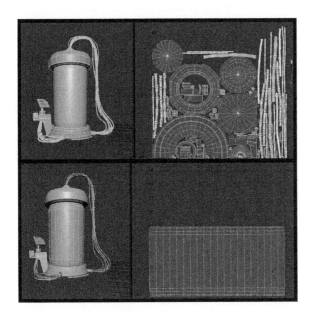

FIGURE 2.29 Pack the UV of the pod.

Step 25: Manual Packing. Other than relying on Maya to layout the UVs for us, we can also manually pack our UVs. Grab all UVs of the pod, switch to Scale tool, hold down D and X, and drag the pivot of the scale tool to the lower left corner of the U1V1 tile. Release the buttons and scale the UVs up. Our UVs now exceed the

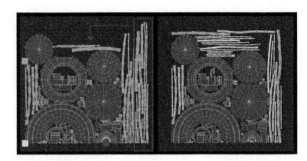

FIGURE 2.30 Manually pack the UVs.

U1V1 range. You want to control how much you are scaling, and the goal is to move the UVs exceeding the U1V1 range back to the remaining empty UV space inside of the U1V1 space (Figure 2.30).

Tips and Tricks

The texel density of our manually tweaked UV layout is 4.7617; the texel density before our tweak is 4.295, that is about 11% increase in resolution. We can always improve our texel density by manually adjusting the UV layout. However, it is going to be a time-consuming process. We need to keep popping out assets to meet the deadline, and sometimes this kind of optimization is not possible with the agenda of the production.

Step 26: Finish all other UVs. Now it is your turn to finish all other UVs. Please ensure that you have similar texel density and give every group of packed UVs a new material. Also, remember to name the materials with the resolution intended for these assets.

Figures 2.31–2.56 are the UVs and texel densities for the rest of the models

Step 27: Organization. Check your outliners and see if there is anything not named. Delete any empty groups; make sure all materials are assigned and appropriately named. When everything is checked, do a File->Optimized Scene Size to clean up redundant history and materials.

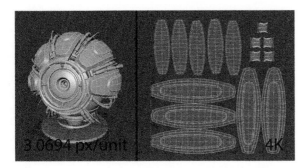

FIGURE 2.31 All the UVs and texel densities for the rest of the models.

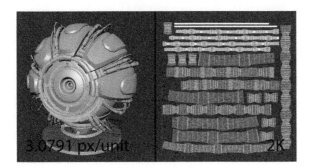

FIGURE 2.32 All the UVs and texel densities for the rest of the models.

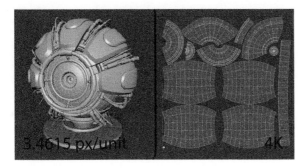

FIGURE 2.33 All the UVs and texel densities for the rest of the models.

FIGURE 2.34 All the UVs and texel densities for the rest of the models.

FIGURE 2.35 All the UVs and texel densities for the rest of the models.

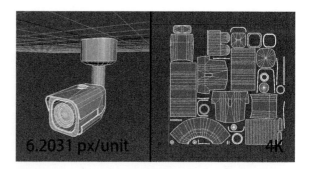

FIGURE 2.36 All the UVs and texel densities for the rest of the models.

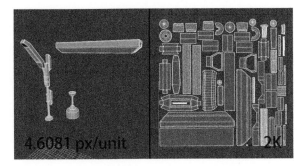

FIGURE 2.37 All the UVs and texel densities for the rest of the models.

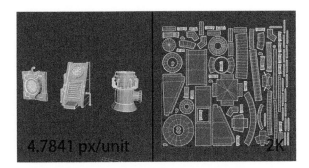

FIGURE 2.38 All the UVs and texel densities for the rest of the models.

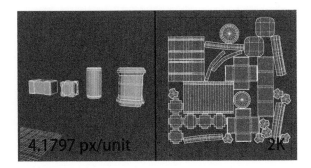

FIGURE 2.39 All the UVs and texel densities for the rest of the models.

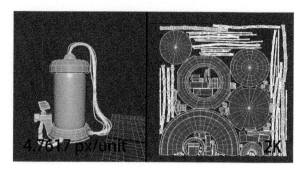

FIGURE 2.40 All the UVs and texel densities for the rest of the models.

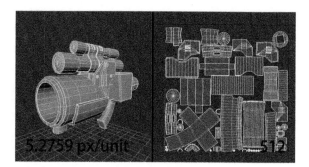

FIGURE 2.41 All the UVs and texel densities for the rest of the models.

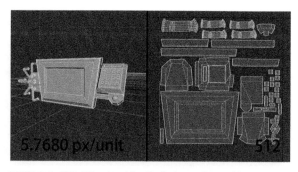

FIGURE 2.42 All the UVs and texel densities for the rest of the models.

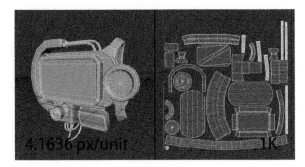

FIGURE 2.43 All the UVs and texel densities for the rest of the models.

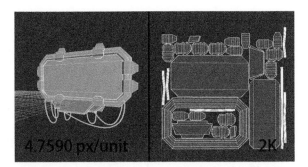

FIGURE 2.44 All the UVs and texel densities for the rest of the models.

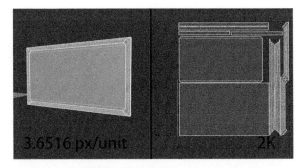

FIGURE 2.45 All the UVs and texel densities for the rest of the models.

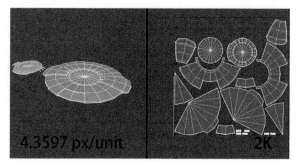

FIGURE 2.46 All the UVs and texel densities for the rest of the models.

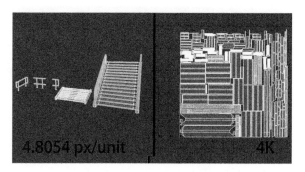

FIGURE 2.47 All the UVs and texel densities for the rest of the models.

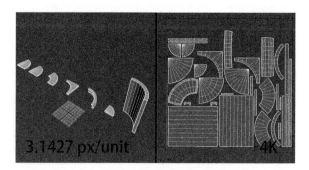

FIGURE 2.48 All the UVs and texel densities for the rest of the models.

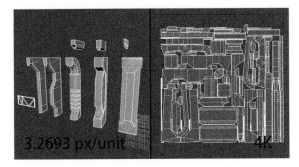

FIGURE 2.49 All the UVs and texel densities for the rest of the models.

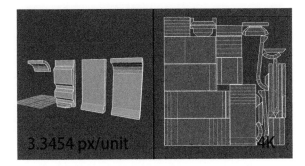

FIGURE 2.50 All the UVs and texel densities for the rest of the models.

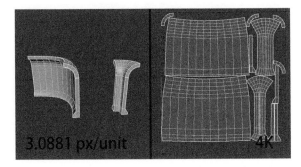

FIGURE 2.51 All the UVs and texel densities for the rest of the models.

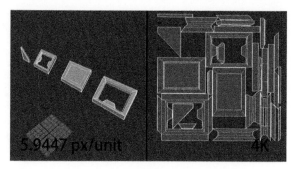

FIGURE 2.52 All the UVs and texel densities for the rest of the models.

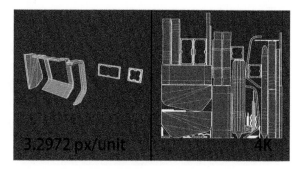

FIGURE 2.53 All the UVs and texel densities for the rest of the models.

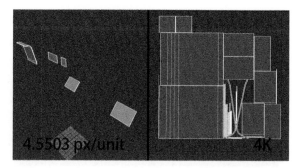

FIGURE 2.54 All the UVs and texel densities for the rest of the models.

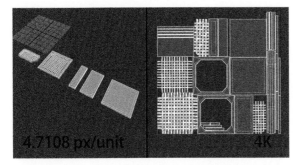

FIGURE 2.55 All the UVs and texel densities for the rest of the models.

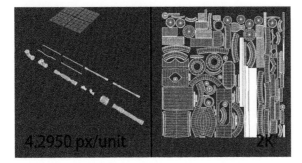

FIGURE 2.56 All the UVs and texel densities for the rest of the models.

Conclusion

The UV part of the model may not appear on the surface of the artwork. However, it is the foundation of the texture of the model and cannot be overlooked. There is an automatic UV command under UV->Automatic; it is wishful thinking that automatic UV can get you to a decent stage. Please don't use it unless you have a good reason. Based on the previous experience of teaching UV, the author already regrets mentioning this command. The students always think automatic UVs are fine – they are not.

Once UVs are done, the fun task of texturing starts. Let's jump into that in the next chapter.

CHAPTER 3

Set Texturing

UV Mapping is generally the painful, or at least annoying, part of making 3D art. However, once we are done with it, we can now jump into texturing, which is a real joy with modern texturing tools.

Texturing is the process by which we define the color, roughness, metalness, height information, and other aspects of the surface of the model. All those aspects are images that can be mapped to the surface of the model with the UV we created. Textures are applied to a material. The material will use the information on the texture to determine the lighting and shading behavior of the model. What is the color of the surface? Is the surface shiny? Is it metal? All these factors play a significant role in how the model looks.

Texturing is considered as important as the modeling part. There are many ways to do texturing. You can paint the texture in 2D with a UV snapshot, or in 3D with some dedicated software. We primarily use a 3D painting software called Substance Painter.

PBR

In the modern workflow, texturing has to define all aspects of a material, like the color, roughness, and metalness. In the game industry, we use a standard called PBR to define a material. PBR stands for Physically-Based Rendering. It enforces the result of the rendering to be physically correct by limiting the number of inputs allowed to be adjusted. Other related material properties are calculated internally to ensure that the energy from the light is reflected, refracted, and absorbed by the surface of the model based on the laws of physics. For example, if you know the color and roughness of a metal surface, you can already calculate the brightness and color of the reflection using the laws of physics. There are variants of this standard, but the most popular one is called PBR – Metallic Roughness, and it is composed of five surface attributes:

> *Base Color*
> *Height*
> *Roughness*
> *Metallic*
> *Normal*

Height and Normal attributes are surface shape details. Strictly speaking, you don't need any information in them to describe a material. However, some renderers still want to have them even they are only a flat color for consistency.

In this book, we will primarily be using Unity's new High-Definition Render Pipeline (HDRP), which uses a variety of channels to store all of this information. This means that, sometimes, the way shaders are built in software like Substance Painter will feel a little disjointed from how they will actually be assembled in Unity. Not to worry though, Substance Painter has built-in export presets that will output the appropriate PBR attributes into HDRP-consumable shaders.

Baking

Texturing often requires another process called baking. Baking is a process that generates textures that contain different information about the geometry; they are as follows:

Normal	Extract high-definition detail in tangent space, the rendering process will use this map to calculate the lighting and make the high-definition detail appear on the low-definition model as an illusion.
World Space Normal	Extract normal coordinates relative to a fixed frame in the object space.
ID	Identification map to quickly isolate areas on the model.
Ambient Occlusion	Becomes darker when the surface area is closer to other surfaces. Used to enhance detail.
Curvature	Extract a map that contains convexity/concavity information of the mesh
Position	Extract the x, y, z world coordinates of all points at the surface of the mesh.
Thickness	Extract the thickness of the different parts of the model.

The effect of the maps can be more evident if we have a high-definition mesh with some sculpted detail on it. You can add sculpting details to a model using sculpting software. Currently, the best sculpting software is ZBrush. Although ZBrush is a powerful piece of software, it's beyond the scope of this book; so we won't be covering it. However, in the long term, if you plan to work in the game industry as a modeler, be sure you start working with this powerful piece of software.

For now, let's jump into texturing with Substance Painter, where we will cover more essential aspects of texturing in the process.

Tutorial 3.1: Texturing Modular Pieces

Step 1: Set up a Maya project. Open our model file in Maya, go to File->Project Window, in the pop-up Project Window, click on the new button at the top row, and type in Game_Maya_Project. Click on the Folder icon in the second row to define a place to save our project, leave the rest as default, and click on Accept. Press Ctrl+Shift+S to save our file again, click on the scenes folder on the bottom left column of folders, and save our file there.

Why?

So far, we have been modeling with Maya with one single file. It is because model files are relatively small, and so managing them in one file is tidy and straightforward. Another reason to have our models in one file is due to the scale of our game being small enough. At some point, we have to have more files for different models, characters, and rigs. When we are creating more and more assets and files, it is going to be harder and harder to trace stuff, so we need to have a way to manage our files. Step 1 creates a folder structure that contains subfolders for us to manage our files; we won't need most of them. However, since we are doing textures, the sourceimages folder it creates is where we put our texturing file.

Step 2: Arrange our models. We are going to texture multiple assets in one file to help ensure consistency. However, to do that, we have to move them away to avoid overlapping models. Select all the modular pieces of our models, press Ctrl+1 to isolate them. Use the Move tool to arrange them so that similar pieces are put together but not overlapping each other (Figure 3.1).

Step 3: Export models. Grab all the modular pieces, go to File->Export Selection. In the pop-up Export Selection window, chose the sourceimages folder. Click on the yellow folder button at the top left corner of the window to create a new folder and rename it as

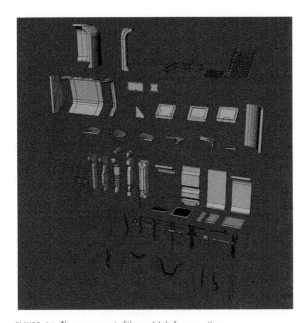

FIGURE 3.1 The arrangement of the models before exporting.

set_texturing. Go to the bottom of the window, and type in modular_pieces in the file name, click the drop-down menu of the Files of type settings, chose FBX export. Go to the right side of the window and under the Options, check on the Smoothing Groups under the File Type Specific Options->Include->Geometry section. Click on the Export Selection at the lower right corner of the window to export the file.

Why?

What about the other models you may ask. Well, texturing files are, unfortunately, super big, and the performance is slow when there are so many models. We need to break our models into multiple texturing files.

Step 4: Import to Substance Painter. Open Substance Painter, go to File->New. In the pop-up New Project window, set the Template to Unity HDRP, or Unity URP based on your engine of choice. You can change this later upon output.

Click on the Select button, find and select the modular_pieces file we export in Step 3, and press the Open button. Change the Document resolution to 2048 and press the OK button.

Why?

You may think, wait a minute, don't we require some of the models to have 4096×4096 (4k) textures? The answer is yes, but 4k is a heavy texture resolution for computers to handle. One of the superpowers of Substance Painter is the ability to upscale the resolution at any stage without losing any detail. It achieves that by remembering every stroke you did while painting your texture and upgrades them to 4k.

The Substance Painter UI

Substance Painter's UI is somewhat like Maya. As shown in Figure 3.2, the area in the red box is the menu where we load and change our models. The area in the yellow box is the Status Bar, which has generic controls like brush size, pressure sensitivity, symmetry, perspective. The column of buttons in the purple box is the Tools bar. This bar has essential painting tools like paint, erase, project, polygon fill. The viewport is in the middle area inside the

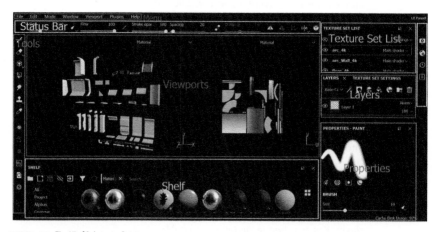

FIGURE 3.2 The UI of Substance Painter.

blue box. It has a 3D viewport and a 2D viewport almost identical to our Maya UV Editing layout. The shelf is below the viewport in the cyan box. It contains brushes, alphas, grunge maps, materials, and other useful assets to help with texturing. Move to the right side. The brighter green box is the Texture Set List. You can see that the names of the materials we created in Maya are listed here. Every material you created for the models in Maya ends up as a Texture set in the Texture Set List. You can think of the Texture Set List as Maya's outliner. Substance Painter only cares about different materials and treats their associated models as different objects. The darker green box is the Layers. This is the area we go to a lot to stack multiple layers of textures together to get a final look. In the orange box is the properties panel, which contains brush or layer-specific settings; things like tiling, channel toggles, alphas can be defined here. Finally, on the far right in the white box, we have the UI Panel. The UI panel lists all the panels that are not showing in the main UI. Click on the various buttons to pull out other hidden panels like Display Settings and Shader Settings.

Navigation

The navigation of the 3D viewport is the same as in Maya; the navigation of the 2D viewport is the same as Maya's UV editor. You can press F2 to show only the 3D viewport, press F3 to show only the 2D viewport, or press F1 to show both.

Light Direction

To change the direction of the light, hold down Shift, click and drag the right mouse button.

> *Step 5: Baking. Click on the TEXTURE SET SETTING tab on the left of the LAYERS tab. Find and click the Bake Mesh Maps button. In the Pop-up Baking window, set the Output Size under the Common parameters section to 4096, check on Use Low Poly Mesh as High Poly Mesh, and set the Antialiasing to Subsampling 8×8. Click on the Bake all texture sets button. Substance*

Painter now starts baking, and it may take a while. We set the output size of the texture to 4096 because it is the highest resolution we are after. The Use Low Poly Mesh as High Poly Mesh setting makes the baker bake all mesh data from the mesh we imported to itself; this way, relevant mesh data like Curvature and AO are generated. Antialiasing is crucial because it is going to reduce artifacts. It is also going to increase the baking time. After baking, the model looks slightly different; its cavities or concave areas appear to be darker. The darker color is the result of the baked AO map, and it enhances the detail of the model.

Ambient Occlusion

Ambient Occlusion is a natural phenomenon. It is caused by the concaved surface or faces close to each other sucking the lights in. Lesser light rays can bounce out from these areas, which causes these areas to be darker. This phenomenon is almost like what an acoustic Sound-absorption Panel will do to sound.

PBR Material Channels

Go to the TEXTURE SET LIST and click on floor_4k; this switches to the material of the floors. Notice that the 2D viewport switches to the UVs of the floors. You can also hold down Alt+Shift together and click on any model of the floor to switch to the floor. Press Alt+Q to toggle on isolation (press Alt+Q again to toggle off). Go to the LAYERS panel, click on the button with a tilted bucket icon, and you can see a new layer called Fill layer 1 created above Layer 1. A fill layer is a layer that allows you to assign solid colors or textures to the model. Go to the PROPERTIES panel, scroll down to the MATERIAL section. There are five buttons right under the MATERIAL section: color, height, rough, metal, and nrm. These five buttons are the toggles of the channels we mentioned in the PBR section of this chapter. For every layer, you can click on the buttons to toggle the channels on or off, which adds or removes that channel's effect from the layer.

The Base color defines the color of the model. You can change it to any color you want to test.

The Height is how far the surface is elevated. Height map is an illusion and is invisible unless there are some variations. Click on the Height uniform color button, in the search bar, and type in Metallic Grate wide. This should filter out others, only giving you the texture named Metallic Grate Wide. Click on Metallic Grate Wide to use it as our heightmap; the patterns are now showing up on the surface of the model. We can assign textures like this to any channel we want. Change the direction of the light, and you can see how the height map reacts to the direction of the light – almost like there are actual height variations on the surface. If you zoom in and look at the model from a side angle, you can see it is still a flat surface.

Roughness defines how rough the surface is: a higher value makes it rougher, and a lower value makes it smoother. Go ahead and drag the roughness slider to see the differences.

Metallic defines the metalness of the surface. In the natural world, surfaces are either full metal or not metallic at all. However, sometimes when a metal surface is covered with dust, we can use a middle value. Go ahead and drag the Metallic attribute to see the difference.

Normal map is like a height map but with more information about the directionality of the surface shape variation.

Right above the MATERIAL section, you can drag the Scale, Rotation, and Offset values to tweak the repetition, rotation, and offset of the applied textures.

> *Step 6: Floor base material. Double-click the name of the Fill layer 1 and type in Metal; this renames the layer to Metal. Set the base color of the layer to a dark grey. Click on the Roughness uniform color, in the pop-up menu, and type Leak Dirty in the search bar on top. Chose the first one called Grunge Leak Dirty. Set the Metallic value to 1. We have just created a dark metal material with some variations on the roughness (Figure 3.3).*

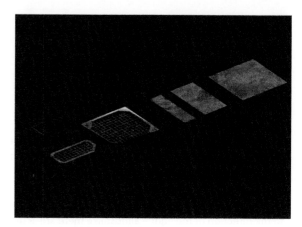

FIGURE 3.3 Basic dark metal material.

Why?

Notice that we only had variations on the roughness, and it can create fine details already. It is always worth noting that roughness should never be overlooked. It is, in some sense, as important as the color, if not more important.

> *Step 7: Floor scratches. Create another fill layer, name it Scratches, and set the Roughness value to 0.25 and Metallic to 1. Because this layer is above the Metal layer, it is blocking the Metal layer. We want this layer to only appear on the sharp edges. Right-click on the layer and chose Add black mask (this adds a mask to the layer). A mask with black color means completely see-through or transparent; that is why we are now seeing the Metal layer again. Right-click on the black mask, and chose Add generator. Go to the PROPERTIES panel and click the Generator button and choose Mask Editor. We can now see how the edges of the model are showing our scratches layer (Figure 3.4).*

Generators

Generators are an essential feature of Substance Painter. Generators generate colors based on the information and setting you give. The most common usage of generators

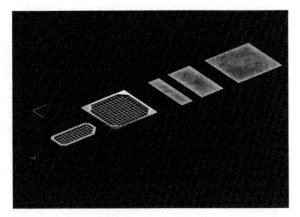

FIGURE 3.4 A new scratches layer.

is to generate masks based on the baked mesh data to create things like edgewear or dust. We are going to cover more details of generators further along the way.

> Step 8: Tweak scratches. The Mask Editor is the essence of the procedural texturing workflow in Substance Painter; it is also the most commonly used generator. Click on the Mask Editor under the mask of the Scratch layer, and the PROPERTIES panel is now showing up all the settings it has. The settings may appear to be intimidating at first, but notice that there are just two sliders that are not 0: Global Balance and Curvature Opacity. Global balance is used to tune up or down the amount of opacity of the generated mask. Curvature is currently the only information used to generate the mask. Set the Global Balance to 0.6 and the Global Contrast 0.2 to make the edge wear look stronger and slightly tighter.
>
> Step 9: Add variation to the mask. Right-click on the mask of the Scratches layer and select Add fill. Go to the PROPERTIES panel, click on the grayscale button on the bottom, Search and chose Grunge Scratches Fine. Click on the Norm button on the right side of the Grunge Scratches Fine and chose Multiply. This setting is called the blending mode. Blending mode defines how to blend the current layer to the layers below it. The default blending mode is Normal, which blocks everything underneath. The Multiply blending

FIGURE 3.5 Add extra scratches to the scratches layer.

mode multiplies the value of the current layer with the layer underneath as the result. This new layer adds subtle scratches to the mask, which makes it more detailed (Figure 3.5).

Tips and Tricks

We have created a decent dark metal material without drawing a stroke; this is called procedural texturing. Procedural texturing has two main drivers: layering and masks. With procedural texturing, not only can we get faster and cleaner results but we can also tweak any step of the process without having to redo other parts. Procedural workflow is also none-destructive because of that.

Step 10: Create a Smart material. Hold down Shift, click on the metal layer, and then the scratches layer, press Ctrl+G to group them into a folder; rename the folder Dark Metal Scratched. You can click on the folder icon to expand or collapse the folder. Right-click on the folder and select Create smart material. A smart material is now added to the shelf with the same name as the folder. You can see many other smart materials shipped with Substance Painter over there. A smart material is fundamentally a group or folder of layers. After creating our smart material, we can drag it from the shelf and add it anywhere we want. Delete our Dark Metal Scratched group in the LAYERS panel. Drag our Dark Metal Scratched smart material from the shelf above Layer 1 again. You can see it just created the same thing.

Step 11: Top panels. Go the SHELF and under the Smart materials section, look for Steel Painted Scraped Dirty; drag it to the top of our layer stack in the LAYERS panel. Open the Steel Painted Scraped Dirty folder, click on the layer named Paint to select it. In the PROPERTIES panel, click on the color bar under the Basie Color, a color pane pops out. Click and drag the three vertical sliders on the right to change the hue, saturation, and value (brightness) of the color. You can also click and drag anywhere in the color gradient box on the right to pick a color there. Change its color to an orange color. This new material now covers almost all areas of our model.

Step 12: Paint height map. Create a new fill layer above the layer named Base Metal. Rename the new layer to OuterPanel. In the PROPERTIES panel, toggle off all channels except the height channel. Drag the slider of the Height setting up to 1. Give this layer a black mask. Right-click on the black mask; select Add paint. Go to SHELF. Click on the Brushes section, click Basic Hard to use the Basic Hard brush. In the PROPERTIES panel, scroll down to the bottom and change the grayscale of the brush to white. Hold down Ctrl + right mouse button and drag left and right to change the size of the brush. You can now try to click and drag on the model to paint extra height (Figure 3.6).

Why?

We created a fill layer; make the value of its height 1, and use a mask to define where the height is. By doing so, we are now able to go back to the fill layer and change its height value to anything else. We could choose to create a new paint layer and define the height we want to paint in the brush settings, but then it is harder to change the height value later.

Tips and Tricks

There are some basic short cuts to tweak the brush. Hold down Ctrl + right mouse button and go left and right to

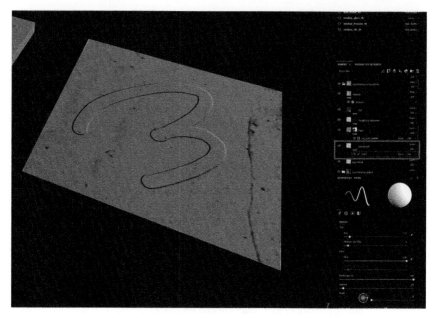

FIGURE 3.6 Test paint some height information on the model.

change the size of the brush. Hold down Ctrl+right mouse button and go up and down to change the softness of the brush. Hold down Shift+left mouse button and go up and down to rotate the brush. Hold down Shift+left mouse button and go left and right to change the opacity of the brush.

> *Step 13: Use the height as the mask of the outer panel. Right-click on the mask of the OuterPanel layer, select Add anchor point. Scroll up and find the group called Steel Painted Scraped Dirty (this is the group of the smart material we dragged in). Give the group a black mask. Right-click on the mask, and select Add fill. In the PROPERTIES panel, click on the grayscale button, and under the ANCHOR POINTS tab, select OuterPanel Mask. What we should see now is the orange outer panel should only appear in the area we painted the height (Figure 3.7).*

FIGURE 3.7 Using anchor point to share masks.

Why?

Anchor points are references of a texture. Our Outer Panel Mask anchor point is a reference of the result of the layers under it and inside the mask of the OuterPanel layer. The fill layer we added to the mask of the Steel Painted Scraped Dirty folder is using that anchor point. So it is referencing the same mask we painted for the OuterPanel layer. That is why where we paint white for the mask of the OuterPanel, we also see the Steel Painted Scraped Dirty appear.

Step 14: Set up symmetry. Press the L button to toggle on symmetry (you can also find it in the Status Bar, see what's toggled on after you press the L button). A Red plane shows up somewhere in the scene (you may have to zoom out to see it). Whatever you drew is going to be mirrored over to the other side of the plane. We want to draw the patterns symmetrically for the square floor piece on the right side. Press the Q button to toggle on the gizmo (blue handles to move the plane). Drag the blue arrows to the right to position the plane to the middle of the square floor piece (Figure 3.8).

Step 15: Paint panels. Press F6 to switch to the Orthographic view (you can also find the switch at the right side of the Status bar). The orthographic view has no perspective distortion, which makes it perfect for painting precise shapes. Press the number 2 button to switch to the Eraser (it is also at the Tools bar). Click and drag to erase the painting we did earlier. Hold down Shift while changing the viewing angle to snap the viewing angle to a straight top view. Move the brush outside and below the shape of the Square floor piece and click to select. Hold down Ctrl + Shift and move the brush up. A dashed line shows up from where we clicked to the current position of the brush; it also snaps every 5 degrees when you move the brush. Make sure the dashed line is vertical and covers the entire floor piece and click again. A straight line is now drawn across the dashed line. Keep doing this until we have covered a good portion of the floor with a square panel (Figure 3.9).

FIGURE 3.8 Toggle symmetry and place it for the square floor piece.

FIGURE 3.9 Draw a square panel with precision.

Tips and Tricks

You may have to go up and down twice to draw a line all the way across. There are many ways we can fill a square. We use the Ctrl + Shift combination to help us draw straight lines. Once we have marked out the edge, how you fill in the middle is all up to you. You can switch to a bigger brush to free draw it to fill the gap.

> Step 16: Paint extra panel Detail. Using Ctrl + Shift combination, we can quickly draw some extra detail to the panel (Figure 3.10).

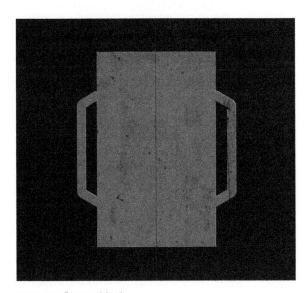

FIGURE 3.10 Extra panel detail.

Tips and Tricks

There is no way you can position the mirror plane at the center of the floor accurately, but we can get close enough. We have to texture individual pieces in different substance files to have a perfect symmetry. However, it is hard to manage that way for our one-man-army approach, but if you have a team, then it is better to have them work on their files.

Step 17: Anchor as micro detail. Our panel looks fine except that there is no edgewear (the scratches or other imperfections on the model). In the Default settings, only baked height and normal maps are used for finding edgewear. To include our painted height, go to the layer named Paint and click on its mask. Select mg_mask_builder. This mg_mask_build generates a mask that makes the edgeware appear on the edge of the model; it achieves this by using the baked normal and curvature maps. At the bottom of the PROPERTIELS panel, click Micro Height and choose the anchor point we created for OuterPanel. The edgewear effect should now appear on the panel we painted (Figure 3.11).

Step 18: Use alphas. Go back to the Paint layer of the masks of the OuterPanel by clicking on it. Go to SHELF and click on the Alphas section. Type in Shape Gradient in the search bar, and choose the first one in the search result. The shape of the brush is now the shape of the Shape Gradient alpha. Press the X button to invert the color of our brush. In our case, it changes from white to black. Hold down the Ctrl+left mouse button to go up or down to change the orientation of our brush. Hold down Ctrl+right mouse button to go left and right to change the size of the brush. To get accurate orientation, go to the Angle setting of the brush in the PROPERTIES panel, hold down Shift while dragging the pin of the circular shaped dial to snap to a certain angle. With an angle of 180 and black color, we can paint a cool ramp on the side of the panel (Figure 3.12).

Step 19: Try other alphas. There are many other alphas; try them out and see if you can create more breakups. Figure 3.13 shows the result of some new shapes added using alphas.

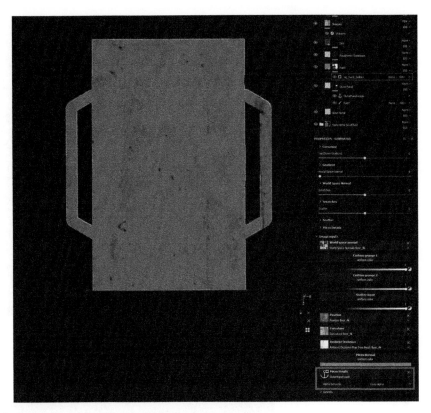

FIGURE 3.11 Use anchor point as extra micro detail.

*Step 20: Normal detailing. Click on the button on
the left of the button that we use to create fill
layers to add a paint layer. While a fill layer
only allows us to use a solid color or a texture, a
paint layer is a layer we can paint anything on.
Name the new paint layer NormalDetail. In the
PROPERTIES panel, turn off all channels but the
nrm (normal) channel. Go to the Hard Surfaces
section in the SHELF. Find Niche Rectangle Top
Wide Rounded (you can search to find it or use
other shapes if you don't like this one). Drag it
from SHELF to the normal in the PROPERTIES
panel. Click the X button on the Alpha of the
brush to get rid of the alpha of the brush. We
should now see the normal shape appears on the
brush fully. You can now click on the model to
stamp that shape (Figure 3.14).*

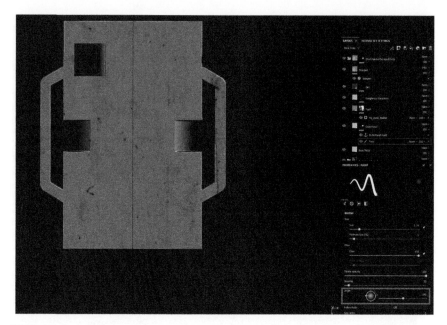

FIGURE 3.12 Ramp added using an alpha.

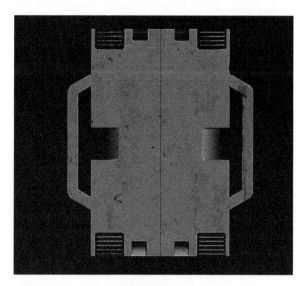

FIGURE 3.13 Extra details added with alphas.

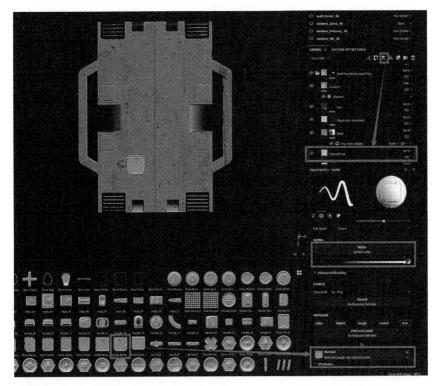

FIGURE 3.14 Stamp normal details to the model.

Tips and Tricks

Through height map and normal maps, we can add a whole lot of surface detail to the model; that is why we do not have to model very complicated shapes in Chapter 1. It is crucial to design your workflow with the tools at hand to determine the best way and best place to do certain things.

> Step 21: Edgewear for the normal map detail. Right-click on the NormalDetail layer and choose Add anchor point. Go to the mg_mask_builder under the mask of the layer named Paint. In the PROPERTIES panel, click on the Micro Normal, and in the ANCHOR POINTS tab, choose our NormalDetail anchor point. Set the Referenced channel to Normal; this ensures we are getting

111

the normal information instead of the base color. The edgewear should now appear on the panels we painted with the normal map. Scroll up to the Micro Details section in the PROPERTIES panel. Set the curvature Intensity down to 0.15 and Height Details Intensity to 10 to tighten up and sharpen our edgewear effect (Figure 3.15).

Step 22: Add more normal panel details. Please go ahead and try to use other normal maps in the Hard Surfaces section in the SHELF to add more detail to the model (Figure 3.16).

Step 23: Add cables. Create a new fill layer and drag it down to reposition it right above our Dark Metal Scratched group and below our Steel Painted Scraped Dirty group. Rename the new fill layer Cables. Set the Base Color of the layer to a darker gray, and set the Roughness to 0.2 and Metallic to 1. Give the layer a black mask and add a paint layer to the mask. Go to the Brushes

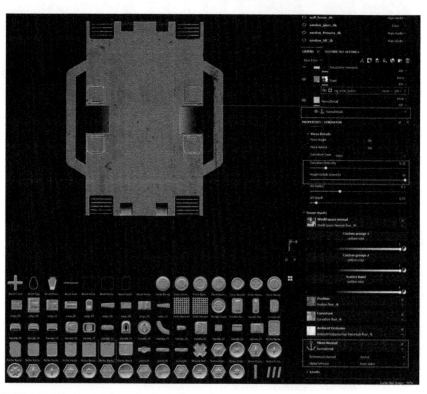

FIGURE 3.15 Add edgewear to the panels painted with normal.

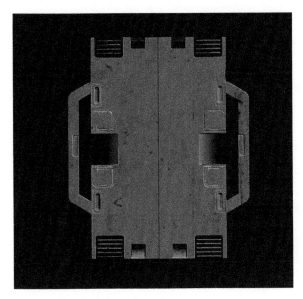

FIGURE 3.16 Extra details done with normal map.

section of the SHELF and chose Basic soft. You can now use the Ctrl + Shift button combination to draw straight lines to lay down some cables (Figure 3.17).

Step 24: Fix height blend mode. There is a problem of our blend mode of the height; the height map of the cable we painted out is showing on the orange panel. To fix that, Select Steel Painted Scraped Dirty. Click on the drop-down list right below the label of the LAYERS panel and change it to Height. We are now viewing and tweaking the height channel. Click the drop-down list on the right side of the Steel Painted Scraped Dirty layer, and change the setting to Normal. The blending mode of the height channel of this group is now normal, which blocks what is happening under it. Our orange panel should now block the cables (Figure 3.18).

Step 25: Extra layer of cables. Click on the number 100 on the right side of the paint layer of the mask of the Cables layer. Drag the slider down to 30; this makes it only 30% visible, or in other words, makes it weaker. Add another paint to the mask of Cables, and start drawing out new cables. The new cables should now above the previous cables (Figure 3.19).

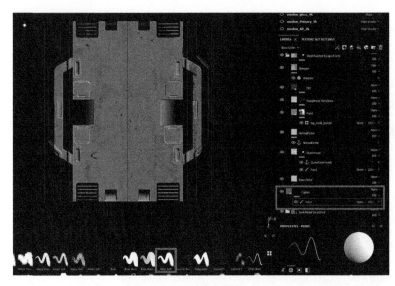

FIGURE 3.17 Paint out some cables.

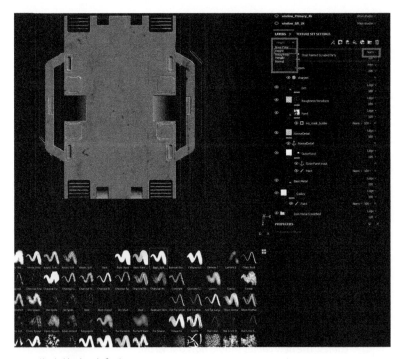

FIGURE 3.18 Height blend mode fixed.

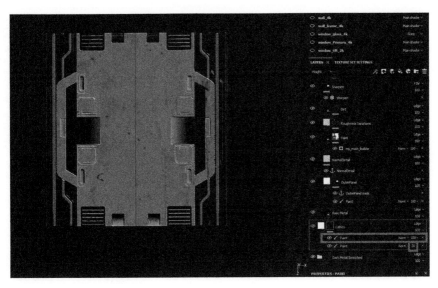

FIGURE 3.19 Extra layer of cable added.

> *Step 26: Cable holders. Select Cables and press
> Ctrl + D to duplicate it. Rename the duplication
> CableHolders and make its Base Color slightly
> brighter and crank up the Roughness to 0.65.
> Right-click on the masks of CableHolders and
> choose Clear mask; this operation deletes the
> paint layers or other things in the mask. Add
> a new paint layer to the mask. Use the Basic
> Hard brush and paint some horizontal bands
> to mimic the holder for these cables. Press the X
> button to switch to black color and click on the
> two sides of the cable holders to add two holes
> (Figure 3.20).*

Tips and Tricks

We used a painted approach to get the cables; it is fast
and clean, but may not have the best shape. We could
choose to model some cables instead, but it is going to be
more cumbersome for the engine to handle. A different
way to achieve this is to bake a normal map from a model
that has cables modeled. To save time and reduce the
volume of this book, we choose to omit that workflow.

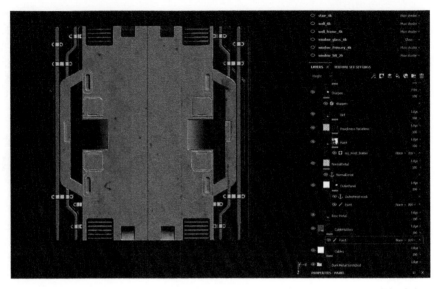

FIGURE 3.20 Added cable holders.

Step 27: Painter other panels. Using the same technique, we can create many details already. Go back to the various layers we added and painted and paint panel and cable details for our other two floor pieces. You do not need additional layers to do this. Figure 3.21 shows the result of the final design; the color of the panel was slightly changed.

Step 28: Limit the details to the top of the floors. Select all the layers except the Dark Metal Scratched and press Ctrl + G to group them. Name the new group Detailing. Give the group a black mask and add a paint layer to the mask. Press the number 4 button to switch to the Polygon Fill tool. The Polygon Fill tool allows us to select elements of the model to fill in colors. In the Properties panel, toggle on the square button of the Fill mode and set the color to 1. We can now click on any face of the model to fill that face to white color and keep clicking until the details we painted all reappear on the top faces of the floor pieces. By doing this step, we have limited our painted details to the top faces. We have also got rid of the overshoot artifacts. Now we have a clean edge cut right at the edge of the top faces (Figure 3.22).

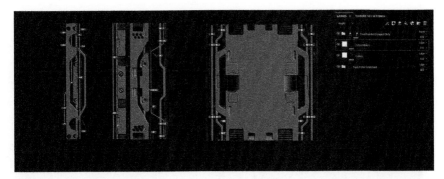

FIGURE 3.21 Paint the other two floor pieces.

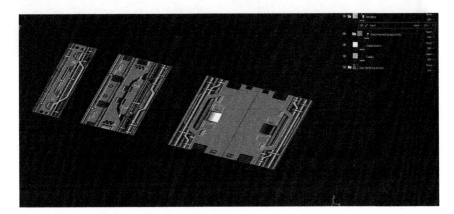

FIGURE 3.22 Limit the details to the top faces of the floors.

Tips and Tricks

The Polygon Fill tool is a clean way to define masks. There are four fill modes: Triangles, Quads, Objects, and UV shells, each represented by a triangle, a square, a cube, and a checker button. Switching to these modes allows you to click to fill these different elements with the color defined by the Color setting. For example, if you chose UV shell mode, change the color to black, click on any part of the model. This is going to fill the UV shell that contains that part of the model to black color.

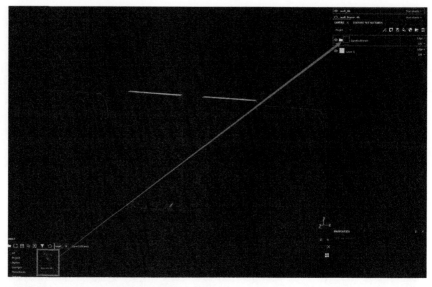

FIGURE 3.23 Use the same material to get started on the walls.

Step 29: Create a smark material. Select all the
layers and press Ctrl+G to group them and call
it GameScifiPanels. Right-click on the new group
and select Create Smart Material.

Step 30: Use the same material on the walls. Hold
down Alt+Shift and click on any model of the
walls to switch to the wall_4k texture set. Press
Alt+Q to Isolate it. Go to the Smart materials
section of the SHELF, and search for our
GameScifiPanel. Drag GameScifiPanels to the
layers. We should now see the dark metal appear
on the walls (Figure 3.23).

Why?

So, where are the orange panels? The answer is they have
no proper mask yet; neither do the cables. All Substance
Painter remembers is that we painted something in the
area of the floors, not on the walls; they are physically
not at the same spot in the scene. Even if they were, the
painting we did for the floor would not work for the walls.
We have to repaint them for our wall models.

Step 31: Paint wall Panels. Go to the various layers and paint the panels for our wall model; don't forget that you can press the *X* button to switch to black color to cut the panels out. Make sure you also try different alphas. We chose not to have cables on the walls, and so we hid the layers of the cable. You can click on the eye-shaped icon in front of the layers to toggle their visibility (*Figure 3.24*).

Step 32: Add extra panels to the walls. Add another fill layer on top of the *OuterPanel*. Name it *ExtraPanel*. Toggle off all the channels except the height channel, set the height value to 1. Add a black mask to the layer, and add a paint layer to the mask. Switch to the *Basic Hard* brush. Hold down *Ctrl + right* mouse button and drag down a little to make the brush softer. Start painting some extra panels on top of the current panels (*Figure 3.25*).

Step 33: Create edgewear for the extra panels. Right-click on the masks of the *ExtraPanel* layer and select *Add Anchor point*. Go to the layer named *Paint*, right-click on it and add a generator. Click on the *Generator* button in the *PROPERTIES* panel and chose *Curvature*. Click the off button after the *Use Micro Details* setting to toggle it to On. Click the *Micro Height* button, under the *ANCHOR POINTS* tab, chose *ExtraPanel* mask. We should now see orange colors appear only on the sharp ridges of the model and the height of the extra panels we painted. Toggle the *Global Invert*

FIGURE 3.24 Toggle the visibility by clicking on the little eye icons.

119

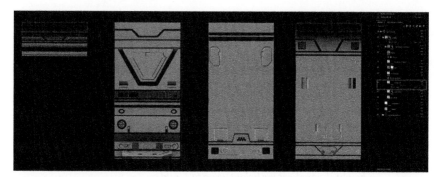

FIGURE 3.25 Creating the ExtraPanel layer.

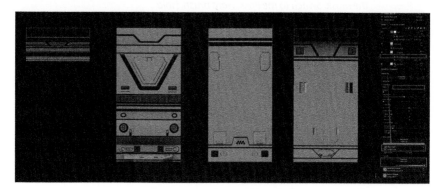

FIGURE 3.26 Extra Curvature generator to create edgewear for the extra panels.

setting On. Go to the bottom of the PROPERTIES panel. Click on the X button of the Curvature map to unload it, and then drag the slider under it down to 0. Now the edgewear should appear only on the extra panels we painted (Figure 3.26).

Why?

We unloaded the curvature map because we do not want the baked curvature to affect the mask. We only want the painted height of the extra panel to have edgewear. Given the proper Micro Height, the Curvature generator is perfect for generating edgewear.

Step 34: Fix the blending mode of the curvature layer. Notice that the only place we see edgewear is on the extra panel we created earlier.

The effect of the new Curvature layer is blocking the Mask Builder layer under it. To get the edgewear we set up earlier back, simply change the blending mode of the Curvature layer to Multiply (Figure 3.27).

Step 35: Cables base material. Switch to the cables. Go to the Materials section of the SHELF; find and drag the Iron Diamond Armor to the layers. In the PROPERTIES panel, drag the slider of the Scale setting all the way up to 128 to repeat the pattern more. In the LAYERS panel, set the channel to Height and set the opacity of the height channel of the Iron Diamond Armor layer to 30 (Figure 3.28).

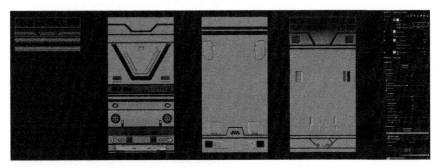

FIGURE 3.27 The result that shows all the edgewear for the panels.

FIGURE 3.28 Base material for the cables.

Why?

You may argue that using an existing material shipped with Substance Painter is not a good idea. After all, other people may use it too. But we are not using it as it is, we can combine multiple materials and get something unique enough.

> *Step 36: Add another variant. Add another fill layer to the layers, name it straps. Change the blend mode of its height channel to Normal. Make the Base Color darker, reduce the Roughness to 0.2, and crank up the Metallic up to 0.7. Go to the Procedurals section of the SHELF. Find and drag Strips to the Height input of the fill layer in the PROPERTIES panel. Set the Scale to 16. It is too strong. Trying to lower down the opacity makes it weaker but also reveals the Iron Diamond Armor below it. Instead, right-click on the Straps layer, and select Add levels. In the PROPERTIES panel, set the Affected channel to Height. Drag the black pin at the bottom of the graph to the right; the more you drag it to the right, the weaker the height becomes. Drag the black pin really close to the right side so the height is weak enough (Figure 3.29).*

Levels

Levels is a typical color adjusting tool. The graph of the levels shows the color distribution of the color from black (left side) to white (right side). There are three Pins on top of the graph. The black pin represents the total black color of the spectrum. The gray pin represents the mid-tone, and the white pin represents the total white color. Dragging them around clamps and shifts the color of the image. For example, drag the black pin to the middle, and any color darker than the mid-tone before becomes total black. Drag the gray pin anywhere, and the color of that point becomes the mid-tone. The two pins at the bottom of the graph remap the color again. The color the black pin is at is used as black. The color the white pin is at is used as white color. The rest of the color is interpolated between these two colors.

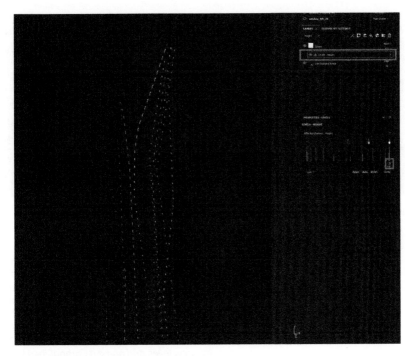

FIGURE 3.29 Add a straps layer with strap patterns.

Step 37: Create a random mask for the Straps layer. Give the Straps layer a black mask. Right-click on the mask and add a Generator. Click on the Generator button under the PROPERTIES panel and select UV Random color. Add a level above the UV Random Color, drag the black and white pins at the top of the level to the middle. This setup makes half of the cables show our Straps and the other half show our Iron Diamond Armor. If you don't like the result, click on the UV Random Color and click the Random button of the Seed setting in the PROPERTIES panel to have a different result (Figure 3.30).

Why?

First of all, the UV Random Color generates a random color for each UV island. The Levels then tighten the colors up to either black or white. This way, half of the cables have a mask of white, and the other half have black.

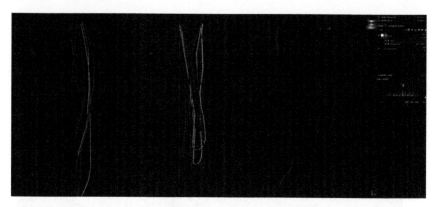

FIGURE 3.30 Create a random mask for the Straps layer.

Step 38: Add carbon fiber band layer. Drag the Carbon Fiber material from the Materials section of the shelf to the top of the layers, change its Scale setting to 128 to repeat the pattern more. Notice that Carbon fiber has no height channel. We want to make it higher than the rest of the cables. Add another fill layer above it, toggle off all channels except the height channel of this new layer, and name it CarbonFiberHeight and set its height value to 1. Select both CarbonFiberHeight AND Carbon Fiber. Press Ctrl + G to group them and name the group CarbonFiberWithHeight. Change the blending mode of CarbonFiberWithHeight to Normal. Give CarbonFiberWithHeight a black mask and add a paint layer to the mask.

Step 39: Paint the mask of the carbon fiber. Press F3 to go to the 2D view. Switch to the Basic Hard brush. In the PROPERTIES panel, set the Alignment setting to UV. Use the Ctrl + Shift button combination to draw a few straight lines across all the cables. Press F1 to see both the 3D and 2D views. We should now see bands get randomly placed on the cables. To make them more visible, click on the Carbon Fiber layer, and set Color 1 and Color 2 to darker colors (Figure 3.31).

Step 40: Create material for the cable base and cable wrapper. For the cylindrical cable wrapper and the base, we can throw a Steel Gun Material at the top of the layer stack. Give the Steel Gun Matte group a black mask, and add a paint layer to it. Switch to the Poly Fill tool. Don't forget to

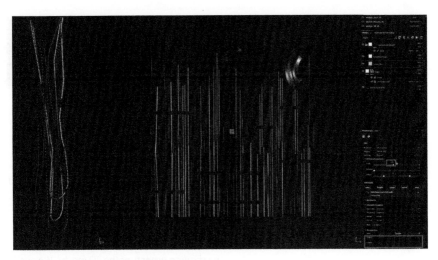

FIGURE 3.31 The result of the placements of the carbon fibers.

change the color to white and change the fill
mode to Objects this time (the button with the
cube icon). Click on the two models to make the
material show up on them (Figure 3.32).
Step 41: Pipe Material. We can use the Steel Gun
Painted also as the material of the pipes. Just
switch to the pipes and drag the Steel Gun
Painted smart material to the layers (Figure 3.33).

FIGURE 3.32 The material created for the cable base the cable wrapper.

FIGURE 3.33 Use Steel Gun Painted as the material for the pipes.

Step 42: Glass Materials. Hold down Alt + Shift and click on one of the glass models to switch to the classes. Press Alt + Q to isolate them. In the TEXTURE SET LIST panel, click on the Main shader drop-down list on the right side of the window_ glass_4k texture set. Select New shader instance. The setting now shows as Main shader (Copy). Main shader (Copy) is a new shader. A shader is a collection of algorithms that calculates all the shading aspects of the 3D model. We need a new shader because the glass is fundamentally different – it has transparency. Click on the Sphere icon on the UI Panel to pull out the Shader Settings panel. Click on the pbr-metal-rough button and change it to pbr-metal-rough-with-alpha-blending; this shader supports transparency. Change the Instance name to TransparentShader (Figure 3.34).

Step 43: Add Opacity channel. Go to the TEXTURE SET SETTINGS panel (on the right side of the LAYERS panel). Click on the + button on

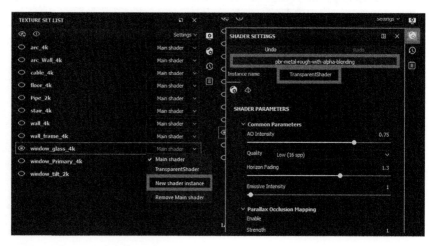

FIGURE 3.34 Create a new shader for our glasses.

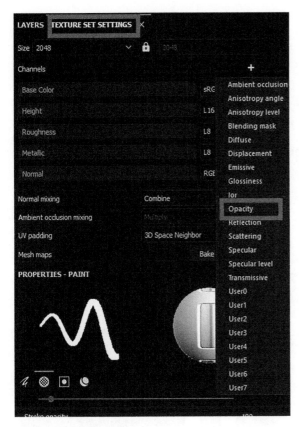

FIGURE 3.35 Add the Opacity channel.

the right of the Channels setting and chose
Opacity (Figure 3.35). An opacity channel
is needed to feed opacity value to our
TransparentShader.

Step 44: Create Glass Material. Go to the LAYERS
panel and add a new fill layer. Name the new
layer Glass. Under the MATERIAL section of the
PROPERTIES panel, you can now see an extra
channel called op. The op channel is the Opacity
channel we added in Step 43. Set the Base
Color of the fill layer to a mid-gray. Click on the
Roughness button, search and use Grunge
Fingerprints Smeared as the Roughness input.
Set the Opacity setting to 0.1 to make it more
transparent. Glasses are generally non-metallic,
so keep the Metallic setting 0 (Figure 3.36).

FIGURE 3.36 A new glass material.

Why?

We don't have too much happening on this glass material. The shader of the game engine is going to be very different for things like transparency. We are going to define these attributes in the game engine when we create these materials.

> *Step 45: Create materials for all other modular pieces. We have covered enough techniques. It is now time for you to finish all the other materials. Figure 3.37 shows our result for the modular pieces, and Figure 3.38 shows a close-up shot of the textures of the stairs.*

FIGURE 3.37 The texture result for the modular pieces.

FIGURE 3.38 The close-up view of the stairs.

Assignment: Texturing the Rest of the Models

The way we texture the props and the hero asset is the same way we texture our modular piece. Figures 3.39–3.44 show the result of the textures we did. The only new thing here is that for the screens, we added an Emissive channel to the shader to allow emissive input to make

FIGURE 3.39 Completed versions of screens.

FIGURE 3.40 Completed versions of rounded set pieces, including glass shaders.

FIGURE 3.41 With a dark base, objects like this will contrast well with the orange components.

FIGURE 3.42 Using a similar pallete keeps elements part of the same universe while providing contrast with the orange walls.

FIGURE 3.43 Finished gun and camera.

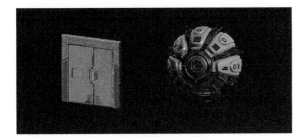

FIGURE 3.44 Complete Hero asset and multi-part door.

the screen a bright blue color. We end up with five substance files:

> *Modular_pieces_texturing.spp (Contains all of our modular pieces.)*
> *Props_texturing.spp (Contains all the prop meshes that are not supposed to move in the game.)*
> *Security_camera_texturing.spp (Contains only the security camera.)*
> *Door_texturing.spp (Contains only the door.)*
> *Hero_asset_texturing (Contains only the hero asset.)*

There is no particular reason why we separate the camera, the door, and the hero asset other than some organization flaws we had during the production. You can have a completely different distribution. Please go ahead and have some fun texturing the rest of the models.

Conclusion

Texturing takes time, but it is more fun to do. However, while textured models are great to see, we're not done. Now, we need to get our textured assets into the game engine, set up the materials, and assemble the completed modules into a playable level.

In the next chapter, we are going to focus on importing and assembling our level in the game engine.

CHAPTER 4

Unity Asset Creation

In this chapter, we finally get to get into the game engine. Until now, we've spent our time building geometry, unwrapping UVs, and finally texturing that geometry. You've learned a lot and come a long way, but now it's time to start moving our assets from the realm of asset creation to the realm of interacting with those assets in a game scenario.

It is important to point out that effective work in game engines is predicated on effective and efficient work in the previous steps. If the geometry has been messily assembled with problems in topology or inefficient UV layouts, there is nothing the game engine will be able to do to compensate for that. On your first round with the game engine, you may find that there are problems in your model that need to be fixed. Not to fear. If something isn't looking like you want in game, go back and take a look at the model/UV/texture and fix it. As you gain more experience, you'll know how to avoid these issues in the future.

Game Engines

Game engines are software packages built to *assemble* games. Think of a game engine as "middleware" where not a lot of visual assets are created, but rather a place where assets are assembled and made interactive. Game engines have built frameworks or modules for rendering, inputs, physics, AI, networking, UI (user interface), VFX, and audio. Usually this framework is leveraged in an "editor" that allows for asset assembly to happen. Importantly, this is where interactivity through scripting is created.

Unity

For this volume, our game engine of choice is Unity. Unity has made a name for itself with its nimble authoring cycle and ease of use. While Unity has always been playing catchup with its biggest competitor (Unreal Engine) in visual fidelity, the benefits in creating efficient, lightweight, and quickly iterated games has made Unity a quick riser in the world of game engines. Particularly in the world of mobile, AR, and VR, Unity has nabbed a big part of the market.

Because different devices have different levels of power (measured in computations per second on a processor, amount of data stored in random access memory, and both for video cards), games are built with target devices in mind. A game build for an PS5 is not going to run on your iPhone (or presently, even on most PCs for that matter). Similarly, a game that passes for beautiful on an Android device feels woefully under-designed on your large gaming PC. Despite both Unity's and Epic Games' (the maker of Unreal) efforts, Unity has dominated in the mobile (lightweight, but extremely profitable) arena but Unreal continues to lead the AAA market for non-proprietary engines. However, with both engines, you can build mobile-based and high-end PC builds.

In this volume, we will be creating a game for Windows or Mac distribution with Unity. Making the leap to mobile would not be hard, but it requires some extra layers of working with touch input (for example) that are beyond the scope of this book. With a PC or next-gen console as our target audience, we need to take a moment to talk about Unity's new Rendering Pipelines. Rendering pipelines reference how a computer deals with drawing assets onto your player's screen. Lately, Unity's approach has been to develop multiple rendering pipelines for different deployment strategies. For years, Unity used one rendering pipeline – the built in one upon which a developer could bolt other modules on to expand its capabilities. Recently though, Unity has introduced Scriptable Rendering Pipelines that allow for much more customization and control. Unfortunately, for a beginner, this can be much too much information to process or wrestle with. But understanding the basics of the two rendering pipelines will be important as moving between the pipelines is a labor-filled process:

> **Universal Render Pipeline (URP)** – *The pipeline will ultimately replace Unity's current built-in rendering pipeline. It is designed to be a one-stop workflow that allows a developer to develop once and deploy across multiple devices. It is more efficient that Unity's old built-in pipeline but also has a few limitations, particularly in how it deals with lights. If you have an underpowered PC, for the upcoming tutorials, you may want to build the project using URP as it generally has lower hardware requirements.*
> **High-Definition Render Pipeline (HDRP)** – *This is a higher-end rendering pipeline with much higher fidelity. HDRP looks better, but it requires better hardware. In early iterations, it also required quite a bit of technical programming know-how. However, in its most recent iteration,*

it works well with built-in settings with Substance Painter. An HDRP project will not run on a mobile platform; thus, Unity advises clearly defining where you plan to deploy your asset from the beginning as HDRP assets are not compatible with URP. HDRP has some interesting new capabilities, including a shader editor that allows for sophisticated shader creation (URP also has these), and some interesting and beautiful implementations of new lighting and physical-based rendering techniques. It's new implementation of physically based camera systems and built-in Post Processing Effects (visual filters and visual interpretation processes that add new levels of visual sophistication to each frame) are particularly exciting. And yet, with all of this excitement come the inevitable bugs to be discovered and squashed. This HDRP is young, and while promising, it has its persnickety corners.

For our uses, we will be using the HDRP. It is no longer in Beta and has been approved for production. However, if you are on a machine that you are worried about carrying the load, you may choose to use URP instead. Most of the strategies we employ in constructing the level (in HDRP) can still be used in URP, and all of the coding we do later will work well in both rendering pipelines.

Alright! Enough discussion, let's get installed and building.

Tutorial 4.1: Installing Unity, Visual Studio, and Starting a Project

Step 1: Download and install Unity Hub. Unity uses something called the Unity Hub to manage Unity installs and Unity project. As URLs can change, the best way to always find this is Google "download Unity Hub". This will take you to Unity's download page (https://unity3d. com/get-unity/download). There look for a "Download Unity Hub" button and download the UnityHubSetup.exe.

Step 2: Launch UnityHubSetup.exe from your Downloads folder. Follow the Installer prompts to install the Unity Hub.

Step 3: Unity Hub will then launch and ask where you want to install Unity. For now, look for a small option at the bottom left called "Skip Install Wizard" (Figure 4.1).

Step 4: Unity Hub will open (Figure 4.2). On the left will be four options: Projects (where we'll set and open Projects to work on), Learn (where you can watch Unity-built tutorials), Community (where you can go for some problem-solving help), and Installs (where you decide which versions of Unity you want installed). For now, click Installs.

Step 5: In the Installs section, click the Add button. This will pull up an Add Unity Version window. At the time of this writing, the most recent Latest Official Release is Unity 2019.3.13f1. If yours is higher than that, go ahead and choose that release and hit the Next button.

Step 6: The next window will invite you to add modules to your installation. Eventually, if you choose to develop for Android, iOS, Linux, Vuforia, etc., you will want to check these modules (Figure 4.3). For now, don't install any of them (you can come back and install them

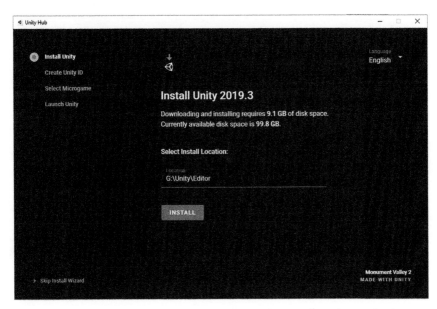

FIGURE 4.1 Unity Hub's installation window. For now, just Skip Install Wizard so we can choose what to install with more control.

FIGURE 4.2 Unity Hub.

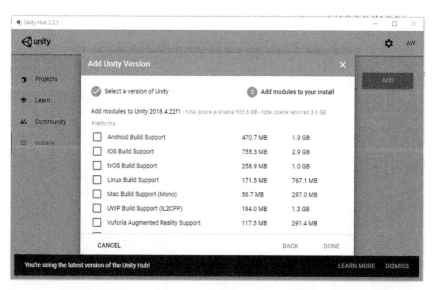

FIGURE 4.3 Unity inviting you to install modules. For now, only make sure that Documentation is checked – leave the rest off for now.

later if needed). Do make sure to scroll down and ensure that Documentation is checked. We'll be referencing this often.

Why?

After checking, several things will actually be installed. Unity Hub will install Unity (of course), but will also install a version of Visual Studio, which we'll use later to write code. Go ahead and run through all the steps for this installation. We will talk much more about Visual Studio later.

> Step 7: When Unity is installed, the Unity Hub will indicate it in the Installs section. You can come back here to install new modules, install new updates of Unity, or uninstall versions of Unity. For now, click on Projects on the far left of the interface.
>
> Step 8: Create a new HDRP project. The Projects window is where we will create new projects and where you should always open Unity projects from. For now, click on the New button. In the following screen, give your project a name, decide its location, and click on the High-Definition RP in the Templates section (Figure 4.4). After hitting next, Unity will take a while as it sets up the project and imports some default scenes and other files.

FIGURE 4.4 Creating a new empty HDRP project.

Why?

From now on, whenever you plan to work on this Unity project, access it via the Unity Hub. Open Unity Hub and this new project should appear in the list of projects. Double-click its name there, and this will open Unity for you and open the project within it.

> *Step 9: Close HD Render Pipeline Wizard, since we aren't converting any old project.*
> *Step 10: Optimize layout. The default layout of Unity is inefficient (and frankly simply mimics UE4 without leveraging the advantages of Unity's leaner UI). To change this, choose Window>Layout>2 by 3 (Figure 4.5).*
> *Step 11: Continue to optimize the Project window. Look for the Project tab and, at the top right-hand corner, look for three vertical dots. Click on those dots and choose One-Column Layout (Figure 4.6).*

A Bit about the Unity UI

Each part of the interface is labeled with a small tab at the top left. Each of these interface parts, Scene, Game, Hierarchy, Project, and Inspector, has a specific and important function. Below is a quick overview of each:

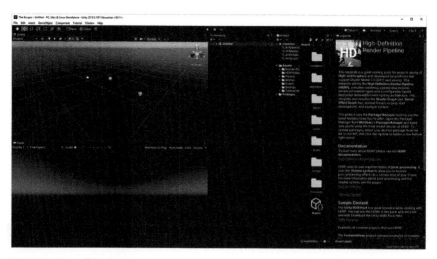

FIGURE 4.5 A more efficient layout.

FIGURE 4.6 Optimizing the layout so that the Project window shows a single-column layout.

Scene – Imagine this as the creator's view. You are the creator, and from this view, you can see visual representations of all the objects currently in the game. In this window, you'll see not only geometry but also icons to represent cameras, lights, particles, effects, volumes, and any other element that is present in your scene. This also includes some other helping UI elements including a grid, and navigation tools in the top right corner. Although, usually I don't use that navigation method. Instead using the very Maya-esque Alt-left, middle, and right mouse-drag will allow you to move around the Scene window. Alternatively, in a very game-like fashion, you can hold the right-mouse button down and use the WASD keys to fly through the scene. Similar to Maya if any object is selected, hitting the "F" key will frame that element in the interface and make it the new center of rotation if you are orbiting around it. Similarly, the keyboard shortcuts of Maya (w-Translate, e-Rotate, r-Scale) are also in effect. If you know Maya, you can maneuver in Unity.

Game – This is what the player will see when playing your game. It is the view of one of the cameras in the scene. When you play the game (using the Play/Pause/Step buttons at the very top of the interface), it is this window you will be interacting with. If you have two monitors, it is often helpful to drag this tab (just click and drag the tab that reads Game) onto that second monitor. This allows you to play full-screen on one screen, while still observing what's happening in the Scene window. In this Game window, there are lots of pull-down and button menus at the top that we will be exploring in the future.

Hierarchy – This shows the current elements in your game. The top-most object listed there will be the name of the level you are editing; when expanded, this will show you the objects currently in your scene. This will be a text accounting of objects you can see in the Scene window.

Project – The project window is like your library shelf. This shows elements (models, textures, materials, scripts, particles, scripts, etc.) that Unity knows about and that are associated with this project. An asset must be in the Project window before it can be incorporated into the level.

Inspector – This provides the details of any selected object. When any object is selected (in the Scene, Hierarchy, or Project windows), the exposed attributes (the attributes you can change) will show up in the Inspector window.

To explore the interface, you might try rotating, panning, and flying around the Scene view of the default level Unity provides. Notice that if you click on any object, you can see the specifics of it in the Inspector. When you're done getting familiar with moving around inside the space, move onto the next step to get started constructing our own game.

> Step 12: Create a new scene. Unity calls game levels "scenes". Although scenes can be more complicated than simply one level of a game (via additive level loading, etc.), for our purposes we're going to create one new scene and think of it as a level of our game. Do this by selecting File>New Scene.
> Step 13: Save it as MainLevel. Choose File>Save. This will open a Save Scene dialog menu. Navigate to the Scenes folder, enter "MainLevel" in the File name: input field and hit save.

Why?

Notice that this is inside the folder that is storing this Unity project. Specifically, it is saving it inside a folder called Assets. It is important that you don't save anything outside of the Assets folder for use in this Unity project. In fact, it's important that generally you don't mess with where files are placed within your Unity project folder in any other place but Unity. If you need to delete an asset, do it in Unity (not in your Finder). This will ensure that you keep your project clean and Unity is able to keep track of where it expects assets to be.

> Step 14: Clean up the Unity project. Unity has provided a sample scene and a load of other sample assets to get your started. Unfortunately, these make the project needlessly large. To keep things a bit leaner, in the Project window select and delete (just hit the Delete button on your keyboard) the following assets: Example Assets (folder), Readme (file), and TutorialInfo (folder). Also expand the Scene folder and delete samplescene (scene file) and sample scene (folder). Your remaining Hierarchy should look something like Figure 4.7.
>
> Step 15: Prepare Unity for asset import. Keeping an organized project is important once we get hundreds (and even thousands of assets). In the Project window, create folders called Models, Textures, Materials, and Scripts. Do this by right-clicking in the Project window and choosing Create>Folder, or clicking on the + button at the top left of the Project window and selecting Folder from the pop-down menu (Figure 4.8).

FIGURE 4.7 Streamlined project. We've eliminated assets Unity included as tutorial files to keep the project lean.

FIGURE 4.8 Our organized Unity project. Folders here have been created into which we'll import a variety of assets to build our level.

Tutorial 4.2: Exporting Asset from Maya and Substance Painter into Unity

Now that our Unity project is created and we're ready to import assets, we can begin exporting assets from Maya and Substance Painter. The steps here are not difficult, but without a little bit of file preparation we can have trouble down the road. So, making sure files are properly prepared before importing into Unity is critical.

If you have been following the past tutorials and have completed all the extra assignments, you can work on your own file. Or if you've (ahem) skipped some of your homework, you can use the files included on the support website for this chapter to download and work with.

> Step 1: Open Maya file. In Maya, set your project and open Models_Complete_ReadyToExport. mb. A quick snapshot of this file shows the assets all separated as they were before export into Substance Painter. This scene is also carefully organized with geometry in groups as per the materials that we created and painted in Substance Painter.
> Step 2: Delete History. Choose Edit>Delete All by Type>History.

Why?

History can be of great help when modeling in Maya, but is not of help when working in a game engine. A model with History will bring in strange empty nodes into your game engine that can cause problems later. For static meshes – meshes that don't move, getting rid of any nodes that might still be hanging on will make sure you only push geometry (with its UV layout) to the game engine.

> Step 3: Freeze the Transformations. Older engines (like UE4) require that all models be actually sitting at 0,0,0 in world space. Unity, as a newer engine doesn't have this restriction; however, it

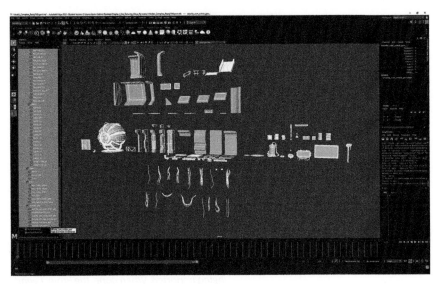

FIGURE 4.9 Marquee select all the geometry (not the groups) and then freeze the transformations.

> is important that the assets report themselves as
> being at 0,0,0. To do this, marquee-drag around
> all the assets in the scene. This will select just
> the geometry (not the groups (Figure 4.9)). Now
> select Modify>Freeze Transformations.

Why?

Freezing Transformation resets the Translate X, Translate
Y, and Translate Y to 0. Unity will interpret these models as
being at "the origin" or 0,0,0 in world space. This will make
for easy placement and manipulation later.

> Step 4: Export as FBX. Choose File>Export All....
> As before, make sure that Files Of Type is set to
> FBX Export. In the Options section, expand File
> Type Specific Options>Include>Geometry and
> make sure that Smooth Mesh and Triangulate
> are checked. Additionally, in that same Include
> section turn off Animation, Cameras, Lights,
> Audio, and Embed Media. Navigate to your
> Unity project and into the models folder (...\The
> Escaper\Assets\Models). Enter "RawModules"
> for the File name, and hit Export All.

Why?

Again, our goal here it to export just the geometry. We'll get the textures from Substance Painter, and other elements like cameras, lights, and audio will be created or assembled in Unity. We want to pass along just the polygons at this point.

Notice that we are also exporting directly into the Unity project – and specifically into the Assets/Models folder. This keeps the process fast, and we don't have to be moving files around out in the finder.

> *Step 5: Check import in Unity. By saving into the Unity project, when Unity is activated again, it will say, "Aha! There's something new in Assets. Let me take a look at that!" You may get a brief progress bar that shows the RawModules.fbx being imported. When done, the Project window will show RawModules as an FBX ready for you to work with. Just for fun, drag the RawModules from your Project window into the Hierarchy (or Scene window) to place it in your scene (Figure 4.10).*
>
> *Step 6: Adjust import settings. In the Project window, select RawModules. The Inspector will show the Import Settings Unity used to import the FBX. To keep the scene lean, click on the Rig button and change Animation Type to None. Click the Animation button and turn off Import Animation. Finally hit Apply.*

FIGURE 4.10 Geometry imported into Unity. It's not ready to use yet, but Unity knows about it and is ready to work with it.

Why?

Of course, this is still missing textures and shaders. We haven't brought those in from Substance Painter yet. And currently it's all one big file, which defeats the purpose of a modular layout. Not to worry. We still have some work to do before we can actually build with these modules. By turning off Rig and Animation, we can make sure that we only have the geometry in this file and nothing else.

> *Step 7: Make sure you're running the latest version of Substance Painter. Open Substance Painter and go to Help>Check for Updates. If you need to download and install an update, do so.*

Why?

Our plan is to use Substance presets for output. As Unity has adjusted their Render Pipelines, Substance has updated their presets to match. For the smoothest move from Substance Painter to Unity, we should have the latest presets in action.

> *Step 8: Find and open the Substance Painter texture files. In Substance Painter, open the files created in previous chapters. If you'd like to use the versions we built, they are on the website as part of the Maya project for this chapter. The files are stored in the sourceimages folder and called props_texturing, modular_pieces_texturing, Hero_asset_texturing, door_texturing, security_camera_texturing.*
>
> *Step 9: Export texture files from Substance Painter into Unity. Figure 4.11 shows Substance Painter with modular_pieces_texturing open. To export the textures, choose File>Export Textures. In the Export Textures window, first make sure that all the materials created in this file are checked on the left side. Then set the Output Director to your Unity project's Textures folder (…/The Escaper/Assets/Textures). Change the Output Template to "Unity HD Render Pipeline (Metallic Standard)". Change the File Type to Targa and 8 bits. Leave the size as Based On Each Texture Set's Size and*

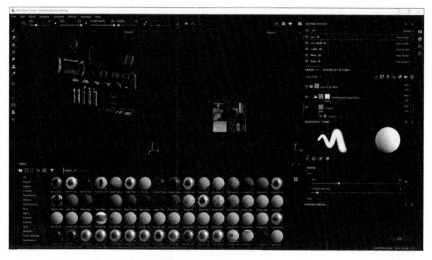

FIGURE 4.11 Where we left off in Substance Painter for the modular_pieces_texturing file.

leave the Padding at Dilation infinite. Hit Export. Depending on how many textures you have, this can take a while to export.

Why?

Lots of "why's" here. We're exporting directly into the Unity project to streamline the asset movement process. In the next steps, we'll look at how Unity imports these new textures it will discover in its Assets/Textures folder. By leveraging Substance Painter's output templates, we can make sure and export the assets we need for our HDRP workflow. Targas are my preferred file format as it is lossless and will maintain its fidelity, although Unity is pretty good at bringing in almost any image file format. Unity only deals in 8-bit textures, so no need to export anything larger than that.

> *Step 10: Repeat export process for all Substance Painter files. Be sure to mimic the settings shown in Figure 4.12.*
> *Step 11: Import textures into Unity. This is actually pretty easy: just go to Unity, and when it realizes, there are new files in its Assets folder it will import them. This may take a while to complete.*

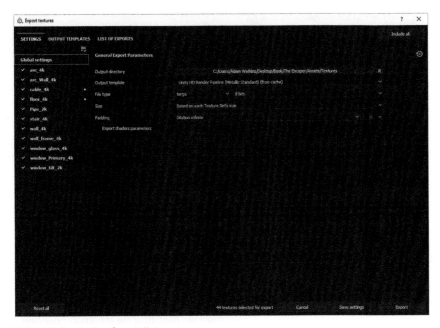

FIGURE 4.12 Export settings for use in Unity.

Step 12: Mark Normal maps as Normal Maps. At the
top of the Project window is a small input field
with a magnifying glass on it. In that input field,
type "normal". This will show all the files that
have "normal" in their name. Notice that there
is likely one file that looks different than the
rest – a preset called NormalTexture. We won't
mess with that one. But in the Project window,
select the first of the displayed normal maps and
then shift select the last. Deselect NormalTexture
(by Ctrl-clicking it). Then in the Inspector, change
the Texture Type to Normal Map (Figure 4.13).
Finally, in the Project window's search input field,
click the little "x" to return the Project window to
regular view.

Why?

Normal maps are strange beasts with much more data in
them that meets the eye. Marking these normal maps that
Substance Painter output helps Unity know how to deal
with these maps and how to use them.

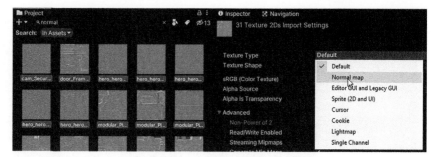

FIGURE 4.13 Setting all the normal maps to be imported as normal maps and not default texture maps.

Step 13: Extract the materials for editing. In the Project window, select our imported FBX RawModules (in the Models folder). Then, in the Inspector, in the Import Settings click the Materials button. Click the Extract Materials… button. In the Select Materials Folder, navigate to the Materials folder within your Asset folder of your project and click Select Folder. You'll see that all of the materials have been filled in beneath that (Figure 4.14). Notice also that in the Project window, if you expand the Materials folder, there are lots of new files there.

Why?

By extracting the materials in this way, we now are able to manually rebuild them to use the textures we exporting from Substance Painter. Until they are extracted like this, they cannot be edited. Notice that these materials (if selected in the Project window) are a shader called HDRP/Lit and make use of the HDRP Metallic workflow.

Rebuilding Materials

So now you have a folder full of materials. These materials are already applied to the geometry in the scene, but without textures to define the various attributes of the materials, they all look gray. The task now is to rebuild the materials using the textures generated from Substance Painter.

FIGURE 4.14 Extracting the materials so we can adjust them and plug in our textures.

> *Step 14: Rebuild hero_sphere_4K material with textures. In the Project window, select hero_sphere_4k. This will bring up that material in the Inspector. Expand the section called Surface Inputs. Notice that several of the inputs have a dark gray to the left of their name.*

To assign a texture to these attributes, find the appropriate texture in the Textures folder (so hero_hero_sphere_4k_BaseMap) and drag the texture from the Project window into the appropriate slit in the Inspector window (Figure 4.15). Repeat for the Mask Map (hero_ hero_sphere_4k_MaskMap) and the Normal Map (hero_hero_sphere_3D_Normal).

Step 15: Untint the Base Color. By default, materials in Unity are a 50% gray. This is defined (in this case) with the Base Map being tinted (Figure 4.16) gray. But now we are defining the Base Map with a texture map, and so need to untint it. Do this by double-clicking on the little gray swatch (to the right of the words Base Map and to the left of the Eye Dropper icon) and use the Color picker to change this to white.

Step 16: Repeat the last two steps for all of the hero asset. Notice that (in our demo scene) there are multiple materials (in the Materials folder)

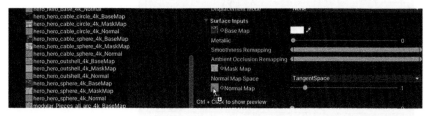

FIGURE 4.15 Plugging in the textures for each material. The naming is fairly straightforward, so plugging each texture in is just a matter of dragging from the Project window into the appropriate slot in the Inspector window.

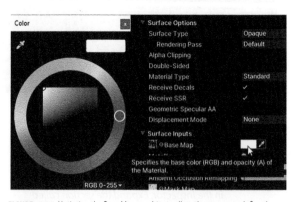

FIGURE 4.16 Untinting the Base Map to white to allow the texture to define the color of the surface.

called *hero_base_4k1, hero_cable_circle_4k1, hero_cable_sphere_4k1, hero_outshell_4k,* and *hero_sphere_4k. The textures for each of these should be easy to identify and plug in. Take your time and be careful; it's easy to zone out and plug the wrong texture into the wrong place and get weird results. Also remember to untint the Base Map as you go.*

Step 17: *Check out the results. In either the Scene window or the Hierarchy window, find the object named "hero", click it and hit F. This will frame the asset. You should have a shape with materials that is much more exciting than the gray plastic we had just minutes ago (Figure 4.17).*

Step 18: *Repeat for all the materials. I know, I know. Boring and will take a while. I understand, and usually in a case like this we would write a script to automate this process for us. But with what we know now, the good ol' fashioned manually-plugging-in-textures is the way to do it. Remember that the name of the textures often is related to the group the geometry is in.*

FIGURE 4.17 Results of our handiwork rebuilding materials.

FIGURE 4.18 Finished rebuilt materials. Notice that this screenshot was taken on the other side as earlier images. To be able to see this, the Directional Light was selected in the Hierarchy and rotated.

As you go, take a look at the models in the scene. If something doesn't look right, its usually an error in plugging things in, so just double-check the material and the textures you have plugged in. When it's all done, it should look like Figure 4.18.

Tips and Tricks

Notice that in each material, not only is there a little gray swatch where a texture can be dragged in, but there is also a little bullseye target icon next to each channel (like Base Map). If you click that little target icon, a window will pop up that will allow you to select a texture by name for the textures Unity knows are in the project. Sometimes, this can be an easier way to populate material channels.

Moving On…For Now

We're not done with materials yet. You've probably noticed that we have shapes that should be clear glass that aren't. And there are surfaces that should be emissive and illuminated, but that aren't yet. We'll be back to revisit and refine the materials later, but for now we'll move on to other tasks. Materials are highly dependent on the lighting situation that is illuminating them, and even the camera settings of the camera looking at them. Before we spend too much time delving into the fine tuning, we'll start building the set and make adjustments as we go.

Tutorial 4.3: Creating Prefabs

Prefabs are a powerful tool within Unity. What they are are objects that might have simple attributes like geometry and materials, but they can also be an object that has scripts, and colliders, and visual effects, and animation, and the list goes on. The idea of a prefab is that the developer can construct an object and hang all the components needed and then store this prefab in the Project window. Then, when needed, prefabs can be dragged out into the Scene or Hierarchy window, and it brings all the preparation with it. There's lots more to the power of a prefab, including the ability to make a change to one instance of a prefab in a level and propagate that change to all the other instances (think changing the color light and everywhere using that same light bulb updates), but we'll get to more of that later.

For now, the important idea is that we want to split the textured geometry off of the FBX they came in on. While we do that, we'll create some very efficient collision detections and prepare the files to modularly build out our level.

> Step 1: Create a Prefabs folder. In the Project window, create a new folder called Prefabs. Remember, you can do this by clicking on the "+" sign at the top of the Project window and choose Folder. We'll store our prefabs here so we don't get mixed up with our non-prepared geometry.
> Step 2: Create a folder called Floors in the Prefabs folder. In the Project window, with the Prefabs folder selected, again choose the "+" button and create a new folder called Floors. This folder should be inside the Prefabs folder. If it is not, just drag it into that folder.
> Step 3: Repeat and create new folders for each of the categories of our imported assets: Arcs, Cables, Pipes, Stairs, Walls, Windows, and Props. You can organize differently if you desire (Figure 4.19).

FIGURE 4.19 Organizing our folders before creating our prefabs.

A Bit about Colliders

In the Hierarchy, click on the object floor_01. Move your mouse over to the Scene object and hit F on your keyboard to frame the object. If you now look at the Inspector, you can see some information about this floor_01. There are several components there: Transform, a Mesh Filter, Mesh Renderer, and the material. Each of these components tells this object how it is to appear or behave in the scene. Currently it knows where it is (in the Transform node) and how it is supposed to appear (the Mesh Filter and Mesh Renderer along with the Material do that). But it currently doesn't know how to be involved in collisions. This means that if we play the game, and walked on this floor, we'd fall right through it. Colliders are components the game engines use to know when objects have bumped into or penetrated each other. In our case, they will be important so we can't walk through walls or fall through the floor.

By default, Unity imports meshes without colliders as it assumes that if you want a collider, you'll add one. Not all colliders are equal, however, and some are much more expensive than others. In most commercial games you play, the colliders have been carefully designed to be as efficient as possible. So, for instance, this floor would usually have a Box Collider that is very cheap. There are several cheap colliders in Unity based on basic shapes: Box Colliders, Sphere Colliders, and Capsule Colliders. We point this out because we're about to take a quick but expensive shortcut. Mesh Colliders are colliders that makes every polygon detect collision. This is the most

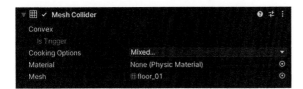

FIGURE 4.20 Newly added Mesh Collider. This is the quickest, but most expensive collider to add.

accurate collision detection, but also the most expensive. For our purposes, this will be quick and easy, but it is only fair to point out that it's also fairly inefficient to the performance of most games.

> *Step 4: Add Mesh Colliders and Lightmap UVs to everything. In the Project window, select RawModules (in the Models folder). In the Inspector window, click on the Model button at the top. These are options that set how the geometry is interpreted or edited upon import. Here, leave everything at its default setting, but also make sure and check Generate Colliders and Generate Lightmap UVs. Click Apply. Take a break as this can take a while to process. Notice that after this is done, if you select any of the meshes in the Scene window the Inspector will now show a new Mesh Collider component (Figure 4.20).*

Why?

We've already talked about collisions, but what are Lightmap UVs? Later we are going to bake some of our lighting (real-time light calculations are expensive). Lightmap UVs are a separate UV set that will store the lighting information when we bake. Right now, this will seem like a strange and esoteric step, but it will become clear later.

> *Step 5: Unpack the RawModules prefab. In the Hierarchy window, right-click on the RawModules object and choose Unpack Prefab. This will allow us to then start moving individual parts into their own Prefabs. Noticeably, the texture for RawModules will change from blue*

*(the color of a prefab) to gray (an instance of
an object).*

*Step 6: Create Prefabs for door and hero and pot.
Do this by dragging each object from the
Hierarchy into the Project window. Sometimes
this will be a group; so for instance start with
door and (from the Hierarchy window) drag
door (the parent door, not the individual parts)
into the Prefabs/Modular Pieces folder. You'll
see a new "door" object appear in the Project
window, and door will appear in blue text
again in the Hierarchy. Repeat for "hero", "pot",
and "security_cam" (the pot and security_cam
groups are inside the Props group if you're using
our tutorial file).*

Why?

We're doing these three first because they are groups.
The rest of the meshes will be their own prefabs, but
these three objects are composed of multiple meshes,
but meshes that will usually be placed *as a group*.

*Step 7: Create individual Prefabs for the rest of the
objects in RawModules. This is easy but boring.
For the rest of the objects in the Hierarchy
(that are currently gray text), drag each one
(one at a time) from the Hierarchy window into
their accompanying folder in the Project window.
When you are done, you'll have all the assets as
ready-to-place modular pieces (Prefabs) in the
Project window.*

Tips and Tricks

As you go, it can be helpful to further organize the Project
window. Making new subfolders can help keep your
separated assets organized. Notice also that the process
of dragging an object from the Hierarchy to the Project
window doesn't need to be terribly accurate at first.
You can drag an object from the Hierarchy window into any
empty space in the Project window and a prefab will be
created. I usually find it easier to quickly drag each prefab
into an empty spot in the Project window and then move
these prefabs into their appropriate folder afterwards.

*Step 8: Delete RawModules **from the Hierarchy**.
It is important to keep track of which one you
are deleting here. We never want to delete
RawModules from the Project as this is the
library of geometry we build these prefabs from.
However, the instance of RawModules that is in the
Hierarchy/Scene window is no longer of use to us.
So in the Hierarchy window, select RawModules
and hit Delete on your keyboard. Note that the
original FBX is still in the Project window, and all of
our newly created individual prefabs are also still in
the Project window ready to be used.*

Tutorial 4.4: A Bit of Material Adjustment

Up to this point, we've been painting with a pretty
broad brush. All the objects have come in with the same
import settings (except the normal maps), and while
this usually works fairly well using the Maya->Substance
Painter->Unity workflow, there are a few things that we
need to get adjusted. Namely, we need to adjust objects
that were glass (like the pot), and emissive surfaces (like
the monitors and lights). To explore these and fix the
problems, we will create a very simple hallway.

*Step 1: Adjust the camera exposure. Go to Edit>Project
Settings. In the Project Settings window, on the
left, choose HDRP Default Settings. On the right,
look for Volume Components and expand the
Exposure area. Change the Mode to Use Physical
Camera (Figure 4.21).*

Why?

Auto Exposure is the idea that the virtual camera we are
using to see the scene is automatically adjusting its virtual
aperture depending on the amount of light it senses.
Many real cameras do this (as does your eye). However,
I find it to be a real problem in virtual environments.
Both UE4 and Unity now start with Auto Exposure
activated, and it means that as you change the light
intensities of the lights in the scene, the camera is
automatically adjusting at the same time. This means

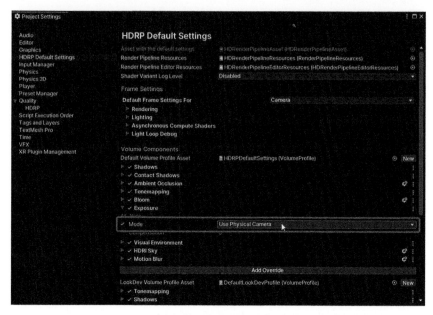

FIGURE 4.21 Adjusting the camera to Use Physical Camera. We'll change this later.

that once you get above a certain intensity of light, as you make it brighter and brighter, the camera closes the aperture, untill it becomes smaller and smaller, and the resulting light doesn't seem to change. This is maddening when designing a lighting scheme. Changing the Mode to use a Physical Camera gives you all the power of a more sophisticated virtual camera, but doesn't automatically adjust the amount of light the camera picks up.

> Step 2: Place a floor prefab. In the Project window, find the object floor_01. Drag it from the Project window into either the Hierarchy or Scene window. In the Hierarchy window, select it and then in the Inspector window change the Positions X, Y, and Z to 0. Hit F to frame it in the Scene window.

Why?

It's not necessary, but getting the first piece in the middle of the world makes for easier understanding of where all the pieces are laid out.

Tips and Tricks

Now that we've adjusted how the camera sees the lighting, you might find your scene a bit dark. If this is the case, select your Directional Light (in the Hierarchy) and then in the Inspector increase its Intensity (I'm using 100,000 as its Lux value).

> *Step 3: Duplicate the placed floor. In the Scene window, select the newly placed floor by clicking on it. Hit Ctrl-D to duplicate it. It will not seem like much has changed, but if you look at the Hierarchy you'll notice a new object called floor_01(1). Unity has indeed duplicated the object, but it's sitting at the exact same place as the original. Hit W on your keyboard (to shift to the Move/Translate tool) and move the second floor away from the first (Figure 4.22).*
>
> *Step 4: Snap the floors together. Press-and-hold the V key on your keyboard. You'll notice the handles on the object begin to move around. What its actually doing is moving to vertices on the selected object. Move your mouse to one of the vertices you wish to snap **from**. Then (still holding V down), click-drag to the vertex on other floor that you want to snap **to**. This will snap the first floor to the second (Figure 4.23).*

Tips and Tricks

Some other game engines (like Unreal) work on the assumption that you are going to be snapping to grids.

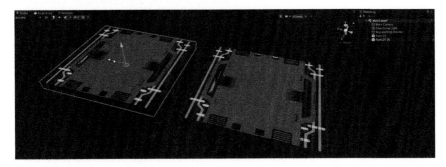

FIGURE 4.22 Moving the duplicated floor away from the first just to see the two separate pieces.

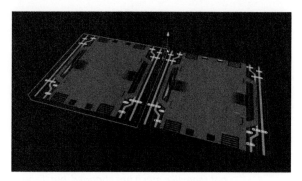

FIGURE 4.23 Using the Vertex Snap method to snap one floor to another.

And, in fact, the model has been built on a grid-assembly assumption. However, Unity offers more sophisticated snapping methods. They are different than most 3D tools, but very effective once you get the hang of it

> Step 5: Place and rotate first wall. From the Project window, drag wall_03 into the Scene. Hit the E key to swap to the Rotate tool. Hold the Ctrl key down (to snap) and rotate along the Y axis (by click-dragging the green circle on the rotation handle) to match Figure 4.24. Then hit W to change to the Move/Translate tool and using the snap method from Step 4, snap the wall into place (Figure 4.25).
>
> Step 6: Duplicate the wall and place on the other side of the hall. Again, Ctrl-D to duplicate. E to rotate, holding Ctrl down to snap the rotation. W to Move, holding V down to snap by vertices.
>
> Step 7: Create a ceiling with rotated floor pieces. Select each of the floor pieces, duplicate them, and flip them 180 degrees on their X axis, so the orange side is facing down. Use the Move tool and snap them to the top of our module group (Figure 4.26).

Tips and Tricks

Your scene might be getting a little dark. If you notice in Figure 4.26, the lighting has been turned off. To do this, just check the little light-bulb button at the top left of the Scene window. Remember though that you've turned this off. It will be important that we turn it back on later.

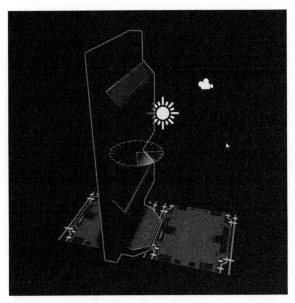

FIGURE 4.24 Rotating the placed wall module. Note that holding Ctrl down will snap the rotation by 15 degrees at a time.

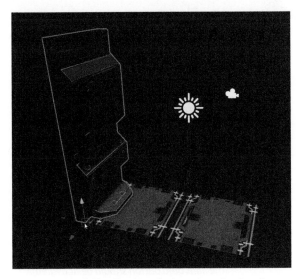

FIGURE 4.25 Using the Move/Translate tool and snapping to place the wall.

FIGURE 4.26 Duplicating the floor to make the ceiling. Notice that lighting has been turned off for this screenshot (see Tips and Tricks).

Step 8: Duplicate this module to create a hallway. Either 1) Marquee drag around our wall and floor pieces in the Scene window (making sure not to grab the camera or lights) or 2) select each element (shift-select) in the Hierarchy. Hit Ctrl-D to duplicate all of them and then hold the V key down and use the Move tool to snap the newly duplicated shapes over. Repeat eight or ten times to create a long hallway (Figure 4.27).

Step 9: Create a simple lighting scheme. We'll talk much more about lighting later, but for now choose GameObject>Light>Point Light. Be sure that lighting is enabled in the Scene window (the light bulb button should be activated). The results will likely be a very dark scene.

FIGURE 4.27 Hallway created by duplicating one section. Be sure to use vertex snapping to make sure they are snug with each other.

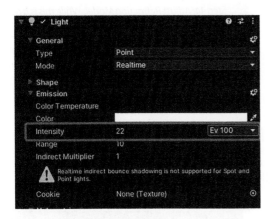

FIGURE 4.28 Adjusting the intensity of a point light.

Step 10: Adjust the settings of the new Point Light. Select the new Point Light in the Hierarchy. In the Inspector, look for the Light component, and expand the Emission section. In the Intensity area, change the unity pulldown to Ev 100 and change the intensity to around 23 (Figure 4.28). If you need to adjust the point light's position to make sure it's in the hallway, do so now.

Why?

HDRP has some new ways of measuring light intensities – not all of them easy to use. The default unit for lights are Lumen. But the values needed for these are huge (six million or so). Numbers that large are goofy to work with, so I prefer using Ev 100 as the unit. This means, sometimes, fine-tuning lights is tweaking in the tenths, hundredths, or even thousandths of a unit, but it's still preferable to Unity showing a value of "1.31768e+07"!

> *Step 11: Duplicate and move the point light to illuminate the hallway. Don't get too worked up over this...just provide some light in the hallway.*
> *Step 12: Place the pot in the hallway.*
> *Step 13: Make the glass material transparent. The pot prefab actually has two meshes: pot_body and pot_glass. In the Hierarchy, expand pot and choose pot_glass. In the Inspector, scroll down to the pot_glass_2k material and expand Surface Options. Change the Surface Type to Transparent (Figure 4.29).*
> *Step 14: Adjust Refraction Model. While this is a good start, it doesn't really look like glass yet. In the Inspector in the pot_glass_2k material section, continue scrolling down and look for Transparency Inputs. Change the Refraction Model to Box and shift the Index of Refraction to 1.7 (or so). The results should be a much more realistic look (Figure 4.30).*

Tips and Tricks

For fun, try playing with this section. Change the Refraction Model to Sphere and change the Index of

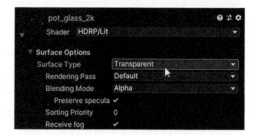

FIGURE 4.29 Tracking down the glass material and changing it to a Transparent shader.

FIGURE 4.30 Adjusting the Transparency Inputs by controlling the Refraction Model (Box) and Index of Refraction (1.7).

Refraction to 1 and change the Transmittance Color to some non-white color and see the results. Be sure to rotate around the object in the Scene window to see the results. It's easy to see how the shader can be adjusted to make the pot go from an empty glass container to one filled (Figure 4.31).

Finally, remember that at this point you can delete the pot from the scene (or not) and the changes made to the Material will be remembered by Unity.

FIGURE 4.31 Continued exploration with the Transparency Inputs (using Sphere Refraction Model and a non-white Transmittance Color).

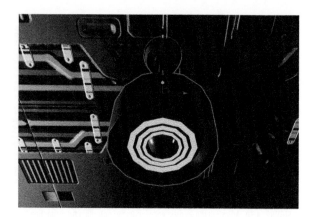

FIGURE 4.32 Placement of the wholly unconvincing light.

> *Step 15: Place ceiling_light_01 into scene. Place this prefab into your scene by dragging it from the Project window (Prefabs folder) into your scene. Move it to some reasonable place on the ceiling (Figure 4.32).*
>
> *Step 16: Adjust the Light_2K texture to appear lit. In the Scene window, make sure the ceiling_light_01 is selected. In the Inspector, scroll down and notice that there are two materials attached to this single mesh: Light_2k and light_geo_2k. The Light_2k is the one of interest to us, as it doesn't look like this light is turned on. Expand the Light_2K material and change the Shader to HDRP/Unlit. Then scroll down to Emission Inputs. Expand it and check on User Emission Intensity and Emission. Change the new Emission Intensity unity to EV100 and enter Emission Intensity: 25. Finally, change the Global Illumination to None (Figure 4.33).*

Tips and Tricks

At this point, the shader for the light looks better; but if you back up in the scene, it's still largely unconvincing. Just for fun, delete the four point lights, and instead create a Spotlight (GameObject>Light>Spotlight). Move the spotlight so that it is at the bottom of the geometry and adjust its angles and intensity so that it makes sense for the geometry. Duplicate a few of these for the hallway (Figure 4.34).

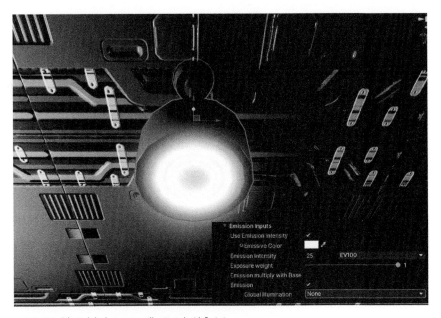

FIGURE 4.33 Adjusted shader to appear illuminated with Emission.

FIGURE 4.34 Adding a few finished lights to the hallway.

Conclusion

There's plenty more to do. Notice that there are other lights that need adjusted materials, and there are things like monitors that also likely need emissive materials. Get in there and start experimenting. Sometimes, learning works best by pushing buttons and sliding sliders once you know where they are and observing the results.

We've introduced some things in this chapter that we will talk much more about later. Namely, we've started using the modules to do some layout and we've made some very basic lights. All of this has been glossed over fairly quickly, and we need to talk much more about them in the upcoming chapters. For now, experiment with shaders and materials. We can always change them later. Once you're happy with the prefabs we have imported and adjusted, move onto the next chapter and we'll start building our level in earnest.

CHAPTER 5

Unity Level Creation

In the last chapter, we imported and refined the modules created in the first part of this book. In this chapter, we get to start to see all that hard work assembled. If you followed the modeling tutorials and built to the specifications Jingtian Li designed the assets to, you will find great flexibility in this chapter as the parts will fit together neatly in a variety of scenarios. You'll be able to build an infinite number of variations of spaces. Here, we will use the modules to design the level for our game. This process is usually called "layout" and is the process of designing how a player will move through the spaces.

The art of layout is one that we won't have time to work with here. However, it is important to acknowledge the importance of level flow and keep the player oriented and know where to go within the level. Here, we will simply look at how to use the modules to lay out one version of the level. If, along the way, you decide you want to make changes to the layout and how we are building the level, go for it. Once you get the hang of how the modules are designed to be assembled, you can "kitbash" the entire level as you desire.

However, as we go, there are some organization tools that will be important to create a reasonable project. Yes, we could just start slamming all the modules into the scene, but the scene would quickly get out of control and the Hierarchy would be unmanageable later when we needed to build interactivity. So, take a while in this chapter and follow along to gather some of the organizing and Prefab-manipulation techniques.

A Quick Review on Snapping

Remember that in the last chapter we looked at snapping modules together using vertex snapping. Older engines rely heavily on snapping to a grid, and Unity can do that too. To use Grid Snapping in Unity, just hold the Ctrl key down when moving an object.

However, the most flexibility comes from being able to snap any element to any other element as we've built. So, remember, when using the Move tool, select the object you want to move, hold V down and move your mouse to the vertex you want to use as your reference snapping point. Then, click-drag and snap that object (by that vertex) to the vertex of the object you wish to snap it to. If you're still having problems with this powerful workflow, take a minute to be sure you're familiar and efficient with it.

Similarly, remember that when using the Rotate tool, holding the Ctrl button down will snap in 15-degree increments. This will allow you to carefully be rotating to 90 degrees so that your geometry snaps together. From here on out in this book, every object moved will be snapped to avoid gaps in the level. Be sure that you are snapping as you go – don't be satisfied with "close-enough."

The Long View

The basic design of this game is that you are attempting to escape the laboratory in which you – a sentient experiment – were grown. The thing that lets you out is a freak accident that cuts power to the facility. You'll sneak your way out with the facility in backup-power mode, avoiding cameras and other previously grown obedient sentient guards. While we aren't going to spend a lot of time on the game-play design, knowing this up front gives us some guidelines. First, we need to make sure that we have plenty of places to hide as we attempt to escape. Second, we're going to need to have a couple of different lighting schemes to switch between. And third we'll need to have cameras throughout. As you're building, keep these things in mind as you adjust your set.

Tutorial 5.1: Level Layout

We'll be doing lighting in the next chapter; so for now, we'll be focusing just on layout out the parts. To do this, we want to make sure that the set is as easy to see and work in as possible. We're going to make some changes to the project settings, but we'll get back to our currently dark and brooding setting later.

> Step 1: Adjust the camera to assist in construction. Select Edit>Project Settings. In the resulting Project Settings window, select HDRP Default Settings on the left, and then look for Volume Components. Expand the Exposure section and change the Mode to Automatic. Then, still in the Project Settings window, scroll down to the Visual Environment (section right beneath Exposure). There, check the Ambient Mode checkbox, and change the drop-down to Dynamic (Figure 5.1). Finally, look for the HDRI Sky section. There activate Intensity Mode: Exposure, then activate Exposure, and change the value to 20.

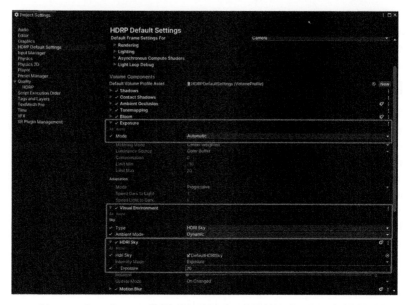

FIGURE 5.1 Adjusting our Project Settings to allow for ambient light throughout (although we'll get rid of this later).

Why?

There are lots of ways to override these default settings. Unity works with an idea called Volumes (Post Processing, Sky and Fog Volumes, etc.), but for the scope of this book, we'll generally work with adjusting the default settings at this point. There may be times you want to swap profiles as you move from Level to Level (Scene to Scene using Unity's language); but for now, since we're working with one Scene, adjusting the default settings works like a Global effect and will be easier to manage.

Note that after changing this setting, if any object is in the scene (try putting the door out there for instance), the dark side of the door will still appear dark until you zoom in close on it. Then the camera will adjust.

Tips and Tricks

So, sometimes (and we think this is a Unity bug), when a scene is reopened, the HDRI Sky Exposure settings seem to have been forgotten. There seems to be some conflict between the default profile that we just edited in the Project Settings and other Global Volumes (Unity's method of controlling effects) that might be in the scene. If you don't get good HDRI lighting, or open the file and everything is dark, in the Hierarchy, find the object Sky and Fog Volume. There, find the Volume component, and the HDRI Sky attribute. Adjust the Exposure there (try 20), and often this will update the lighting settings.

> Step 2: If there is still any geometry left in your scene, delete it. You should be left with Main Camera, Directional Light, and Sky and Volume. Alternatively, you can create a new Scene (File>New Scene) and then save the Scene over your old MainLevel scene.
> Step 3: Place floor_01 at 0,0,0. In the Project window, find the prefab floor_01 from the last chapter and drag it into the Scene window. In the Inspector, set its position to 0,0,0 for its Positions X, Y, and Z.
> Step 4: Flip the floor over. Select the floor and either use the Rotate tool (and hold down Ctrl to snap the rotation) and rotate the floor 180 degrees in X, or in the Inspector enter 180 in the Rotation X input field.
> Step 5: Duplicate, move, and snap two copies. Swap to the Move tool (W), and then Ctrl-D to duplicate. Move (with snapping (V)) the duplicate so that it snapes to the edge of the first. Repeat (Figure 5.2).
> Step 6: Duplicate this row of three tiles three times to create a square room. In the Scene window, marquee drag around the three floor_01 objects

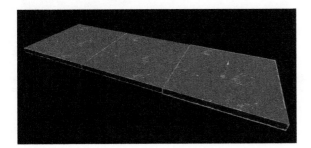

FIGURE 5.2 Three floor_01 prefabs duplicated and snapped into place.

and then duplicate them, and move the three over to match Figure 5.3. Repeat.

Step 7: Snap the corner pieces down to allow room for grates. Select one of the corner tiles and then Shift-select the other three. Snap with the move tool and move these down so the top of them lines up with the bottom of the rest of the tiles (Figure 5.4).

Step 8: Place the grates (floor_04) in the gap. Drag the floor_04 prefab into the scene and vertex snap into place as seen in Figure 5.5.

Step 9: Add extra pizazz by replacing the area under the grate with floor_02 prefabs (Figure 5.6).

Step 10: Using floor_02 and floor_03, add trim around three sides of the room (Figure 5.7).

Step 11: Group and name the floor. Set the Tool Handle Position to Center. This is at the top of the Unity interface (above the Scene window (Figure 5.8)). Notice that it might say Pivot... click it until it says Center. Marquee select all the geometry we have currently built. Hit F to frame it. Choose GameObject>Create Empty. This will create a new GameObject in the Hierarchy. In the Hierarchy window, select all the placed floor elements and drag them onto GameObject to make them children. Rename GameObject to StartRoom_Floor.

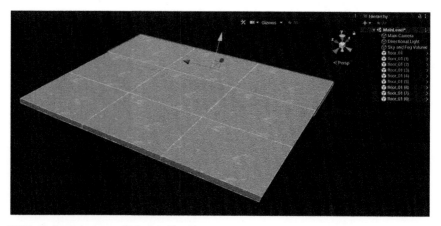

FIGURE 5.3 Roughed out room with duplicated floor tiles.

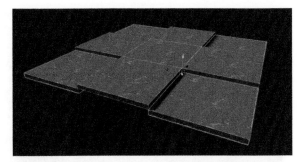

FIGURE 5.4 Snapping the corner tiles down to make room for grates.

FIGURE 5.5 Finishing off the grate.

FIGURE 5.6 Adding extra visual interest by swapping out the units beneath the grates. Alternatively, you could also use floor_03 (although you'd need to place more of them).

177

FIGURE 5.7 Adding trim around three size of the room.

FIGURE 5.8 The Tool Handle Position settings to change where the tool handles appear on selected objects or (importantly) groups of objects.

Why?

Lots going on in this step. Let's break it down. The Tool Handle Position (Pivot/Center) determines where the handle (Move/Rotate/Scale) is displayed. If this is set to Pivot, and a group of objects are selected, the handle will appear on the last object selected. If set to Center, Unity finds the geometric center of the group of objects centered and displays the handle there. Then, when F is pressed, Unity will center its view on the geometric center of the group of selected objects. This becomes handy because when a new object is created in Unity, it is created at the view center. So being focused on the geometric center of a group of objects means the empty GameObject (no geometry of its own – just a container) is created right in the middle of the objects its meant to contain.

Making objects children of an empty GameObject is very similar to how Maya handled groups. The objects will move with the parent object, but can also move independently of the parent. For us, this renamed GameObject (now called Start_Room_Floor) can be minimized to save space in the Hierarchy. We can also select the StartRoom_Floor parent gameobject, and move all the floor at once. However, it's important to see that to select the parent group; you need to select it in the Hierarchy (not the Scene window).

> Step 12: Create wall pieces. Use the wall_01 prefab to create the walls shown in Figure 5.9. Roughly, there is one above every one of the outer floor trim pieces. Be sure to snap into place on top of the floor pieces.
> Step 13: Fill in the corners with Turning_wall_01 (Figure 5.10).

Tips and Tricks

Originally, Turning_wall_01 was designer to be used on the outer corner of a wall. But it's a nice look for the inside corner of this room. It's the power of a modular workflow – you can mix and match modules or parts of modules in whatever way you wish.

FIGURE 5.9 Wall placement using wall_01. Notice that lighting has been turned off for this screenshot by hitting the Toggle Scene Lighting button (the little light bulb at the top of the Scene window).

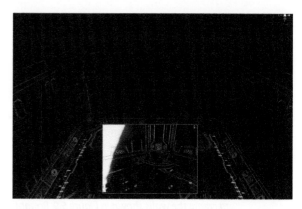

FIGURE 5.10 Filling in the corners with Turning_wall_01. The inset shows the vertex used to snap most efficiently.

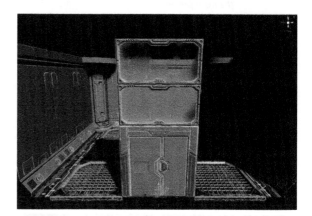

FIGURE 5.11 Roughing out the door and windows above.

Step 14: Build the door. Figure 5.11 shows the door prefab and window_01 (with window_01_glass) stacked above it.

Tips and Tricks

Figure 5.11 actually has a bit of adjustment we haven't explicitly covered in earlier tutorials. The glass and frame are two different shapes, and the glass has its Material attributes adjusted. Be sure you make the window_01_ glass a child of the window_01 prefab. Also, be sure to adjust the material on the window_01_glass shape to be Transparent (if you haven't done already). Finally, on the window_glass_4k material, try experimenting with the Smoothness Remapping attribute to get the look you're comfortable with. Remember that lighting in the Scene view must be activated to see the glass shader in action.

Finally, because many of the shapes here are beveled, vertex snapping might not be the best solution. You can snap to grid by holding the Ctrl key down while moving an object.

Step 15: Finish out the door with door frames. The ones used in Figure 5.12 are the prefabs door_frame_flat.

Step 16: Finish off the wall. Figure 5.13 uses two more wall_01 and two wall_corner_frame.

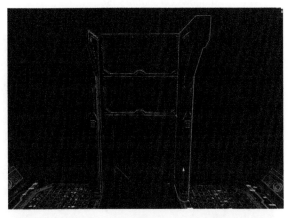

FIGURE 5.12 Door frames (door_frame_flat) to round out the door.

FIGURE 5.13 Finishing off the walls using wall_01 and wall_corner_frame prefabs.

Step 17: Organize the walls by creating a new GameObject (renamed to StartRoom_Walls) and making all the walls a child of it.

Step 18: Use floor prefabs to create the ceiling. Be sure the dark sides of the prefabs (if you're using floor_01, floor_02, and floor_03) are facing into the room (Figure 5.14).

Step 19: Group the ceiling pieces into a new group called StartRoom_Ceiling.

Step 20: If you haven't lately, save your Scene (File>Save). Unity is fairly stable, but why tempt fate?

Step 21: Ensure light can pass through the windows. In the Hierarchy window, find the glass prefabs (arc_window_glass, Tilt_window_02_glass, Tilt_window_03_glass, window_01_glass, window_02_glass) and select them. In the Inspector, look for the Mesh Renderer section and the Lighting area. There change Cast Shadows:Off (Figure 5.15).

FIGURE 5.14 Creating ceiling from floor prefabs.

FIGURE 5.15 Ensuring that our glass prefabs will let light pass through it by setting the geometry to not Cast Shadows.

Why?

Now that there's a ceiling on the room, it's dark in there. Well, it's dark until the camera compensates. Even though the material for the glass panes may be set to be transparent, the geometry still thinks it should stop light. By making sure Cast Shadows is set to off, light can stream through the glass. Importantly, by doing this to the prefabs, every place we have placed the prefabs will automatically use these settings.

The Directional Light that is default in the scene should now be streaming through the windows above the door. Try rotating the Directional Light to see the effect (Figure 5.16).

> *Step 22: Add light geometry into the room. Drag ceiling_light_01 into the room. Select it and, in the Inspector, go to the Light_2k material, and in the Emission Inputs area, change the Emission Intensity back to 0. Figure 5.17 shows one potential lighting scheme. It uses ceiling_light_01 and ceiling_light_02 placed at the ceiling.*

Why?

You probably noticed that before we turned the Emission Intensity back to 0, those lights were all aglow. This is

FIGURE 5.16 Light streaming through our newly non-shadow casting glass panes.

183

FIGURE 5.17 Placing some lighting geometry in the scene.

because of our Adaptive Camera. We want to leave it adaptive for a while longer as we build the geometry out, but it can cause trouble in a room with low light like this one. Later, when we are lighting the scene, we will turn the Emission for the light materials back up.

> *Step 23: "Dress" the scene. Dressing the scene is the process of putting props, boxes, vents, pipes, etc. in the scene to finish it out. Remember to not put too much stuff in there (the player will need to move around eventually), but putting some objects in the scene helps it feel finished. Figure 5.18 is the solution we built – feel free to vary to taste. Just be sure to group into a group called StartRoom_Dressing.*

FIGURE 5.18 Dressed set. Feel free to adjust as you see fit.

Tips and Tricks

The lighting is likely an annoyance at this point. You'll likely see some volumetric lighting artifacts and other things that will bother you. Not to worry. After we get a bunch of this geometry placed we'll start in on the lighting and give the space some real volume and ambiance.

Kitbashing

To "kitbash" is to take a kit of modules and bash them together into endless variations. You can buy kits to bash, although here we've created our own (which is really the professional way to work). Hopefully in the previous steps you got a good idea of the process of placing prefabs, snapping them into position, and/or rotating, moving, scaling the parts into a cohesive whole.

For the rest of this chapter, we will move quite a bit faster. The reason is the specific pieces of the kit that you bash together aren't terribly important and you can deviate from the proposed spaces all you want. However, we will provide some quick suggestions on putting shapes together to provide some guidance of the usefulness of the various pieces of our kit.

> Step 24: Create a floor block to roughly match Figure 5.19. Notice that the center is two floor_01 prefabs. There are pairs of floor_03 on either side of those with the grate (floor_05) on top of that.

Why?

A module here that is two units long allows for the grates to be mirrored so the long hallway will have a more interesting breakup.

Tips and Tricks

Figure 5.19 shows some elements, like the floor_05 grates mirrored (both from across the walkway and from the one closest to them). Mirroring is pretty simple in 3D packages,

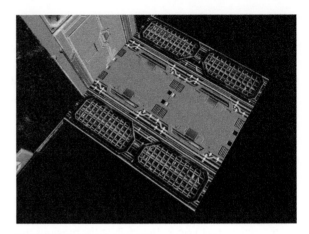

FIGURE 5.19 Start of a hallway module.

just change the Scale (in the Inspector) to −1 in any one direction and you'll have a mirrored mesh along that axis.

> *Step 25: Fill in some curved walls. Pairs of wall_02 are shown in Figure 5.20.*
> *Step 26: Fill in the ceiling. Select the two center floor modules (floor_01), duplicate them, and slide them up to fill in the hole. This will use the dark side of the floor modules for the inside of the ceiling. Perfect (Figure 5.21).*

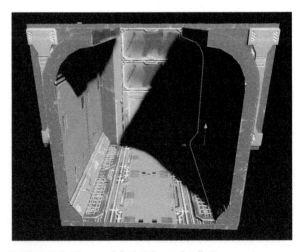

FIGURE 5.20 Building up walls for the hallway with wall_02.

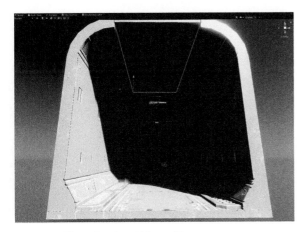

FIGURE 5.21 Filling in the ceiling with floor prefabs.

Step 27: Duplicate and organize. Select all the placed prefabs of this hallway and duplicate (Ctrl-D) and move. Repeat approximately three times (Figure 5.22).

Step 28: Organize into EntryHallFloor, EntryHallWalls, and EntryHallCeiling. Remember the process is to select the elements of, say, the walls; hit F to frame and then create a new GameObject (GameObject>Create Empty). Rename the empty GameObject and place the relevant modules as children by dragging them onto the parent. Finally, create one more GameObject called EntryHall and make these three groups a child of it.

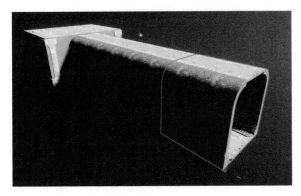

FIGURE 5.22 Duplicating the hall module.

FIGURE 5.23 Dressed hallways.

> *Step 29: Dress the hallway. Pipes, lights, boxes, vents. You know the drill (Figure 5.23). When complete, make the dressing a child of a new EntryHallDressing and make it a child of EntryHall.*

Tips and Tricks

There are few rules to this sort of dressing. Dress until you get tired of the space. However, make sure that objects are not penetrating each other, and remember that a player is going to need to walk through this space; so don't leave any boxes too far out to trip on.

> *Step 30: Create the floor for a corner in the hallway. This requires a little bit of extra real estate beyond four floor_01 modules; note the four floor_03 modules tacked onto the edges (Figure 5.24).*
>
> *Step 31: Use Turning_wall_01 and Turning_wall_02 to create the inner and outer wall of the turn. Notice that you need to rotate each of these 90 degrees in Y. Remember to snap by vertex to match the end walls of the hallway (Figure 5.25).*
>
> *Step 32: Use floor_01 and floor_03 modules to put a roof on the turn. Don't worry about parts sticking out; when we're inside the hallway we won't be able to see them (Figure 5.26).*

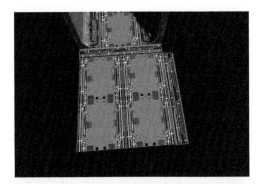

FIGURE 5.24 Building out the extended floor for a turn in the hallway.

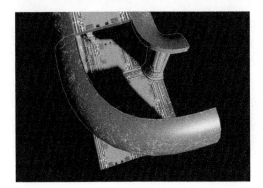

FIGURE 5.25 Building in the curves of the hallway with our pre-built curved wall modules.

FIGURE 5.26 Putting ceilings on using floor modules.

Step 33: Group all of these into a new
HallwayLeftTurn group. This will make this easily
used again later if desired.

Step 34: Duplicate EntryHall, rotate the group
90 degrees and put it on the end of our turn
(Figure 5.27). Tweak as desired.

Step 35: Use wall frame prefabs to provide other
variation to the space. Figure 5.28 shows one
solution using door_frame_flat, door_frame_
top, and wall_corner_frame. Notice the door

FIGURE 5.27 Leveraging effective grouping allows us to duplicate the hallway
quickly, rotate it, and build another long chunk of the level. Note that the pipes have
been removed in this version to allow for some other variation.

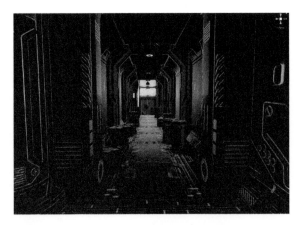

FIGURE 5.28 Further variations of the hallway using frame modules.

and window solution at the end of the hall (just duplicated from the StartRoom).

Step 36: Create the CameraRoom. This room will contain a monitor that the player can come in and check out security monitors of the facility. Make sure there is an exit besides the one used to enter the room, but the specifics are up to you. My solution is in Figure 5.29.

Step 37: Finish off the room with a bit of height (floor_02 turning on its side added to the top of the walls) and some Tilt_02 windows (Figure 5.30). Finally, duplicate the floor and move it up for the ceiling.

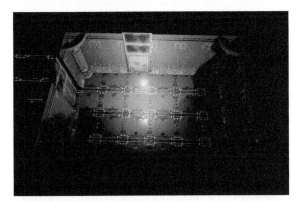

FIGURE 5.29 Roughed out CameraRoom. Note that "CameraRoom" refers to the name of the group all of these assets end up being the children of. Note that there's a temporary Point Light in the scene to help us see what's happening in there.

FIGURE 5.30 Finishing out the room.

FIGURE 5.31 Built platform with stairs. Build to taste.

Step 38: Build a platform with stairs. Build per your own design, but give some difference of height here for variation. We'll put the monitor up on this platform (Figure 5.31).
Step 39: Save.

Tips and Tricks

At this point, we're starting to have a lot of closed off spaces. With our adaptive camera, sometimes the lighting can be goofy to work with. If you find this to be the case, drop some Point Lights into the scene (I'm using 25 EV100 for its intensity). We'll delete them later, but they can be useful while constructing inside a closed room.

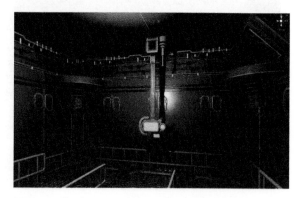

FIGURE 5.32 Placed monitor using Monitor_02 and monitor_mounter.

Step 40: Add a monitor. Figure 5.32 uses Monitor_02 and monitor_mounter.

Step 41: Dress the room. Jingtian Li's original design of the space uses lots of dangling cables and vents. Design as you prefer (Figure 5.33). Be sure to group the dressing (CameraRoomDressing) and make the dressing a child of CameraRoom.

Step 42: Create a new long hallway as we move towards the entrance to the StorageHanger (which we haven't built yet). This time, use the techniques we've looked at before but look at creating a more complicated wall unit (Figure 5.34) for one side, and use glass windows for the other (Figure 5.35).

FIGURE 5.33 Dressed out CameraRoom.

FIGURE 5.34 More complicated module collection for one side of the long hallway.

FIGURE 5.35 Utilizing some of the other modules we have to allow us a glimpse outside, although we'll adjust this in a bit to allow for the Armory.

Step 43: Create a small armory (where the player will get their first weapon in the game) towards the beginning of this newly created long hallway (Figure 5.36). Try using some of the modules we haven't used yet, particularly the arcs.

Step 44: Assemble the entry way and staircase to the StorageHangar (Figure 5.37). This should be at the end of the StorageHangarHallway.

Step 45: Map out the general shape of the StorageHangar by building the floor. The specific size is unimportant, but this is meant to be a large storage space (Figure 5.38).

Step 46: Create some lower wall modules. Explore new pieces and combinations (Figure 5.39).

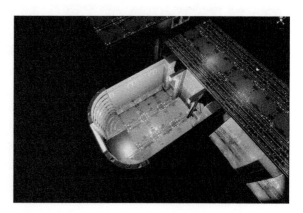

FIGURE 5.36 Creating the small armory using some of the arc modules.

FIGURE 5.37 StorageHangarEntry.

FIGURE 5.38 StorageHangar floor mapped out.

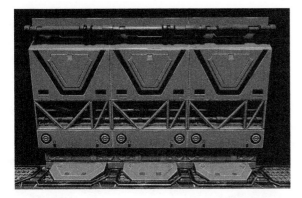

FIGURE 5.39 New combinations of modules to create more sophisticated combinations.

> *Step 47: Finish off the lower walls. Figure 5.40 shows one solution that includes some glass to see outside. Notice that importantly, there is another entrance (or for us exit) on the far side where we will face the final boss.*

FIGURE 5.40 Finishing off the lower walls of the StorageHangar.

> *Step 48: Create a vaulted ceiling using the tilted window collections. No rules here besides completing the roof, but Figure 5.41 shows one solution.*
> *Step 49: Fill the ends of the roof off using windows and the previously unused Tilt_04 (Figure 5.42).*
> *Step 50: Begin filling in the StorageHangar with stairs and catwalks. Remember that among the prefabs is one called floor_5_support to make sure there aren't any floating objects (Figure 5.43).*

FIGURE 5.41 Creating the roof using tilted windows.

FIGURE 5.42 Finishing off the dormers with windows and Tilt_04.

FIGURE 5.43 Catwalks and stairs to begin filling out the space. This screenshot taken with the ceiling turned off in the Inspector.

Tips and Tricks

In a big closed in space like this, a bit of rough lighting will make the process much easier. For the screenshots given for this section, there are several Point Lights placed within the scene. Later we'll get rid of those, but it makes this part much easier.

It's also fairly tricky to be figuring out where to place the catwalks. In fact, it's likely that once you start to play your game, you will find that the flow of the level needs to be adjusted. Not to worry, since the scene is entirely modular, if we need to come back and adjust later, we certainly can.

One note to keep in mind is that we want to help the player know where the other exit is. So if the layout of catwalks and later boxes and other props can help guide the player just a little bit, they will fail to curse your name as they wander, lost through the space.

> Step 51: Dress the set. Add boxes, crates, pipes, cables, etc. Take special note to make sure the exit door is easy to identify and that it looks important (Figure 5.44). Be sure to be organizing with groups as you go along.
> Step 52: Build an entryway to the final boss room. This is just the typical quiet respite space games often provide players before the final battle. To continue to provide vertical variation, we've

FIGURE 5.44 Dressed StorageHangar with emphasis on exit door.

FIGURE 5.45 Entryway to the final boss space.

used a sequence of stairs (Figure 5.45). Adjust as you'd like.

Step 53: Build the FinalBossRoom. Design the space as you'd like. Do keep in mind, however, that this area will need enough open space for the player to run around during the final battle. So while you're designing the space and dressing it to be a visually engaging experience, be sure that you allow for plenty of play area too. Figure 5.46 is the space we built. Organize as you go, and be sure to use the Hero prefab (obviously).

Tutorial Conclusion

There are lots of ways to build an interpret this level. Jingtian Li's modules are designed in a way to allow for most any configuration. Jingtian Li's layout of the boss room, for instance, differs significantly than the interpretation seen in Figure 5.46 – and yours undoubtedly will as well. No matter how you layout the level, you'll likely eventually adjust.

FIGURE 5.46 FinalBossRoom.

Tutorial 5.2: Walking Through

Up to now, we've been moving through the level using Alt-Left, Middle, Right Mouse drag, or Right-Mouse+WASD to fly through the space. However, neither of these are the way the game will be played. The design of this game is a first-person shooter, and we should make sure we can move through the space and experience it like the player would. Plus, it's a bit of a thrill to move through the space as a player.

Historically, Unity had built in a couple of controller mechanisms. In recent years, they released a ball roll, third-person, and FPS controller in a package called Standard Assets. This was a bloated package of tools, but once it was in your scene, you could easily pick a lot of ways to move through a space, and explore a bunch of sample assets. Unfortunately, at the time of this writing, Standard Assets has been discontinued. Unity was soliciting feedback on what to include in an updated package; but it hasn't yet been released. This is shameful for Unity and they need to get this put right soon; but for now we need to look at how to work around this problem.

On the Unity Asset Store (Window>Asset Store), there are thousands of assets created specifically for quick import into Unity. Some are free, and some are not; but the assets are built for use in Unity, and usually implementation is fairly painless. There are quite a few FPS Controllers within the asset store, and some are quite expensive (although very powerful). For us, we will be using the FPSController that originally shipped with Standard Assets. We've pulled it out of the old Standard Assets package, cleaned it up a bit, and made it available for download.

Step 1: Download FPSController Unity Package. To get it, just go to the support website and look into this chapter's support assets. Look for FPSController and download it.

Why?

This file is a Unity Package File, which are zipped archives that can include anything from models to animations, to scripts, to all of the above. Although up to now we've simply saved things that we planned to use in Unity into the Assets folder, for Unity Package Files we need to do this just a little differently.

Step 2: In Unity, import the FPSController package. Go to Assets>Import Package>Custom Package...Track down where your downloaded package is (likely in your Downloads folder) and click Open. You'll be presented with an interface like Figure 5.47. Click Import.

Why?

Notice that this includes quite a few items. There are several scripts in there, readme, and even some geometry. This is the power of a Unity Package – it's not only an import, but it maintains the proper file structure for the imported assets.

When this is done, you will notice a new folder in the Project window called Standard Assets. In general, don't move anything into or out of this Standard Assets folder. The organization is important to the functionality of the FPSController we've just brought in.

Step 3: Put the FPSController into the StartRoom. In the Hierarchy, select the StartRoom and hit F to frame it. Navigate so you can see inside of it. In the Project window, expand the windows to

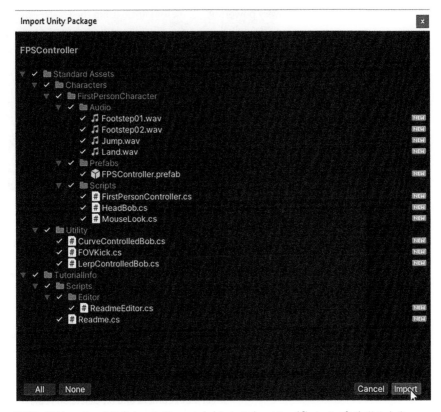

FIGURE 5.47 Importing a Unity Package. In this case, we're bringing in the scripts and file structure for the Unity-built FPSController.

navigate to Standard Assets>Characters>FirstP ersonCharacter>Prefabs. Drag the FPSController prefab from the Project window into the Scene window. You may need to move it up so that it isn't sitting in the floor (Figure 5.48).

Why?

FPSController is a weird looking thing at first glance. There are a lot of gizmos drawn there. You can see the green capsule shape that is the collider, the camera, the audio source, the frustum of the camera, etc. Don't get too caught up on any of it for now. We'll be looking at all the components attached to this over time.

201

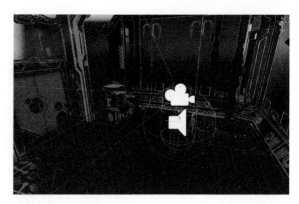

FIGURE 5.48 Placed FPSController.

The one note that is important here though is that when you want to move the FPSController, be sure to select it in the Hierarchy (not the Scene) as you want to make sure you get all of it (not just, say, the camera).

> *Step 4: Delete the Main Camera. When we first created the scene, Unity created a Main Camera. If you've been noticing the Game Window, the view presented there was from this camera. For now, we only want one camera – the one attached to FPSController. So, in the Hierarchy, select Main Camera and hit Delete on your keyboard.*

Why?

Two cameras in a scene can be bad news. For one thing, it means that the scene is being drawn twice (more work than we want for the computer to do). For another, both cameras have Listeners on them that define how the player hears sound in the game – think of them as microphones. If there are two Listeners, Unity isn't sure which to capture sound from. For now, we want to make sure the only camera in the scene is the one attached to FPSController.

> *Step 5: Resize the FPSController. In the Hierarchy, select FPSController and then in the Inspector change the Scales X, Y, and Z to 0.8.*

Why?

Unity's default FPSController is two units tall. Two units in Unity is 2 meters. This means the default character is over six and a half feet tall. Resizing to 0.8 makes the character much closer to the size of the character we will actually play as.

> *Step 6: Make a Point Light a child of FPSController. Select GameObject>Light>Point Light. Make the Point Light a child of the FPSController in the Hierarchy. Select the Point Light and change its Intensity to 25 Ev100. Expand Shadows and, under Shadow Maps, click Enable and under Contact Shadows click Enable again (Figure 5.49).*

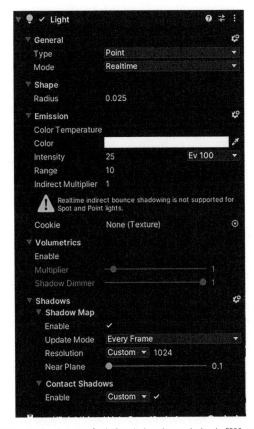

FIGURE 5.49 Rough settings for the Point Light we've attached to the FPSController in the scene.

FIGURE 5.50 The Play button in Unity to try experiencing your work in the Game window.

Why?

So far we've done a lot of modeling, but no real lighting. You may have created a few point lights in the scene to help with modeling, but otherwise the level is going to be pretty strange. This Point Light is a crude way of sticking a lantern on our head so we can see things as we move around. It's not going to be a terribly flattering way to view our level (that will come next chapter when we light it), but we'll be able to see what's happening in the scene.

> Step 7: Play the game to discover you're locked in the room. At the top-center of your Unity interface are three buttons (Figure 5.50). The one on the left is the play button, which will allow you to play your game. Notice that Ctrl-P is the keyboard shortcut for this and is generally the best way to jump in and out of the game. When you hit play, look in your Game window and use your mouse to look around and WASD to move. You'll be able to move around in the room, but not leave it.

Why?

Because everything has a collider on it, we luckily don't fall through the floor. But that means we also, unluckily, can't walk through the doors. Later, we'll create some script that will open the doors as we get close. For now, we need to adjust them so we can walk through them.

> Step 8: Turn off the Mesh Collider for the doors. In the Project window, track down where your door prefab is (in mine it's in the Prefab folder). Double-click it to open the Prefab in the Prefab Editor window. Don't worry, your scene is still there, we're just editing attributes of this prefab. Notice that the Hierarchy only shows the parts

FIGURE 5.51 To exit the Prefab editor, just click on Scenes at the top left of the Scene window.

of the door. Select door_l and in the Inspector, check off the Mesh Collider component (to turn it off). Repeat for door_r. Notice that in the top left of this window you can see something similar to Figure 5.51. When "Scenes" is clicked, you'll exit the Prefab editor and get back to your Unity scene.

Why?

By turning off the Mesh Collider for the door prefab, all the doors that we've place everywhere in the scene will now no longer have a collider. This means we'll be able to just walk through the doors. It's the power of the prefab. If we make changes to the original, all the instances of that prefab inherit that change.

Step 9: Play the game again and you'll be able to pass through the doors.

Conclusion

Lots still to do. Hopefully, at this point, you feel accomplished that you've built the level, but unsatisfied as the lighting is so lame. Lighting is a critical part of the design process that has not only functional uses (if we can't see it's a boring game) but also artistic functions as it can be one of the most effective ways to add ambiance and mood to a scene.

In the next chapter, we'll tear into Unity's lighting tools. Using HDRP, there are some really yummy functions to explore. We'll move our scene from clunky to gloriously spooky.

If you'd like to see the results of this chapter, we've included the Unity project in the Support files on the website.

Post Script

In the next chapter, when we do lighting, our concept is that our incursion is happening at night under the cover of darkness. The lighting schemes are more dramatic that way. However, there certainly is a case for a daytime lighting scenario. The problem is that we can look out the window and see the outside of our facility and it doesn't look good. We've constructed the facility to be lovely from the inside, but the outside is just the backsides of our interior shapes (Figure 5.52).

Lots of solutions here: we could make the windows less transparent, we could swap them out with a solid shape instead of windows, or we could mask out the rest of the building. Masking might be the most fun. It's really beyond the scope of this book, but Unity has a fun Terrain modeler that allows for the creation of Terrain objects (GameObject>3D Object>Terrain) that, using a variety of built-in brushes, allow for the quick painting of rises in altitude (Figure 5.53). Grab a few free assets from the Asset Store (just search for Terrain maps or terrain trees) and the terrain can quickly take shape (although there are some restrictions in HDRP).

Alternatively photogrammetry is a technology that is very exciting in game engines right now. Epic Games (which makes the competing engine Unreal) recently purchased

FIGURE 5.52 Lovely daytime lighting – except that we can see parts of the facility we oughtn't.

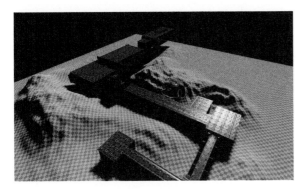

FIGURE 5.53 Roughing out using Unity's Terrain.

Quixel, which had a great library of scanned objects. It is subscription only, and since Epic now owns it, Quixel MegaScans are not as easy to get into Unity as they once were. However, scanned objects can still be downloaded and placed into Unity. Or take a quick search on the Unity Asset store and search for "photogrammetry." Lots of free and inexpensive scanned objects.

Importing into HDRP sometimes take a little bit of tweaking. The objects will usually come in all pink as they are using another type of shader. But with a little bit of rebuilding (change the Material type to HDRP>Lit, and then plug in the Abedo maps into the Base Map), you can produce some nice output (Figure 5.54).

Having said that, we are likely to not see much of this in our version of the next chapter because of our lighting choices there. But it's an easy thing to implement if you need it.

FIGURE 5.54 Blocking out unsightly areas with a bit of free downloaded photogrammetry.

CHAPTER 6

Lighting and Baking

Time for the sexy stuff: lighting! Lighting can be one of the most effective ways to add a visceral, emotional, and impactful atmosphere. Bad lighting can make the most beautifully modeled and textured assets look like ancient technology, while good lighting can make a mediocre asset look AAA. Of course, by the time you're done with the scene, your incredibly crafted assets are going to look even better!

There are some core ideas that we need to cover before diving into Unity's lighting system. The first is that lighting, and its accompanying shadows, bounced light, ambient occlusion, and other natural phenomena, can be expensive to render – particularly in real time for games.

High-end software rendering solutions like VRay and Arnold have been used for years in film, and the output there is amazing. However, it's not unusual for a beautiful VRay frame to take 12 hours to render. In games, where we expect 60 frames to be rendered every second, this is clearly not a workable solution.

When we play games, we are heavily reliant on the video card to make the lighting and rendering calculations quickly. And while video cards are becoming increasingly sophisticated (just take a look at Realtime Raytracing that is just now making its presence felt on games), we still need to do some careful thinking about hardware-driven lighting to make it useful, effective, and, most important of all, keep the game moving.

At its core, there are two and a half different ways of thinking about lighting:

> **Real time** – *This is lighting that is calculated every frame. Every pixel on the screen is the results of all the lighting sources in the scene being accounted for, including where the lighting emission is blocked by some other geometry (resulting in shadows). You want a flashlight in the hands of the player? Gotta be real-time lighting. Want to be able to hit a hanging light so that it swings wildly? Gotta be real-time lighting.*
>
> *Some forms of real-time lighting are not prohibitively expensive and can be used in games. A direct light ray that shoots off in a direction and dies when it hits a surface is not going to break the rendering budget. But if we expect that light ray to bounce off a surface and that surface absorb the light spectrum that represents the color we see, and then have the resulting light ray repeat as it strikes another surface with different color attributes, well, this is beautiful, but computationally heavy and therefore pricey.*
>
> **Baked** – *This is a lighting scheme in which a game engine pre-computes lighting (including the complex scenario of bounced light). The pre-computed lighting is then "baked" into the texture information of the surfaces of the game. Think of this like painting a shadow on the floor (or wall). Because these shadows and*

illumination are painted onto the surface, the computer can take much longer to calculate much more sophisticated renderings. Want a photorealistic interior? It's probably baked. Want effective bounced light that picks up color as it hits a red wall? It's probably baked.

Baking light puts all the rendering time up front on the developers side, so the player's machine doesn't have to work quite so hard. This can make for very sophisticated lighting schemes and visual impact for the player – as long as nothing moves. You see, with baked lighting, if a shadow of a chair is baked onto the floor, when the chair moves the shadow remains where it was baked. So baked lighting is most effective in a truly static environment where lighting and geometry are not going to change.

Mixed *– This is a combination of the two. Mixed lighting schemes bake much of the lighting in, but leave some of it to be rendered in real time. This means that looking down a long hallway can display beautifully pre-rendered lights, but the hanging light right above the player can be bumped, and then the lights and shadows it causes change. This usually take a little more work on the developers side, but the results can be very effective.*

What It Means for You?

Many feel that baked lighting will eventually go away and that all lighting will become real time as the hardware grows in power and sophistication. This is likely true, although we've been told for decades that eventually polycounts won't matter as computers will just get fast enough to draw anything. But, as each generation of hardware emerges, our expectations of visual accuracy and artistry evolves. What once was cutting edge (seen the original *Toy Story* lately?) seems quaint and flat today. The point here is that understanding lighting, baking, and how to effectively use it will definitely still be around for several years to come. And while the game engines arms race continues to rage (we, the users, benefit by this), exploring the different techniques in lighting will always be part of the game.

Unity Lights

Let's start by first taking a quick look at the different types of lights that Unity provides. For a quick exercise, Save your scene (File>Save) and create a new scene (File>New Scene) as a playground. In this playground, create a plane (GameObject>3D Object>Plane). Hit F to focus on it.

Create a few simple shapes (I created four spheres) and set them atop the plane (Figure 6.1).

Notice in the interface there are lots of Gizmos (the little symbols that represent construction objects (in this case the Main Camera, Directional Light, and Sky and Fog Volume)). Each of the Gizmos shown in the Scene window is represented in the Hierarchy.

There is already some light in the scene. Some of it comes from the Directional Light, and some comes from the HDRI Sky that we activated in the Project Settings.

> **Directional Light** – *Think of directional lights as things like sunlight or moonlight. If you select the Directional Light, you can see that it has little rays that indicate the direction the light is coming from and going to. Directional Lights produces light rays that are all in parallel to each other. The illumination from Directional*

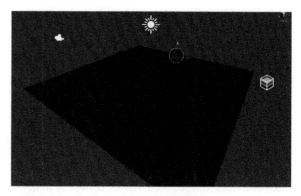

FIGURE 6.1 Playground with the default scene lighting.

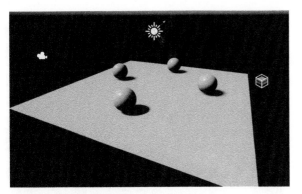

FIGURE 6.2 Directional lights throw parallel lights from infinitely far away an infinite distance. Notice by default they don't cast shadows.

Light comes from infinitely far away and is thrown for an infinite length (no falloff).

Depending on how your camera is interpreting the scene, the default intensity of the directional light can be very low (as it is in Figure 6.1). Notice that, by default, Unity lights to not cast shadow, but they can be activated in the Inspector under the Shadows>Shadow Map>Enable. With the Directional Light selected, you can adjust the brightness in the Emission area and add a couple 0's to the Intensity value (Figure 6.2). Since we're doing an interior scene, we won't worry too much about this lighting type; but while we're here, notice that there's a Color Temperature area that, when activated, will allow you to adjust the color temperature of the light. Finally after you've played with it, delete the Directional Light from the scene.

Point Light – *Point lights are most analogous to a light bulb. The light comes from a point in space and emits in every direction. Try and create one (GameObject>Light>Point Light) and place it in your scene in a place that makes sense. Select it and then, in the Inspector, change the Intensity to 25 Ev100. Again notice, no shadows, but they can be added under Shadows>Shadow Map>Enable (Figure 6.3). There is one other point to note with this light: notice that there is a big light yellow sphere centered on the light. This is the Range of emission for the light. Any objects*

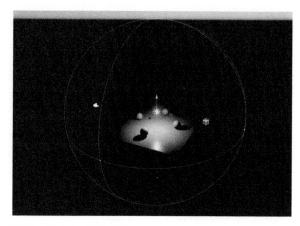

FIGURE 6.3 Basics of a Point Light.

outside of this range (which can be adjusted by dragging the tiny yellow squares on the Range sphere or in the Inspector in the Emission section and the Range numerical value) will not receive any illumination for this particular light source. The combination of increasing/decreasing the Range and increasing/decreasing the Intensity is part of the balance for controlling the brightness for lights in Unity. Play with the light for a minute and then delete.

Spot Light – *Figure 6.4 shows a Spot Light placed in the scene (GameObject>Light>Spot Light).*

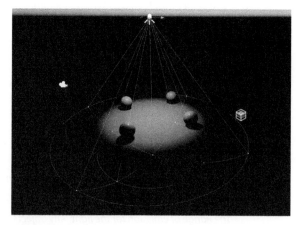

FIGURE 6.4 Spot Light in action.

This light works like the lights we've looked at (Intensity, Range, Shadows, etc.), but it also has a Shape attribute. The shape attribute allows you to change the shape from a Cone to a Pyramid or Box, and it also (importantly) allows for the Outer Angle and Inner Angles to be changed. Try it and see how these angles can be changed in the Inspector or the Scene view. Notice that if the Outer and Inner angles are a long way from each other, the edge of the illumination is soft. But if these get to be the same value, the light becomes focused and the edges hard. Experiment and delete.

Area Light – *Real-time Area Lights are an interesting evolution in lighting. In previous versions of Unity, Area Lights could only be baked, but now this light (that you can think of as a light box) can be used in real time. Create one, turn on Shadows, and turn up the Intensity (Figure 6.5 shows 30 Ev100). Notice that the shadows are very soft. This is because an area light produces light that doesn't come from a single point in space (like a Point or Spot Light), but rather frames a rectangle shape. This rectangle shape can be adjusted in the Shape part of the Inspector although the other shapes have limitations on whether they work only in Real time (Tube) or Baked (Disc). For most cases, the Rectangle shape is going to be the winner.*

As an experiment, change the size of the Rectangle. You'll see that the size of the Area Light has a direct correlation to the amount of illumination it provides.

FIGURE 6.5 An Area Light.

Tutorial 6.1: Lighting the Scene

For the remainder of this chapter, we're going to be using these lighting instruments in our scene. There are other attributes to these lights that we didn't cover in the above discussion, but we'll get to many of them in the course of the following steps.

Further, in this tutorial we will be Baking to see the effects of the lighting choices we make in a baking situation and how to actually bake a mixed lighting situation. Finally, we'll look at completing the look of the game by wrangling Unity's postprocessing effects to refine the look of the scene.

Step 1: Close the experiment scene (Don't Save) and open MainLevel.

Step 2: Get to a blank lighting slate. At the top of the Hierarchy is a search field. There type "Point Light". This will identify all the point lights we may have created as we were modeling. Select them and delete them. In the search input field, click the little "x" to show everything in the scene again.

Why?

We're working on lighting this for the evening. As such we don't want a bunch of random lights we may have inserted during building in our scene. We will be working with practical lights (lights the player can clearly see the source of), and mood lights, but we want to start with a tabula rasa.

Step 3: Disable the Directional Light. In the Hierarchy find Directional Light, and then in the Inspector check off the check-box next to the words Directional Light. This will turn the light off, but not delete it (we'll use it again later).

Step 4: Import alternate skyboxes/HDRI skies. Go to the Asset Store (Window>Asset Store). There, search for AllSky; you'll find a free asset "AllSky Free – 10 Sky/Skyboxes". Click it, then Download, and Import. In the Import Unity Package window, click the Import button. This import can take a little while. When this is done, there will be a new folder in the Project window called "AllSkyFree".

Why?

AllSky is a nice collection of assets for – you guessed it – skies. The paid version is worth every penny, but the free version has some nice assets we can make use of. Incidentally, skyboxes (the asset used to contain skies) can be created from many other downloadable assets. Using something like HDRI (high dynamic range images) can determine how the ambient light in the scene appears. As an example, Figure 6.6 shows the sample scene using a variety of HDRI-based skies. Besides the obvious changes to the color of the sky, the results on the geometry are also clearly seen.

> *Step 5: Plug in AllSky_Night_MoonBurst_Equirect as the HDRI sky. In the present scene, the HDRI sky is stored in the object Sky and Fog Volume. In the Hierarchy, find this object and expand the HDRI Sky section; there is an input field called "Hdri Sky" that should be checked. In the AllSkyFree folder, expand any of the folders and look inside for the cubemap asset (Figure 6.7). Drag that cubemap into the HDRI Sky input field. Experiment with several to see the effect, but in the demo we ended up with the asset in the Night_MoonBurst folder (Figure 6.8).*

Tips and Tricks

This is definitely a bug. Closing the Unity project and then opening it up again will yield the HDRI sky reverted to default. Hopefully that is fixed by the time you are

FIGURE 6.6 Identical lighting, with different HDRI-based skies and the resulting changes in ambient light (global illumination).

FIGURE 6.7 A Cubemap asset. Notice there are lots of other assets in the folder, but the Cubemap is the required one to define the sky.

FIGURE 6.8 Results of the Night MoonBurst HDRI Sky.

reading this; but if not, and you open the scene to see all the lighting seemingly changed, just remap as above upon reopening the file.

> *Step 6: Change the camera to a fixed exposure. Choose Edit>Project Settings. On the left, click on HDRP Default Settings. On the right, scroll down to Volume Components>Exposure. Change the Mode: Fixed and the Fixed Exposure: 8.5 (Figure 6.9).*

Why?

That Automatic exposure we were working with was fine while modeling. But with a camera that is continually adjusting, it is impossible to light. For instance, with

FIGURE 6.9 Setting the camera exposure to a fixed amount. Notice the inside of the level will be very dark – just like we need it.

Automatic exposure selected, the HDRI Sky exposure could be changed to almost any value and the output would remain the same – the camera would simply be adjusting to let the same amount of the light into the camera even though there was more light in the scene. Fixed mode (although you may choose to go back to Physical camera later) will provide us a constant intensity as we build the lighting scheme.

The Power of Prefabs

The power and workflow of prefabs has been covered in earlier chapters, but it is worth repeating. When a prefab is placed in the scene, Unity is *instancing* that prefab. That is, it is creating an instance (or a copy that is still linked to the original) of the prefab. This means, if we adjust the prefab, all the instances of that prefab are also updated.

This will be useful for us as we have been placing the geometry for lights throughout the scene. Now, if we add a light object to the light geometry prefab, every place that we placed a prefab light will suddenly also have a Unity light attached. It will be so effective, in fact, that we might find that we need to delete some of the lights.

Let's start figuring out our lighting choices in the StartRoom (where the FPSController is at). In the Scene window, you may need to turn off lighting (light bulb button at the top left) since the scene will be very dark. Then navigate so you are inside the room (Figure 6.10).

Step 7: Add a Spotlight to the prefab ceiling_ light_01. In the Project window, find the ceiling_ light_01 prefab (Prefabs>Props). Double-click it to open the Prefab Editor. Create a spotlight with

FIGURE 6.10 Getting ready to light (the Game window will be really dark). This is the Scene window with lighting temporarily turned off.

FIGURE 6.11 Placed Spot Light.

GameObject>Light>Spotlight. In the Inspector, change the Position X, Y, Z to 0 to make sure it is lined up with the geometry. Then move it down in Y to approximate Figure 6.11.

Step 8: Adjust the spotlight settings. In the Inspector (with the Spot Light still selected), change the Outer Angle so that it roughly approximates the bottom of the geometry (with my placement this ended up being about 70). Adjust Intensity: 25 Ev100. Enable Shadow Map and Contact Shadows (Figure 6.12). Finally, go back to the Scene window by clicking Scene at the top left of the Prefab Editor window.

Step 9: Re-enable lighting in the Scene window to observe the mess (Figure 6.13).

Why?

What a mess. It's actually pretty easy to clean up, but this is often what happens with first guesses. Let's break down what is happening there. The dirty volumetric light and big rings on the floor are because the light course is up inside of the geometry and the rings of the light are casting a shadow. The intensity might be a little hot as well.

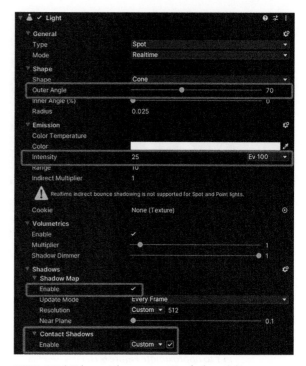

FIGURE 6.12 Initial guess at the necessary settings for the spotlight.

FIGURE 6.13 The results of our initial pass at lighting.

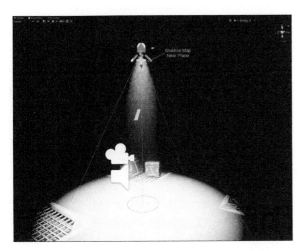

FIGURE 6.14 Adjusting the Near Plane changes where Unity begins calculating shadows from.

Step 10: Still in the scene window, track down the instance of ceiling_light_01 (just click it). In the Hierarchy, the instance will show the Spot Light object that is a child of the ceiling_light_01 geometry. Select it, and in the Inspector, find Shadows>Shadow Map>Near Plane. As that slider is moved to the right, watch carefully in the Scene view. There a circle will descend from the Spot Light's origin to define this near plane (Figure 6.14).

Step 11: Adjust other settings including Outer Angle and Intensity. Figure 6.15 shows the results of increasing the Outer Angle to 80 and reducing the Intensity to 20. It keeps the light from being blown out on the surfaces, but also allows a bit more light in the room.

Make Way for Cookies!

Well, not those kind. Cookies in Unity reference a sort of shadow casting effect on lights. In theater terms, this would be known as a "gobo" – a piece of tin that is put between the bulb and the lens of a theater instrument that can give the effect on the lit stage of leaves that aren't really there, or light coming through a window when there is none. For us in 3D, a cookie will help us steer

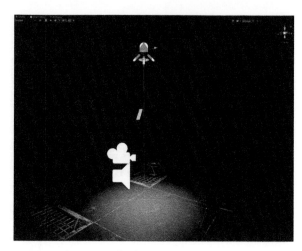

FIGURE 6.15 Continuing to refine the Spot Light.

clear of the too even, too "computery" look that the Spot Light currently has.

Technically, cookies are just images. Although they can be in color, they are usually in grayscale. Usually, they are square images that have a completely black border. There are loads that can be downloaded online (just Google "Unity cookie"), or you can build your own. For this exercise, there are two included on the support website in the Support Files folder for this chapter (SpotLightCookie. jpg and FlashlightCookie.jpg).

Incidentally, there are more effective ways to create more believable lights. IES (Illuminating Engineering Society) files define specifically how different types of lights work in both real and virtual worlds. UE4 allows for IES profiles to be used directly in the engine and is a real shortcoming for Unity. However, IES is on Unity's roadmap and will be welcome when it finally arrives. But since it isn't currently implemented, we'll work with the next best thing: cookies.

> *Step 12: Create space in the Cookie Texture Atlas. Access the Cookie Atlas by going to Edit>Project Settings. On the left, choose Quality>HDRP. On the right, click on the HDRenderPipelineAsset profile near the top and scroll down to the*

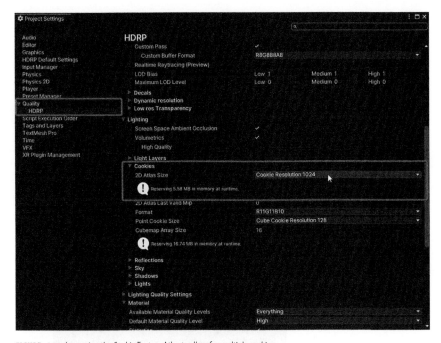

FIGURE 6.16 Increasing the Cookie Texture Atlas to allow for multiple cookies.

> Lighting section and expand Cookies. Change
> the 2D Atlas Size: Cookie Resolution 1024
> (Figure 6.16).

Why?

A Texture Atlas is a single file that holds the textures for multiple objects. In this case, Unity is going to create an atlas to store cookies. A 1024 atlas can store four 512×512 cookies. It stores these cookies in memory (which ties up resources) but doesn't require extra draw calls (the process of actually drawing something) if more than one is in the scene. This is new to Unity, but if you don't clear space in the Cookie Texture Atlas, Unity will complain loudly when it is applied to a light.

> Step 13: Import the cookies. In the Project window,
> create a new folder called "Cookies". Download
> the two images (Flashlight_Cookie and
> SpotLight_Cookie) from the support file for this

chapter and then either drag the files from the finder into your Cookies folder, or right-click on the Cookies folder and choose Import New Asset…and bring them in that way.

Step 14: Adjust the import settings. In the Project window, select both Flashlight_Cookie and SpotLight_Cookie. Then, in the Inspector window, change Alpha Source: From Gray Scale. Change Wrap Mode: Clamp. Finally, in the Default tab, change Max Size: 512 (Figure 6.17). Click the Apply button.

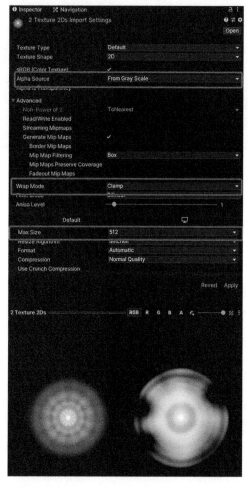

FIGURE 6.17 Important import settings for Cookies.

Why?

In previous versions of Unity, the images actually had to be imported as Cookies. But HDRP prefers that they come in as Default setting. However, the Cookie texture needs to know which parts are to let light through, so changing the Alpha Source to "From Gray School" allows Unity to add an alpha channel to the image and allow light to pass through white pixels but be stopped by black ones. Finally, changing the Max Size to 512 makes sure that both images come in as 512×512 and fit into our 1025 Cookie Texture Atlas.

> Step 15: Apply SpotLight_Cookie to the Spot Light. In the Hierarchy, select the Spot Light we've been working with and look in the Emission section for the Cookie input field. From the Project window, drag SpotlLight_Cookie into the Cookie input field in the Inspector. The results should look like that shown in Figure 6.18. You may need to adjust the Intensity as cookies usually change how bright a light shows.
>
> Step 16: Apply Spot Light changes to all the prefabs. In Hierarchy, select the ceiling_light_01 that is the parent of the Spot Light. In the Inspector, look for an Overrides drop-down menu on the Prefab line (Figure 6.19). Click the Overrides drop-down menu and select Apply All.

FIGURE 6.18 Spot Light with cookie.

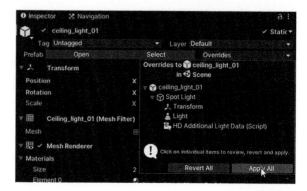

FIGURE 6.19 Applying the changes made to a single instance of a prefab to all instances of a prefab.

Why?

Working in the Prefab Editor has its limitations. We never would have been able to see what intensity was appropriate for the light (for example) in that interface. But when we changed the settings in the Scene window for the Spot Light, it was only changing that particular light (not all the lights attached to all the other ceiling_light_01s). By applying the Overrides, we have instructed Unity to apply these changes to all instances of the prefab (Figure 6.20).

FIGURE 6.20 Applying Overrides to a prefab propagates the changes everywhere that prefab appears in the scene.

Step 17: Repeat the process for ceiling_light_02 but use an Area Light. In the Project window, double-click on ceiling_light_02 to open the Prefab Editor. Create an Area Light (GameObject>Light>Area Light). Move it down below the light cylinders and use the little yellow box handles to change its shape to mimic where the light would be coming from. Change the intensity to about 15 EV100 (we'll undoubtedly change this later) and enable Shadow Map (Figure 6.21). The result in scene should look something like that seen in Figure 6.22.

FIGURE 6.21 Placed area light with adjusted settings.

FIGURE 6.22 First pass at Area Lights.

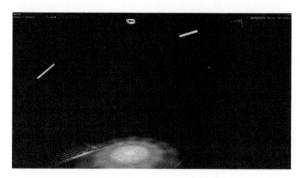

FIGURE 6.23 Results of small tweaks after playing the game.

Step 18: Play the game and see what it looks like from the player's perspective. Make adjustments as needed. Figure 6.23 shows choices where both the Area Light and Spot Light used Color Temperature and were pulled a little colder (bluer).

Tips and Tricks

Cookies don't work in Area Lights. Even though Unity has left a Cookie input field there for the area light, don't even try and add something there. It usually breaks the Cookie Texture Atlas. Hopefully they'll remove this in future versions, but for now, ignore that an Area Light even has the option.

Step 19: Add an area light for the floor light. Figure 6.24 shows roughly the solution we used. Note that because the area light is smaller, the intensity has to be a little higher to compensate. Remember to turn on Shadow Maps.

Tips and Tricks

The Gizmos (the icons that represent things like Lights) can sometimes get in the way. If they are, look at the top of the Scene window for the Gizmos pulldown menu. There you can change the size of Gizmos in your scene.

Step 20: Adjust the material to make the surface look lit. We turned this down and off earlier so we could see what was going on when we were constructing

FIGURE 6.24 Prefab Editor placing another area light.

the level; but now it's time for it to be back. Select any of the geometry for any of the lights and in the Inspector scroll down until Light_2k is visible. Under the Emission Inputs, make sure the Emission Intensity is set to a non-zero value. Since our scene used a slightly blue color temperature, we also adjusted the Emissive Color a bit (Figure 6.25). Season to taste (Figure 6.26).

Step 21: Make sure all of your prefab lights have passed the changes made in the Scene window to all the prefabs. Remember to do this by selecting the altered prefab (in Hierarchy) and then, in the inspector, choose Overrides>Apply All. Do this for each prefab (remember the

FIGURE 6.25 Making the geometry appear emissive again.

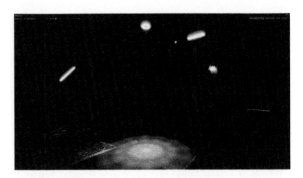

FIGURE 6.26 Lighting so far with emissive shaders again.

prefab – not the light – has to be selected to do this).
Step 22: Save.
Step 23: Reward yourself by running around the level. Play the game. You'll find all the places you had already put lights in will now be lit. In general, the level is likely too dark (we haven't baked in any bounced light). But the scene should start to take shape.
Step 24: Make some decisions about the directional light. Now, try turning the Directional Light back on in the Inspector. It likely is way, way too bright, and the Intensity will need to be brought down considerably (Figure 6.27 uses an intensity of 5000). But give it a look. Rotate it to create different angles in the scene and make the Color Temperature very, very cool (blue, like moonlight). There are definitely reasons for and against it. If you use it, you'll need to consider masking the outside of the buildings as discussed in the last chapter. But it can have some lovely effects through the windows. Explore your preference.

FIGURE 6.27 Without and with the Directional Light. Each tells a different tale, and there isn't necessarily a better choice. You chose.

232

Baking

Currently, everywhere the player looks they are seeing real-time lighting. There are some benefits to this. For instance, if we wanted to design game play that allowed some of the boxes to be moved, real-time lighting would be needed to update as the pieces moved. However, there are also some drawbacks. For instance, if you have a small video card you might be starting to run up against some performance issues where your machine is unable to draw the scene smoothly or interact quickly. Further, the lights that are in the scene light the surfaces they strike, but that light largely dies there. It does not bounce and further illuminate other surfaces. This means that the ceilings (that were already dark) are completely black (which in most cases would not be accurate in the "real world").

Baking allows us to do some of that expensive calculations before runtime. This will bake the illumination into the surfaces, including bounced light. It can be a slow process for a really robust level like we currently have, but the results can be worth it.

Now a quick disclaimer before we get started. There is a lot that can be done to decide what parts of the map get the most lightmap real estate. We've already Generated Lightmap UVs when we imported the meshes which means there is a separate UV set to store the baked lightmap information. But we're currently letting everything have equal space on that baked lightmap UV set (including the outside of walls). Long term, if you are a lighting artist, understanding how to control who gets what texel space will be an important skill. For us now, we'll paint with broad strokes.

> Step 17: Mark the lights as Mixed. Open the Prefab Editor for each of our lighting prefabs. Select the Unity light in each and in the Inspector go to General and change Mode to Mixed (Figure 6.28).

Why?

Mixed lights are those that react to movement when close, but the results of the light can be baked into the

FIGURE 6.28 Setting the lights in each prefab (and therefore all the lights in the scene) to be Mixed. This means they will be involved in the baking process.

surfaces when they are a long way away. By default, Unity now creates lights as Real time only so they need to be changed before baking.

> *Step 18: Tell the geometry in the scene to be "bakeable". In Hierarchy, select the all the groups you've created. Then in the Inspector, look at the top right corner for a Static check box. Check it. A pop-up window will ask if you wish to apply this to the children of the selected object; click Yes, Change Children.*

Why?

If an object moves, the light shouldn't be baked for it (remember the example of moving a chair and leaving the shadow behind?). By marking the room (and all of its children) Static, we are indicating to Unity that these objects will not move and should be used in the baking calculation.

> *Step 19: Set up the Baking parameters. Go to Window>Rendering>Lighting Settings. Leave most of the settings at default except for Mixed Lighting>Lighting Mode:Baked Indirect, Lightmapping Settings>Lightmapper> Progressive GPU (Preview). Also change the Indirect Intensity: 1.25. Click Generate Lighting (Figure 6.29).*

Tips and Tricks

Walk away. Progressive CPU (the default baking engine) is terribly slow (it could take your machine all night to bake), but it's stable. The Progressive GPU we just activated is much, much faster, but is prone to crash. Unity implies

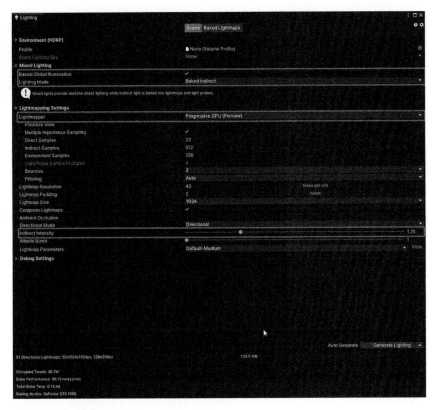

FIGURE 6.29 Quick baking settings.

that users can continue to work in the engine while the baking is occurring, but in our experience, this is a recipe for crashes. Set it to bake and then take a break. Don't believe the estimated remaining time either. On my machine, the first estimate was 54 minutes to complete the bake, but it was done in less than 12.

One other bug that sometimes shows up: occasionally, with a complex scene (like this is), partway through the bake, Unity will suddenly shift back to Progressive CPU (and explode the baking times). If this happens, in the Window>Rendering>Lighting Settings window, uncheck "Prioritize View" and even though the console with throw a couple of errors, the scene will continue to bake with Progressive GPU (Figure 6.30).

FIGURE 6.30 One hallway prebaked on the left and postbaked on the right.

Camera Adjustments and Postprocessing

Step 20: Adjust exposure. There is no need to be satisfied with the results of the bake – especially if it is too dark. Remember that we can work with the exposure settings for the camera as well. Open Project Settings (Edit>Project Settings) and again go down to Volume Component and expand Exposure. There, change the Fixed Exposure up or down. Figure 6.31 on the left shows a Fixed Exposure setting of 8.5 and the one on the right shows 7.5. No baking, no relighting, just adjusting how the camera sees the extant lighting scheme.

Step 21: Create a Global Volume to better control the Post Processing. Choose GameObject and choose Global Volume. In Hierarchy, rename this CameraEffects. In the Inspector, under the Volume section create a new Profile by clicking the New button.

Why?

Creating a Global Volume like this allows us to control things like the Post Processing Effects. Postprocessing is

FIGURE 6.31 Adjusting the camera's exposure time to change the light intensities. The left image is using a Fixed Exposure of 8.5, while the right is showing 7.5.

how Unity gives the last bit of polish to a scene. It can also be a very expensive process. The default HDRP has loads and loads of postprocessing going on (including irritating things like Motion Blur). By creating a Global Volume and then creating a Profile for that volume, we can take more direct control over how the image is processed after the geometry is rendered but before its shown to the user.

Once the Profile is created, Overrides can be added that override whatever the default settings are for the project.

> Step 22: Adjust Tonemapping. With the new CameraEffects object selected, in the Inspector click the Add Override button and choose start to type "Tonemapping". When it's selected in the list, it will show up as a new attribute. Try activating Mode and change Mode: ACES. Figure 6.32 shows a before and after of this sort of postprocessing.
>
> Step 23: Add Vignette. Again, click the Add Override, start typing "Vignette". Activate the Mode: Procedural, and activate Intensity, setting its value to taste.
>
> Step 24: Turn off Motion Blur by taking control of it in this Global Volume. Do this by hitting the Add Override button, typing "Motion Blur". Then once it's an attribute, activate Intensity and set its value to 0.
>
> Step 25: Explore other Overrides. Figure 6.33 shows the solution we finally ended up with. It adjusts the color (reduces the Saturation) using Color Adjustments. We changed the shadows to be a bit brighter, but more towards the blue side using Shadows, Midtones, and Highlights. We also added a film-like grain using Film Grain. This is a nondestructive process; so go crazy. Play the game ever so often to see the overall effect (Figures 6.34–6.38 are beauty shots of one lighting scheme).

FIGURE 6.32 Without ACES Tonemapping and adjusted Ambient Occlusion on the left. With adjustments on the right.

FIGURE 6.33 Extensive control over postprocessing effects can allow for a lot of detailed look development.

FIGURE 6.34 Beauty shot of lit and baked hallway.

Tips and Tricks

A few notes on performance: At the top right-hand side of the Game window are a few buttons of interest. The first is a button called Maximize on Play. If this is pressed, when the game is played, this fills the screen. This can be desirable in that the game play gets your full attention, but also because the computer is only drawing the scene once (in the Game window) rather than once in the Game

FIGURE 6.35 Beauty shot using some volumetric light to shield the empty outside.

FIGURE 6.36 Beauty shot of the finished warehouse.

window and once in the Scene window. This will become obvious if you check the Stats button (also in the top right corner). Among other things, this will show you how many frames per second you are getting. This is a critical measurement. If, when playing the game, you get consistently less than 60 fps, your game is outstripping your hardware's capability. Here are some things that can be done to reclaim your frames per second:

239

FIGURE 6.37 Beauty shot of a dramatically lit entrance to the final boss.

FIGURE 6.38 Beauty shot of the final, lit boss.

1. Change the Max Resolution of all the textures. In this case, it's easy as they are all in the Textures folder. Select all of them and change the Max Size from 2048 to 1024 or even 512 (although this can really start to degrade the textures).

2. Reduce the Far Clipping plane of your camera. In this case, the Camera is called FirstPersonCharacter and is a child of the FPSController. Under the General

section is an area called Clipping Planes. Reducing the Far to 100 or smaller means that the camera isn't drawing objects that are a long way away – particularly those that are behind walls that the player can't see anyway.

3. Change the Shadow Settings to On Demand. For each of the lights in the light prefabs, look down it the Shadows area and change the Update Mode to: On Enable.

4. Bake all your lighting using lights whose mode is Baked. Not just using Mixed, but Baked. This doesn't take long to set up. Just change all the Lights that are children of the light prefabs to Mode:Baked. Then, after marking your scene as Static (all of it), use Windows>Rendering>Lighting Settings and bake. Without any real-time lights and shadows to calculate, the game will play much faster. The player won't be able to shoot boxes and watch them bounce around, but if the game plays at 100 fps, this could be a reasonable compromise.

Hopefully, you have superhuman computing hardware and your target player also is well equipped. But finding the balance between performance and beauty is always part of the balancing act of game design.

Final Challenge

Another design choice could be a very low lighting situation full of dark and foreboding shadows. The player, luckily, has a flashlight so that everywhere they look, the scene (and the resulting spooky shadows it creates are built). Think about creating a Spot Light (make sure to use the Flashlight_Cookie) and attaching it to the player's camera (FirstPersonCharacter). Be sure that its casting shadow, and bit of light adjustment can help too (Figure 6.39).

Really into lighting? Although we won't cover it here, there is a powerful idea called Lighting Probes. These are imaginary objects that are set throughout the scene and the lighting for that area of the scene is baked into them. What happens then is that when a nonstatic object

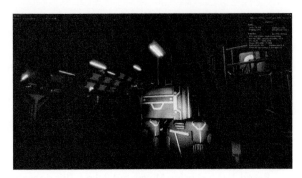

FIGURE 6.39 Alternative lighting challenge using a flashlight attached to the character.

(like a character) gets close to the probe, it informs the object how it should be lit. This means that all the light could be baked (great performance increase), but the character would still yield excellent lighting looks.

If you're getting a dramatic performance decrease, take a look at this technology. It's a great way to get ahold of some frames again in the game. The final build included in the support files will utilize Light Probes. The setup for them will also be included in the final Unity project (although not included in the support files for this chapter). Take a closer look if you need it.

Conclusion

Time for you to explore. Now that the basic tools are in your possession, you can start twisting and tweaking them to your nefarious will. Much of the creativity process of lighting is via experimentation so try something; if it doesn't work, tweak and try again.

For now we're going to leave the set behind. It's time to work on characters for our scene.

CHAPTER 7

Character Modeling

Hello, and welcome to the character modeling chapter! Character is always one of the critical aspects of a game. It may not take a lot of screen space, but it is what the player looks at for a long time; it is also what the players imagine as themselves. Therefore, developing a compelling character is an essential task of production.

Making characters requires dedication and patience so that every little detail is thought through and perfect. To keep the scope of this book suitable for all types of games, we will develop a full-body character that can fit into any camera placement. We will also ensure that it can be rigged and animated fully.

Concept Art

Concept art is one of the most critical steps of character development and should never be overlooked. The back story, environment, occupation, and all other parts of a character are thought through before the visual is touched. Visual appearance also takes many iterations to achieve the desired result. Our concept here is Ellen Mara. She is one of the genetic clones of a mindless killing army but somehow becomes self-aware and want to escape from fate. The design we settled on is shown in Figure 7.1.

Style Sheets

It is critical to have a clean style sheet that lays out the full character, and it is more practical to avoid fancy shading and use clear lines to represent the shapes. It is also essential to have different views of the character to match each other accurately. For example, the bottom of the chin should be in the same location in both the front and side view. There are two different poses we can model our character in: T pose and A pose. T pose has the arms straight, while A pose has the arms down naturally. We choose A pose for a better definition of the shape of the shoulder. Otherwise, the shoulder of the character in a natural pose has to be defined by rigging.

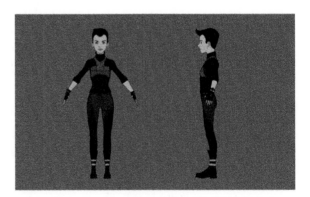

FIGURE 7.1 The design of Ellen Mara.

Workflow

Through the years of development, the workflow to make a character has changed a lot. The modern workflow mostly has a sculpting software called ZBrush involved. However, to limit the amount of software and the cost to follow this book, we are going for a more traditional approach – box modeling. Box modeling may not be the state-of-the-art workflow, but it is the best practice to teach topology, which is technically critical for rigging and animation. On the other hand, it is also going to force the artist to think about big shapes and proportions first.

Polycount

Polycount is one of the first things to think about before start making the model. It is drastically different based on the targeted platform, engine, and how many characters are going to appear on the screen. Polycount becomes lesser of a performance hit compared to the amount of lighting, shadowing, and textures, and we can safely assume an amount of 30k tris acceptable. This is not to say that we should reach 30k tris, finding the right balance between quality and performance is always needed.

Setting Up Image Plane in Maya

Step 1: Open a new Maya scene and save it as Ellen_Mara.mb.

Step 2: Go to the front view, choose View->Image Plane->Import Image, and load Ellen_Style_Sheet_Front.jpg.

Step 3: Switch to the right view, choose View->Image Plane->Import Image and load Ellen_Style_Sheet_Side.jpg.

Step 4: Create a cube, scale it up to 160 units, and move it up 80 units. The size of the cube is roughly the size of our character.

Step 5: Go to perspective view, select the two image planes, and scale and move them up so that the size of the character is roughly the size of the box.

Step 6: Go back to the front view and select ImagePlane1 in the outliner. Move it so that

FIGURE 7.2 Import and arrange the image planes.

the front view of the character is aligned to the center of the grid.
Step 7: Switch to the right view and select ImagePlane2 in the outliner. Move it so that the side view of the character is aligned to the center of the grid.
Step 8: Go to the perspective view and delete the cube. Move ImagePlane1 away from the center on the Z-axis and move ImagePlane2 away from the center on the X-axis (Figure 7.2).

Why?

The two image planes are references we need to get an accurate result. We are moving them away from the center to avoid clipping between our geometry and image planes.

Step 9: Select imagePlane1, press ctrl+a to open the attribute editor. In the Image Plane Attributes section, change the Display attribute to look through the camera. Do the same thing for imagePlane2.

Why?

This step is to keep the perspective view clean, but it is optional. Some modelers may think having image planes visible in the perspective view is more helpful.

Eyeball

> *Step 10: Create a polygon sphere and rename it Ellen_l_eye_geo. This sphere is going to be the eyeball (Create->Polygon Primitives->Sphere).*
> *Step 11: Reduce eyeball polycount. Select Ellen_l_eye_geo, go to the channel box, under the INPUTS section, click polySphere1, and change the subdivision Axis and Subdivision Height to 16.*

Why?

Although eyeball is important, our gamer is very unlikely to see it terribly close; reducing its polycount can help increase the frame rate in the game. Note that based on the type of the game, the subdivision level can very.

> *Step 12: Fix eye topology. Select the top center vertex of the eyeball (this is the front of the eye), holding down Ctrl, and then hit the delete button on the keyboard. We are now rid of all the triangles in the center. Switch to the Multi-Cut tool and connect the points to a grid-like topology (Figure 7.3).*

Why?

Any vertex that has more than four edges connected is called a pole. Pole is notoriously bad for smooth shading, especially when it has a lot of lines connected to it. Because the eye is one of the most important parts of a character, we choose to recreate the topology of the front.

> *Step 13: Fix curvature. Go to the front view, select the vertices of the top row, and holding down shift + right mouse button, in the marking menu, select Average Vertices. The Average Vertices command*

FIGURE 7.3 Recreate the topology of the front of the eye.

FIGURE 7.4 Change the shape back to spherical.

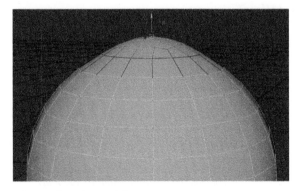

FIGURE 7.5 Create the cornea bulge.

averages the position of the selected vertices and give you some curvature. They are also collapsed down; use the move tool to move them back up. Repeat the Average Vertices and move operation until the eyeball is back to a spherical shape (Figure 7.4).

Step 14: Add cornea bulge. Switch back to the perspective view. Select the vertex at the top center, holding down the B button to enable soft selection. Drag the left mouse button to make the falloff range roughly the size of the cornea. Use the move tool to move up just a little bit to create the form of the cornea bulge (Figure 7.5).

Why?

The shape of the eyeball is not exactly a ball. The corneal area is bulging out a little bit more, mimicking the same shape that will help the refraction and highlight of the eyeball.

FIGURE 7.6 Match the eyeball model with the reference images.

Step 15: Rotate the eyeball 90 degrees on the X-axis. Move and scale the eyeball until it matches the left eyeball in both the front and side image planes (Figure 7.6).

Step 16: Duplicate the eyeball, name the new one Ellen_r_eye_geo, change its translate x from positive to negative (mine went from 3.938 to −3.938).

Create the Eyelids

Step 17: Make eyeball live. Select Ellen_l_eye_geo, go to the Status-Line and click on the last Magnetic Icon. Our eyeball model is now live; when the geometry is live, any creation or movement will be snapped to its surface. Making the eyeball live helps us to get the correct curvature of the eyelid.

Step 18: Draw eyelid geometry. Press the number 5 button on the keyboard to go to the solid shading mode, in the viewport menu, select Shading->X-Ray to turn on X-Ray. With nothing selected, hold down the Shift button and the right mouse button, select the Quad Draw Tool. Go to the front view, click on the eyeball to the drop-down points; create four points and then holding down Shift and click in the middle of the four points to fill in a quad geometry (Figure 7.7).

Step 19: Finish the eyelid loop. Create two more points and fill another quad that connects to the first quad. Keep doing the same thing until you get a loop wrapping around the contour of the eyelid (Figure 7.8). You can drag any point or edge to move them, hold down Ctrl+Shift, and click on any point or edge to delete them.

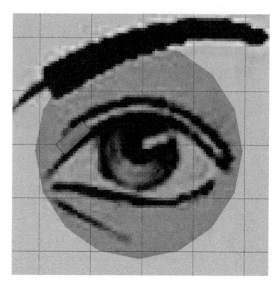

FIGURE 7.7 Use the Quad Draw Tool to draw a face for the eyelid.

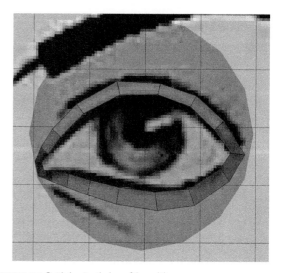

FIGURE 7.8 Finish drawing the loop of the eyelid.

Why?

Quad Draw Tool is a re-topologizing tool that allows us to create the topology for any geometry. We use it to get the correct curvature of the eye. One important usage of this

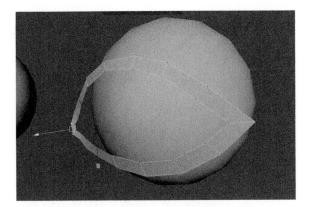

FIGURE 7.9 Drag the inner corner of the eyelid forward.

tool is to re-topologize a high-resolution model sculpted from a sculpting software like ZBrush, and we call that high to low workflow.

> *Step 20: Refine the eyelid shape. Turn off the live object, switch to the Selection tool, and go to object mode. Move the eyelid model forward a little, so there is a gap for the thickness of the eyelid. Go to side view and drag individual points to match the shape to the contour of the eyelid in the side view.*
>
> *Step 21: Refine the inner corner. Select the two endpoints of the inner corner; use Move, and soft selection to drag the inner corner area forward (Figure 7.9).*

Why?

Although the outer corner of the eyelid rests on the side of the eyeball, the inner corner does not. Underneath the inner corner of the eyelid, there are structures like caruncle and Papilla lacrimalis, which displace the inner eye corner forwards. That's why we drag it forward.

> *Step 22: Extrude the thickness of the eyelid. Go to edge mode, and double click to select the inner edge loop of the eyelid. Extrude the loop towards the eyeball, do another extrude to extend the inner surface to warp around the eyeball (Figure 7.10).*

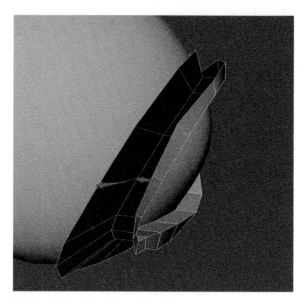

FIGURE 7.10 Extrude the thickness of the eyelid.

Step 23: Create the caruncle. Follow the steps shown in Figure 7.11 to create the caruncle.

Here, we first add an edge loop in the middle of the eyelid thickness face loop. We then select the top and bottom second faces from the inner corner and do a bridge face. After that, we select the loop of the hole between the inner corner and the new bridged face and delete it. We then double click the resulting hole and do a fill hole command, don't forget to fill the hole on the back as well. Finally, we add a horizontal edge loop to the new structure created, and move the vertices to make it looks like a flat oval shape.

FIGURE 7.11 Create the caruncle.

Why?

*Step 23 seems to be a lot of work, but this part is a
must-have to make the eyes look good. We are
trying to achieve high-level results here; feel free
to skip this if you are not trying to make a very
detailed eye.*

*Step 24: Round up the ridge of the eyelid. Select the
loop at the turning edge of the upper eyelid that
transitions from its front to its thickness, drag it
up a little bit. Select the same loop of the lower
eyelid and drag it down. This is to make the
correct curvature of the transition of the eyelids;
see Figure 7.12 for detailed illustration.*

*Step 25: Soften the normal. Go to object mode, make
sure Ellen_body_geo is selected, hold down
Shift + right mouse button, and then choose
Soften/Harden Edges->Soften Edge.*

Why?

We tend to limit our polycount, but we do not want to see
hard polygon edges. Soften Edge command helps smooth
out the shading between edges of the faces.

Create the Eye Socket

*Step 26: Mark the edge of the eye socket. Select
the outer edge loop of the eyelid, extrude out*

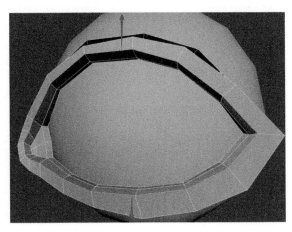

FIGURE 7.12 Drag the edges to round up the ridge of the eyelid.

another loop of faces, and move the vertices so that the new outer edge loop is at the edge of the eye socket (Figure 7.13).

Step 27: Eye socket Inter Detail. Add an edge loop in the middle of the face loop extruded in the previous step, and tweak the vertices to give it a correct curvature (Figure 7.14).

Step 28: Refine the inner structure. You can add more loops to any part around the eye to support more detail. In our case, three more loops around the eyelid were added and tweaked to support the bottom edge of the lower eyelid and the fold above the upper eyelid (Figure 7.15).

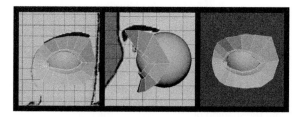

FIGURE 7.13 Create an edge loop that extends to the edge of the eye socket.

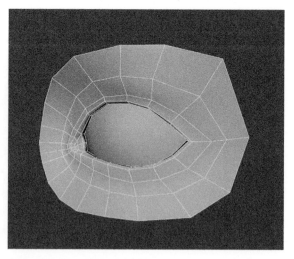

FIGURE 7.14 Add additional loop to define the inter detail of the eye socket.

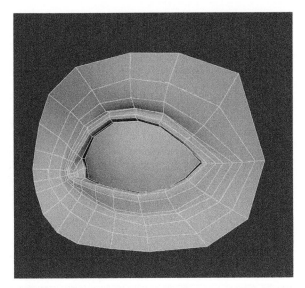

FIGURE 7.15 Add more loops to define the curvature of the eye socket.

Why?

From Step 26 to Step 28, we used a workflow of mark the edge first and then added detail in the middle. This workflow ensures that we can get the bigger shape first and never lose control.

> *Step 29: Mirror. Select Ellen_body_geo, go to Modify->Freeze Transformations. Go to the front view, holding down D and X and use the Move tool to move the pivot to the center of the grid. Go to Edit->Duplicate Special□. Change the geometry type to Instance, and change the scale to −1,1,1. This setting creates an instance of the model so we can see the full face while modeling on one side.*

Tips and Tricks

After modeling a while, your model might become heavy due to all the construction histories. Make sure you press Alt+Shift+D to delete history from time to time to avoid performance issues, strange behavior, or crashes.

Forehead and Nose

Step 30: Root of the Nose. Select a few edges on the center side of the model, and extrude out these edges towards the center of the grid. Scale them down on the X-axis to flatten them, use Move, and grid snapping to snap them to the center. Go to the side view and drag them forward, move individual vertices to align them to the bridge of the nose (Figure 7.16).

Step 31: Add curvature to the root of the nose. Add a vertical loop to the root of the nose, and move it forward to distinguish the front and side plane of the nose. Keep adding new loops and tweak the vertices until it can represent the curvature of the nose. Two more loops were added, as shown in Figure 7.17.

Step 32: Connect nose to the eyebrow. Extrude the top loop of the eye socket twice and merge them

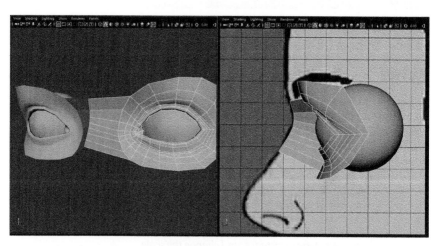

FIGURE 7.16 Create the root of the nose.

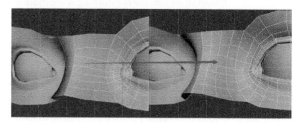

FIGURE 7.17 Add curvature to the root of the nose.

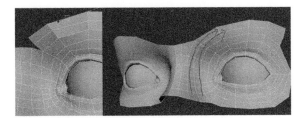

FIGURE 7.18 Connect the nose to the eyebrow.

> with the side loop of the root of the nose. We now
> have a geometry flow that went through the side
> of the nose to the brow ridge (Figure 7.18).

Why?

The edge flow is the only tool to represent turns of any
structure. We built the loop in Step 32 to accurately
represent the structural change of the nose and eyebrow,
almost like how you would place the bricks on an arch.

> Step 33: Forehead. Extrude the top loops upwards to
> the edge of the forehead. Add more horizontal
> edge loops to support the curvature, just like
> what we did for the root of the nose (Figure 7.19).

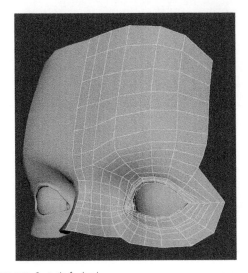

FIGURE 7.19 Create the forehead.

Step 34: Nose bridge. Extrude the bottom edges of the root of the nose downward and forward. Adjust the vertices to match it with the shape of the nose bridge (Figure 7.20).

Step 35: Mark the loop of the nasolabial fold. Extrude an edge downwards from the bottom of the nose bridge. Select the side edge of the new face, and extrude sideways around the side of the nose. Don't forget to rotate it after extrusion, so the loop's edge flows naturally as the direction of the face changes. Keep extruding until the entire nasolabial fold is created and extended around the mouth area (Figure 7.21).

Step 36: Tweak the loop of the nasolabial fold. Go to the right view. Drag the vertices of the nasolabial fold loop to adjust its shape, so it lays around the mouth nicely (Figure 7.22).

Step 37: Mark other essential loops. Extrude a few loops to represent the contour of the side of the nose, nostrils, and bottom of the nose. These loops help us define the primary areas of the nose (Figure 7.23).

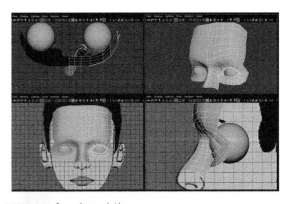

FIGURE 7.20 Create the nose bridge.

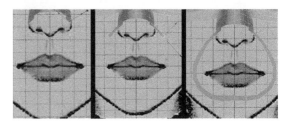

FIGURE 7.21 Mark the loop of the nasolabial fold.

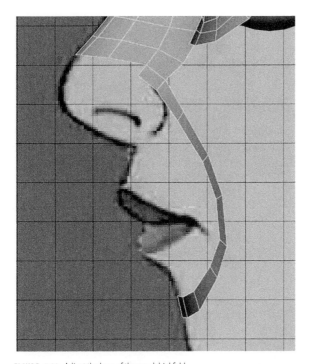

FIGURE 7.22 Adjust the loop of the nasolabial fold.

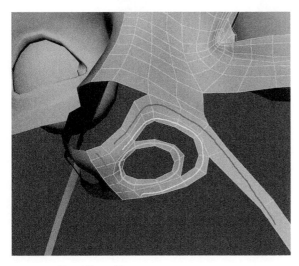

FIGURE 7.23 Essential loops of the nose.

Note that this is not a trivial task, and it takes careful moving of the vertices in all different views to ensure the shape is good at all angles. Some of the loops are touching, so their edges are fused.

Why?

Making the contour of different parts gives us the framework of the shape. Once finished, all we need to do is to fill in the gaps. Topology is basically edge loops like what we did in Step 36 with grid-like internal fills.

Step 38: Fill the side of the nose. Select the hole of the side of the nose, hold Shift + right mouse button, and choose Fill Hole. Use the Multi-Cut tool to fill in the geometry. In Figure 7.24, highlighted lines are the newly added lines to get a clean topology. Drag the vertices around to refine the shape of the side of the nose.
Step 39: Fill the tip of the nose the same way we did in Step 38 (Figure 7.25).

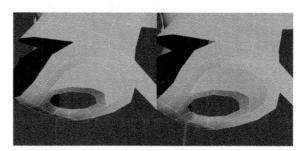

FIGURE 7.24 Fill the side of the nose.

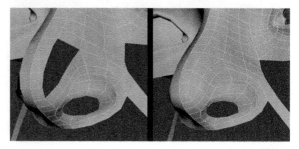

FIGURE 7.25 Fill the tip of the nose.

Mouth

Step 40: Mouth. Extrude from the bottom of the nose to create the philtrum. From the bottom of the philtrum, extrude out the loops for the lip. Add extra loops to help define the shape better. Be careful about the curvature of the model from different angles. It is very easy to end up with a flat result, so make sure that the arc of the contour is always managed (Figure 7.26).

Step 41: Fill in the gaps between the mouth and the nasolabial fold. Bridge the outer edge of the lips to the inner edge of the nasolabial fold; if there is a mismatch on polycount, just add more loops. A pole is needed to sort out the upper right corner mesh flows (Figure 7.27).

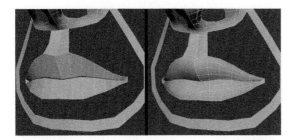

FIGURE 7.26 Create the topology of the mouth.

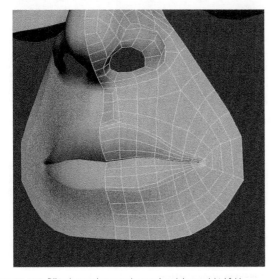

FIGURE 7.27 Fill in the gaps between the mouth and the nasolabial fold.

Rest of the Head

Step 42: Frame the rest of the head. Create more loops around the head to mark the edge of the side of the face, ear, top, and back of the head. Create loops for the neck and the jawlines as well (Figure 7.28).

Step 43: Fill in the front of the face. Start bridging faces of the front of the face using the Bridge, Extrude, Fill Hole, and the Multi-Cut command. Find the crucial loop that needs to be established first, and then fill in the gaps. Make sure that everything you added must be tweaked on some level to have the correct shape (Figure 7.29).

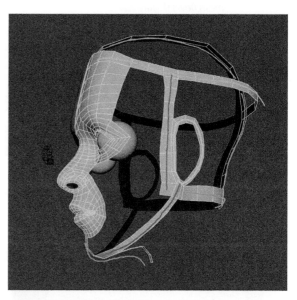

FIGURE 7.28 Frame the rest of the head.

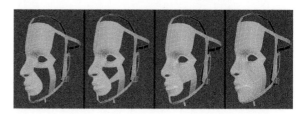

FIGURE 7.29 Fill the front faces.

Tips and Tricks

After filling in the gaps, the face might not look smooth at all. Select the model with object mode, hold down Shift+right mouse button and choose Sculpt Tool, hold down Shift+right mouse button again, and choose Grab. You can now drag any part of the model like you are sculpting it. Hold down B button, and then drag to change the brush size; be aware that the size of the brush might be too big, so you need to zoom out a lot to see it changing. You can also hold down Shift and then drag on the surface of the model to smooth it. Remember that shape is always more important, don't drown yourself in topology. You will get better and better at topology, but if you don't pay enough attention to shapes, you may not get better at it.

Step 44: Fill in the side of the face. We can fill the side of the face using the same method as in previous steps (Figure 7.30). The outer corner of the eye does not have enough polycount to connect to the other side, so two more loops were added to compensate that. They are marked in Figure 7.30.

Step 45: Fill in the top of the head. The topology of the top is basically a cube smoothed twice. The important thing is to find the two corner points, and they are indicated in Figure 7.31. It is these two points that redirect the flows of the polygons. After these two points, geometries either go from front to the back or from side to middle. Note that Grab and Smooth sculpting were used to achieve a smooth result after getting the topology working.

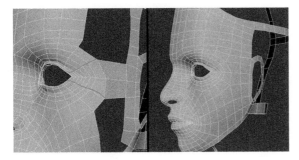

FIGURE 7.30 Fill the side of the face.

263

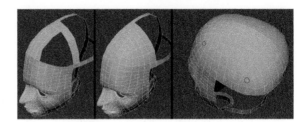

FIGURE 7.31 Fill in the top of the head.

Step 46: Fill in the back of the head.

Ear

The ear might be not as important as the eyes and nose, but it is something that if you do not do well, it jumps out and ruins your model. We will address the ear carefully in detail.

Step 47: Create the main loop of the ear. Just as how we did the nose, the ear can also be modeled by first laying out the primary structures using poly loops. Extrude from the back of the ear, and then start building the loops from there. There is a color-coded version of the ear loops in Figure 7.32.

Step 48: Fill the ear. We can use the bridge and extrude command to fill in the gaps between the loops; don't forget to leave a hole open to extrude out the ear hole (Figure 7.33).

Step 49: Connect the ear. Keep bridging and extruding faces to connect the ear to the face

FIGURE 7.32 Create the main loop of the ear.

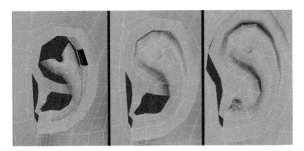

FIGURE 7.33 Fill the ear.

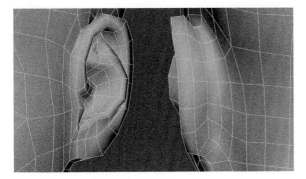

FIGURE 7.34 Connect the ear.

(Figure 7.34); the polycount might not match exactly, and you will need to choose to add or delete edge loops.

Neck

Step 50: Fill the bottom of the head. There are many lines coming down from the head. However, we do not want that much happening on the neck. Redirecting these edge flows to turn to the center and meet on the other side is a good way of getting rid of them altogether (Figure 7.35).

Step 51: Extrude the neck. We chose to make the neck as simple as possible because the turtleneck collar is covering it. All we do is to extrude from the bottom of the neck hole to the base of the neck, and add extra loops in the middle to match the shape of the concept (Figure 7.36).

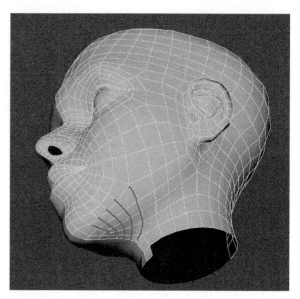

FIGURE 7.35 Redirect the line of the face loop to the center and fill the bottom of the head.

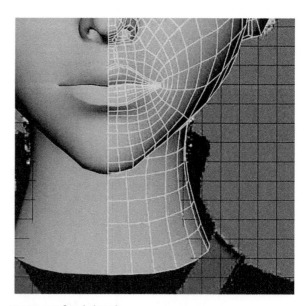

FIGURE 7.36 Extrude the neck.

Internal Structures

Step 52: Nostrils internals. Select the loop of the hole of the nostrils and extrude up and inwards a little bit; do it two more times so that the hole looks extended all the way, and make sure the end is not visible (Figure 7.37).

Step 53: Mouth internals. The mouth Internal is the same topology as the nostrils but needs more loops and inflation of the space inside. Select Ellen_body_geo, press Ctrl+1 to isolate it. Then select the edge loop of the seam between the lips, extrude inwards, and then expand out. Make sure that there is space for the teeth. Keep Extruding more until the oval mouth internal cavity is constructed (Figure 7.38).

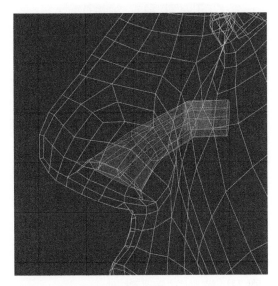

FIGURE 7.37 Extrude the internals of the nostrils.

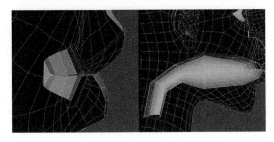

FIGURE 7.38 Extrude the internals of the mouth.

Body

Step 54: Create the center loop of the torso. Extrude from the front bottom of the neck; keep extruding until the geometry wraps around the contour of the right view. Merge to the back of the neck (Figure 7.39).

Step 55: Chest. Create loops around the chest and the armhole, then bridge a loop from the neck to the armhole to mark the range of the chest. Fill the hole of the chest; use the Multi-Cut tool to fill in the missing topology; add extra lines if the polycount does not work. Use the sculpting tool to smooth and refine the shape after getting the topology done (Figure 7.40).

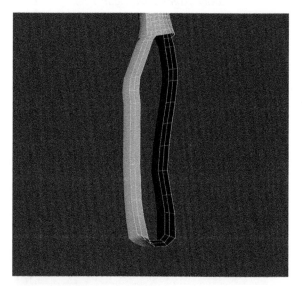

FIGURE 7.39 Create the center loop of the torso.

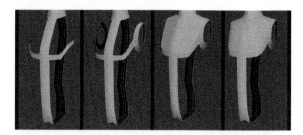

FIGURE 7.40 Create the chest.

Step 56: Fill the back. Using the same method of Step 55, we can fill the back of the body (Figure 7.41).
Step 57: Fill the torso. Using the same method of Step 55. We can fill the waist (Figure 7.42).
Step 58: Tweak the flow of the pelvis. Extrude out a loop from the bottom hole of the torso, and tweak the shape so that there is a loop around to represent the upper edge of the pelvis (Figure 7.43).

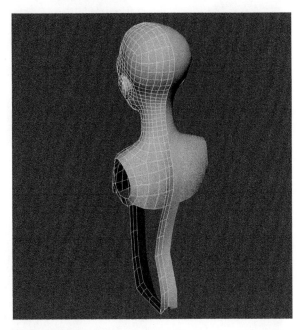

FIGURE 7.41 Fill the back.

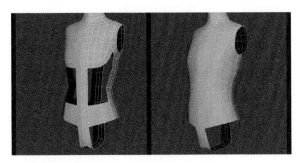

FIGURE 7.42 Fill the torso.

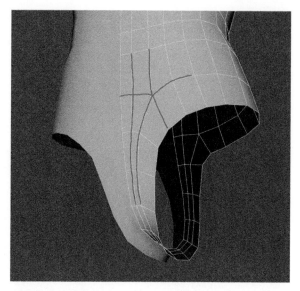

FIGURE 7.43 The tweaked topology of the pelvis.

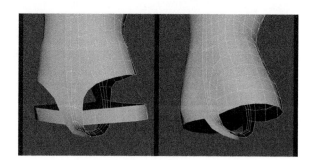

FIGURE 7.44 Create the loop of the leg hole.

Step 59: Loop of the leg hole. Create a loop of the leg and fill the gap between the pelvis loop to the leg loop (Figure 7.44).

Step 60: Create the leg. Extrude from the leg hole to make the leg. We can use a very simple cylinder-like topology to represent it; keep in mind that at least three loops are needed to bend the knee and ankle properly (Figure 7.45).

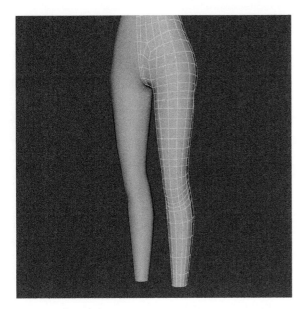

FIGURE 7.45 Create the leg.

Tips and Tricks

After we create the loops that outline different structures, it is critical to define its profile properly so that further extrusion or fills have the perfect shape already.

> *Step 61: Ankle. Extrude down from the leg, make an angle shape at the bottom. The bottom vertex will be the primary turning point of the edge loops – the pole (Figure 7.46).*

Tips and Tricks

One thing to always keep in mind is to have the same polycount on the two sides you know that will merge. In Step 61, you need to make sure that the front and back of the bottom point have the same polycount. Otherwise, you are going to have to add extra lines or delete lines later.

> *Step 62: Create the feet. We use the same technique we have been using to create the framework of the feet first and then fill in the gaps after (Figure 7.47).*

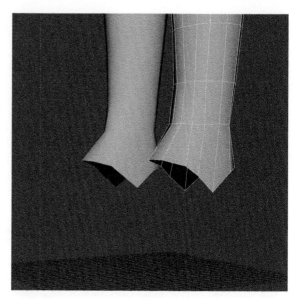

FIGURE 7.46 Create the ankle.

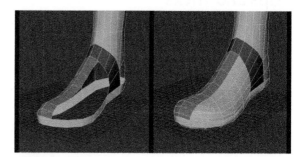

FIGURE 7.47 Create the feet.

Step 63: Create the deltoid. Go to edge mode, select the top half of the armhole. Extrude out two loops, bridge the side of the second loop to the edge right below the previously selected edges. Tweak the shape so that the contour matches the image plane and has a tilted armhole (Figure 7.48).

Step 64: Create the arm. Extrude from the armhole to create the arm. The process is exactly like how we did the leg (Figure 7.49).

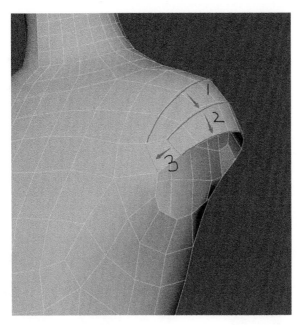

FIGURE 7.48 Create the deltoid.

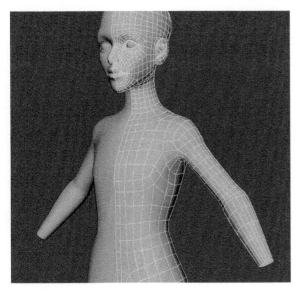

FIGURE 7.49 Create the arm.

Hands

Step 65: Palm. Extrude from the wrist to create the palm; add a few loops to define the size change of the palm (Figure 7.50).

Step 66: Thumb. Add one more loop to mark out the base of the thumb and then extrude the faces out to create the first segment of the thumb. Go to Edit->Circularize to make the extruded face more rounded, keep extruding, adding edge loop, and tweaking to finish the thumb (Figure 7.51).

Step 67: Thumb Tip Topology. Delete all the lines the tip of the thumb has, and use the Multi-Cut tool to create a new topology like Figure 7.52. Make sure that you tweak the shape afterward.

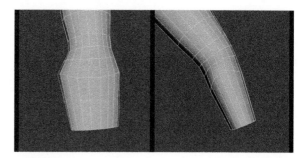

FIGURE 7.50 The base of the palm.

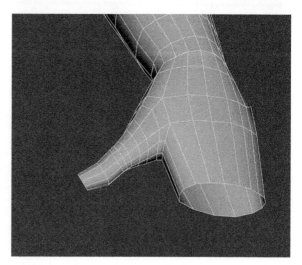

FIGURE 7.51 Extrude out the thumb.

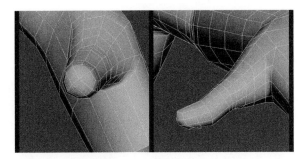

FIGURE 7.52 The topology of the tip of the thumb.

> *Step 68: Create the index finger. Start with a cube, move it to the base of the index finger, and extrude the tip out twice to mark the three segments of the finger. Tweak the size of the different segments (Figure 7.53).*
>
> *Step 69: Add finger detail. Delete the face at the root of the finger. We need it to open to connect to the palm. Switch to Insert Edge Loop tool; hold down Shift, and add two more edge loops to round up the finger (Figure 7.54).*

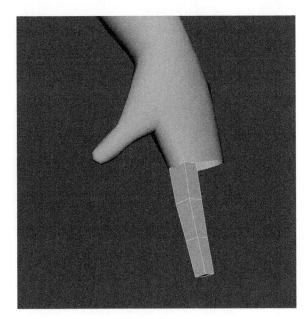

FIGURE 7.53 Create the base of the index finger.

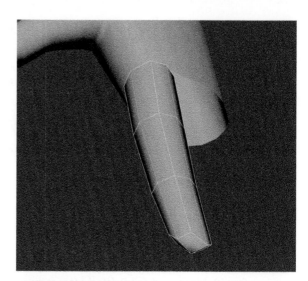

FIGURE 7.54 Add details to the finger.

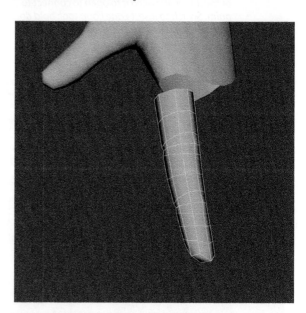

FIGURE 7.55 Add the finger loops to support bending.

Step 70: Add the finger loops. Add more loops to the finger; at least three loops are needed for the bending of each segment. Tweak the shape after adding new loops (Figure 7.55).

Step 71: Duplicate the fingers. Duplicate the index finger, move, and scale the duplication to the position of the middle finger. Keep in mind that the base of the four fingers is not a flat plane but rather a convex arc (Figure 7.56).

Step 72: Combine fingers. With all fingers selected, select Mesh->Combine. Select the inside two edges of the two adjacent fingers and bridge them. Add one vertical edge loop to the bridged faces and drag it inwards to mimic the gap between the fingers (Figure 7.57).

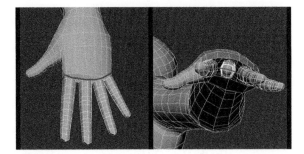

FIGURE 7.56 Duplicate the index finger for the other three fingers and arrange them properly.

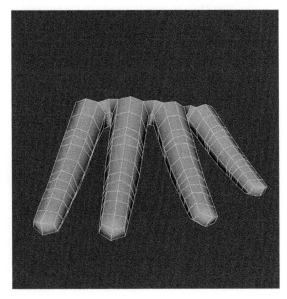

FIGURE 7.57 Combine the fingers.

Step 73: Attach fingers to the hand. Select both the body and the fingers; select Mesh->Combine. Press Alt+Shift+D to clean up the history. After combining, some redundant groups may remain. Delete all empty groups and name the combined model Ellen_body_geo. Bridge the faces of the two ends of the finger geometry and closest faces of the palm and fill the two holes left (Figure 7.58).

Step 74: Refine hand topology. Use Multi-Cut to connect the lines from the finger to the palm. It is obviously going to have different polycount; just cut through the edge of the palm for now. Make sure you spend some time evening out the vertices (Figure 7.59).

Step 75: Reduce polycount. Merge the two adjacent points to the point that belongs to the line that goes across the gap between the fingers (Figure 7.60).

Step 76: Clean up the triangles. Please reference the result of Figure 7.61. What we do is to delete the middle line of the resulting triangle shape in the previous step and drag the bottom point down. Use the Multi-Cut tool to add an extra loop that goes across the middle of the previous triangle shape and has a line connected to the middle line between the fingers.

Step 77: Fix N-gons. Use the Multi-Cut tool to redirect the extra lines that do not meet with the bottom structure sideways. These lines can meet and cancel each other out without having to add extra lines to the arm. One more edge loop is also added to the big gap between the fingers and palm. Figure 7.62 highlights all the new lines added.

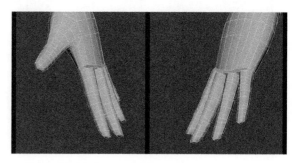

FIGURE 7.58 Attach the fingers to the palm.

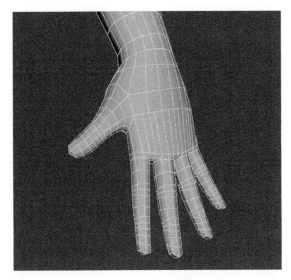

FIGURE 7.59 Use the Muti-Cut tool to fill the missing topology.

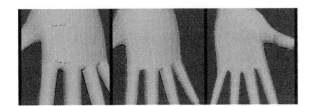

FIGURE 7.60 Reduce the polycount on the palm.

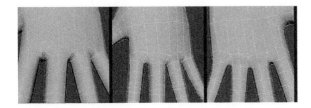

FIGURE 7.61 Clean up the triangles.

Step 78: Mirror. Select all the edges in the middle of the body, scale them along the X-axis to flatten them. Hold down X and drag them along the X-axis to snap to the center of the grid. Switch to object mode, hold Shift + right mouse button, and choose Mirror. In the floating setting menu, set the Merge Threshold to 0.01 (Figure 7.63).

279

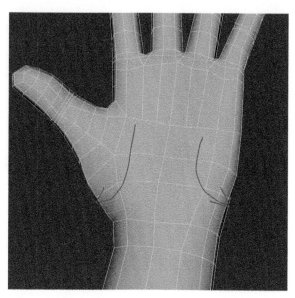

FIGURE 7.62 Fix the N-gon of the palm.

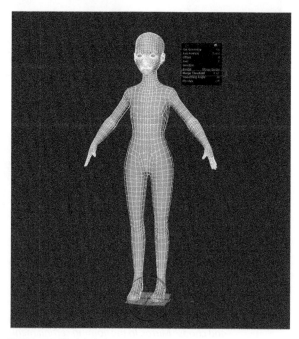

FIGURE 7.63 Mirror the body.

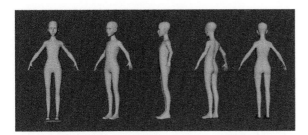

FIGURE 7.64 Tweak the body of the character.

> Step 79: Tweak the overall shape. After the body is
> all done, it is a good time to tweak the global
> shape and proportion. Hold down W and drag
> the left button up and up again; this should turn
> on the symmetry and allow you to tweak the
> model symmetrically. Start tweaking the body
> with whatever tool you feel comfortable with
> (Figure 7.64).

Hairs

> Step 80: Hair Sculpt. Create a cube, move, and scale
> it to roughly the location and size of the hair.
> Smooth it four times (Mesh->Smooth), so we
> get many polygons to work with. It may shrink
> after smoothing, so scale it up again. Go to
> the Sculpting shelf, pick the grab tool to sculpt
> the shape of the hair. We only care about the
> shape of the hair for now. We can give it proper
> topology later (Figure 7.65).
> Step 81: Auto re-topologize the hair. Select the
> hair, choose Mesh->Retopologize. Maya now
> automatically creates a topology for us. After the
> retopology is done, more tweaks can be applied
> to make the shape of the hair better.
> Step 82: Add hair detail. Smooth the hair twice, and
> now you can use all the sculpting tools to tweak

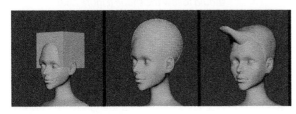

FIGURE 7.65 Sculpt the hair shape.

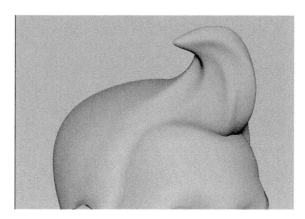

FIGURE 7.66 The sculpted hair shape.

and add more detail to the hair. In Figure 7.66, sculpt brush was used to add some basic clumping details to the hair.

Tips and Tricks

Maya is not the best tool to sculpt; if you want to create detailed hair, ZBrush is going to be the tool you use.

> *Step 83: Final Hair topology. Select the hair model. Go to Status-Line, click on the last magnetic icon to make it live. With nothing selected, hold down the Shift+right mouse button, and choose the Quad Draw tool. Click and drag on the hair to create new points, and hold down Shift to fill a quad between any points. Start re-topologizing the hair and make sure the loops flow with the direction of the clumps (Figure 7.67).*
> *Step 84: Finish hair topology. Keep re-topologizing the hair; keep in mind that the flow of the loop should follow the shape (Figure 7.68).*

Tips and Tricks

When doing topology for games, it is acceptable to end up with some triangles to save polycount. It is always possible, though, to avoid having triangles. After all, the cause of having a triangle is mismatched polycount.

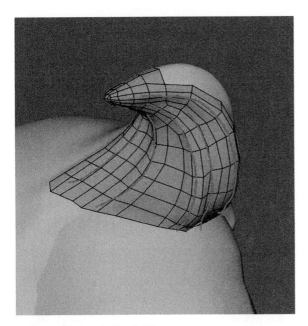

FIGURE 7.67 Start retopologizing the hair.

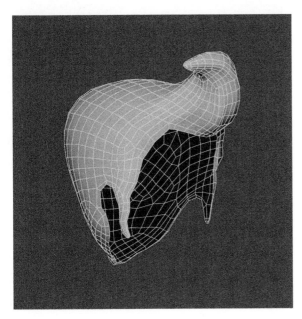

FIGURE 7.68 Finished hair topology.

Step 85: Eyebrow. Select the model and make it live. Use the Quad-Draw tool again to layout the geometry of the eyebrow. Extrude the eyebrow faces to give it thickness. Add a few edge loops across the eyebrow and drag the vertices to round it up; give the hair and the eyebrow a darker material (Figure 7.69).

Step 86: Eyelashes. Eyelashes can be done the same way we did the eyebrow, but more dragging is needed to make the shape stick out (Figure 7.70).

Step 87: Sweater base. Duplicate the model, and name it Ellen_sweater_geo. Delete the faces that are not part of the sweater. Do an extra tweak of the topology and the shape to give the sweater a clean edge on the chest. Select all vertices of the sweater model, hold down W + right mouse

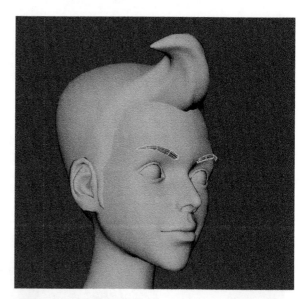

FIGURE 7.69 Create the eyebrow.

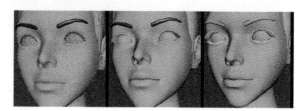

FIGURE 7.70 Create the eyelashes.

button, and choose Axis->Normal. Drag the N axis just a little to inflate the sweater (Figure 7.71). Don't forget to switch the moving axis back to the object.

Step 88: *Sweater collar and rolling sleeves. Extrude from the top edge of the collar inwards and then downwards to mimic the thickness of the turtleneck. Add extra edge loops in the middle; drag the face of the collar out to give it the correct volume. Make extra adjustments to add variations and crevices. It should appear to be thicker on the top and bottom, and narrower in the middle. The rolling sleeves can be done the same way (Figure 7.72).*

Step 89: *Outer garment base. Duplicate the Ellen_ body_geo, name it Ellen_outfit_geo. Delete the faces above the chest. Make the Ellen_body_geo live again, select Ellen_outfit_geo, hold down Shift+right mouse button, and choose the Quad Draw Tool. Use retopology to create the missing upper part of the outfit and refine the already existing shapes. Tweak the shape so that it is above the sweater, and add thickness by extruding the edge of the outfit inwards twice (Figure 7.73).*

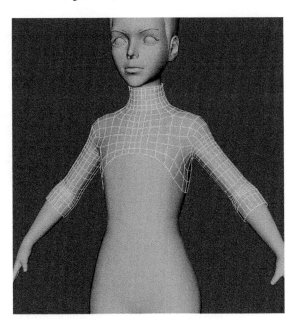

FIGURE 7.71 Create the base of the sweater.

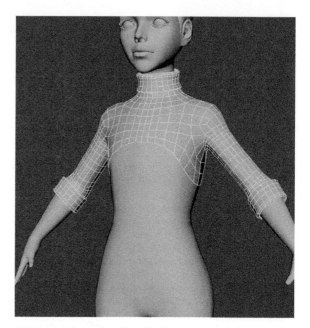

FIGURE 7.72 Add the collar and the rolling sleeves.

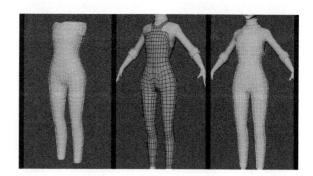

FIGURE 7.73 Create the base of the outer garment.

Step 90: Preview materials. Hold down the right mouse button on different models and choose Assign New Material; click on Lambert on the pop-up window. Go to the Attribute Editor and change the color of the material based on the reference. Assigning different colors can help us spot clipping geometry and better visualize our model (Figure 7.74).

FIGURE 7.74 Assign different colors for the garments.

> *Step 91: Belt. Duplicate the Ellen_outfit_geo; delete everything but the loop around the belt. Extrude it out to make the belt. Extrude the middle two loops of the belt to mimic the buckle. Give it a new lambert material, make it darker, and name the belt Ellen_belt_geo. Select all the faces below the belt, assign a new lambert material to them, and change the color to the color of the pants (Figure 7.75).*
>
> *Step 92: Create the patterns of the boots. Select Ellen_body_geo and make it live; use the Quad Draw tool to draw out the patterns of the shoes. Turn off the live object, adjust the shape of the boots to match the concept, and name the model Ellen_boots_geo (Figure 7.76).*
>
> *Step 93: Boots bottom. Duplicate Ellen_body_geo one more time, and delete everything but the bottom of the foot. Adjust its edge so that it matches the shape of the bottom of the boot. Extrude all the faces down to give it thickness; select the faces on the back and extrude again to create the heel.*

FIGURE 7.75 Create the belt.

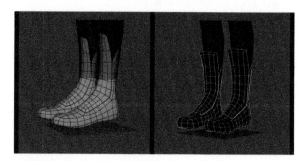

FIGURE 7.76 Create the patterns of the boots.

Select the edges of the upper and lower rim of the model, hold down the Shift+right mouse button, and choose Bevel Edge. In the pop-up menu, reduce the Fraction attribute to make the bevel smaller. Fix the N-gon generated by the bevel command (Figure 7.77).

> *Step 94: Add thickness to the patterns. Select the outline edges of the patterns of the boots, and extrude out the thickness. Bridge the edges of*

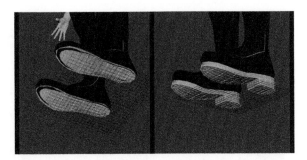

FIGURE 7.77 Create the bottom of the boots.

the seam lines, select the rest of the outline, and extrude in again for extra thickness (Figure 7.78).
Step 95: Boot Belts. *Select Ellen_body_geo and make it live; use the Quad Draw tool to draw the upper belt out and extrude the thickness, duplicate, and move it down for the bottom one (Figure 7.79).*
Step 96: Create the base shape of the gloves. *Duplicate Ellen_body_geo, select all faces that you wish to be the glove, press Ctrl+Shift+I to reverse the selection, and press delete button to remove all other faces. Select all points on the hand, hold down W+right mouse button, choose*

FIGURE 7.78 Add thickness to the patterns.

FIGURE 7.79 Add the belts of the boots.

Axis->Normal, and drag the N axis to move the points out (Figure 7.80).

Step 97: Add details to the glove. Add more loops at the wrist part of the glove; scale them up and down to mimic a layering effect. At the opening of the glove, extrude more loops, and scale them to create a ridge. Eventually, add thickness to the glove by extruding the edge loops on all the openings to add thickness (Figure 7.81).

Step 98: Glove belt. Create the belt of the glove using the same method as in Step 97 (Figure 7.82).

Step 99: Watch. Follow the steps shown in Figure 7.83 to create the watch.

Start with a cube, add edge loops in the middle, and expand the loop in the center. Bevel the four corner loops to create the base shape of the watch. Extrude the top face in and down to create the area of the watch panel. Don't forget to use the Multi-Cut tool to fix the N-gon in the center. Extrude from the side of the watch to add the connections for the watchband. Select the primary turning edges of the watch and bevel it; move it to the right hand when it's all done.

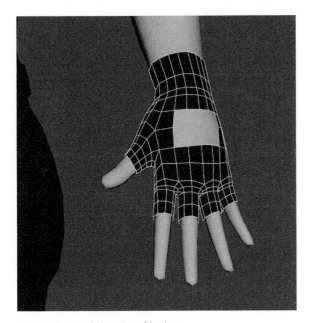

FIGURE 7.80 Create the base shape of the gloves.

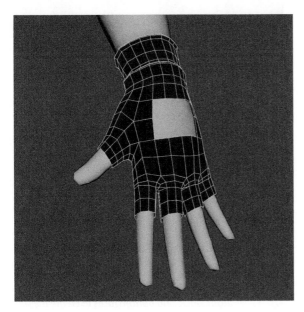

FIGURE 7.81 Add details to the glove.

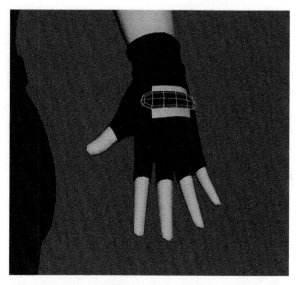

FIGURE 7.82 Create the belt of the glove.

FIGURE 7.83 Steps to create the watch.

Step 100: Watchband. The wrist band can be easily done the same way we created the boot belts in Step 97 (Figure 7.84).

Step 101: Final body adjustment. Spend some time to adjust the whole body; if you have a team, it is also an excellent chance to talk with them. The adjusted result of the character looks like that seen in Figure 7.85. A few pockets were added to the belt.

Weapon

Step 102: Create the base shape of the gun. Create a cube, name it Ellen_gun_geo, scale it down on its X-axis to make it narrower, and extrude from its front, back, and bottom faces to create the slide and handle. Keep adding loops and extruding to

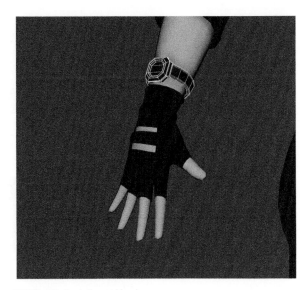

FIGURE 7.84 Create the watchband.

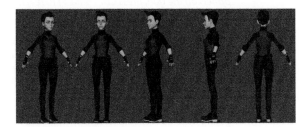

FIGURE 7.85 The finalized model.

FIGURE 7.86 The process to create the base shape of the gun.

add extra detail. Figure 7.86 shows the process of the shape evolving.

Step 103: Add extra detail to the gun. Duplicate the gun, select the faces that could be the extra

293

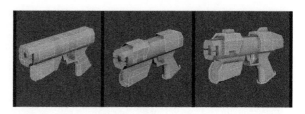

FIGURE 7.87 Add extra detail to the gun.

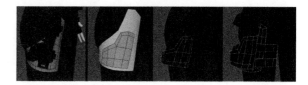

FIGURE 7.88 Create the gun holster.

panels on the gun, press Ctrl + Shift + I to reverse the selection, and press delete to get rid of other faces. Extrude out the thickness of the panels, drag the vertices around to make the shape more interesting, add new edge loops, and extrude out extra detail (Figure 7.87). Combine the body and the panels together, delete the history, and name it Ellen_gun_geo.

Step 104: Gun holster. Follow Figure 7.88, move the gun to the side of the right leg, and make the Ellen_outfit_geo live. Use the Quad Draw tool to layout the shape of the base of the gun holster, and move it outwards a little afterward to separate it from the leg. Using the same method, we can get the profile of the outer layer of the holster. We need to move points out to wrap it around the body of the gun. A few loops were added to support the curling shape. Two straps were created around the leg afterward.

Tips and Tricks

When making weapons, it is crucial to make sure that the size of the weapon is suitable to the character. The handle of the gun was extended to make sure it fits in the hands of the character.

Final Clean Up

Step 105: Delete hidden geometry. Duplicate the Ellen_body_geo, name it Ellen_full_body_ref, and press Ctrl + H to hide it. Select Ellen_body_geo, select the faces that are hidden under the garments, and delete them (Figure 7.89).

Why?

We have a copy of the full body and hid it as a backup in case something needs to be changed or added. We rely on the body to add all the garments and props. For rigging, it is easier to bind the joints with a full-body, do the skin weighting, and copy the weight over to the garments.

Step 107: Separate and rename. Select Ellen_body_geo and Click on Mesh->Separate. The model now separates to multiple ones based on connectivity. Combine the hands and arms, and name the new model Ellen_hands_geo. Select the head and name it Ellend_head_geo. Press

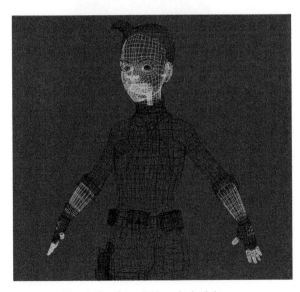

FIGURE 7.89 Delete the faces that are hidden under the clothing.

FIGURE 7.90 The outline of the finished model.

Alt + Shift + D to delete the history. Select the resulting group Ellen_body_geo, and click Edit->Ungroup to ungroup it. The outliner ends up as shown in Figure 7.90.

Tips and Tricks

Facial Expression rig requires something called Blendshape. It is much cheaper to do Blendshape on a simpler model; that is why, if possible, separate the head from the body.

Conclusion

We made it! We have a character that is ready to go for UV texturing, rigging, and animation; the polycount is 29,250 Tris, a little lesser than our prediction. The whole character is designed and modeled in a week. We have used many techniques. However, there are far more areas of character modeling we have not touched, like ZBrush sculpting and Marvelous Designer, to name a few. If you ever want to have more advanced knowledge on character modeling, ZBrush is the next to jump in, and it is a super fun software. Feel free to stay here and do more tweaking of the shape of the character before moving on. It is critical to have a good-looking character with proper topology for rigging and animation. The final model is shown in Figure 7.91.

In the next chapter, we will go over the UV Mapping of the character. UV is the foundation of texturing and is of great importance to bring life to our solid colored character.

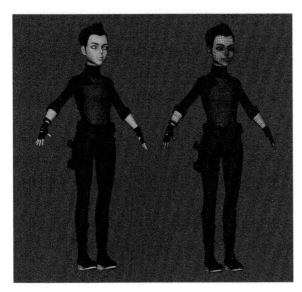

FIGURE 7.91 The final model.

CHAPTER 8

UV Mapping

UV for characters is particularly important. It is the foundation of good texture mapping, which is the primary way we add color and detail to our character. With a proper texture set, we can make a 30k tris polygon looks like a million tris.

It is, however, safe to say, modeling is more critical now than it was 10 years ago. This is the last time we are asking you to check your model before moving on. Make sure that you and your team are 100% happy with the shape of the character. Once we move further on, changing of the shape will need you to change the UV to avoid stretched textures.

UV Mapping

UV mapping algorithm has been improved through the years; so, all artists need to do is to define the seam properly and lay out the UV the efficient way. There are other tools like Unfold 3D that are dedicated for UV Mapping, but Maya's UV tools are already amazingly good. So, we will stick with Maya for the ease of not having to move to a different package.

Tutorial 8.1: Character UV Mapping

In this tutorial, we will jump into UV mapping of the character. We are going to do a basic error checking of the model, define seams of the UV shell, unfold them, layout and organize the UV, and assign shading groups. Along the way, we could discover more modeling problems, and we will address it right away.

Mesh Inspection and Cleanup

Based on how experienced you are at modeling, there could be many problems in your model. Let's review some of the common problems in case you have them on your model.

> *Step 1: Flipped faces. In the viewport menu, go to Lighting and check off Two-Sided Lighting; if any faces of the model appear to be black, select these faces and do Mesh Display->Reverse.*
>
> *Step 2: Check N-gon. Select the model you want to check, go to Mesh->Clean Up□. Change the Operation to Select matching polygons and check on Faces with more than four sides in the Fix by Tessellation section. Press the apply button. If there is any face that is selected, they are N-gons.*
>
> *Step 3: Fix N-gons. N-gon is basically caused by polycounts that are not matching; to fix N-gon, you either add more loops on one side or delete loops on the other side. Figure 8.1 shows two options to fix a pentagon; unless there is a particular reason to add a new loop, deleting one is a better choice. Another option is to use*

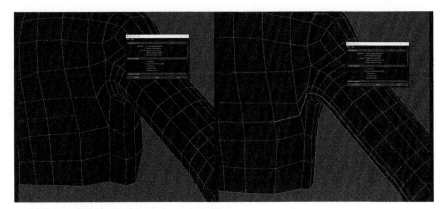

FIGURE 8.1 Two ways to fix an N-gon.

> the Multi-Cut tool to cut the N-gon to triangles and quads.
> Step 4: Overlapping faces. There could be a chance that you have two faces stacked right on top of each other and sharing the same edges. Select the model and hit 3 to smooth preview the model and check the flow of the wireframe. If you find something irregular (Figure 8.2), you know that something must be wrong. It is recommended to delete these faces and redo them to ensure it is bug-free.

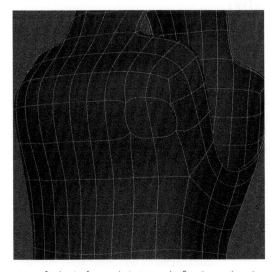

FIGURE 8.2 Overlapping faces results in strange edge flows in smooth preview.

FIGURE 8.3 Potential topology errors that could happen to the middle of the model.

Step 5: Middle line problem. Select the model you want to check, go to edge mode, double-click to select the vertical loop in the center. If the selection is not all the way to the other side, go check the breaking point and fix it. The problem could be that the points there are not merged; an extra face is extruded, or more lines are overlapping in there (Figure 8.3). It is also recommended to delete the problematic area if it is unclear what is wrong.

Step 6: Clean up the history and freeze transformation. Select all models and press Alt + Shift + D to delete their history. Go to Modify->Freeze Transformations to clean up their transformation.

Why?

Topology error occurs all the time, even for industry veterans. It's important to fix them before moving on to the next steps to avoid having to redo things like rigging, UV, and more.

We have done UV mapping with the environment already, and the techniques we will be using here are not that different. In the author's opinion, it is sometimes easier to do UV for organic shapes because there are no clear hard edges. Most of the times, we think of only three things: hide the seam, avoid stretching, and texel density.

Body UV

Step 7: Setup workspace. Go to the upper right corner of the UI, and under workspace, select UV Editing. Move the cursor to the UV editor, press

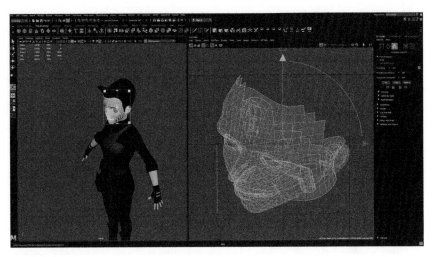

FIGURE 8.4 Project the UVs.

the number 5 button to toggle on the Shaded
viewing mode. This view mode gives every
different UV shell a different solid color.

Step 8: Projection. Select Ellen_head_geo; navigate
the view to a 3-quarter view, go to UV->Planar☐.
Under the Project from section, choose Camera.
Click on apply to project the UV from the
perspective camera that we are currently looking
through (Figure 8.4).

Step 9: Cutting the ear. Go to object mode, hold
down W, and drag the left mouse button up and
up again to turn on symmetry. Choose UV->3D
Cut and Sew UV Tool. Click and drag the lines
around the ear until it is cut off. You know it's
completely cut off when it turns a different color.
Double-click the loop of the earhole to cut it out
to avoid stretching. Don't forget to double-click
on one of the inner loops of the ear hole to cut it
open like a cylinder (Figure 8.5).

Tips and Tricks

When using 3D Cut and Sew UV Tool, click and drag cuts
the lines under the cursor. A double-click cuts an entire
edge loop. Holding down Ctrl while doing the previous
operations sews the lines back together.

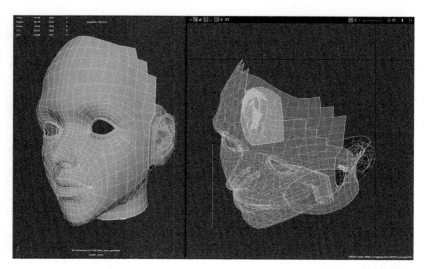

FIGURE 8.5 Cut the UVs of the ears.

Step 10: Cut the mouth and the nostrils. Double-click to cut the edge loop that is the touching edge loop on the inner side between the upper and lower lip; this will cut off the mouth cavity. Double-click to cut the center loop of the upper part of the mouth cavity. Using the same method, we can cut the inner part of the nostrils out (Figure 8.6).

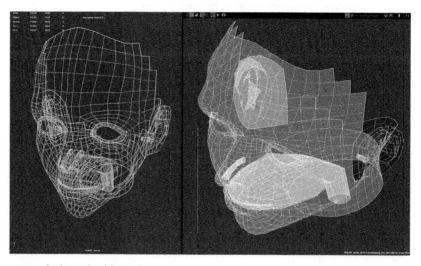

FIGURE 8.6 Cut the mouth and the nostrils.

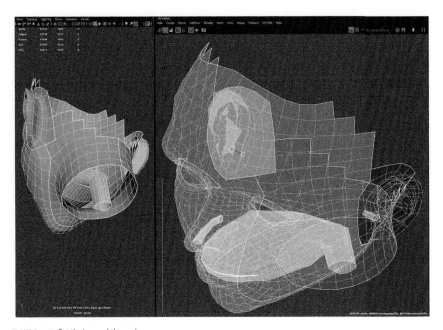

FIGURE 8.7 Cut the jaw and the neck.

Step 11: Cut the jaw and neck. Cut the loops under
the jawline and the back of the neck (Figure 8.7).

Step 12: Cut arms and hands. Project the UV of Ellen_
hands_geo the same way using UV->Planar. The
arm is basically a cylinder. Go to UV->3D Cut and
Sew UV Tool and double-click the bottom loop of
the arm to cut it open. Cut the middle line on the
side of the fingers to separate them into up and
bottom shells (Figure 8.8).

Step 13: Unfold and optimized the UVs. Turn off
symmetry, go to object mode, and select both
Ellen_hands_geo and Ellen_head_geo. In the
UV Editor, hold down the right mouse button
and choose UV, and drag-select all the UV points.
Hold down the Shift + right mouse button, go to
unfold->unfold☐, and set the Method to Unfold
3D; press the Apply and Close buttons. The shells
should now be unfolded nicely.

Hold down the Shift + right mouse
button, go to Optimize☐. Under the Optimize
Options section, set the Iterations setting
to 30, press Apply and Close (Figure 8.9).
You can do optimize many times to reduce
stretching further.

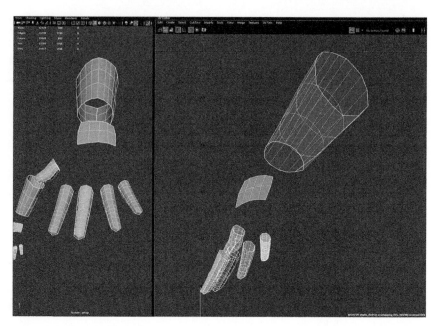

FIGURE 8.8 Cut the arms and the hands.

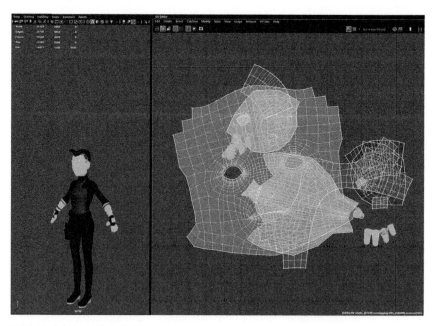

FIGURE 8.9 Unfold and optimize the UVs.

Tips and Tricks

When using Optimize to help reduce stretching, it may cause some UV to overlap each other. Make sure that you check for overlapping UV after using the Optimize command.

> *Step 14: Layout UV. With all the UVs selected in the UV Editor, hold down the Shift + right mouse button, go Layout->Layout☐. Under the Pack Settings section, change Packing Resolution to 4096; under Layout Settings section, set Texture Map Size to 4096, Shell Padding to 30, and Tile Padding to 30. Click on Apply. The UVs are now arranged for us automatically (Figure 8.10).*
> *Step 15: Manually adjust the UV layout. The UV laid out is technically fine but could be enhanced. We can see some unutilized space and some tilted shells that could be more straight. Double-click any UV point of a UV shell to select the entire shell; in the UV editor menu, select Modify-> Orient shells to make it straight. Rotate the shell*

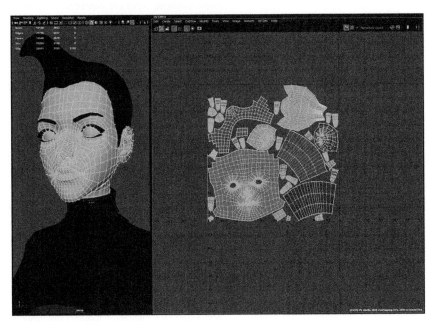

FIGURE 8.10 Layout the UVs.

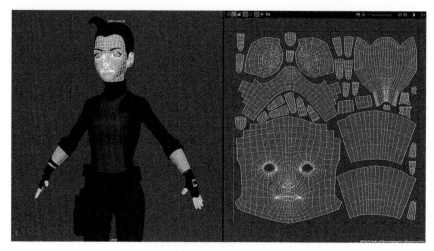

FIGURE 8.11 Manually adjust the UV layout of the character.

while holding down the J button on the keyboard to snap it to the correct orientation. Scale all UV up a little bit, and move and rotate the shells around to get maximum UV space utilization. Avoid overlapping of the shells and keep all shells inside of the UV space (Figure 8.11).

Why?

We want to squeeze all the possible performance and quality out. That means even a little better UV space utilization is a win; that's why manually adjusting the UV is necessary.

Eye UV

Step 16: Eyeball UV Mapping. Select Ellen_l_eye_ geo, go to UV->Planar to project it to the UV Space. Go to UV->3D Cut and Sew UV Tool, and double-click to cut the vertical loop in the middle of the eyeball. Select all the UV vertices, hold the Shift + right mouse button; go Unfold->Unfold. Double-click any UV point of the front shell to select the entire shell, hold the Shift + right mouse button, go Layout->Layout. Scale the shell down just a little bit to avoid it touching the edge. Select the back shell, scale it down, and move it to any corner (Figure 8.12).

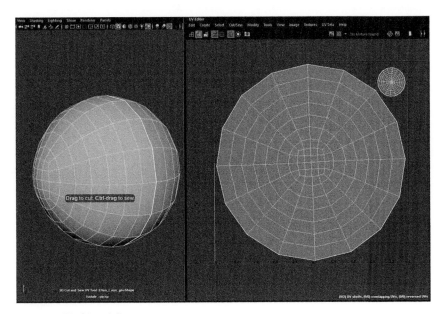

FIGURE 8.12 UVs of the eyeball.

Why?

We will never see the back of the eyeball, so there is no point in wasting UV space; that's why we scaled it down and moved it to a corner.

> *Step 17: Copy UV to the other eyeball. Select Ellen_l_eye_geo, add select Ellen_r_eye_geo. In the main menu, go to Mesh->Transfer Attributes□. Under the Attribute Settings section, set the Sample space to Component, and press the Transfer button. Press Alt+Shift+D to delete the history. After the operation, both eyeballs should have identical UV Layout.*

Hair UV

> *Step 18: Hair UV. Project the hair UV to the UV Editor the same way we did for the body and eyeball. Go to 3D Cut and Sew UV Tool, find a relatively hidden loop to cut the frontal hair clump open; it is also helpful to cut the back half of the hair open. With all UV vertices of the hair selected, do*

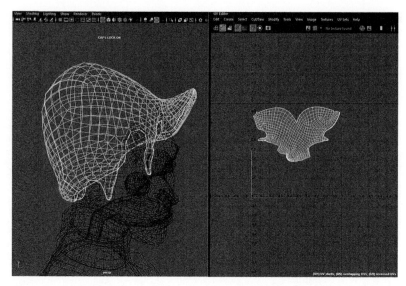

FIGURE 8.13 Create UVs for the hair.

*an Unfold command and an Optimize command
to unfold it. Move it, so it fits in the UV space
nicely (Figure 8.13).*
*Step 19: Eyebrow UV. Select Ellen_eyebrow_geo, and
do a planner projection. Go to 3D Cut and Sew
UV Tool, cut the backside and bottom edges to
open it. Select all the UV vertices of the eyebrow,
do an Unfold, Optimize, and Layout command
(Figure 8.14).*
*Step 20: Eyelash UV. Do the eyelash UV the same way
we did in Step 19 (Figure 8.15).*
*Step 21: Combine the UVs of the eyebrows,
eyelashes, and the hair. Select Ellen_hair_geo,
Ellen_eyebrow_geo, and Ellen_eyelashes_geo.
In the UV Editor, select all UV vertices. Do a layout
command. Select all the eyebrow and eyelash
UVs. Scale, rotate, and move them to take over all
the UV space (Figure 8.16).*

Why?

We have scaled the eyebrow and eyelashes up, and this
will result in uneven UV distribution. However, it gives us
more resolution for the eyebrow and eyelashes. It is going
to help us to add more detail to them if necessary.

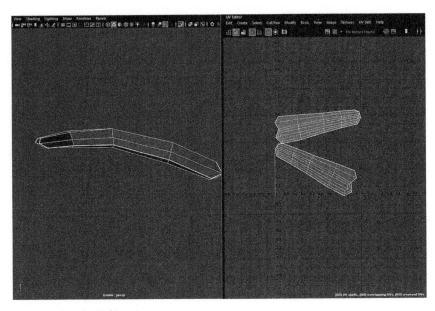

FIGURE 8.14 Create the UV of the eyebrows.

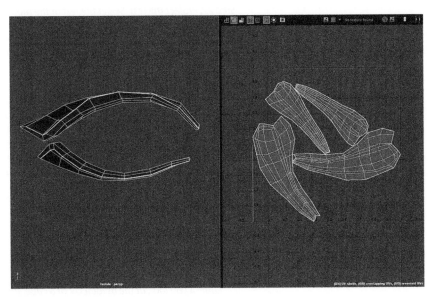

FIGURE 8.15 UVs of the eyelashes.

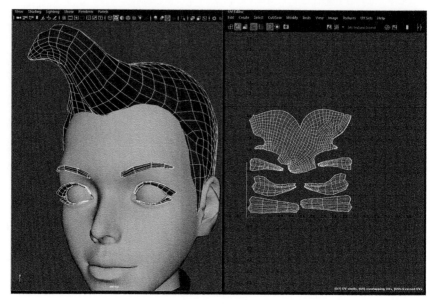

FIGURE 8.16 Combine the UVs of the eyebrows, eyelashes, and the hair.

Garment UV

Step 22: Project the rest. Select the rest of the models together, go to UV->Planner to project them all at once (Figure 8.17).

Step 23: Cut the sweater. Select Ellen_sweater_geo; use the 3D Cut and Sew UV Tool to cut the sweater. Cut the two arms, two rolled back sleeves, and the collar out; these parts are basically cylinders. Just find a relatively hidden loop to cut them open. Cut the rest of the body to front and back pieces in the middle (Figure 8.18).

Step 24: Cut the outfit. Select Ellen_outfit_geo, Cut the model to front and back pieces through the middle on the outside and between the legs. Cut through the loop of the waist where we have the separation of the color of the pants and the upper part (Figure 8.19).

Step 25: Cut the UVs of the belt. Select Ellen_belt_geo, cut the loop on the inner side of the bottom of the belt, cut the center vertical loop on the back, and cut the buckle out (Figure 8.20).

Step 26: Cut the pockets. The pockets are basically a cube; if you look at the default UV of a cube, that is going to be exactly how we cut the pockets,

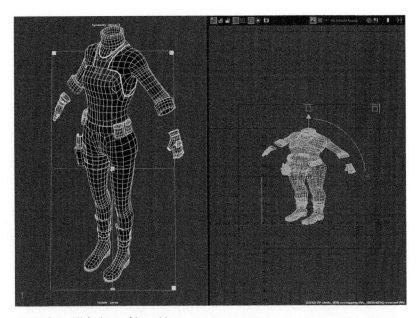

FIGURE 8.17 Project UVs for the rest of the model.

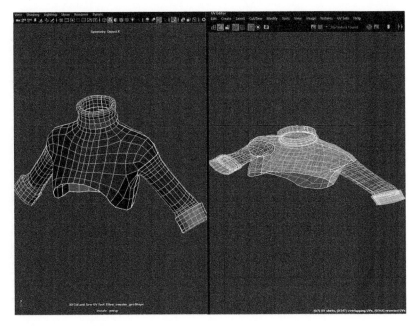

FIGURE 8.18 Cut the UVs of the sweater.

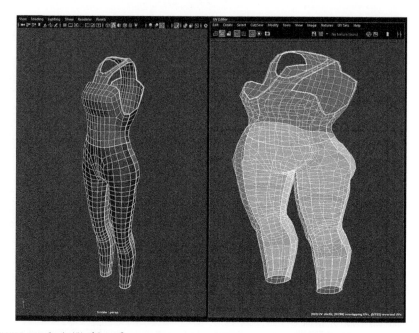

FIGURE 8.19 Cut the UVs of the outfit.

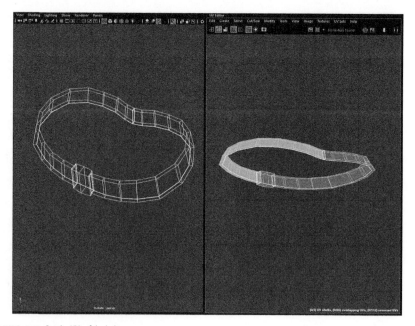

FIGURE 8.20 Cut the UVs of the belt.

almost exactly how a pizza box is opened
(Figure 8.21).
Step 27: Cut the gun. The gun is a bit complicated,
but just like any hard surface UV we have done,
we can deal with individual pieces one by one;
the cutting choices we've made are shown in
Figure 8.22.

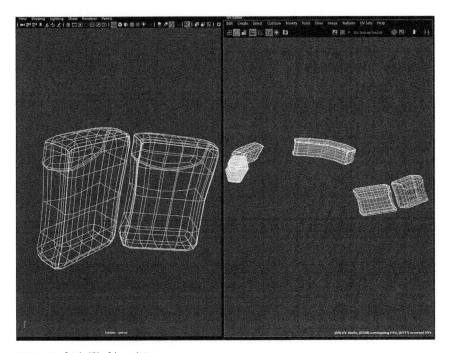

FIGURE 8.21 Cut the UVs of the pockets.

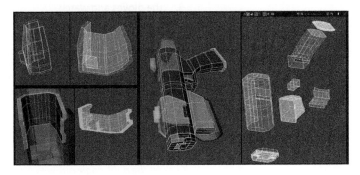

FIGURE 8.22 Cut the UVs of the gun.

Tips and Tricks

When we are trying to figure out where to cut the UV, there are three things to think of:

1. **Stretching** – Find the primary turning part of the shape and cut there. If not, stretching is most likely to happen.
2. **Hide the Seams** – Cut places that are hard to see if possible. Try to cut less if possible.
3. **Texel Density** – Make sure there is a consistency of the resolution of the textures on the 3D model.

It is also up to the texturing habit of the artist and the nature of the tools to determine some of the cutting rules. Texturing with photoshop will require lesser seams while texturing in Substance Painter is pretty much free from seam problems, or the seam is at least easily fixable.

> *Step 28: Cut the rest of the model. Using a similar method as before, we can cut the rest of the models. Figure 8.23 shows all the cutting choices we've made.*
>
> *Step 29: Unfold, optimize, and layout. Grab all the garment models we projected and cut. Select all UV vertices, do an Unfold, Optimize, and Layout command (Figure 8.24).*
>
> *Step 30: Separate the UVs. We can Separate the UVs of all the garment into four UV sets:*
>
> 1. *the upper body.*
> 2. *the pants, shoes, and belts.*
> 3. *the gloves and watch.*
> 4. *the gun.*
>
> *First, move all the UVs away from the U1V1 space. Start with selecting the upper body parts, and this includes the sweater and the upper part of the outfit. After selecting, do a Layout command to lay out the UVs selected to the U1V1 space. Don't forget to do some manual arrangements afterward.*
>
> *Go to the UV Toolkit on the right side of the UV Editor. In the Transform section, change the value of the Move setting to 1. Click on the right-angle arrow to move the UV*

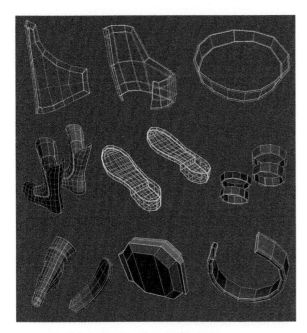

FIGURE 8.23 All the cutting choices of the rest of the models.

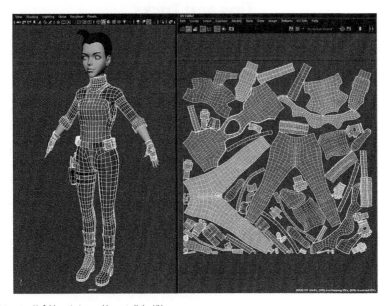

FIGURE 8.24 Unfold, optimize, and lay out all the UVs.

FIGURE 8.25 Separate the UVs and put them into different UV tiles.

set to the next UV space on the right; click six more times to move it to the seventh UV tile on the right. Keep doing this until all four tiles are created (Figure 8.25).

Why?

We have purposely arranged the UV to the four tiles to get more resolution. The gloves, the watch, and the gun also have higher resolution because they are close to the viewer in the game. We can check the relative resolution by checking on the Checker Map option in the Textures menu in the UV Editor. The smaller the checker pattern is, the higher the resolution.

Tips and Tricks

When it comes to arranging the UV sets, it is helpful to arrange them based on material type. Fabric, metal, and leather should be put into their separate UV sets.

Step 31: Assign garment materials. We will give each UV set we created a different material. Starting by selecting all the faces of the gun in the UV Editor, hold down the right mouse button in the perspective view, and choose Assign New Material. In the pop-up window, select Lambert. In the attribute Editor, name the material Gun_mtl, and drag the slider of the Color attribute of the material down to make it darker to differentiate it from others. Do the same thing for the other three tiles. Then, name them as Lower_body_mtl, Glove_and_watch_mtl, Upper_body_mtl, and Gun_mtl. After assigning the materials, grab the UVs of each UV set and use the Move button in the Transform section of the UV Tool Kit editor to move these all back to U1V1 space.

Step 32: Assign all other materials. Grab Ellen_ hands_geo and Ellen_head_geo, give them a

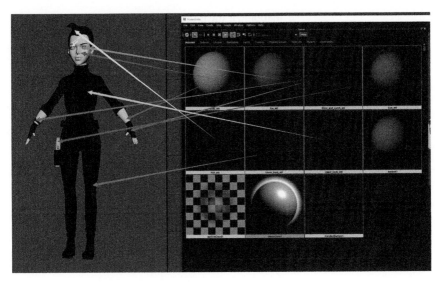

FIGURE 8.26 Final Material distribution of the character.

*Lambert material and name the material Body_
mtl. Grab the two eyeballs, give them a Lambert
material and name the material Eye_mtl. Finally,
grab the hair, eyebrow, and eyelash models, give
them a Lamber material and name the material
Hair_mtl. The final material distribution is shown
in Figure 8.26.*

Why?

There are seven materials created for the character; it is a
little heavy to use, but we are going to get good quality.
How many materials are used is based on the engine and
the target platform. For our desktop game, we can spoil
ourselves a little.

Conclusion

We have now finished the UV Mapping process. It takes
some time but is often not considered difficult to do.
All we did here is to project, cut the seams open, unfold,
and layout. However, the arrangement and the packing
of these UV pieces require some serious thinking. UV

319

Mapping is the foundation of the texturing process and cannot be overlooked. Please double and triple check your UVs and material assignments to ensure that there are no overlapping UVs and all materials are named properly. We are going to move on to the next exciting chapter – Character Texturing.

CHAPTER 9

Character Texture Painting

Character texturing is very similar to the set texturing we did in Chapter 3. However, a more complicated process might be needed to get a good-looking skin and enough detail on the clothing. It is also a fun part of doing 3D art. Since we have talked about the tools before, we will jump into the texturing process right away.

> Step 1: Export. Select all models except the hidden
> full-body, and go to File->Export Selection. In the
> pop-up widow, change the Files of type setting
> to FBX export, and set the File Name to Ellen_
> Texturing_to_SP.fbx. Click on the sourceimages

under the Current Project list, click on the yellow folder shaped button on the top row of the window to create a new folder, and name it ellen_texturing. Double-click the newly created ellen_texturing folder, then click on the Export Selection button to export the model.

Step 2: Import the model to Substance Painter. Open Substance Painter; here, we import our model with the same setting we used when we import our environment assets.

Step 3: Baking. On the right side of the UI of Substance Painter, find TEXTRUE SET SETTINGS panel; click on the Bake Mesh Maps Button. Change the Output Size to 4096. Check on Use Low Poly Mesh as High Poly Mesh, and change the Antialiasing to Subsampling 8×8. Click on the Bake All Texture Sets button to start baking. We set the best quality, give it a few minutes to finish the baking task (Figure 9.1).

Step 4: Check baking error. Look around the model to check if there are any baking errors. It is very unlikely to see errors if we bake the model using the Use Low Poly Mesh as High Poly Mesh option. Zoom in to the head, the eyeballs may appear to have some baking artifacts. The artifacts on the eyeballs are due to overlapping UVs – both eyeballs are using the same UV mapping. Hold down Ctrl + Alt and right-click on one of the eyeballs to select the Eye_mtl. Go to TEXTURE SET SETTING, and under the Mesh maps section, click on the X button on all the maps in the list to get rid of the baked maps.

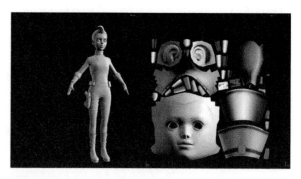

FIGURE 9.1 The baking result of the character.

Why?

The eyeballs can look around, baking an ambient occlusion map and other maps would not make much sense. There are other moving parts like the mouth that we should, in theory, open when baking so that no dark ambient occlusion is baked on the part where the upper and lower lips meet.

Skin Texturing

Step 5: Basic skin color. Hold down Ctrl+Alt and right-click on the face to switch to Body_Mtl. Go to the LAYERS panel. Click on the bucket icon to add a fill layer. Double-click on the name of the Fill layer 1 to rename it as Skin_Base. Go the PROPERTIES panel, change the base color to a basic skin color, and drag the Roughness slider higher to make it less shiny (Figure 9.2).

Step 6: Skin red tint base. Create another fill layer, rename it to Red_Tint, change the color to a pure red color. Under the MATERIAL section, click on height, rough, metal, and nrm to turn off these channels. Right-click on the Red_Tint layer and select Add black mask. Right-click on the black mask and select add fill. On the right side of the fill, set the visibility percentage to 80. In the PROPERTIES panel, click on the grayscale, type in clouds in the search bar and click Clouds 1, set the Projection to Tri-planar projection, and set the Scale setting to 16 (Figure 9.3).

Why?

It may appear to be crazy after Step 6. However, we are going to layer multiple textures together to get a proper final skin result. And we can get very rich color variation by doing it this way. Tri-planar projection projects the texture from the front, side, and top views of the model; this enables the avoidance of any seams.

Step 7: Paint red color distribution. Right-click on the mask of Red_Tint, and select add paint. Press 1 button to switch to the paint brush. Go to SHELF,

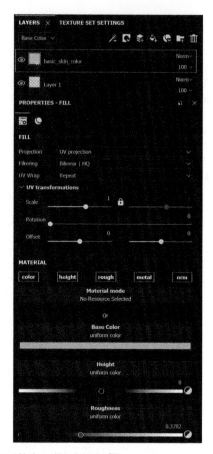

FIGURE 9.2 Add a basic skin color with a fill layer.

under Brushes, find and click on the Dirt 1 brush. Turn on symmetry, and start painting on the redder areas. These areas are the cheek, tip of the nose, lips, ear, and anywhere with more blood, typically the muscles and higher areas of the face (Figure 9.4).

Step 8: Paint blue color distribution. Select Red_Tint, and press Ctrl+C and then Ctrl+V to duplicate the layer. Name the new layer Blue_Tint, and change the color of the layer to a pure blue color. Click on the mask of the layer, and select Clouds 1. In the PROPERTIES panel, click on the grayscale Clouds 1 button, switch it to Clouds 3 so that the blue color uses a different noise.

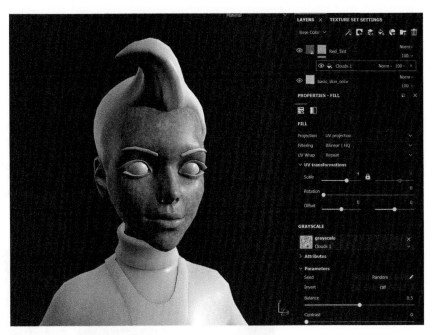

FIGURE 9.3 Add a fill layer with red noises.

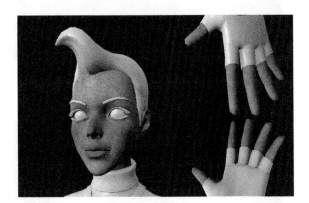

FIGURE 9.4 Paint the redder area.

Click on the X button on the right side of the Paint mask layer to delete it. Create a new Paint layer and start paint the variation of the blue color. The areas on the face that have more blue tint are the eye socket, jaw, and typically low areas or cavities. Some of

325

the areas of the face like the cheek and nose may need lesser blue tint; hit the X button to change the color of the brush to black and erase blue off these areas (Figure 9.5).

Step 9: Paint yellow color distribution. Copy paste the Blue Tint layer, and name the new layer Yellow_Tint. Change the color to a slightly greyed out warm yellow color. The color should be close to the color of the bone but more saturated. Click on the mask of the layer, select Clouds 3, and set its visibility to 30; under the PROPERTIES panel, change the Scale setting to 3. Delete and recreate the paint layer and paint the variation of the yellow color. Yellow color mostly appears on the bony area (Figure 9.6).

FIGURE 9.5 Paint the blue area.

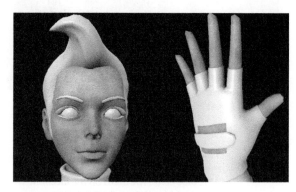

FIGURE 9.6 Paint the yellow color distribution.

Tips and Tricks

The color variation of a human face is complicated. However, you can follow this rule of having the high areas red, low areas blue, and bony areas yellow.

> Step 10: Add a white color overlay. Copy and paste the Yellow_Tint layer, name it White_Cover, change the Cloud 3 to Fractal Sum 1, and reduce the opacity to 50. We do this to add an overall white coverage to even out the color variation (Figure 9.7).
>
> Step 11: Balance skin variation. Select Red_Tint layer, hold down Shift, and click on White_Cover layer to select all the color layers. Press Ctrl+G button to create a group. Name the group Color_Variation. Add a black mask to this group and add a fill layer to the mask. In the PROPERTIES panel, change the GRAYSCALE value to 0.15. Add a paint layer to the mask; use the paint brush to make the color tint more visible on the cheek, nose, and eye socket (Figure 9.8).
>
> Step 12: Overall adjustments. Add a new paint layer on top of the Color_Variation folder. Change the name to Overall_Adjust. On the upper right corner of the layer, change the blending mode

FIGURE 9.7 Add a white color overlay.

FIGURE 9.8 Balance the skin variations.

from Norm to Passthrough. Any adjustment we apply to this layer should affect all layers below with the Passthrough blend mode.

Right-click on the Overall_Adjust layer, and select Add Filter to add a filter to it. Select the Filter layer added to it; under PROPERTIES panel, turn off height, rough, metal, and nrm. Click on the Filter button, and chose HSL Perceptive. We can now use the setting in the PROPERTIES panel to tweak the hue, saturation, and lightness of the texture. The Hue, Saturation, and Lightness are set to 0.51, 0.53, and 0.51, respectively. Add another adjustment layer, and chose Blur as the filter; set the Blur Intensity to 2. The visibility of the Blue_Tint layer is also reduced to 80 (Figure 9.9).

Why?

It seems a huge waste of time doing all the blending and eventually blurring it. However, it can make a substantial difference with all the noisy blendings. It is also because of the stylized art style that we blurred our texture quite a bit to make it look clean.

FIGURE 9.9 Skin appearance after adding the adjustment.

Step 13: Lips. Create a new fill layer, and name it Lip, set its color to a darker red color, and set its roughness to 0.2. Give the layer a black mask, and add a paint layer to the mask. Go to the Brushes shelf, chose the Basic Soft brush, and paint on the lips to make them red.

Reduce the visibility of the Lip layer to 50 to have better blending. Add another filter to the mask; in the PROPERTIES panel, change the Filter to Blur, and set the Blur Intensity setting to 1.5 (Figure 9.10).

Tips and Tricks

Instead of trying to figure out the color of the lip, it is easier to control by adding a pure red color first and then reducing the visibility to determine the color. After all, the reason the lip is redder is because it has more blood vessels.

Step 14: Fingernails. Create a new fill layer, and name it Fingernails. Set the color of the layer to white, and set its roughness to 0.3. Give the layer a black mask and add a paint layer to the mask. Go to the Brushes shelf, chose the Basic Hard brush, and paint on the fingernails. Finally, reduce the visibility of the Fingernails layer to 40 to have better blending (Figure 9.11).

FIGURE 9.10 Add color to the lips.

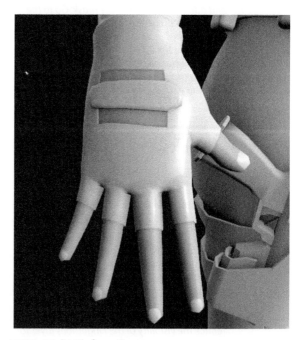

FIGURE 9.11 Paint the fingernails.

FIGURE 9.12 Draw lines to mimic the edge of the various clumps of the hair.

Hair

> *Step 15: Hair base color. Hold down Ctrl + right mouse button on the hair to switch to the Hair_ mtl. Add a new fill layer, and name the new layer Hair_Base. Set the Base Color of Hair_Base to a dark red and set the roughness to 0.45.*
>
> *Step 16: Hair dark color. Copy and paste Hair_Base and name the duplicate as Hair_bottom. Make the color darker and change its Height to −0.5. Right-click on the layer and give it a black mask. Add a paint layer to the mask. Press the D button to toggle the steady stroke; steady stroke makes your stroke more fluid. Start drawing lines to mimic the edge of the various clumps on the hair (Figure 9.12).*

Tips and Tricks

When drawing the hair clumps, make sure that the lines are fluid and flow with each other. When a line meets another, make sure its direction is gradually aligned with the other line when they meet instead of cutting into the other line directly.

> *Step 17: Blur the hair clumps. Right-click on the mask of Hair_Bottom, and chose Add filter. Click the Filter layer, go to the PROPERTIES panel, change the Filter to Blur, and set the Blur value to 1.5 (Figure 9.13).*
>
> *Copy and paste the Hair_Bottom layer; name the duplicate as Hair_Bottom_Sharp. Change its Blur value of the Blur filter of its mask to 0.5. Make another duplication*

331

FIGURE 9.13 Blurred hair clumps.

FIGURE 9.14 Add more layers to refine the curvature of the hair clumps.

and name it Hair_Bottom_Soft, change its Blur value of the Blur filter of its mask to 3 (Figure 9.14).

Why?

We used three layers to add the height information and utilized different blur values to achieve good control

FIGURE 9.15 Add bright tint to the high ground of the hair clumps.

of the slope of the hair clumps. It would be difficult to achieve both defined and soft results at the same time with only one layer.

> Step 18: Hair bright color. Copy and paste the Hair_bottom layer, name the duplicate Hair_Top, change the color to a brighter color, and change the Height to 1. Right-click on the Paint layer in the mask, select Add filter, change the new filter layer to Bevel, and change the Distance setting of the Bevel to 1. Add another filter layer on top of the Bevel layer and change the Filter to Invert. Set the visibility of the Hair_Top layer to 10. The hair should now have a subtle bright tint on the high ground of the hair clumps (Figure 9.15).
>
> Step 19: Eyebrow and eyelashes. Create another paint layer on top of the mask stack of the mask of the Hair_Top layer; paint black color over the eyebrow and eyelashes to make them dark.

Eye

> Step 20: Eye white. Switch to the Eye_mtl, create a new fill layer, and name it Eye_White. Change the color of the layer to a red color, give it a black

mask, and add a fill layer to the mask. In the
PROPERTIES panel, click on the grayscale button.
In the search bar, type in polygon 2, and select
polygon 2. Toggle the Invert option on, and set
the Histogram position to 0.65. Under the Pattern
section in the PROPERTIES panel, change the
Sides setting to 32. The eye white should now
have some red tint on the corner.

Step 21: Iris group. Click the folder icon under the
LAYERS panel to create a new folder, and name
it Iris. Create a new fill layer, drag it into the Iris
folder, and rename it as Iris_Base and change the
color of Iris_Base to a dark brown color. Right-
click on the Iris folder and add a black mask; give
the black mask a fill layer, and make it polygon 2.
This time, set the Histogram position to 0.28,
Histogram contrast to 0.96, and Sides to 32. The
mask now constraints everything under the Iris
group in the circle area defined by polygon 2
(Figure 9.16).

Why?

We chose polygon 2 as the mask instead of painting
it ourselves with a brush. Using polygon 2 makes it
more flexible and cleaner; this is also something we call
procedural texturing.

Step 22: Iris contour. Copy and paste Iris_Base and
name the new layer Iris_Contour. Make the color
darker, and give it a black mask. Right-click
on the mask of Iris folder, chose Copy mask,
right-click on the Iris_Contour, and chose Paste
into mask. The polygon 2 from Iris group is now
copied to Iris_Contour. Add another fill to the
mask of Iris_Contour, chose polygon 2 again,
and change the fill layer blend type to Subtract.
In the PROPERTIES panel, set the Histogram
position to 0.23, Histogram contrast to 0.9,
and Sides to 32 (Figure 9.17). Again, we have
procedurally made the dark rim of the iris with
the polygon 2 texture.

Step 23: Pupil. Copy and paste Iris_Base, name the
new layer Pupil, make the color darker, give it
a black mask, and add a fill layer to the mask
with polygon 2. In the PROPERTIES panel, set the
Histogram position to 0.1, Histogram contrast to
0.85, and Sides to 32 (Figure 9.18).

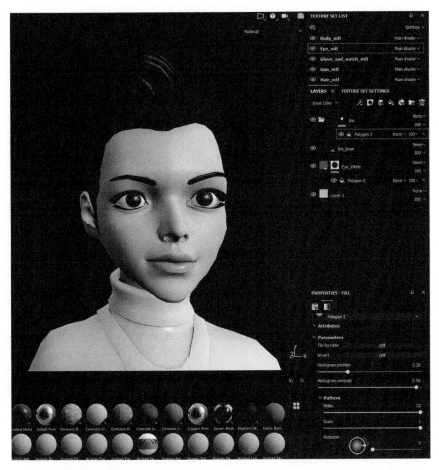

FIGURE 9.16 Create a folder for the iris and add a mask to it.

Step 24: Iris top shading. Copy and paste Iris_Base,
name the new layer Iris_Dark and make the color
darker. Give the new layer a black mask, and
add a fill layer to the mask. In the PROPERTIES
panel, click on the grayscale, search, and choose
Gradient Linear 1. Under the Parameters section
in the PROPERTIES panel, set the Balance to
0.475, and the Contrast to 0.9 (Figure 9.19).
Step 25: Iris bottom light. Copy and paste Iris_Base;
name the new layer Iris_Bright. Make the color
brighter, click and drag it to move it above
Iris_Dark. Give Iris_Bright a black mask and add
a paint layer to it. This time, we use the Basic

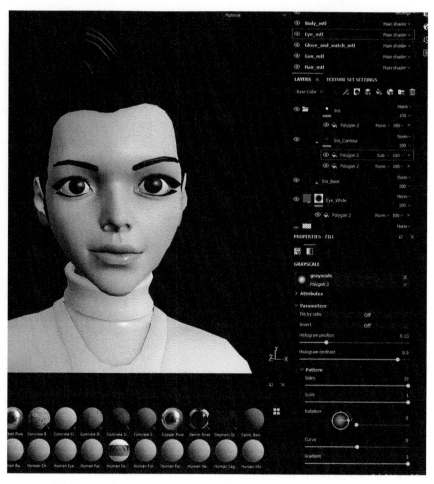

FIGURE 9.17 Add the contour of the iris.

Soft brush to paint around the bottom portion of the Iris to mimic lights traveling out of the Iris (Figure 9.20).

Add another filter to the mask of Iris_Bright and change the filter to Blur to blur the mask (Figure 9.21).

Why?

In theory, the darkness of the upper portion of the iris is caused by shading. The brighter color on the bottom part

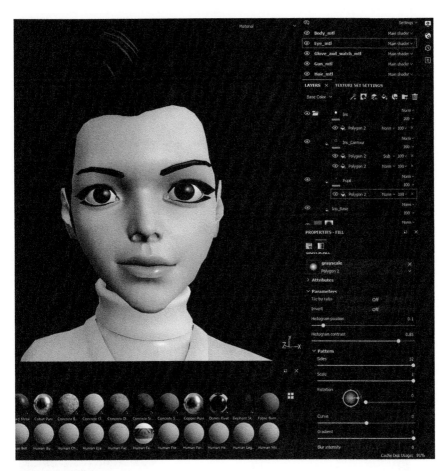

FIGURE 9.18 Add pupils to the eye.

of the iris is lighting traveling out. Our model is too simple to support such accurate shading, so we faked it using textures.

> Step 26: Iris fiber. Create a new fill layer above Iris_Bright, name it Iris_Fiber, change its color to a dark brown, and set the height value to −0.3. Give the layer a black mask and add a fill layer to the black mask. In the PROPERTIES panel, click on the grayscale, search and select Circular Stick. In the Parameters section, set the Number to 64, Offset to 0, Bar Length to 1, and Bar Width to 0.005. We now have a dense fiber covering the

337

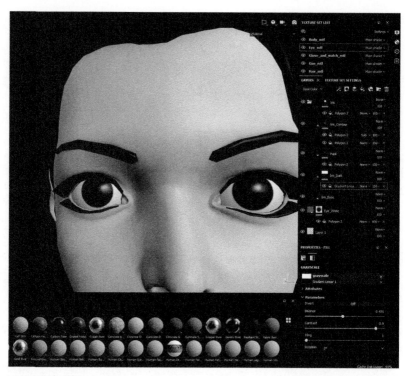

FIGURE 9.19 Add top shading to the iris.

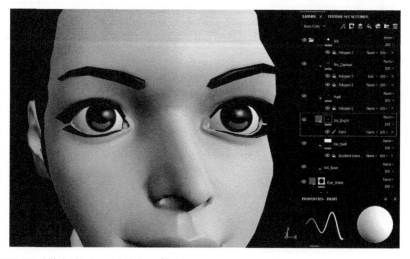

FIGURE 9.20 Add a brighter layer at the bottom of the iris.

FIGURE 9.21 Blur the brighter color at the bottom of the iris.

iris. Add a blur filter to the mask to make it softer (Figure 9.22).

Step 27: Fix height error. Select the Iris_Contour layer, under the LAYERS panel, right beneath the LAYERS label, and change the Base Color to Height. Change the blending mode of the Iris_Contour to Normal to make the dark contour block the height information below it.

Select the bottom Polygon 2 in the mask of the Iris_Contour layer, set the Histogram Position to 0.3 and Histogram contrast to 1 to cover the outer edge of the Iris (Figure 9.23).

Step 28: Eye roughness. Create a new fill layer at the top of the layer stack and name it Roughness. In the PROPERTIES panel, turn off the color, height,

339

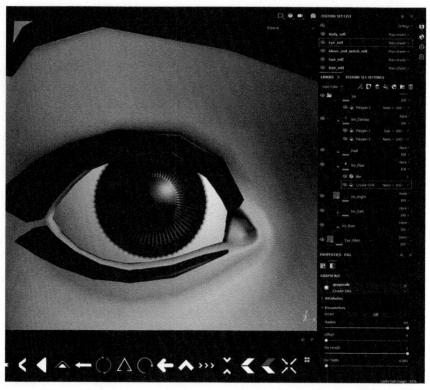

FIGURE 9.22 Add fibers to the iris.

metal, and nrm channels. Set the roughness to 0.25 to tighten up the highlight (Figure 9.24).

Upper Body

Step 29: Sweater base. Switch to the Upper_body_mtl, add a new fill layer and name it Sweater_Base, change its color to a dark gray, and roughness to 0.8. Press Ctrl+G to group it under a folder; name the folder Sweater. Add a black mask to the folder and give the mask a paint layer. Hit the number 4 button on the keyboard to toggle the polygon fill tool; in the PROPERTIES panel, click on the checker box button to switch to UV shell selection mode. Change the Color to 1, go to the 2D view, and click on the UVs of the sweater (Figure 9.25). The mask should now be white on the sweater.

FIGURE 9.23 Make the contour of the iris block the height of the fibers.

Step 30: Sweater pattern. Go to Materials, find Scarf wool, drag it above Sweater_Base, and rename it as Sweater_Pattern. In the PROPERTIES panel, change the color to a dark gray; under the Technical Parameter, change the Height Range to 0.25 (Figure 9.26).

Step 31: Fix the pattern direction of the left sleeve. Add a white mask to the Sweater_Pattern and add a paint layer to the mask of Sweater_Pattern. Hit the number 4 button to switch to polygon fill tool, change the color to black, and click on the sleeves and the collar. The pattern should now be removed from these parts.

Duplicate the Sweater Pattern, name the new layer Sweater_Pattern_Sleeve_L, delete the paint layer of the mask of the new

341

FIGURE 9.24 Tweak the roughness of the iris.

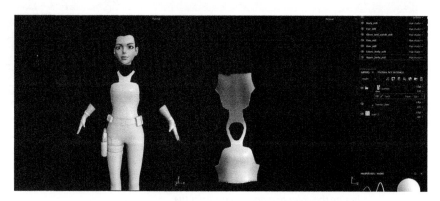

FIGURE 9.25 Create a layer and a folder for the sweater.

layer, and add a new paint layer. Hit the 4 button, change the color to black, and click on the UV shells that are not the left sleeve to mask them out. Go click on the icon of the new layer and change the rotation in the PROPERTIES panel so that its direction is aligned with the left sleeve. Create two more duplications of the layer to fix the pattern direction of the right sleeve and the collar (Figure 9.27).

FIGURE 9.26 Add the Scarf wool material to the sweater.

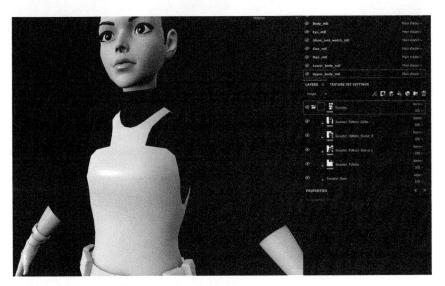

FIGURE 9.27 Fix the direction of the patterns with new layers.

Step 32: Add smart material to the outfit. Go to
the SHELF, select Smart materials in the left
column, and find Fabric UCP. Drag it to LAYERS
and move it below Sweater. Open the folder
added called Fabric UCP, find Fabric UCP
layer, go to PROPERTIES, and change Color 01,
Color 02, Color 03 to three different blue colors
(Figure 9.28).

343

FIGURE 9.28 Add Fabric UCP as the material of the outfit.

Step 33: Edge variation. Duplicate Fabric UCP and name the duplicate as Fabric UCP_Edge. Right-click on the layer and click add levels. Select the newly added Levels – Base Color, drag the middle pin of the top row of the level graph to the left just a little to make the color brighter.

Create a new black mask to Fabric UCP_Edge, go to the Smart Masks in the SHELF, and drag Fabric Edge Damage to the mask of Fabric UCP_Edge. The edge of the garment should now become brighter, which mimics real-life scratches (Figure 9.29).

Step 34: Top strap height. Create a new fill layer below Fabric UCP_Edge, name it Top_Strap_Height. Turn off the color, rough, metal, nrm channel of the layer, and change its height value to 0.75.

Create a black mask for Strap_Height and give the mask a paint layer. Use the Basic Hard brush and white color to paint on the areas that belong to the top strap layer (Figure 9.30).

FIGURE 9.29 Add subtle edge wear to the outfit.

Tips and Tricks

Don't worry about painting over the sweater, we can change the height blend mode of the Sweater folder to normal to override it.

> *Step 35: Sewing seam. Duplicate Top_Strap_Height, name it Sewing_Seams, set its height to 1, delete, and recreate the paint layer in the mask. Hold down Shift while clicking to create the sewing seams (Figure 9.31).*

FIGURE 9.30 Add height to the top strap.

FIGURE 9.31 Add Sewing seams to the outfit.

Why?

It is difficult to paint clean lines, so we use the Shift-click trick to draw straight lines instead of trying to create a fluid arc line.

> Step 36: Waist patch color variation. Duplicate Fabrick UCP and name the duplication Fabrick UCP_Waist. Make the color of the new layer

FIGURE 9.32 Add color variation to the waist patch.

> darker and more saturated. Gave the new layer
> a black mask and add a paint layer to the mask.
> Use Brush Hard to paint over the area on and
> below the horizontal seam in the middle painted
> in Step 34 (Figure 9.32).
>
> Step 37: Waist side patch. Create a new fill layer
> above Fabric UCP_Edge, name it Waist_Side_
> Patch. Go to the PROPERTIES panel, set the
> Scale value to 25, click on the height uniform
> color button, in the search bar, type in Circles
> to find the Circles mask, and click on it to
> use it as our height. Set the height blending
> mode of Waist_Side_Patch to Normal, give
> it a black mask and add a paint layer to the
> mask, and use the Basic Hard brush with white
> color to paint over the side patch of the outfit
> (Figure 9.33).

Tips and Tricks

Whenever we need to paint something clean, we can hold
down the Shift button and do left mouse clicks to draw
straight lines to mark out the contour of the area and then
fill in the middle.

FIGURE 9.33 Add circular patterns to the side patch of the outfit.

Pants

Step 38: Pants base color. Switch to the Lower_body_ mtl, go to SHELF, click on the Materials section, search for Fabric Baseball Hat, and drag it to the layers. Name the new layer Pants_Base, change the Scale of the layer to 3, and tweak the rotation value so that the direction of the lines in the pattern becomes vertical. Finally, change the color to a darker grayed out blue color (Figure 9.34).

Step 39: Pants gradient. Duplicate Pants_Base, name the duplication Pants_Darker, and make the color of Pants_Darker darker and bluer. Give the layer a black mask, add a generator to the mask, in the PROPERTIES panel, and change the generator to Mask Editor. In the PORPERTIES panel, set the Curvature Opacity to 0 and the Position Gradient Opacity to 1. Open the Position Gradient section, turn on the Invert, and set the contrast to 0.7. Tweak the Balance value so that the transition of the brightness of the color starts around the knee (Figure 9.35).

FIGURE 9.34 Add the material for the pants.

FIGURE 9.35 Add a gradient to the color of the pants.

Tips and Tricks

Gradients are happening all of the places in nature, they are great for add detail.

> *Step 40: Pants front flipper. Create a new fill layer above Pants_Darker, name it Pants_Height_ High. Toggle off the color, rough, metal, nrm channel of the layer, and change the Height to 1 to make it a high ground. Add a black mask as well as a paint layer to the mask.*
>
> > *Draw a long square at the front of the hip to mimic the shape of the flipper. Create a new fill layer above Pants_Height_High, name it Pants_Height_Low, change its height to −1, and give it a black mask and add a paint layer; make the brush smaller and draw a vertical line on the side of the flipper (Figure 9.36).*
>
> *Step 41: Pockets. Add a new paint layer to the mask of Pants_Height_High and name it Pocket_ Height. Drag it beneath the previous paint layer, turn on symmetry, and use the Basic Hard brush to paint over the area of the pockets. Make sure the brush size is big and covers much more area around the pocket.*
>
> > *Add a Blur filter above Pocket_Height and below the Paint layer; set the Blur Intensity to 7.*
> >
> > *Add another paint layer to the mask, call it Pocket_Opening. Make the brush smaller, press the X button to flip the color from white to black. Paint across the opening of the pocket to cut the seam open, and paint off all the high areas behind the opening of the pocket (Figure 9.37).*

FIGURE 9.36 Create the high ground and the seam of the flipper of the pants.

FIGURE 9.37 Add the shape of the pockets.

Tips and Tricks

Whenever we need to paint something more complicated, we can break it down to multiple steps, just like we did in Step 40. We create the soft bump with the combination of a harsh brush stroke and a blur filter. We then paint half of it out to mimic the opening of the pocket.

> *Step 42: Seams. Go to the paint layer of the mask of Pants_Height_Low, use a small brush to cut the seams on the side of the pants (Figure 9.38).*
> *Step 43: Back Pocket. Use similar techniques we used for the pockets and flipper; we can create the back pockets with ease. Don't afraid to paint over to other parts because we will cover these with materials on top (Figure 9.39).*
> *Step 44: Stitches. Create a new layer on the very top and name it Stitches. In the PROPERTIES*

FIGURE 9.38 Add seams to the pants.

FIGURE 9.39 Create the back pocket.

panel, toggle off metal and nrm, set Base Color to white, set the Height, and the Roughness to 1. Give it a black mask with a paint layer. In the Brushes section of the SHELF, find and click on Stitches 1. Reduce the size of the brush to 0.9, use the Shift-clicking techniques to draw stitches out on the sewing lines of the pants (Figure 9.40).

Step 45: Organization. Select all layers we created so far, press Ctrl+G to group them in a folder, and name the folder Pants.

FIGURE 9.40 Add stitches to the pants.

Belts, Straps, Pockets, Holster, and Boots

Step 46: Leather material. Go to the Smart materials section in the SHELF. Find Leather Stylized, drag it above the Pants folder, and give Leather Stylized a black mask with a paint layer. Press the number 4 button to switch to Polygon Fill tool. In the PROPERTIES, click on the checker box button to switch to UV shell mode. Set the color to white, click on the Belts, Straps, Pockets, Holster, and Boots to make the leather show up on these parts. Open the Leather Stylized folder, select Base Color, change its color to a darker brown color (Figure 9.41).

Step 47: Refine curvature. Add a paint layer to the mask of the Curvature layer inside Leather Stylized. Select the Basic Soft brush in the Brushes section of the shelf. Change the color of the brush to black and paint out the overgrown edge wear on the pockets and gun holster (Figure 9.42).

Step 48: Boots bottom. Go to the Smart materials under the SHELF. Drag Rubber Dry to the top of the layer stack and name the group Boots_ Bottom. Give it a black mask with a paint layer.

FIGURE 9.41 Add leather material to the leather parts.

FIGURE 9.42 Refine the edge wear of the leather materials.

FIGURE 9.43 Add the Rubber Dry material to the bottom of the boots.

Use polygon fill tool with UV shell selection mode to assign the rubber material to the bottom of the shoe (Figure 9.43).

Gloves

Step 49: Glove Base. Switch to the Glove_and_watch_ mtl and drag Leather Stylized into the layer stack. The result should look like Figure 9.44.

FIGURE 9.44 Glove material artifacts.

We can see many bad triangular artifacts. These artifacts are due to us baking using the low-resolution geometry as the high-resolution one. It is all fine if our texture does not rely heavily on the curvature map. Pull out the baked curvature map, and you can see the artifacts already existing on the baked map (Figure 9.45).

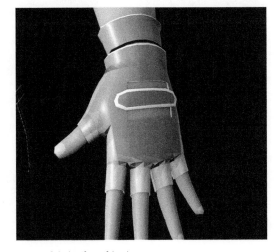

FIGURE 9.45 Baked artifacts of the glove.

We have two solutions:

1. Go to TEXTURE SET SETTINGS, under the Mesh maps column, click on curvature, set the Algorithm to Per Vertex, this will give us a much clean curvature map (Figure 9.46).

2. Go back to Maya, select the glove models, go to Mesh->Smooth, smooth the glove model twice (Figure 9.47).

We can use this smoothed model as the high-resolution model. Grab both the gloves and the watch, export them out as an fbx file. Back to Substance Painter; go to TEXTURE SET SETTINGS and click on Bake Mesh Maps. In the common settings, check off Use Low Poly Mesh as High Poly Mesh. On the side of the High-Definition Meshes list, click on the file icon to load the file exported from Maya, then bake again (Figure 9.48).

Solution 2 was used to get a better curvature map, and the result is that the leather material on the glove looks like Figure 9.49.

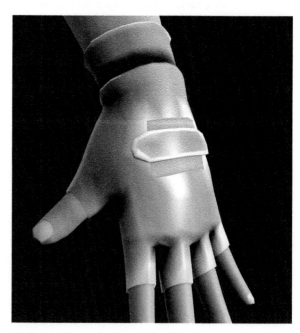

FIGURE 9.46 Baking result with the Per Vertex Algorithm.

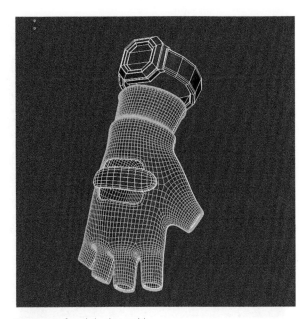

FIGURE 9.47 Smooth the glove model.

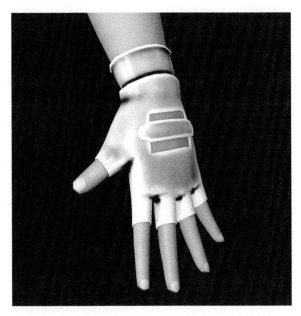

FIGURE 9.48 New baking result with the smoothed mesh as the high-resolution model.

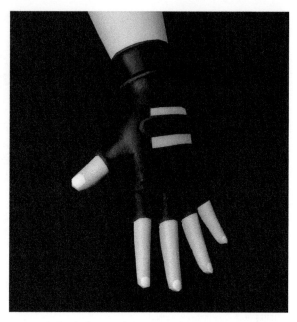

FIGURE 9.49 New leather material appearance with the new curvature map.

Step 50: Refine the amount of edge wear. Open the Leather Stylized folder and select the Mask Editor of the Curvature layer. In the PROPERTIES panel, change the Global Balance to 0.35 and the Global Contrast to 0.83. Go to the mask of the Darker Touch layer and select its Levels layer. In the PROPERTIES panel, drag the three pins on the top of the LEVELS graph to the right to minimize the amount of darker touch. Go to the Base color layer and change it to a darker color (Figure 9.50).

Step 51: Add extra height to the glove. Create a new fill layer above Base Color, name the new layer Glove_Extra_Height. In the PROPERTIES panel, toggle off color, rough, metal, nrm, and change the Height attribute to 1. Add a black mask with a paint layer, and use the Basic Hard brush to start painting in some extra layers around the finger and palm. Add a Blur filter above the paint layer to blur out the slope of the height (Figure 9.51).

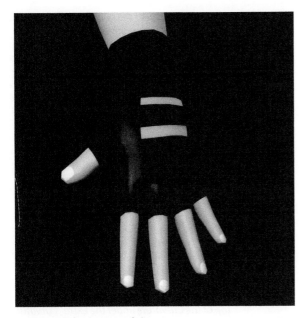

FIGURE 9.50 Refine the amount of edge wear.

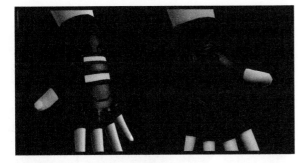

FIGURE 9.51 Add extra height detail to the glove.

Tips and Tricks

The Shift-click trick was used a lot to create clean straight lines. Now, hit the X button and erase to create valleys. We use the Hard brush first to lay out the patches, and then we blur it using a blur filter. This workflow gives us the flexibility to tweak how blurred we want it to be.

Step 52: Extra scratch to the new patches. Duplicate the Curvature layer, name the duplication Extra_Curvature, and toggle its height on and set the height value to −0.05. Delete the Mask Editor under its mask and add a new Generator to the mask. In the PROPERTIES panel, add a Curvature as the Generator; under the PROPERTIES, set the global balance to 0.7 and global contrast to 0.45 to get a basic color variation on the edge and high grounds.

Right-click on the mask of Glove_Extra_ Height, select Add Anchor Point (we have covered anchor point before). Back to the Curvature mask of Extra_Curvature, in the PROPERTIES panel, toggle on Use Micro Detail. Under the Image inputs, click Micro Height, go to the ANCHOR POINTS tab, and select Glove_Extra_Height mask. Go to the Micro Detail section, drag Curvature Intensity up to 5, and set the Height Detail Intensity to 1.8 (Figure 9.52).

Step 53: Refine the edge wear. Add a paint layer on top of the Curvature under the Extra_Curvature. Use Dirt1 brush to paint extra edge scratch and imperfections (Figure 9.53).

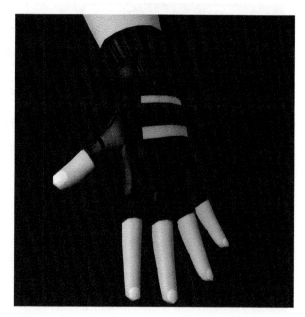

FIGURE 9.52 Use anchor point to create edge wear for the heightmap we painted.

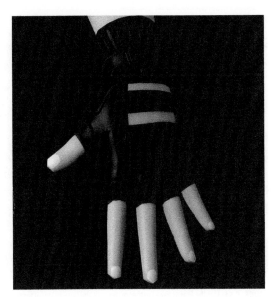

FIGURE 9.53 Hand paint more details to the edge wear of the glove.

Watch

Step 54: Add a basic material to the watch. Go to the shelf, drag the Plastic Fake Leather material on top of the Leather Stylized. Give it a black mask with a paint layer, press the number 4 button to use Poly Fill tool, and change the mode of the Poly Fill tool to UV shell mode. Set the color to white, and click on the watch to assign the material to the watch (Figure 9.54).

Step 55: Add material to the screen of the watch. Create a new fill layer and name it Watch_ Monitor. Change the Base Color of the layer to a dark gray, height to −0.35, roughness to 0.01, and the blend mode of the Height channel to normal. Give it a black mask and use the Poly Fill tool to make it appear only on the screen of the watch (Figure 9.55).

Step 56: Add extra height to the watch. Create a new fill layer, name it Watch_Extra_Height, and drag the Height down to −1. Add a black mask with a paint layer and start to paint extra detail on the watch. After painting, drag both Watch_Monitor and Watch_Extra_Height to Plastic Fake Leather and rename the folder Watch (Figure 9.56).

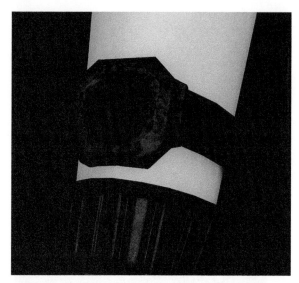

FIGURE 9.54 Use the Plastic Fake Leather material as the base material for the watch.

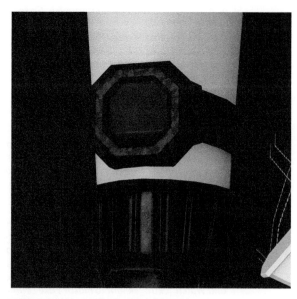

FIGURE 9.55 Add material to the screen of the watch.

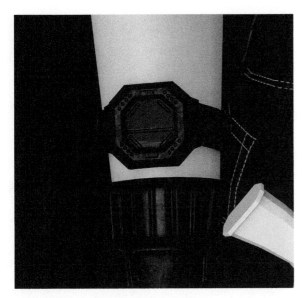

FIGURE 9.56 Paint extra height to the watch.

Gun

> *Step 57: Gun rebake. Switch to the Gun model and press Alt+Q to isolate the gun. The portion inside of the holster is darker due to the baked Ambient Occlusion. Open Maya and load the model in there, grab the Ellen_gun_geo, go to File->Export Selection, use the FBX format, and export with the name Gun_High. Back to Substance Painter, go to TEXTURE SET SETTINGS, and click Base Mesh Maps. Check off Use Low Poly Mesh as High Poly Mesh, load Gun_High in the High-Definition Meshes, and click on Bake Gun_mtl Mesh Maps to bake the mesh maps for the gun again.*
>
> *Step 58: Texture the Gun. The Method we use to texture the gun is the same we used to texture our environment modules. Go ahead and finish texturing it; Figure 9.57 shows our result.*

Other Details

> *Step 59: Chest Logo. Switch back to Upper_body_mtl and create a new fill layer above Fabric UCP. Name the new layer Chest_Logo, change its*

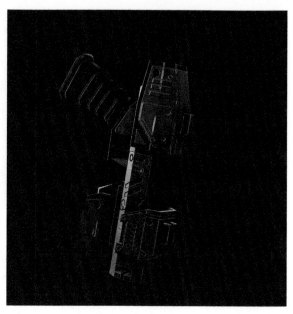

FIGURE 9.57 The finished texture of the gun.

color to a darker gray, height to 1, and give it a black mask with a paint layer. Use the Basic Hard brush to paint out the circle of the logo, shrink the brush size, and hit the X button to reverse the color. Paint out the middle to create the outer ring of the logo.

Change the Stroke opacity slider above the viewport to 50 and hit the X button to reverse the color back to white. Make the brush a little smaller and paint over the middle of the circle to add a half-transparent and half-height circular pattern. Change the Stroke opacity back to 100 and use the Shift + Left click combinate to draw a letter "A". Finally, hit X again to switch back to black; make the brush small and paint the dots across the outer circle (Figure 9.58).

Step 60: Metal bolts. Switch to the Lower_body_mtl, go to the Materials of the shelf, find and drag

FIGURE 9.58 Paint a chest logo.

FIGURE 9.59 Add metal bolts.

Nickel Pure to the top of the layer stack, and name it Bolts. Change the height blending mode of this new layer to replace. Toggle on the height channel and set the Height value to 0.5. Change the color to a darker brown and increase roughness to 0.3.

Give Bolts a black mask with a paint layer, and press the number 1 button to switch to the paint brush. Use Basic Soft as the brush, hold down Ctrl and drag right mouse button up to make the brush sharp. You can now left-click to add bolts or paint any areas that are supposed to be metal. Do the same thing to the gloves (Figure 9.59).

Export Textures

Step 61: Export Textures. Go to File->Export Textures. In the pop-up Export Document settings window, go to CONFIGURATION and choose the same configuration we did in Chapter 4. Go back to EXPORT, change the format from png to targa, click on the directory, and change it to the sourceimages folder of the Maya project. Add a new folder there and name the folder

Ellen_Textures. Select Ellen_Textures, and press Select Folder. Change the resolution of the Eye_mtl and Hair_mtl to 1024×1024 to save some performance; press Export to export all maps.

Step 62: Test the textures in Maya. Open our character scene in Maya, select Ellen_head_geo, and press Ctrl+A to open the attribute editor. Select the Body_mtl and click the checker box icon after the color to pull out the Create Render Node window. Select File in the list and click on the Folder button on the right side of the Image Name setting in the Attribute Editor; choose Ellend_Body_mtl_BaseColor.tga and press open to load it. Press the number 6 button on the keyboard to show the texture.

Hold down right mouse button on the model and select Material Attributes to go back to the material. In the Attribute Editor, click on the checker box to assign a file node to the bump mapping. Maya creates a bump2d node automatically. Change the Use As setting to Tangent Space Normal in the Attribute Editor. Click on the button with a square and an arrow on the left side edge to go to the file node. Load the Ellen_Body_mtl_Normal.tga; for a normal map, we need to change the Color Space setting to Raw.

Do the same to all other materials (Figure 9.60).

Step 63: Move the gun to the origin. We have placed the gun to ensure that the gun works with the proportion and color scheme, but for rigging and game mechanics, the gun should be placed at the origin. Select Ellen_gun_geo, and switch to the Move tool, hold down D button, and click on a side face of the barrel to move the pivot to that face. Go to Modify->Bake Pivot. Maya then generates transformation values based on the current location and orientation of the pivot.

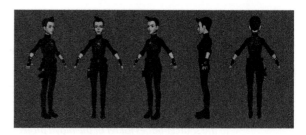

FIGURE 9.60 Test the textures in Maya.

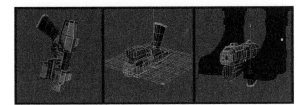

FIGURE 9.61 Move the gun to the origin.

> Go to the Channel Box and zero out all the translate and rotate values; the gun should now no longer be tilted. Do a Modify->Center Pivot, hold down D and drag the Y and Z axes to move the pivot to the handle; do another Bake Pivot and zero out the translate and rotate values. Finally, rotate the gun back if it is flipped and do another Modify->Freeze transformation (Figure 9.61).

Why?

Bake pivot calculates the location and rotation of the pivot relative to the origin and overrides the translation values with that. We can use it to get the rotation of a tilted model back, even if we have done a freeze transformation on it.

Conclusion

That's it, we have finished our character texturing! Overall, with Substance Painter, the texturing process should be a joyful one. With smart masks, generators, height map painting, and PBR workflow, we can get many things done. Be aware that we have seven texture sets, or materials, each with 2k images to achieve this crisp, high-resolution result. It is a pretty ambitious setup and would not be recommended for low-performance platforms. However, we could spoil ourselves on a PC game like what we are doing.

Moving on from here, we will jump into a pretty technical process – Rigging.

CHAPTER 10

Rigging

Now that we have the 3D model created and UV mapped and textured, we can begin the rigging process. Rigging is essentially placing joints inside the character so that the animator can then animate those joints and bring the character to life. Each joint will influence a nearby polygon vertex and cause the deformation of that polygon. Once there's enough joints influencing enough vertices, the character will appear to be in motion. This will make more sense as we go on. Let's first take a quick look at how joints behave in Maya.

Joint Behavior

Create a new Maya file and go to the side view. In the rigging module, click Skeleton, create joints. Click in the side view once, then move your cursor to a new area above and click again. Do this one final time and press Enter. We now have a three-joint chain created (Figure 10.1).

Take a peek in the outliner; notice that the joints are created in the hierarchy on clicking. The top joint is the first joint you created. Look at the first joint, notice the orientation is pointed in the direction of the next joint. As joints are created, they automatically orient to the direction of the next joint. There are ways to add or remove joints to your joint structure but, for now, the main thing to know is to press Enter to finalize your joint chain.

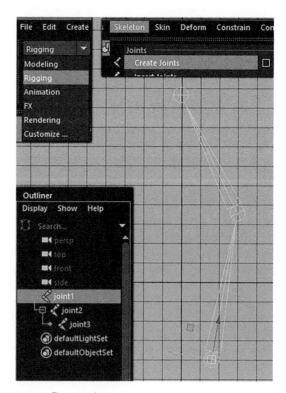

FIGURE 10.1 Three-joint chain.

Few things to note:

1. The best views to create joints are in the top, side, or front views.
2. If you hold down the shift button while creating joints, the joints will be created in a straight line.
3. You can easily change the hierarchy of joints in the outliner. For example, Select joint 3 and press Shift+P. You have now unparented joint 3; it stands alone, as seen in the viewport. To add it back to the hierarchy of joint 1, select joint 3 in the outliner and middle mouse drag it under joint 2. As you can see, we are now back to our original joint hierarchy.
4. You can translate joints in the viewport to get them in the position you want, but generally you do not want to rotate the joints. We'll discuss this more as the tutorial progresses, but, ideally, you want your joint rotations to be at 0,0,0. This will make the animation process go much more smoothly.

To get comfortable with the joint creation process, create a few new joint chains and alter their structure in the outliner. Once you're comfortable with creating joints and moving them into positions, we should be ready to create a skeletal joint structure for our game character.

Joint Placement – Hip, Spine, Neck, and Head

Let's start this chapter by creating joints for the root (the base joint from which all other joints will arise), spinal cord, neck, and head. We will use the create joints tool.

Tutorial 10.1: Create the Joint Chain for Our Character

Step 1: Reference in the model. Create a new Maya file. Then go to File->Create Reference and point towards the 3D character Maya file we created in the previous chapters.

Why?

Referencing is an industry-standard process. We reference in characters, environment, and rigs into scenes so that should the characters, environments, or rigs will be updated. The file that we are working on automatically grabs those updates. This allows us to make sure we are working on the most up-to-date models and rigs.

Step 2: Go to your side view.

Why?

By creating our joints in the side view, the joints will be created directly in the center of the character. This is especially important because we'll be mirroring our left arm and left leg joint to the right side to save some time.

Step 3: Create a spine joint chain. Go to the menu of the viewport, and check on Shading->X-Ray Joints to see the joints through the models. Create the root joint by clicking in the middle of the hip area. Once that's done, while holding down the shift button, add three more joints going straight up and press Enter. You should now have a 4-joint chain (Figure 10.2).

Step 4: Rename the joints. Let's name our joints before we move on, starting with joint 1. Double-click joint 1 in the outline and type in hip. For the rest of the joints, label them spine_01, spine_02, and chest.

Step 5: Make the joints evenly apart. Let's make it so that spine_01, spine_02, and the chest joint are equally apart from each other. We can do this by using the translation attribute in the right-side channel box. Select spine_01, spine_02, and chest, go to the Channel Box, and type in a value of 8 in Translate X. The value may vary depending on the size of your character. The goal here is to get the chest joint to end up a little below the chest area of your 3D character. This is where the chest will rotate from.

Once that's done, we can now move onto the neck and head area. We'll do this by creating a new joint chain.

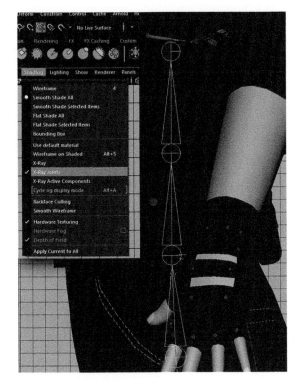

FIGURE 10.2 Root and spine joints.

> Step 6: Create the joint chain of the neck: Hit Create
> joints again and start with the base of the neck.
> Place the next joint right below the w line and
> then while holding shift, make the last joint be at
> the top of the head. See Figure 10.3.
>
> Step 7: Name the joints. Let's name these joints as
> neck, head, and head_end.
>
> Step 8: Parent neck joints to the spine. We have now
> created the joint chain we'll use to animate the
> neck and head of our character. The next thing
> we need to do with this chain is to add it to our
> existing hip joint hierarchy. To do this, we are
> going to go in the outliner and middle mouse-
> drag it onto the chest joint. Your joint system
> hierarchy should now look like this (Figure 10.4).
>
> Before we move on, there's a couple
> of things to note. So far, we've only been
> translating our joints. Double check that all
> your joints have no values in the rotation
> channels (Figure 10.5).

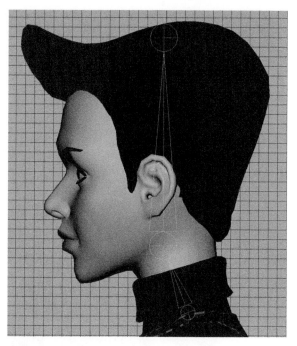

FIGURE 10.3 The joint chain for the neck.

Why?

This is the cleanest way of setting up a rig for animation. By keeping the rotation values at 0, animators can easily reset the joints to their original position by entering values of 0 in the rotation rather than some odd number.

Joint Placement – Left Arm

Let's now move onto creating the left arm joint structure. The goal here is to create a left arm structure along with a simple finger joint setup and then mirror that same setup to the other side for the right arm.

> Step 9: Create the clavicle joint. Switch to the Create Joint tool; in the front view, click in the area where the clavicle would be (between the shoulder and neck areas).

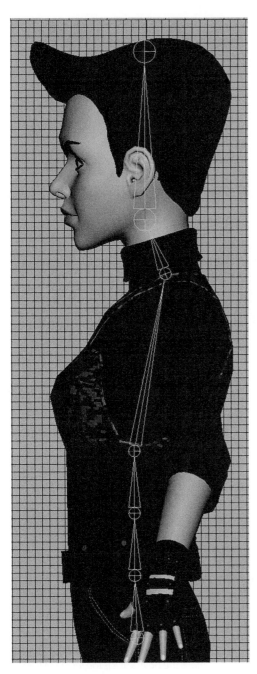

FIGURE 10.4 Parent neck joints to the spine.

Translate X	0
Translate Y	0
Translate Z	0
Rotate X	0
Rotate Y	0
Rotate Z	0
Scale X	1
Scale Y	1
Scale Z	1
Visibility	on

FIGURE 10.5 Before moving on, make sure there are no non-zero rotation values for the joints.

FIGURE 10.6 Create the arm joints.

> *Step 10: Create the arm joints. While holding down the shift button, add the shoulder, elbow, and wrist joint; they should form a horizontal joint chain at the moment (Figure 10.6).*
>
> *Step 11: Rename the joints. Let's relabel these as left_clavicle, left_shoulder, left_elbow, and left_wrist.*
>
> *We now need to rotate the joints to be in their correct direction. However, we do not want to rotate using the regular joint rotation. We want to use what's called joint orient, which can be found in the attribute editor once you select a joint (Figure 10.7).*

Why?

Using joint orient allows us to rotate the joints while keeping the original joint orientation clean.

> *Step 12: Position the arm joints to the right spot. First, move the clavicle if it is too far in the front or in the back. Next, select the left_shoulder joint and*

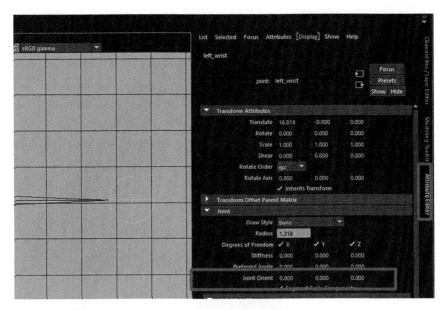

FIGURE 10.7 Attribute editor for the left_wrist joint.

go to the attribute editor. While holding down
the Ctrl key, middle mouse drag the values in the
joint orient box that correspond with the direction
you need to rotate the joint. In our case, we need
to rotate both the joint orientations Z and Y to
get the direction of the shoulder to properly line
up with the arm. Once the direction of the joint
is correct, you can change the translate X of the
child joint (left_elbow) to change the length of the
shoulder joint (Figure 10.8).

Step 13: Repeat the process we did for the shoulder joint
to the elbow and wrist joint until the arm joints are
all positioned in the right spot (Figure 10.9).

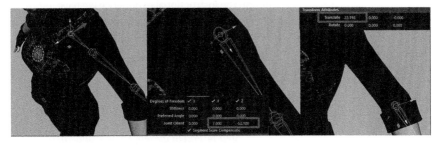

FIGURE 10.8 Position the clavicle and shoulder joint.

FIGURE 10.9 Finish the arm joints.

Tips and Tricks

Through the instructional experience we have, more than half of the students don't follow this rule. So we are going to write this down three times with all capitals:

DON'T ROTATE THE JOINT, CHANGE JOINT ORIENT!

DON'T ROTATE THE JOINT, CHANGE JOINT ORIENT!

DON'T ROTATE THE JOINT, CHANGE JOINT ORIENT!

> Step 14: Parent the left_clavicle underneath the chest joint (Figure 10.10).

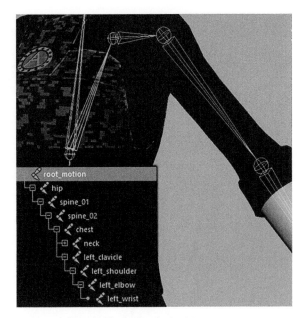

FIGURE 10.10 Parent the left_clavicle to the chest joint.

Now it's time to create the finger joints.
We'll just use a basic setup for the fingers that
consists of three animatable joints for each
finger.

Step 15: Turn on the Snap to Projected Center option.
Let's turn on "Snap to Projected Center" option,
which can be found in the top menu among the
buttons with icons of magnetics. This allows us
to create joints in the "perspective" viewport and
automatically place the joints inside the hand
mesh (Figure 10.11).

Step 16: Create the index finger joints. Create the first
joint at the base of the knuckle; add three more
joints down the finger, with the last one being at
the tip of the finger.

FIGURE 10.11 Turn on the Snap to Projected Center option.

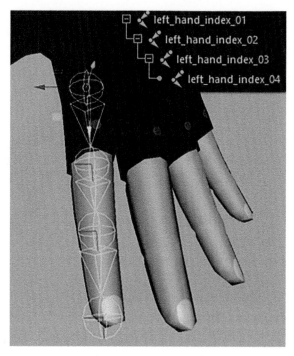

FIGURE 10.12 The joints of the index finger.

Step 17: Name the finger joints. Let's now label these joints left_hand_index_01, left_hand_index_02, left_hand_index_03, and left_hand_index_04 (Figure 10.12).

It's possible that our joint orientations are a little skewed after creation. Let's go and zero out the values of the joint orient of left_hand_index_02, left_hand_index03, and left_hand_index_04.

Why?

Upon doing this, we now have a clean structure wherein the fingers are all straight. Now we can get the orientation correct by changing the joint orientation values in the attribute editor the same way we did for the arm joints.

Now that we got that all cleared up and ready to go, let's duplicate and use that same joint setup for the rest of the fingers.

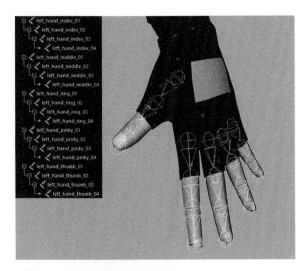

FIGURE 10.13 All fingers duplicated.

Step 18: Duplicate the index finger for the rest of the fingers. Select the left_hand_index_01 and press Ctrl + D. This makes a duplicate copy of that joint system. Move that new system onto the middle finger and adjust the joint orient accordingly. Remember only to translate the joints and use the joint orient to rotate the joints into place. It's your choice to either create the thumb from scratch or use a duplicate from the index finger.

Repeat the same process for the rest of the fingers and name them accordingly (Figure 10.13).

Step 19: Parent the fingers to the wrist. The last step is to grab all the first finger joints in the outliner and middle mouse drag them underneath the left_wrist joint. This will connect all the fingers to the wrist (Figure 10.14).

Tips and Tricks

As you're doing this, be sure to keep your orientations cohesive. Make sure all your fingers rotate the same direction so that, as your animating, you can grab all the fingers and animate them all at once in one axis.

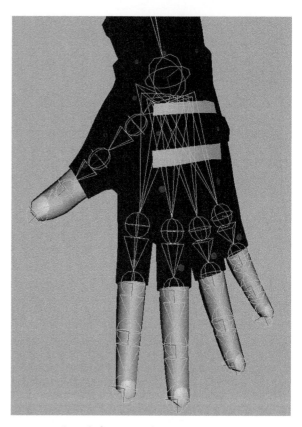

FIGURE 10.14 Parent the finger joints to the wrist joint.

Joint Setup – Right Arm

To get the right arm created, we could run through the whole process again, but we're going to take a shortcut for this one. We're going to do a process called Mirror Joints. This will essentially duplicate one side of the joints to the opposite side and save us much time.

> *Step 20: Mirror the joints. Select the left_clavicle. In the Rigging menu, select Skeleton->Mirror joints☐. Here, set the Mirror across to YZ so the joints are getting mirrored across the Y and Z planes. The other thing we want to do is relabel all of our new joints to start with right, instead of left. In the Search for text field, type in left. In*

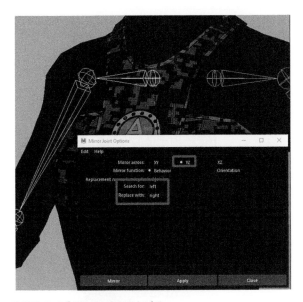

FIGURE 10.15 Settings to mirror a joint chain.

> *the Replace with text field, type in right. If you labeled all of your left joints correctly, all of your new mirrored joints should be properly labeled for the right side (Figure 10.15).*
>
> *Hit the Apply button. And we've finished the right arm.*

Joint Setup – Legs

The legs will be most likely animated using a method called Inverse Kinematics or IK. However, for now, we need to create a basic joint structure. Few things to note: we'll be creating this in the side view, and we need to be sure not to create the joint structure straight down. We need to create a slight bend from the thigh to the knee to the ankle.

> *Step 21: Create the leg joints. In the side view, create a new joint at the center of the hip area and name it left_thigh. Create another joint at the knee and then the ankle; name them accordingly (Figure 10.16).*

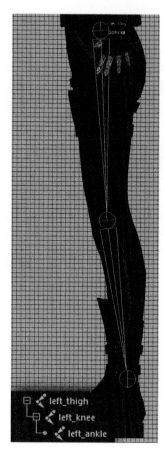

FIGURE **10.16** The naming and hierarchy of the leg joints.

Step 22: Create the foot joints. Add two more joints for the ball of the foot and the toe, name them, and parent the ball joint to the ankle joint after creation (Figure 10.17).

Once our structure is created, we need to go to the front view of the character and move left_thigh to match the leg joints to the left leg and parent it to the hip joint (Figure 10.18).

Step 23: Mirror the leg joints. The next step would be to mirror this leg the same way we mirrored the clavicle.

Step 24: Parent the hip joints underneath the hip joint.

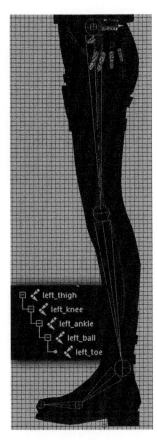

left_thigh
left_knee
left_ankle
left_ball
left_toe

FIGURE 10.17 Final joint chain for the left leg and foot.

Once this is done, we now have the left leg joint structure complete. We can now create what is called an IK chain for the leg. IK works a little differently than the forward kinematics that we've been using so far. IK allows us to move a point or a target and have the connected joints automatically rotate the joint to point to that target. This will make much more sense as we create one, so let's do that for the left leg.

Step 25: Go to Skeleton->IK handle☐, and click on the Reset Tool button. We will only need the default setting of this tool.

Step 26: Apply the IK handle to the leg. Click the center of the left hip joint and then at the left ankle joint. The IK handle has now been created.

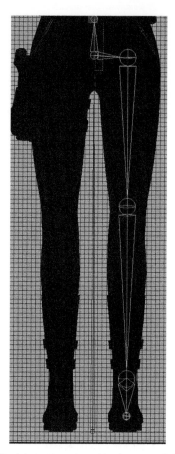

FIGURE 10.18 Match the leg joint to the model and parent it to the hip.

To see how this works, grab the IK Handle1 in the outliner and translate it around. The leg is now animating with inverse kinematics instead of forward kinematics. Go ahead and name this IK handle, left_leg_ankle_IK.

Step 27: Create IK chains for the foot joints. Create another IK handle from the ankle to the ball of the foot. Label the new IK handle, left_leg_ball_ IK. Create a final IK handle from the ball to the toe and label it left_leg_toe_IK. We should now have three IK chains. If you cannot see them, go to the menu of the viewport and check on Shading->X-Ray (Figure 10.19).

Step 28: Make the IK handles sticky. The last step for these IK chains is to make them sticky.

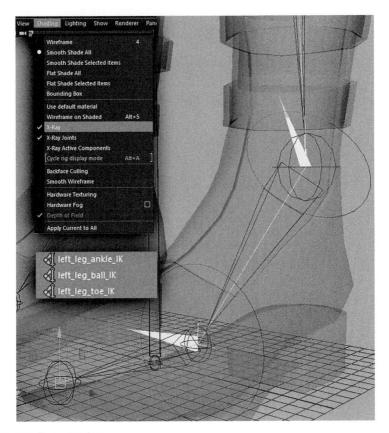

FIGURE 10.19 The new joint chain.

> To achieve this, go to the outliner and select the
> IK handles, then in the attribute editor under the
> IK handle Attributes section, turn on Sticky under
> Stickiness. Do this for each of the IK handles
> (Figure 10.20).

Foot Roll Rig

The next thing we need to do is create controllers for the
foot. We'll be animating these later instead of trying to
grab the IK chains in the outliner.

> Step 29: Create the controller for the left toe. Go to
> Create->NURBS primitives->Circle. This will create
> a NURBS circle at the origin. Let's label this one

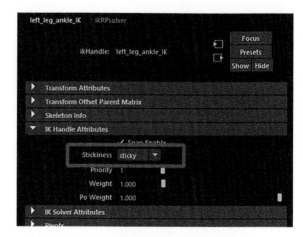

FIGURE 10.20 Make the IK handles sticky.

left_toe_ctrl. NURBS models are mathematically constructed, lightweight, and perfect for creating controllers.

Step 30: Group the controller. After labeling the curve, we need to group it by selecting the NURBS curve and then pressing Ctrl + G. Name the group left_toe_ctrl_group. The group is what we'll use to position the curve where we need it to go, leaving the NURBS curve attributes clean.

Why?

We'll be animating with the NURBS curves later on, and we need those to not have any values on them to make life easier for the animators. By keeping the values empty, we can easily reset the controller back to default by entering 0 in the values.

Step 31: Position the group to the toe joint. Select the left_toe_ctrl_group and then add select the left_toe joint. In the top menu, select Modify->Match Transformations->Match All Transforms. The left_toe_ctrl_group should now be moved to the left_toe joint.

If you don't see the controller, press Ctrl + 1 to isolate the group, and you can see it is just too small. To make it bigger, hold down the right mouse button on the curve and

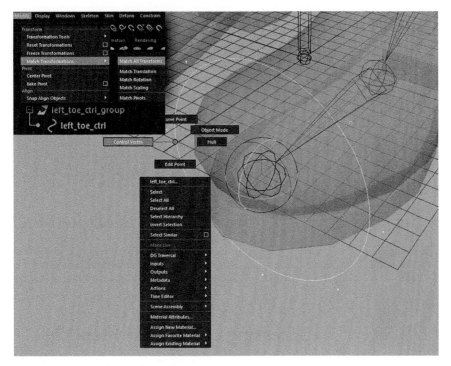

FIGURE 10.21 Position and reshape the controller.

> select Control Vertex. Marquee select all the
> vertices and scale and rotate them, as shown
> in Figure 10.21.

Why?

We could easily scale the controller up, but that introduces
scale values in the Channel Box, which will cause
problems for animation and rigging later on. Always
remember, the Translate X, Y, Z and Rotate X, Y, Z values of
your controller should remain 0, while the Scale X, Y, and Z
values should remain 1.

You can press Ctrl + 1 again to toggle isolation.

> Step 32: Create the controller for the left ball joint.
>   Repeat the same process given in Steps 29–31 for
>   the left_ball joint.

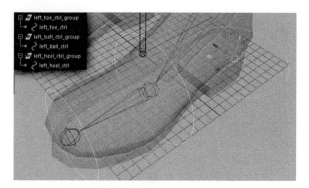

FIGURE 10.22 The left foot controller setup.

> *Step 33: Create the heel controller. Create another controller and group pair, and name them left_heel_ctrl, and left_heel_ctrl_group. This time, instead of match transformation, place the left_heel_ctrl_group to the base of the heel (Figure 10.22).*

Setting Up the Foot Hierarchy

The next part of the process is putting the controllers into the correct hierarchy so they can control the joints.

> *Step 34: Parent IK to the controllers. Make Left_leg_ ankle_Ik a child of left_ball_ctrl. We can achieve this by middle mouse dragging leg_ankleik onto left_ball_ctrl. Follow the same trend, do the following parenting operations:*
> *Make left_leg_ball_IK a child of left_toe_ctrl*
> *Make left_ball_ctrl_grp a child of left_toe_ctrl*
> *Make left_leg_toe_IK a child of left_heel_ctrl*
> *Make left_toe_ctrl_grp a child of left_heel_ctrl.*
> *Your hierarchy should now look like Figure 10.23.*
> *Step 35: Create a main foot controller. Create another controller and group pair. Name the controller left_foot_ctrl and name the group left_foot_ctrl_group. Place left_foot_ctrl_group directly underneath the foot. Hold down the right mouse button on the curve and select Control Vertex. Marquee select all the vertices and scale them to match their size to the bottom of the foot. Finally, parent left_heel_ctrl_group to left_foot_ctrl.*

FIGURE 10.23 Left foot rig setup hierarchy.

Step 36: Repeat Steps 25–35 on the right leg.
Currently, the joints are not influencing any of the geometry. The next thing we need to do is have it such that the joints are now influencing the character vertices or polygons. To do this, we'll be using a method called Bind skin.

Tutorial 10.2: Bind and Paint Skin Weighting

Step 1: Select all the joints and the models. In the outliner, select the root_motion joint and then on the top menu, go to Select->Hierarchy; this will select all the joints. Now, while holding down the Ctrl button, add all the character meshes except the gun to the selection.

Step 2: Bind the models to the joints. In the Rigging menu, go to skin->bind skin□. In the pop-up Bind Skin Options window, click on Edit->Reset Settings to use default skinning options (Figure 10.24).
Press the Bind skinbutton. (Binding skin will bind the vertices to the closest joints so that when you rotate or translate the joints, the corresponding geometry deforms accordingly.)

Now that our geometry is bound to the joints, we need to refine the skin weights. The process is known as painting skin weights, which is the process of adjusting the intensity values on each vertex to the corresponding joint. This part of the rigging process is

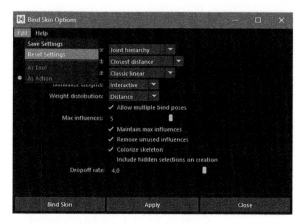

FIGURE 10.24 Bind skin options.

one of the most important as it allows us to make sure each joint is deforming the corresponding geometry properly and smoothly.

Painting Skin Weights

The goal here is to make sure only the specified geometry bends with the corresponding bind joint. Another thing we're going to do is copy the skin weights from one side of the body to the other. So we'll paint the skin weights for the character's left side and copy them to the right side.

To make things easier, we'll paint the skin weights on the Ellen_full_body_ref geometry and then transfer the skin weights to the main character geometry.

> *Step 3: Hide all the geometry except for the Ellen_full_body_ref. Select the geometry pieces in the outliner and press Ctrl + H. Next, be sure to unhide the Ellen_full_body_ref if it's hidden. Select the geometry in the outliner and press Shift + H.*
> *Step 4: Open the Paint Skin Weight Tool. Select the Ellen_full_body_ref in the viewport, hold down the right mouse button, and select the Paint Skin Weights tool. This now activates the skin weighting process for the geometry and joints.*

There are a few things to take note of in the Tool Settings that pop up. The first is that you'll see is a list of all the joints. Select one of the joints in the list, and you'll see which part of the geometry that joint is affecting. The controlled geometry area is displayed in white, as shown in Figure 10.25. We will be mainly using the Add and the Smooth options under paint operation.

Step 5: Paint the weighting for the head. Let's start with the head joint. Select the head joint in the influences list on the paint weight tool settings box that popped open. Once selected, make sure the paint operation is set to Add and the opacity is at 1.0000. We'll also put the Value at 1.0000. The goal here is to paint the head geometry to have a value of 1 so that when the head joint is animated, the head geometry rotates accordingly.

Paint the whole area of the head to white to make the head joint take full control of the

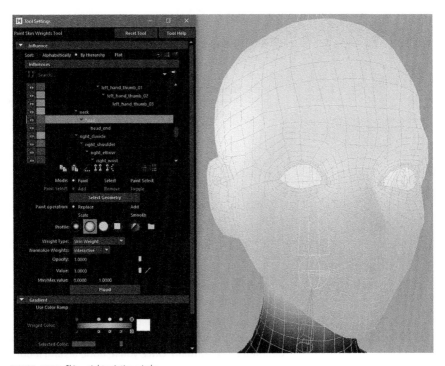

FIGURE 10.25 Skin weight painting window.

393

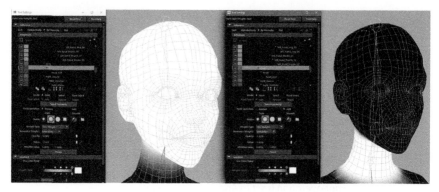

FIGURE 10.26 Paint the weighting for the head and the neck.

head. Moving down to the neck joint, and paint the neck area to white to make the neck joint control the neck (Figure 10.26).

Tips and Tricks

When painting, completely white means that vertex has a weight value of 1.

Step 6: Smooth the weighting between the head and the neck. Now that we've got the head and the neck completely painted with an influence of 1 (white), what we'll want to do is smooth the weighting between the two joints. To do this, select the head joint in the list and switch to the Smooth operation option in the tool settings. Once that's selected, press the Flood button (located under the opacity option) a few times. You'll now see the blend is much smoother to the neck joint. This will allow for a smooth deformation when bending the joint.

Tips and Tricks

You can also hold down Shift and paint to smooth out any area. To verify if your skin weights are looking nice and clean, grab the head joint and rotate it. You'll see how the geometry is deforming. Once you're done testing it out, be sure to set the joint back to 0,0,0 (Figure 10.27).

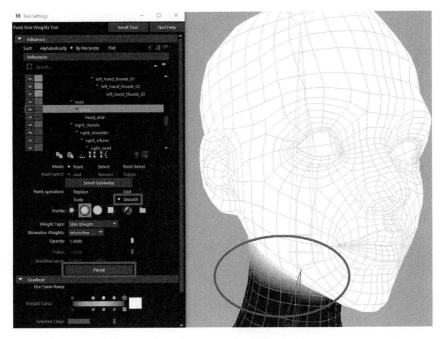

FIGURE 10.27 Head skin weighting smooth to neck joint.

> Step 7: Paint the weight down the chain. The next
> step would be to work our way down the chain.
> The chests would be the next joints to paint.
> Do the same process as before. Use Add, and
> paint the influence of the chest joint. Once
> done with that area, you can smooth out the
> transitions (Figure 10.28).

Tips and Tricks

Sometimes as you're going through your paint weighting
process, you'll see a vertex with influences from an
unwanted joint. In these cases, select the vertice, and go
to the Windows->General editors->Component Editor.
Once there, you'll see a Smooth Skins tab that shows
which joints are influencing that vertice. If there's a joint
that is influencing and you do not want it to, you can enter
0 in the box associated to that joint (Figure 10.29).

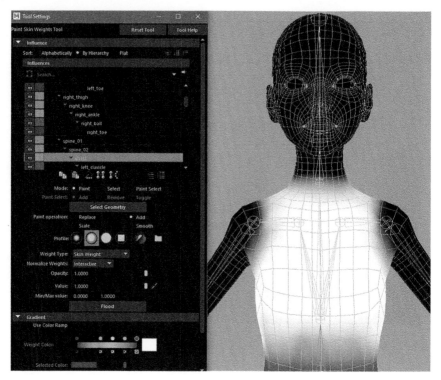

FIGURE 10.28 Chest weighting completed.

Step 8: Repeat the weight painting process for the rest of the spine. You will repeat this process down the spine. Below is an image showing the cutoff points for each joint (Figure 10.30).

Once you're done with the spine, it's time to do the arms and legs. Remember, we're only doing one side, and then we'll copy the weighting to the other side. So, let's do the character's left side.

Step 9: Paint the weighting for the left clavicle. Starting with the left clavicle, repeat the process of painting in Add mode, and then smooth it out (Figure 10.31).

Step 10: Finish the weighting of the rest of the body. The next joint would be the shoulder, then the elbow, wrist, and finger joints. Once the arm is done, the next thing to do would be the left leg, starting from the hips.

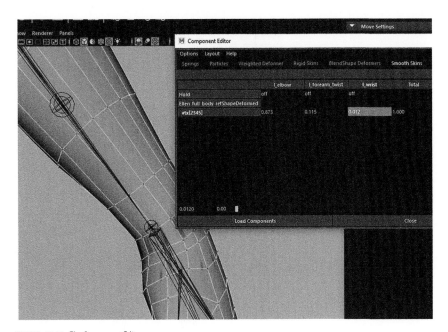

FIGURE 10.29 The Component Editor.

Mirroring the Skin Weights

Instead of painting the right side of the body, we're going to mirror the skin weights from the left side.

> Step 11: Mirror the skin weights. Select the geometry and go to Skin->Mirror Skin Weights□. In the Mirror Skin Weights Options window, make sure the Mirror across option is set to YZ and the Direction Positive to negative (–X to X) is checked so that it's mirroring from Positive to Negative (+x to –x) (Figure 10.32).
>   Hit Mirror. The skin weights have now been mirrored to the right side of the body. Be sure to double-check this is in fact the case. Test it by animating or rotating the joints. Be sure to set them back to 0,0,0 afterward.

Copying the Skin Weights

Now that we've got the Ellen_full_body_ref painted, we're going to transfer the skin weights from this model to the

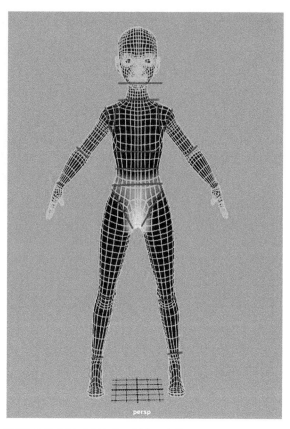

FIGURE 10.30 Full-body joint skin weighting cut-off areas.

rest of the models. This is a simple process that'll only take a few minutes.

> *Step 12: Unhide the models. Unhide the geometry that we hid before. Select all of the geometry in the outliner and press Shift+H.*
>
> *Step 13: Copy skin weight to the sweater. Select Ellen_full_body_ref and then shift select Ellen_sweater_geo. Go to Skin->Copy Skin Weights. The order of selection is important; you must select the source first, then the destination. Once you've hit copy skin weights, the skin weighting should now be applied to the Ellen_sweater_geo. Test it out again by animating the joints.*

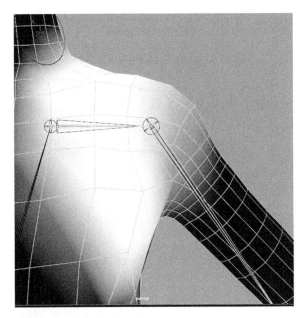

FIGURE 10.31 Left clavicle skin weighting.

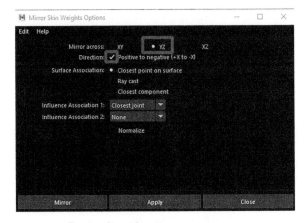

FIGURE 10.32 The mirror skin weights settings.

Step 14: Repeat the same process for all of Ellen's geos.

Once you've copied all of the skin weights over, test out the deformations. While copying the skin weights over does a great job, it's never 100%, so be sure to test out and adjust

*accordingly using the paint skin weights
process that we did before.*

*Now that the skin weighting is out of the
way, let's start creating controllers for the arm.*

Tutorial 10.3: Set Up Arm Controls

*Step 1: Duplicate the left arm joints. Select the
left_shoulder joint and press Ctrl+D to duplicate
it. You should now have a new chain called left_
shoulder1, left_elbow, and left_wrist. The fingers
were also probably duplicated, but we don't
need those. In the outliner, delete the duplicated
finger joints.*

*Step 2: Unparent the new joint chain. Grab
left_shoulder and press Shift+P. This will
unparent the new joint chain that we created
since we want it to function separately from the
deformation joint system.*

*Step 3: Rename the new joints. Rename the
duplicated joints as left_drv_shoulder,
left_drv_elbow, and left_drv_wrist. As a final
step on this joint chain, place it under a group
and name the group left_drv_arm_group
(Figure 10.33).*

FIGURE 10.33 New arm joint setup.

*This new joint chain we created is often
called a driver joint chain. It receives the
controller's input and drives the original
joints. We also call the original joints the
binding joints.*

*What we want to do now is create
controllers to control this driver joint chain.*

*Step 4: Create the controller. Go to the top menu
and select Create->NURBS Primitives->Circle.
This will create a NURBS circle at the origin.
If you do not see it, be sure to go to the
perspective view.*

*Step 5: Delete history. With the circle selected, go to
Edit->Delete by Type->History.*

*Step 6: Rename the controller to
left_fk_shoulder_ctrl.*

*Step 7: Group the controller. With the controller
selected, press Ctrl+G. This creates a group
on top of the controller. Rename that group,
left_fk_shoulder_ctrl_grp.*

*Step 8: Match the group to the shoulder joint. Select
the group and then shift select the left shoulder
joint. Go to the top menu, Modify->Match
Transformations->Match all Transformations.*

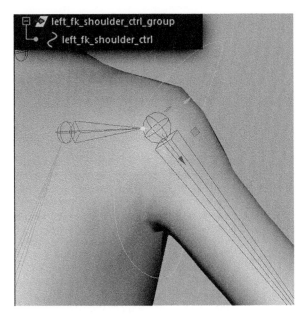

FIGURE 10.34 Arm control setup.

This will place the group and controller in the exact place and orientation of the selected object.

Step 9: Tweak the shape of the controller. You'll want to resize the controller if it is not looking right. Manipulate the control vertices to change its size and shape (Figure 10.34).

Step 10: Duplicate the controller group. Select the left_fk_shoulder_ctrl_grp and duplicate it by pressing Ctrl + D. This creates another group; rename the group to left_fk_elbow_ctrl_grp. Open the group and rename the controller under it to left_fk_elbow_ctrl.

Tips and Tricks

It's important to keep the actual controls clean with zero values on them. That's why we're using the groups to move them into position and adjusting the control vertices to rotate or scale them into your desired size and shape.

FIGURE 10.35 Arm controller hierarchy.

Step 11: Match the left_fk_elbow_ctrl_grp to the elbow joint. Grab the left_fk_elbow_ctrl_grp and add select the elbow joint; do a match all transformations. Then resize the controller to your liking by manipulating the control vertices.

Step 12: Repeat Steps 10 and 11 for the wrist.

Step 13: Put the controller into a correct hierarchy. The last step for the controller set up is the hierarchy of the groups and their controls. It's important that after we do this, we are moving the groups on top of the controls in the outliner. The hierarchy should be from the shoulder down. So first, grab the elbow group and drag it underneath the shoulder controller (not the group, the controller under the group). Then grab the wrist group and drag it under the elbow controller (Figure 10.35).

Step 14: Use the controllers to control the driver joints. Select left_fk_shoulder_ctrl and then shift select the left_drv_shoulder joint and select Constrain->Orient. (Be sure that the maintain offset option is checked in the settings.) Do the same thing for the elbow and wrist. In the end, you should have three orient constraints, one on each joint. If you did things correctly, you should be able to rotate the controllers and see the joints rotate with it. These will be the FK arm setup.

Constrains

After you apply constrains to objects, the second one in the selection starts to follow the first one in the selection. Orient constraint makes the object follow this rotation only. Go to the constrain menu, and you can still see Parent and Point. Parent constraint makes the object follow both the translation and the rotation. Point constraint makes the object follow the translation only.

IK Arm Setup

Now let' setup the IK arm controls.

> Step 15: Create the IK controller for the wrist. Duplicate the left_fk_wrist_ctrl_grp and unparent the new duplicate. Replace the "fk" in the names of the new group and the controller under it with "ik".
>
> Step 16: Reshape the new IK controller by right-clicking and going into the Control vertex mode. All you have to do is make it look different than the left_fk_wrist_ctrl (Figure 10.36).
>
> Step 17: Create the IK controller for the elbow. Duplicate the left_ik_wrist_ctrl_grp and replace the "wrist" in the name to "elbow". Select the new group, match it to the elbow joint with Modify->Match Transformations->Match all Transformations. Select the group and translate it back so it sits behind the elbow. Change the shape of the controller as shown in Figure 10.37.
>
> Next, let's setup the IK control system for the arm.
>
> Step 18: Create the IK Handle. Go to the rigging module, then Skeleton->Create IK handle. Use the default settings. Click on the left_drv_ shoulder then left_drv_wrist (Isolate them so you can easily click on them). This will create an IK handle. Rename it as left_wrist_IK.

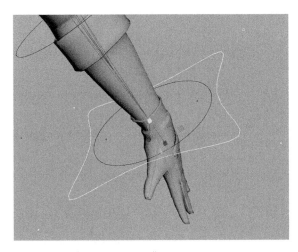

FIGURE 10.36 Reshape the new IK controller.

403

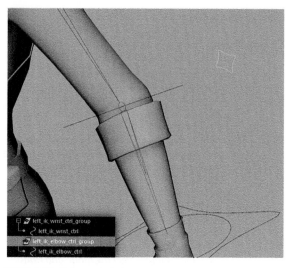

FIGURE 10.37 IK elbow control setup.

Step 19: Parent the IK handle to the IK wrist controller. Select the left_wrist_IK in the outliner and middle mouse drag it onto the left_ik_wrist_ ctrl. Now left_ik_wrist_ctrl should be driving the IK system.

Step 20: Set up the IK elbow control. Select the left_ik_elbow_ctrl you created in the outline. Holding down Ctrl and select the left_wrist_IK, go to Constraint->Pole Vector. This pole vector control should now be able to control the IK elbow position.

Step 21: Apply wrist rotation control. The last thing we need to do is add an orient constraint between the left_ik_wrist_ctrl and the left_drv_ wrist joint. Select the left_ik_wrist_ctrl, then shift select the left_drv_wrist joint, and select Constrain->orient constraint.

> *Now that we have the IK created, one of the last things we need to do is constrain the new duplicate arm driver joints to the original binding joints. What we'll be doing is parent constraining our binding joints to the new driver joints.*

Step 22: Parent Constraint the binding joints to the driver joints. Select the new left_drv_shoulder joint and shift select the left_shoulder binding joint. Select Constrain->Parent Constraint to apply a parent constraint to the binding joint.

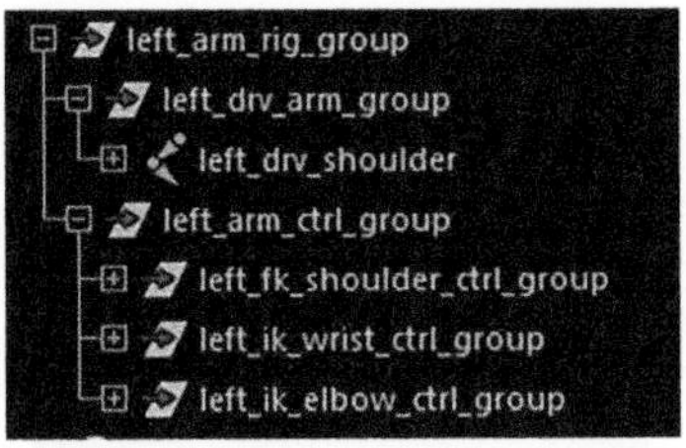

FIGURE 10.38 The final hierarchy of the left arm.

> Go ahead and do the same thing for the elbow
> and the wrist joints.
>> Now that we have our arm rigs done, we
> need to clean up the groups in the outliner.
> Step 23: Group all the controllers. Select left_fk_
>> shoulder_ctrl_group, left_ik_wrist_ctrl_group,
>> and left_ik_elbow_ctrl_group. Group them and
>> name the new group left_arm_ctrl_group.
> Step 24: Group the controllers and the driver joints.
>> Select left_arm_ctrl_group and left_drv_arm_
>> group. Group them and name the new group
>> left_arm_rig_group (Figure 10.38).
>> You will need to repeat the entire Tutorial
> 10.3 for the right arm.

Tutorial 10.4: Finger Controls

Now that we have the arm completed, we need to create
controls for each finger joint.

> Step 1: Create the fk controllers. Create the fk
>> controllers for the fingers the same way we
>> created the controllers for the arm. You can think
>> of the fingers as mini arms. Don't forget to parent
>> the controllers to their correct hierarchy the same
>> way we did for the arm controllers (do not create
>> IK ones).
> Step 2: Parent constraint the joints. Once you're done
>> with all of the fingers' controls, you'll need to
>> parent constraint the joint to each corresponding
>> finger controller. This is the same process that
>> we've been doing for the other controls. The finger
>> joints should now rotate as you rotate the controls.
> Step 3: Group the controllers. Next let's group all
>> finger groups under one group and call it left_
>> hand_group. This group should hold all your
>> finger controls and their groups (Figure 10.39).

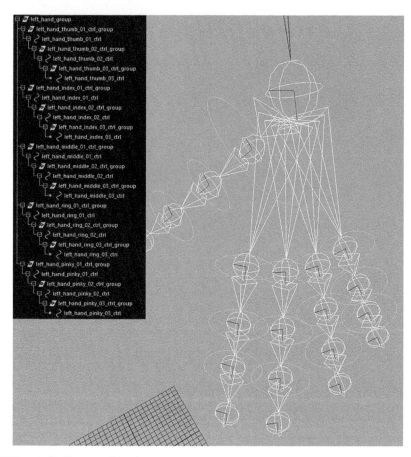

FIGURE 10.39 Final finger control hierarchy.

Step 4: Make the hand follow the wrist. The last step of this process is to parent constrain the left_hand_grp to the left_drv_wrist joint. This will make sure the group follows along with the arm motion.

Tutorial 10.5: Clavicle and Body Controls

Since we have the driver joints and the binding joints for the arm, we need to do a similar setup for the clavicles.

Step 1: Create the driver joint. To start things off, we need to duplicate the left_clavicle joint. This will duplicate the joints underneath. We only need the clavicle and shoulder; go ahead and delete everything else. Once those are deleted, rename the joints to left_drv_clavicle and left_drv_shoulder. Group left_drv_clavicle and rename the group to left_drv_clavicle_group. Finally, unparent the group (Figure 10.40).

Step 2: Creating Clavicle controls. Now we need to create controls for the clavicles using the same method as before. Create a NURBS circle and group it. Move the group to the position of the clavicle joint by matching all transformations. Name the controller and the group following using the same convention we've been using. Finally, group the top group of the controller and the driver joint to a new group called left_clavicle_rig_group (Figure 10.41).

FIGURE 10.40 Left clavicle and shoulder joint setup and hierarchy.

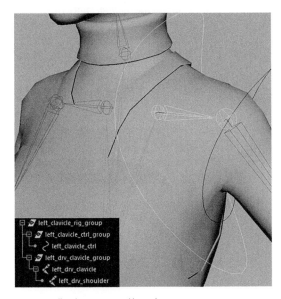

FIGURE 10.41 Clavicle rig groups and hierarchy.

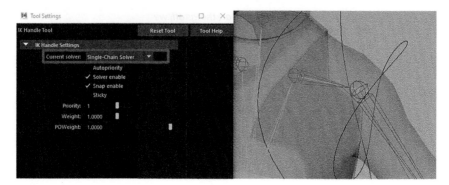

FIGURE 10.42 Clavicle IK and joint setup.

Step 3: Create an IK handle. Next, we are going to create an IK handle to animate the clavicles when the arm is in IK mode. Go to Skeleton->Create IK handle☐. In the Tool Setting window, change the Current Solver setting to Single-Chain Solver. Click on left_drv_clavicle, then left_drv_shoulder to create an IK handle and name it left_clavicle_IK (Figure 10.42).

Step 4: Parent left_clavicle_IK to the left_clavicle controller (Figure 10.43).

Step 5: Constraint the original joints. Next, we need to have these driver joints drive the binding joints. Select the left_drv_clavicle joint and then shift select the left_clavicle joint. Do a Constrain->Parent Constraint.

Step 6: Constrain the shoulder driver joints. Next, we need to select the left_drv_shoulder of the

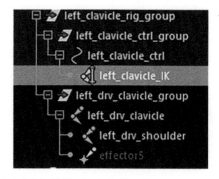

FIGURE 10.43 Left clavicle IK and controller hierarchy.

*clavicle driver joints and then add select the
left_drv_arm_group, and do another parent
constraint. This will allow the driver joints from
the arm to follow the clavicle.*

*Step 7: Constraint the shoulder FK controllers. Select
the left_drv_shoulder of the clavicle driver joints
and then add select the left_fk_shoulder_ctrl_
group, and do one more parent constraint.*

*Step 8: Make the clavicle follow the chest. Now, we
need to make the clavicle group follow the chest
control. Select the chest joint, and then shift
select the left_clavicle_rig_group, and do one
last Constrain->Parent Constraint.*

> *Now you have done the left clavicle, do
the same thing for the right clavicle.*

> *Now it's time to create the root and spine
controllers. Remember, the controls will all
need groups.*

*Step 9: Create the hip controller (NURBS circle), name
it, group it, and rename the group as well.*

*Step 10: Grab the group and match all
transformations to the hip joint.*

*Step 11: Parent constrain the hip joint to the hip
controller.*

*Step 12: Repeat this same process for the joints that
lead all the way up to the head (Figure 10.44).*

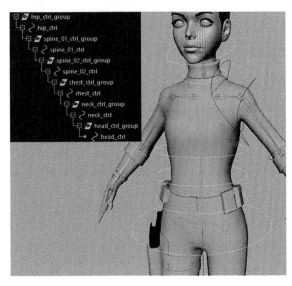

FIGURE 10.44 Body controller setup.

Gun Joint

We now need to add one last joint that will be used for the weapon in the game.

> *Step 13: Select Skeleton->Create joints. Create a joint at the origin and then translate it inside the gun, and rename the joint to gun_joint.*
>
> *Step 14: Bind the geometry of the gun to gun_joint. Select the gun geometry, and add select the gun_joint. Do a Skin->Bind Skin.*
>
> *Step 15: Paint the weight of the gun so that the gun_ joint has complete control of the gun.*

Final Hierarchy

Now that we have all the controls created, we just need to clean them up in the outliner and make sure they're placed in the correct order and under the proper groups.

> *Step 16: Create the world controller. Create a new controller at the origin and rename it as world_ ctrl. Group the world controller and rename it as Ellen_rig_grp.*
>
> *Step 17: Parent other controllers and driver joints under the world controller. The world controller should be the root of the hierarchy. Parent all the controllers and driver joints under the world controller (Figure 10.45).*

Conclusion

We have finished our rig, but bear in mind that this setup is the bare minimum of rigging; we ripped off everything we could to keep rigging simple for you. However, if you want to have more advanced rigs, there are plenty of auto rigs out there. Plug-ins like Advanced Skeleton and Rapid Rigs can make all the controls for you in a matter of minutes. Maya has its own auto rig as well, located at Control->Create Control Rig.

There are more things to explore in the world of rigging. To name a few, we did not do any facial expression controls, and we cannot even move the eyes, or open the mouth. We also did not set up any stretching. However, we

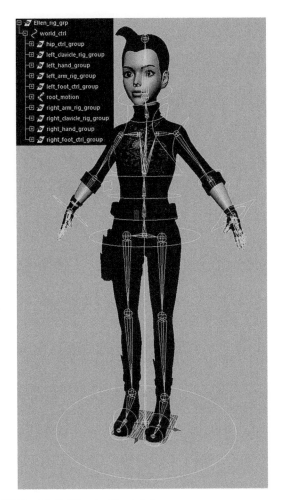

FIGURE 10.45 Final hierarchy of the whole rig.

should always avoid overdoing the rig. If we don't need facial expressions, it makes total sense not to rig the face.

Rigging can be super confusing, so if you don't understand some of the steps, try to read through them again. Also, if you don't feel like rigging at all, we have a finished rig file for you, and you can work the animations with it in the next chapter.

See you there!

CHAPTER 11

FPS Animation in Maya

FPS Animation Overview

First-person shooter (FPS) animations are utilized in games where player immersion is significant. It is as if the player were stepping into the character's shoes and becoming that character. The player will usually only see their character's hands and weapon if the gameplay calls for one. Since we only see a fraction of the character, creating FPS animations is usually simpler than animating characters we will see in full view, such as non-player characters. In the animation phase, our job is to create believable character movement. There are a few technical considerations to think about before starting the FPS animations, but once those are set up, breathing life into our character should be straightforward. Before moving on, if you feel like speeding up the workflow, you can jump to the next chapter where the second half shows how to use motion captured data as our animation instead of doing it manually.

Referencing the Character Rig

Instead of opening Ellen_rig as usual, you have the option of referencing the character rig in a new Maya file. Referencing in the rig will allow you to animate an instance of the character while leaving the original file untouched.

> *Step 1: Start with a clean Maya file, and go to File>Create Reference. Navigate to Ellen_rig and click on Reference to bring in the instanced version of the Ellen rig. This is the file you will begin your animations in.*

Why?

When you start animating and maybe realize that you need to make model or rigging adjustments, you can jump into the original rig file, Ellen_rig, and make those changes. When you return to your animation file with the referenced rig, those adjustments will be reflected on the model and/or rig, and your animation should still be intact. If you do not see those changes immediately, go to File>Reference Editor, right click on the rig name in the newly appeared window, and choose Reload Reference to bring in those changes into your animation file.

Besides the ease of updating the model and rig separately from the animation data, referencing makes it such that altering the rig while you are animating is impossible. You will not be able to delete any controls or any parts of the model by accident.

Tips and Tricks

Referencing character rigs is optional and not required to animate. You can always just animate straight on the original rig file. Be sure to incrementally save your files regardless of which method you decide to go with. For example, let us say you have been working in a Maya scene named AnimationFile_1. After an allotted time, such as 10 minutes, I would recommend creating a new iteration named AnimationFile_2. Sometimes animation files can crash, so if AnimationFile_2 becomes corrupted in an unexpected crash, you will still have AnimationFile_1 as a backup.

Save Files

All the animations for each weapon set will be housed in their own Maya file. When you save this Maya file, name it Ellen_gun_animations to distinguish it from other files.

Display Layers

Seeing your character without any obstructions is important while you animate. Display layers can be used to hide certain aspects of the model or rig when they are not needed, while also removing the need to dig through the Outliner every single time you want to hide those character parts.

> Step 2: Shift-select all the parts of the geometry that we do not need to see for FPS animation creation. Navigate to the Display Layer Editor in the lower right-hand side of the screen, and go to Layers>Create Layer from Selected. A new display layer named layer1 will appear right below the area you just clicked. Let's rename the new layer to something more specific by double clicking on the name layer1. In the Edit Layer window, type RestOfBodyMesh in the Name input box and click on Save to exit the window.
>   The columns of boxes to the right of the display layer name will allow us to quickly control the display layers. The first column containing the letter "V" controls the visibility of the object. To turn off the RestOfBodyMesh display layer, click on the letter "V" so that the box becomes empty. Ellen's upper body and arms should be the only visible parts of the geometry in your viewport.

Step 3: Repeat this process with the controls that are not needed for FPS animations and name the layer NotNeededControls.

Step 4: Let's also create a display layer for the visible parts of Ellen's mesh and instead utilize a different feature of display layers. When you click on the blank third column box, the letter "R", meaning referenced, will eventually be revealed. Turning on the letter "R" will cause the geometry to not be selectable.

Why?

During the animation process, you will want to only move the controls created during the rigging process, not the character geometry. By putting Ellen's upper body, arms, and weapon geometry on their own display layers with the referenced option active, you will not have to worry about setting stray keyframes beyond the controls. Figure 11.1 shows an example of the various display layers created so far.

Tips and Tricks

As you animate, you will need to quickly preview your animation without the controls, which is how we will ultimately see the character in the game. In the Viewport menu bar, click on Show, which will bring up a long list of components that you can hide and unhide, as seen in Figure 11.2. Click on NURBS Curves or use the keyboard shortcut Alt+1.

FIGURE 11.1 List of display layers.

FIGURE 11.2 Show>NURBS Curves to hide the controls.

This will cause both the checkmark next to NURBs Curves and all the controls in the scene to disappear temporarily, which is like turning off the visibility of a display layer. I recommend using the display layer visibility toggle if you want to hide a part of the character for a long period of time. Use the Show>NURBS Curves hotkey shortcut while you are in the middle of animating to do quick checks on movement clarity.

Camera Configuration

FIGURE 11.3 Resolution gate icon.

Step 5: Select the Front/Persp quick layout button, located right above the Outliner button, to bring up two viewports on your screen. We will create a dedicated FPS camera in the left-hand viewport by going to Panels>Perspective>New. Name it FPS_Cam. In that same viewport, turn on the resolution gate by clicking on the icon seen in Figure 11.3. Also click on the gate mask icon, which is to the right of the resolution gate icon, so that a light grey, shaded area will appear around the gate.

Step 6: On the right-hand-side viewport, we will move FPS_Cam so that it mimics the player character's line of sight. If you do not see a floating green camera, check if camera visibility is on by going to Show>Cameras in the Viewport menu bar. Grab FPS_Cam and move it so that is near Ellen's eyes (Figure 11.4). You may turn on the visibility of the RestofBodyMesh display layer temporarily so you can position the camera with Ellen's head geometry on.

Why?

This viewport setup will allow you to see the FPS camera view and your working area at the same time. Since the resolution gate and gate masks are visible on the left-hand side, you will be able to focus on what the player will see in the game. Grabbing controls will be easier in the right-hand-side viewport since you can move freely around the scene.

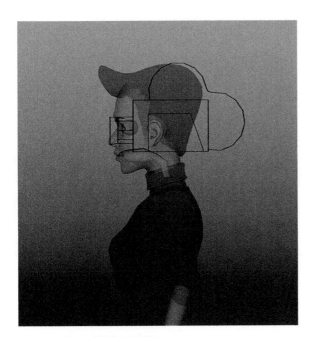

FIGURE 11.4 Line up FPS_Cam with Ellen's eyes.

Step 7: Now that we have a dedicated FPS camera, we will create our own reticle based off this camera's location. In the main menu, create a locator by going to Create>Locator. Locators have a variety of uses, such as acting as a middleman when connecting different parts of a rig. We will be using the locator as our reticle in Maya. Select the locator, shift-select FPS_Cam, and go to Modify>Match Transformations>Match Translation. The locator will snap to FPS_Cam's location. Translate the locator along the z-axis so that it is directly in front of the camera. You should be able to see the locator in the middle of the left-hand-side viewport, as seen in Figure 11.5. Make the locator unselectable by putting it in a referenced display layer. You can also lock its movement by going to the Channel Editor, click-dragging all the channel attributes, right clicking the blue highlighted selection, and clicking on Lock Selected (Figure 11.6).

419

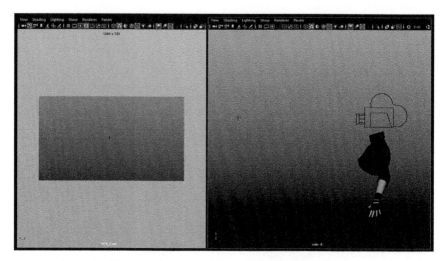

FIGURE 11.5 Creating the reticle.

Why?

In FPS games, a reticle is a small icon, like a crosshair or dot, in the center of the screen that is used to assist the player with aiming. There will be a different reticle created in the game engine, but our locator reticle will still be useful. We can reference it while posing our character and make sure that the weapon is pointed towards the reticle.

Game Animations

We are close to being able to animate full speed ahead. At this point, we can start crafting our first pose. Game characters have a set of animations that will play in the game depending on the circumstances. One of the most important animations will be the idle. An idle animation will be playing when the player has not input any commands. It is meant to keep the character alive even though they are not performing any specific movements. The idle is the first to be created in a set because it will serve as the returning point for most animations. When Ellen is done walking or has finished firing her gun, she will return to the idle animation.

FIGURE 11.6 Right clicking channel attributes to lock the locator's movement.

The only time Ellen will not return to idle is after she is caught by the security cameras and the game is over. The other animations that Ellen will need are attack, walk, "got caught", and reload.

Creating a Pose

Animation is a time-based art form, and the illusion of movement is created when a series of poses are played one after another. When we create a pose, we will need to tell Maya that we want it to be played at a specific time. The Time Slider at the bottom of the screen will be where

421

we define those times. The grey highlight is the current time indicator and can be changed by click-dragging left and right on the Time Slider. The length of your animation can be adjusted by entering values in the entry fields on either side of the Time Slider.

You can create the pose by translating or rotating the character controls that were set up in the rigging stage. When you are ready to save the pose, select all the controls and press "S" to set a keyframe. A red tick will appear at the selected frame number on the Time Slider. The key tick's timing can be adjusted by shift-selecting it and click-dragging it to a new time. If you do not like a pose, you can remove it by selecting all the character controls, right clicking on the unwanted keyframe and pressing Delete. When there are multiple key ticks you would like to adjust, click-drag across those ticks while holding down Shift. This will create a red highlighted selection that can be moved or deleted.

Once you place your first keyframe, do not be afraid to tinker with its original timing later. Getting a feel for the correct timing is an essential part of the animation process.

Weapon Movement Simplified

One thing to consider is how our character will hold her weapons: will Ellen carry her weapons with one hand or both hands? Before attaching the weapon to the character, it is good to begin creating the idle pose first. If she will hold them with one hand, follow Step 8 and skip to Step 12. If she will hold the weapons with two hands, head straight to Step 9 and continue through Steps 10 and 11.

> *Step 8: Move Ellen's right arm to an upright pose. The rigging file we provide has one more feature we did not go over in the rigging chapter. It has an IK FK blend slider, located on the outside of the arm (looks like a lollipop). If you are using your rig done in chapter 10, your arm will not move with the FK controllers. You need to do 2 things to make the FK work.*

The first thing is to find left_ik_wrist_ctrl and select the left_wrist_IK parented under it. In the Channel Box, set the Ik Blend attribute to 0 to switch to FK(set it back to 1 to switch back to IK). The second thing is about the wrist, select left_drv_wrist; in the Channel Box, find the last 2 attributes: Left Fk Wrist Ctrl W0 and Left Ik Wrist Ctrl W1. Set the Fk one to 1 and Ik one to 0 to switch to FK(flip the values to switch back). The lollipop slider we provided in the rig does these 2 things automatically if you drag it up and down. The names of the controllers might be different in the rig we provided. Because of the length restrictions, we removed this lollipop controller in the rigging chapter. However, this animation chapter was developed parallel with the rigging chapter when we have this lollipop controller. Select the shoulder control ac_r_fk_shoulder, use "E" on your keyboard to turn on the Rotate Tool and rotate the arm so that it is almost parallel to the ground. Rotate the elbow and wrist controls, ac_r_fk_shoulder and ac_r_fk_wrist, to help the arm pose look more natural. Translate the gun model group, Gun_grp, so that the gun is resting in Ellen's right palm. Rotate the finger controls so that the fingers are wrapped around the gun handle (Figure 11.7).

Once you have solidified the finger posing, select ac_r_fk_wrist and shift-select Gun_grp in the Outliner. With the Rigging menu set to active, create a parent constraint connection between the wrist control and the gun group by using Constrain>Parent. Now, whenever the right arm moves, the gun will also move.

FIGURE 11.7 Creating the single-handed gun idle pose.

Select all the arm controls and press "S" to save this pose on frame 0. Head straight to Step 12.
Step 9: *For Ellen to hold the weapon with two hands, we will have to switch the arm movement method from forward kinematics (FK) to inverse kinematics (IK). Drag the lollipop sliders on both side of the arms down to switch to IK. (or use the method mentioned at the beginning of step 8 if you are using your rig file).*

Use the ac_r_ik_wrist and ac_l_ik_wrist controls to move Ellen's hands upward so that she can aim the gun in front of her. When you select one of the controls, use "W" to turn on the Translate Tool. When the arms are in IK mode, they can be moved via translation and rotation. Keep in mind that the elbow controls, ac_r_ik_drv_elbow and ac_l_ik_drv_elbow, could be used to help the pose feel more natural. Once you have the arms roughly positioned in the lower right-hand section of the FPS_Cam viewport, translate the gun group, Gun_grp, so that the handle is resting in between Ellen's hands. We will not permanently attach it just yet. Use the gun model as a frame of reference for adjusting both hands and moving Ellen's fingers. Rotate the finger controls so that the fingers are wrapped around the gun handle. The left-hand fingers should be wrapped around the right-hand fingers (Figure 11.8).

Select all the controls that were moved and press "S" to save the pose on frame 0. Continue to Step 10.

Tips and Tricks

Be sure to be check the FPS_Cam viewport as you pose the character in the perspective viewport. The gun and hand should end up in the lower right-hand side of the screen and not be blocking the reticle.

Two-Handed Weapon Setup

If you decided to go the two-handed weapon route, we will need to create a way to move both hands and the weapon all at once. Trying to move the hands and weapon in sync will be hard without tying them together using

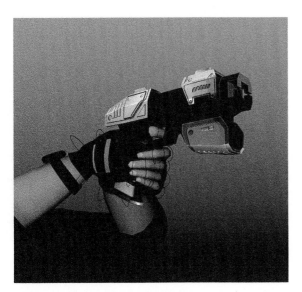

FIGURE 11.8 Left hand wrapped around the right hand.

locators and parent constraints. Our goal is to create a single NURBs curve that will move the hands and weapon all together. In this chapter, we will cover this setup with the handgun, but this system can be applied to both the pipe and grenade launcher.

> Step 10: Create a new NURBs circle named gun_CTRL and translate it so that it is positioned around the center of the gun and scale the circle up so that is slightly larger than the gun mesh (Figure 11.9). This NURBs curve will drive the primary movement of the hands and gun, so make sure it is easy to grab in the viewport. While holding down "D", translate gun_CTRL's manipulator so that the pivot point is at the gun handle, as seen in Figure 11.10.
>
> Now we need to attach the gun to the new control. Navigate to the Outliner, select gun_CTRL first and then shift-select Gun_grp. With the Rigging menu set active, create a parent constraint connection between the two objects by using Constrain>Parent. Whenever gun_CTRL is moved, the gun will now follow.
>
> Step 11: To wrap up the two-handed weapon setup, we will now attach the hands to gun_CTRL.

FIGURE 11.9 Creating a control for the gun.

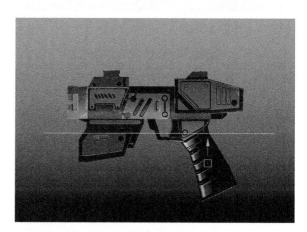

FIGURE 11.10 Changing gun_CTRL's pivot point.

*Create a locator named rightHand_locator,
shift-select ac_r_ik_wrist and match the IK
control's position by going to Modify>Match
Transformations>Match Translation and Match
Rotation. Shift-select rightHand_locator, select
ac_r_ik_wrist_grp in the Outliner and create a
parent constraint so that the locator moves the
right hand while still giving you the freedom to
move ac_r_ik_wrist. Select gun_CTRL, shift-
select rightHand_locator, and then create one
more parent constraint. Now the right hand will*

follow gun_CTRL. The rightHand_locator can now be hidden for the time being. Repeat this process for the left hand. You will primarily use gun_CTRL in your animation workflow.

Frame Rate

Animations created for film and television are generally created at 24 frames per second. Standard playback rates for video games are 30 and 60 fps. Always double check the frame rate in Maya before starting an animation.

Step 12: Change the frame rate from 24 frames per second to 30 frames per second using the drop-down menu below the right-hand side of the Time Slider (Figure 11.11). Go to Windows>Settings/Preferences>Preferences and click on Time Slider in the left-hand column. Under Playback, change the Playback speed to 30 fps×1 (Figure 11.12).

FIGURE 11.11 Standard game animation frame rate is 30 frames per second.

Idle Animation

We will create a breathing idle animation for Ellen. It is possible to create idle breakers that are animations that still play when the player has not input any commands, and they generally show a bit more personality. Our main idle animation will be a simple inhale and exhale with a touch of weight shifting.

Step 13: Since most game animations loop continuously, they need to have the same start and end pose. Select all controls, right click on frame 0 on the Time Slider, which should contain

FIGURE 11.12 Switching Playback speed to 30 fps×1.

427

FIGURE 11.13 Time Slider with the idle key poses.

the pose that was created when we attached the gun to the hand(s), and click on Copy. Drag the current time indicator to frame 60, right click on the Time Slider, and press Paste>Paste. The pose from frame 0 should now be on frame 60. Paste this same pose one last time on frame 120. Frames 0, 60, and 120 will be the inhale moment of the idle. Have the gun move downward on frame 30, set a keyframe for all the controls by pressing "S", and do the same on frame 90. Your Time Slider should look like the one in Figure 11.13.

The shortcut to play and pause an animation is Alt + "V". Play through your animation to make sure that the poses flow together and the overall movement makes sense.

Tips and Tricks

In the beginning stages of an animation, it is smart to set a key on all the controls each time you create a main pose. Adjusting the timing will be easier since you will know that all controls have been accounted for in each of the main poses.

Step 14: Add a simple weight shift to add more variation to the breathing. On frame 60, have the hands and gun move towards our right a tiny bit. From frames 0 to 60, Ellen will weigh shift to our right, and from frames 60 to 120, she will return to the idle pose by weight shifting to our left.

Cleaning Up Odd Jitters

You might start to notice weird glitches in the animation, even if you did not set any specific keys to define that movement. Right clicking on the timeline and pressing Tangents>Auto should remove those hitches.

Ease-In's and Ease-Out's

The main poses have been set for the idle animation, but the movement might feel floaty. There is no sense of weight in the animation yet. We can insert additional keyframes to help show ease-in's and ease-out's. This is important to utilize in your animations because most movements take time to start up and come to a natural stop. Ease-in's and ease-out's can also be used to add a moment of hold. If you take a deep breath in real life, your upper body will hold still for a few seconds before exhaling. That stillness is like an ease-in. When you exhale, you are gradually easing out of the inhale "pose."

Graph Editor

Animators must become acquainted with the Graph Editor to finetune their work. All keyframes are represented on a graph as plotted points that can be adjusted, and the interpolation between each keyframe is represented as curves. With a basic understanding of curves, the Graph Editor can be used to create quick ease-in's and ease-out's.

Tips and Tricks

Try opening the Graph Editor by going to Windows>Animation Editors>Graph Editor. If you have a second monitor available, I suggest having the Graph Editor maximized on one screen. If you have one monitor, you can have it open on one of the viewports by going to Panels>Panel>Graph Editor.

> Step 15: Select ac_r_fk_shoulder if you are animating just one arm or select gun_CTRL if you are animating both hands holding the weapon. Open the Graph Editor. On the left-hand side, select the primary channel that is responsible for the upward and downward movements. For the one-handed weapon setup, select Rotate Y, and for the two-handed weapon setup, select Translate Y. That specific channel is the only one that is visible (Figure 11.14). If you cannot see the

429

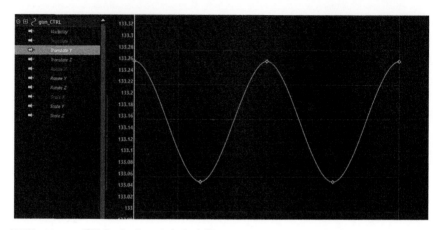

FIGURE 11.14 gun_CTRL's Translate Y curve in the Graph Editor.

green curve clearly, press "F" to quickly zoom in towards the curve.

Similar to scrubbing through the Time Slider, you can adjust the time by click-dragging the yellow Current Time Marker left and right within the Graph Editor. Select the Insert Keys tool in the upper right-hand corner of the Graph Editor and click on the curve to insert keys on frames 13, 25, 35, 46, 73, 85, 95, and 106. Press "W", click on frame 13, and middle-mouse-click-drag it upwards closer to frame 0. Grab frames 25 and 35 and middle-mouse-click-drag those keys towards frame 30. Continue this for the remaining keys that we just added. Refer to Figure 11.15 for a general idea of how your curve should look. Do not worry if it is not an exact replica. The animation should have a slight moving hold each time the character inhales.

Why?

Understanding what the curve shapes represent is more important than just simply copying. The curve shape from frames 0 to 13 is an ease-out. The gentle slope represents small movement over a long period of time. We know that frames 13–25 will be faster due to the steep slope that showcases a large value change over a short period of time. Frames 25–35 is another ease-in. Ease-in's and

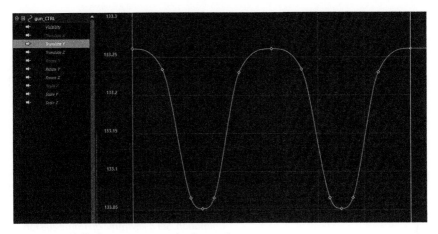

FIGURE 11.15 Added keyframes to create ease-in's and ease-out's.

ease-out's help vary the spacing between each main pose and helps add more weight to the movement.

Keywords Aside

Timing is the object's *speed*, while *spacing* is how the object will move from point A to point B. Spacing will help determine moments of acceleration and moments of hold.

Tips and Tricks

When you are adding ease-in's and ease-out's, you do not necessarily have to select all the controls and press "S". At this stage of the animation, you can be more selective with keyframe placement.

Attack Animation

The attack animation is up next. The gun firing should be rapid and impactful. As soon as the player presses the button to attack an enemy, we want the player to see and feel an immediate response in the gun. A combination

of fast timing and careful spacing consideration help us
achieve this goal.

Step 16: Select all the controls, copy the first frame
of the idle animation, and paste it on frames 200
and 212. Frame 200 will be the start of the attack
animation, and 212 will be the end. On frame
204, create the recoil pose by moving the gun
back closer to Ellen and rotate the gun so that
it is pointing upward. Maya should now show
the initial movement between frames 200 and
204, but it is still too slow. To help show snappy
gunfire, move the gun backwards towards Ellen
on frame 201.

Step 17: Let's add some final touches to the attack
animation. Set a keyframe on frame 208 for
the main movement control. Open the Graph
Editor and create an ease-in using the newly
added keyframe. Go through all the Translate
and Rotate channels on the left-hand-side bar
to check if there is a moving curve to add an
ease-in. Figures 11.16 and 11.17 are two examples
of how this ease-in could be implemented on
frame 208. If there is a horizontal line instead
of a trending curve, this means that there is

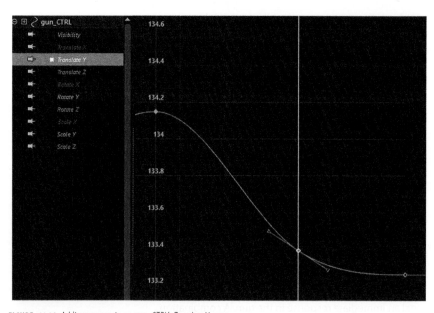

FIGURE 11.16 Adding an ease-in on gun_CTRL's Translate Y curve.

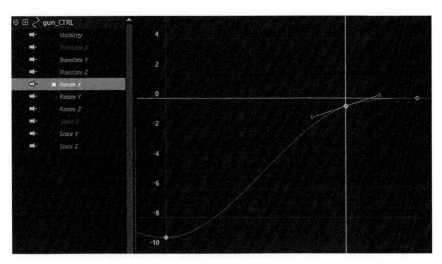

FIGURE 11.17 An ease-in added to gun_CTRL's Rotate X curve.

no movement, so you will not need to add the
ease-in for those specific channels. Once you
have finished this step, the animation should
come to a more natural stop.

Walk Animation

A basic walk animation consists of the following main
poses: contact, down, passing, up, and back to contact
pose to repeat the cycle. This animation will be simpler
to create as first-person shooter animation in contrast
to a full-body piece, but we can still move the arms and
weapon in accordance with the main poses.

> Step 18: Begin the walk cycle by setting down the
> contact poses. Select all controls, copy the idle
> pose from frame 0, and paste a key on frames
> 300 and 331. Slightly rotate the gun so that it
> points to our left on frame 315. On contact pose,
> the upper body will twist the most side to side.
> Step 19: The next pose to block is in the passing pose,
> which is the halfway point between each contact
> pose. On frame 307, translate the character to
> our left, and on frame 323, translate her to our
> right. The character has shifted their weight the
> most to the left or right on passing pose.

Step 20: We will finish blocking in the walk with the down and up poses. The character should translate down on frames 303 and 318, and she should translate upward on frames 312 and 327. The gun should also rotate down and up, but we can add an offset in the rotation's timing so that movement feels looser and more broken up. Rotate the gun down on frames 308 and 324 and add in an upward rotation on frame 316.

Step 21: As a final touch, add ease-in's and ease-out's to make the animation feel less even. Figures 11.18 and 11.19 showcase how the ease-in's and ease-out's could be applied to the contact and passing main keys in the Graph Editor.

"Got Caught" Animation

When Ellen is caught by one of the security cameras, she will raise her hands up in shock. If you are animating her with both hands on the weapon, we will need to detach one of the hands from the gun handle. This animation will be "game over" for the player, so we do not necessarily have to loop the animation.

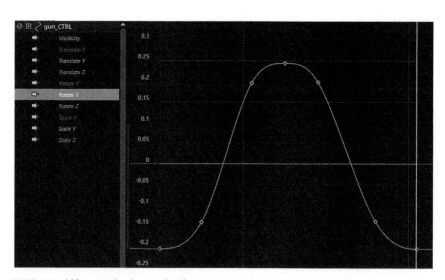

FIGURE 11.18 Adding ease-in's and ease-out's to the contact poses.

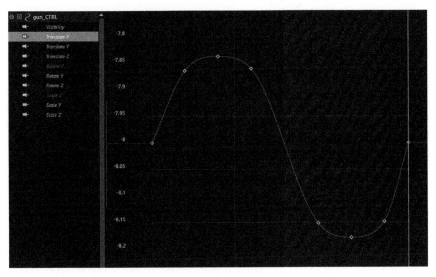

FIGURE 11.19 Additional keyframes to give more weight to the passing poses.

> *Step 22: Select all the controls, copy the idle pose, and paste it on frame 400. If you are animating with the two-handed weapon setup, select leftHand_locator and make sure that it also has a keyframe at 400. If the locator did not have any keyframes placed beforehand, you should notice a new attribute in the Channel Box called Blend Locatorleftparent 1. On frame 400, Blend Locatorleftparent 1 should be set to 1. To detach the left hand from the gun handle, change Blend Locatorleftparent 1 to 0 on frame 401. Hide leftHand_locator while you create the "Got Caught" animation. You can now move ac_l_ik_ drv_wrist independently of gun_CTRL.*

Tips and Tricks

Remember to select leftHand_locator and change Locatorleftparent 1 back to 1 when you want the left hand to be attached to the gun handle again.

> *Step 23: Create the last pose of the animation on frame 426. The right hand still holding the gun will move back and move towards the right of*

the screen. Move the left hand towards the left edge of the screen and spread the fingers out (Figure 11.19).

Keywords Aside

Depending on the speed of an action, we might need to add an *overshoot* pose to give more time to the audience to take in what just happened. The overshoot will move past the last pose we just created and will settle into the last pose more slowly.

> Step 24: Let's add in an overshoot to both hands on frame 413. Select all controls, copy frame 426, and paste it on frame 413. This will be our starting point for the overshoot pose. The left hand's last pose ends up close to the left side of the screen, so the overshoot will be a tiny continuation of that movement. Translate and rotate the left hand ever so slightly to the left, and do the same for the right hand, except towards the right-hand side of the screen. The left-hand fingers can also be a part of the overshoot. Rotate the fingers to the left just a tad bit (Figure 11.20).
>
> Step 25: We can create a more fluid motion in both hands by examining their motion trail. Select the left-hand control, and with the Animation menu set active, go to Visualize>Create Editable Motion Trail. A curve representing the left hand's path of action has now appeared (Figure 11.21). When you add a keyframe to that control, the motion trail should update. Move the hand downward on frame 402 so that it will dip before traveling

FIGURE 11.20 "Got Caught" pose.

to the main pose on 406. In your perspective viewport, zoom in close to the motion trail at frames 413–426. Add additional keyframes to create a more rounded shape in the motion trail (Figure 11.22). Compare Figures 11.21–11.23. The motion trail has more apparent arcs. Go ahead and delete motionTrail1Handle in the Outliner. Repeat this entire step for the other hand.

FIGURE 11.21 Motion trail representing the left hand's path of action.

FIGURE 11.22 Adding more keyframes to round out the motion trail.

FIGURE 11.23 Final motion trail for the left-hand control.

Why?

Most living beings move in arcs, while machinery tend to move in a linear fashion. Exaggerating the arcs of an object's motion trail can be a quick way to add a layer of fluidity to the animation.

> Step 26: Use the Graph Editor to assist in creating a natural settle for the ending of the animation. Add an ease-in at frame 416.

Reload Animation

The reload animation will be a culmination of everything that we have covered, as well as adding one more object for Ellen to interact with. If the two-handed setup is in use, the left hand will need to leave the gun handle once more. The added challenge is that we must get the character to return to the idle pose, in contrast to the "Got Caught" animation that did not have to loop. In this animation, Ellen will first shake the empty magazine out of the gun. Her left hand will temporarily leave the screen to grab the new magazine. Once the left hand returns to the player's view, Ellen will reload the gun, and the left hand should return to its original idle pose.

> Step 27: We will create a system in which the magazine can be attached to either the gun or left hand. Create an empty group named gunClip_CTRL_group. Match the group's transforms to Gun_clip_grp. Create a locator named gunClip_Locator, match its transforms to Gun_clip_grp, and make it a child of gunClip_CTRL_group. Select gun_CTRL, shift-select gunClip_CTRL_group, then create a parent constraint so that the magazine will now follow the main gun control. Select the left-hand control, shift-select gunClip_Locator, and create a parent constraint so that we can tell the magazine to follow the left hand.
> At the start of the reload animation, we will want the magazine to be following the gun control. Let's turn off the gunClip_Locator's constraint for the time being.

With the locator selected, change Blend Parent 1's value to 0.

Step 28: Start off the animation by copying the idle pose and pasting it on frame 500. At frame 510, have the left hand completely leave the screen and raise the right hand up in anticipation for the shake. Create the right hand's lowest point in the shake at frame 515, and have it rise just a little to settle into the main pose at frame 526. Use gunClip_Locator to translate the magazine out of the gun from frames 512 to 522. Select gunClip_Locator, set a key on frame 500 and 512, and ensure that Blend Parent 1 is 0 on those two keys. Change Blend Parent 1 to 1 on frame 529 so that it will be attached to the left hand.

On frame 538, rotate the right hand towards the camera. Bring the left hand back up into view with the magazine resting against the bottom of the gun grip. You can also rotate the fingers so that they have a better grip on the magazine (Figure 11.24).

Step 29: Let's continue the second half of the reload animation. On frame 545, move the left hand up and to our right so that the magazine can be reloaded into the gun. The right hand should also slightly move in reaction to the left hand's movement. The magazine will need to switch parents from the left hand to the gun control. Make sure that gunClip_Locator's Blend Parent 1 is set to 1 on frame 538. Change Blend Parent 1 to 0 on frame 541. If the magazine rotates oddly on frames 539 and 540, go ahead and fix it by rotating the magazine to align with the grip. Paste the idle pose on frame 564.

FIGURE 11.24 Pose before the gun is reloaded.

Step 30: Add final touches to the animation. Track each hand's motion trails and see if you can round out any arcs. Use ease-in's and ease-out's to create a moving hold for the key poses on frames 526 and 538. Finally, have the gun come to natural settle at the end with a gradual ease-in to the last pose.

Considerations and Conclusion

Once you have created your first animation set, animating the grenade launcher and pipe will both be a familiar and new process. While the other weapons' movement will not be the same as the handgun, most of the main poses should remain the same. There are some differences in the story that is told through each weapon. The grenade launcher and pipe might have slower timing since they are heavier than a handgun. The pipe will not have its own reload animation because it is a melee weapon. The grenade launcher will only be able to hold one grenade at a time, so you will not need to animate Ellen shaking away an empty cartridge.

Animation can be easy to pick up, but there are still obstacles to consider from both a technical and artistic standpoint. Have fun and challenge yourself to create believable, responsive movement.

CHAPTER 12

Auto Rigging

In the previous two chapters, we have looked at rigging and the basics of animation. These are some technical art forms that the industry always has need of. Be an expert at either of these, and there will always be work waiting for you. However, they are also areas that not everyone needs to be an expert at. In fact, the two areas are not necessarily inter-inclusive. Most expert riggers are not fantastic animators (some can't animate very well at all), and there are some expert animators who are not great riggers. However, a compelling argument can be made (and we do to our students) that knowing something about both of these areas is in an animator or rigger's interest. The best analogy for this is a racecar driver. Does the driver (say, an animator) need to be an expert mechanic (rigger)? Of course not. But if the driver doesn't know enough about the mechanics of their car to communicate to the mechanics and engineers, they won't be able to tweak the engine to full efficacy for the driver. And so it is with riggers and animators. An animator who has done a bit of rigging will be able to more effectively communicate problems with the rig as they animate. Such knowledge will make the process better for all involved in the rigging/animation pipeline.

Having said all of that, not everyone will be an animator (or a rigger). Many folks are reading this book because they are far more interested in the development side of games and never plan to be involved in the animation process. Fair enough. At most studios, the coder will never animate a character and the animator will run far from code. This chapter is for the prototyper who doesn't have the time or money to hire an animator and rigger. This chapter is for the coder who wants some good looking animation in their scene but doesn't want to purchase a fully animated character from the asset store. And finally, any aspiring animators out there need to realize that motion capture (MoCap) is central to the game industry. And while they might not have their own MoCap rig, there are MoCap libraries out there that they can get into and get started with.

Tips and Tricks

If you'd rather work with traditionally animated clips, the support files for this chapter include some animations for our bad buys animated by Matthew Tovar – an animator formerly with Naughty Dog, Infinity Ward, and other studios. When we get to Chapter 17: AI, if you'd prefer to use Tovar's animations, the process there will be the same. However, at the end of this chapter, we will also have some output files that can be used (and will be used) in that chapter.

Mixamo

Our goals then in this chapter is to use some external tools to auto-rig a character and plug some motion-captured animations into those rigs. Finally we will export those animations and use them later in the production process (Chapter 17 to be exact). This chapter will be short and the process quick thanks for a free-to-use online tool called Mixamo.

A spin-off of Stanford University, Mixamo was acquired by Adobe in 2015. Although it once contained quite a bit of other tools that included facial animation tools, the core remaining tools include an Auto-Rigger and an incredible collection of cleaned-up motion capture clips.

According to Adobe's website, "Mixamo is available free for anyone with an Adobe ID and does not require a subscription to Creative Cloud." Although, "Mixamo is not available for Enterprise and Federated IDs. Mixamo is not available for users who have a country code from China. The current release of Creative Cloud in China does not include web services." So before we get going, go to Mixamo.com and be sure to sign up for an Adobe ID. It's free, doesn't take long and will provide a great collection of free tools to use.

Tutorial 12.1: Mixamo-Based Auto Rigging and MoCap

Step 1: Open UVed character in Maya. If you have been following the tutorials in this book, this will be your results at the end of Chapter 8 (after the character has been UVed). If not, the results of Chapter 8 are included in the support files for this chapter (EllenUVed.mb). Figure 12.1 shows the file from the support files opened and its organization.

Why?

Since the textures were constructed in Substance Painter – the textures will be exported from there and reassembled in Unity. So, we don't need or want a version of Ellen

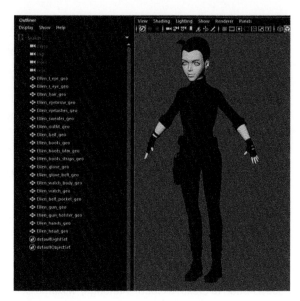

FIGURE 12.1 UVed version of Ellen – the results Chapter 8.

textured in Maya. However, it will be important that those textures are mapped correctly on the mesh once they are united in Unity. So, it is important that the mesh we are exporting to be rigged has already been UV mapped.

> *Step 2: Export as FBX 2013. Quickly make sure there is no History (Edit>Delete All by Type>History). Then export using File>Export All. Make sure Files of Type: FBX Export. In Geometry, make sure Smooth Mesh and Triangulate are checked. Turn off Animation, Cameras, Lights, Audio, and Embed Media. Under Advanced Options, expand FBX File Format. There, change Version: FBX 2013. Export to some neutral location (Desktop is a good place) as "EllenEnemy" (Figure 12.2).*

Why?

We haven't changed the FBX format before; why now? Well, for reasons only known to Adobe at this point, Mixamo requires FBX 2013 or earlier. If you export using FBX 2020 (which is what we've used up to now), Mixamo will complain.

FIGURE 12.2 When exporting for Mixamo, be sure to use FBX 2013.

In earlier chapters, we have exported directly to the Unity project Assets folder. But in this case, we need to do some work in Mixamo before its ready for Unity consumption. Thus, saving it to the Desktop keeps it out of Unity's clutches until its ready.

>   Step 3: Export just the gun. In the Outliner, select
>   Ellen_gun_geo. Use File>Export Selection. Again
>   export as an FBX (FBX 2020 or FBX 2013 will both
>   work) and save to your desktop as "Ellen_Gun".

Why?

There is already a gun on the mesh we're exporting; why do we need another. It's a little tricky to explain at this point, but the gun is about to become part of a rig, which means the gun will be controlled by a joint. Later in this tutorial, we will need the gun in her hand (not on her thigh), and so having a separate gun not tied to a joint chain will make things much easier.

>   Step 4: Begin the import process in Mixamo. In a web
>   browser, go to Mixamo.com and login. At the
>   top left corner of Mixamo's interface, click on the
>   Characters button (Figure 12.3).
>   Step 5: Use Upload Character to import the mesh.
>   Look to the far right of the interface and click on
>   the Upload Character button (Figure 12.4). Either
>   drag EllenEnemy into the Upload A Character
>   window, or use the Select Character File link
>   to upload it. Click Next when it displays the
>   character (Figure 12.5).

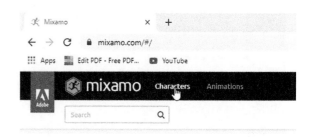

FIGURE 12.3 To begin importing EllenEnemy to Mixamo, log in and use the Characters link.

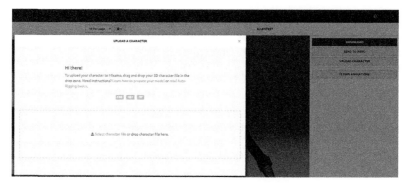

FIGURE 12.4 Sending the EllenEnemy fbx to Mixamo for processing. Mixamo will process for a second before showing Figure 12.5.

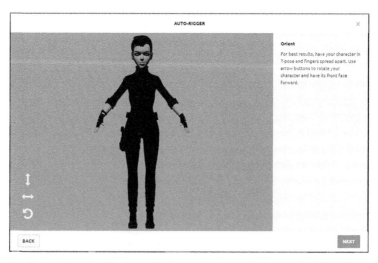

FIGURE 12.5 The imported version of the character. Don't worry about the materials showing up black. We will be reimporting textures later.

Step 6: Move the Chin, Wrists, Elbows, Knees, and Groin identifiers onto the character. It can be a little tricky as much of the body is completely black. But with a bit of adjustment you can usually estimate the right spot (Figure 12.6). Click Next. And then click Next again after the Review window shows your character looking around (Figure 12.7). Continue to click Next until EllenEnemy appears in the main interface.

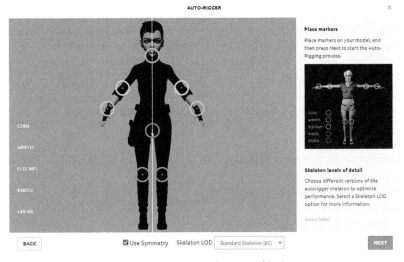

FIGURE 12.6 Placing markers to help the Auto-Rigger determine the anatomy of the character.

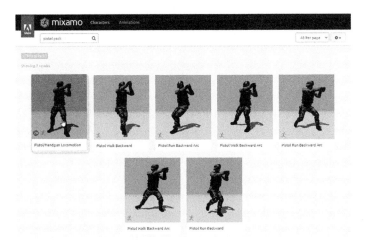

FIGURE 12.7 Select the Pistol/Handgun Locomotion pack.

Tips and Tricks

It will be important that when placing things like the Chin and Groin that the placement is indeed on the mesh (don't get so exact that you miss the bottom of either).

> Step 7: Click on the Animations link at the top left of the interface.
>
> Step 8: Play. Click on any of the animations included there to see EllenEnemy animated. Quickly she can belly dance, throw a football pass, idle like an old man, or drunk walk. We're not going to use any of those, but it'd be a shame to pass up the fun.
>
> Step 9: Search for "Pistol Pack". In the search field at the top left of Mixamo's interface, type "Pistol Pack" and then select Pistol/Handgun Locomotion from the results (Figure 12.7).

Why?

EllenEnemy will likely quickly leave her preview space. And her movements might not make a lot of sense at first. You can follow her by clicking the little camera icon in the bottom left of her preview space. What is happening is that EllenEnemy is running through a whole lot of animations one right after another with little break in between. In reality, she's doing a lot more than we will use in the scene, but bringing in this whole pack will provide a lot of different things for this character to do.

> Step 10: Download the animations and rig. On the far right of the interface is the Download button, click it. In Download Settings, leave all the settings at default except for Format: FBX for Unity (.fbx). Click Download (Figure 12.8). This will download to your system's Downloads folder.
>
> Step 11: In Downloads, find Pistol_Handgun Locomotion Pack. Unzip it.
>
> Step 12: Import the Mixamo-output files into Unity. In Unity, create a new folder called "NPC". Right click the NPC folder and choose Import New Assets. Find the Downloads folder and the Pistol_Handgun Locomotion Pack folder (not the .zip file). Shift select all the assets and click Import (Figure 12.9).

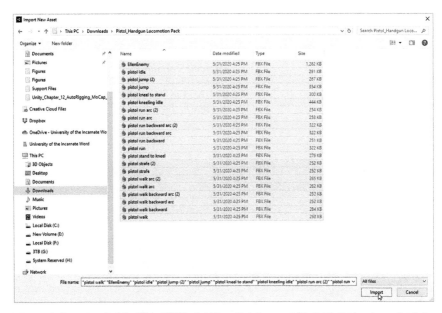

FIGURE 12.8 Mixamo's download settings for Unity.

FIGURE 12.9 Be sure to grab all the different FBX files that Mixamo includes as part of the Pistol_Handgun Locomotion Pack.

Step 13: Extract the materials for EllenEnemy. Select the newly imported EllenEnemy fbx in the NPC folder. Click the Extract Materials button. Because our Materials folder is getting pretty large, extract them into a new Materials folder in the NPC folder.

Step 14: Create another folder inside of NPC called "Textures". We will export the Textures from Substance Painter into this directory.

Substance Painter Output

While we're preparing files for Unity, let's go ahead and get the textures out of Substance Painter. The Substance Painter files used to texture the character and her weapons are huge (and available on the support website in the "Substance Painter Assets" folder). If you don't want to mess with downloading the files just to export them, the exported textures are also available under "Painter Texture Outputs."

> Step 15: Export the textures for the character. Use your own Substance Painter files, or the ones on the support website. Be sure to make the Output Directory the Textures folder in the NPC folder within Assets of the Unity project (TheEscaper/ Assets/NPC/Textures). Also remember to change Output Template: Unity HD Render Pipeline (Metallic Standard) with a File Type:targa (Figure 12.10).
>
> Step 16: Back to Unity. Mark the Normal maps as Normal in the Inspector.

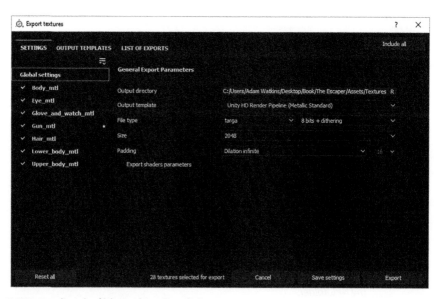

FIGURE 12.10 Reminder of Substance Painter Export Textures settings.

Putting it All Together

Time to put the textures into the extracted materials. In order to get a good idea of how this should look, be sure and find a reasonably well-lit corner of the level to work with. If you need to cheat a little and temporarily put another light in the scene (Real time), go ahead and so that to get setup (Figure 12.11).

> *Step 17: Drag EllenEnemy out into the Scene (Figure 12.11).*
>
> *Step 18: Rebuild the Materials using the Substance Output textures. This is a review, and shouldn't take long. Plug the BasemMaps, MaskMaps, and NormalMaps into their respective channel for the new materials for EllenEnemy (Figure 12.12).*
>
> *Step 19: Make the skin a Subsurface Scattering material. Select Body_mtl (in NPC/Materials). Scroll down and change Material Type: Subsurface Scattering. Don't worry about the scary green for a minute.*
>
> *Step 20: Scroll down the Surface Inputs and click on the Target icon for Diffusion Profile. Pick Skin from the presets available (Figure 12.13).*

FIGURE 12.11 EllenEnemy placed in the scene with a cheater light to see and understand the shaders.

FIGURE 12.12 Plugged in textures to create materials.

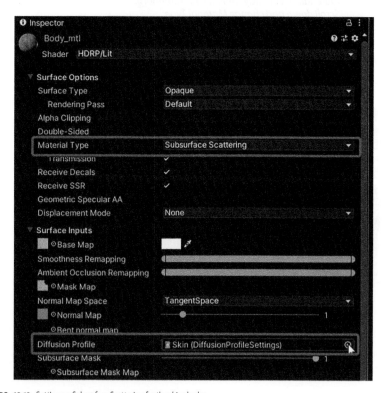

FIGURE 12.13 Setting up Subsurface Scattering for the skin shader.

Why?

Subsurface Scattering is the ability of some surfaces to scatter light that penetrates their surface. Think of the difference between a glass full of white paint and a glass full of milk. The milk allows light to penetrate the surface and then diffuses it through its volume. Human skin is a good example of subsurface scattering and is a great place to use this material type. The results are subtle (Figure 12.14 left is Standard and right is Subsurface Scattering), but important.

Step 21: Adjust the Base Maps of all the new materials so that the Color swatch is white. It will bring the eyes back up to alive (Figure 12.15).

FIGURE 12.14 The effects of subsurface scattering.

FIGURE 12.15 Adjusting the Base Map color tints from the default gray tint to white.

Setting Up the Animator

There's a lot of files that came in just now. EllenEnemy is there, but there is also a big collection of FBX files there that all start with "pistol" (pistol idle, pistol jump, etc.). Let's take a moment now to set up a simple animation scheme to see at least the idle in action. We will leave this unsatisfyingly unfinished after that because the rest of the animations are those that we'll want to tie into the AI system in Chapter 17; but if we can get the basic setup structured here, it will allow us to focus on AI then.

The process here will be to assign a Humanoid rig to EllenEnemy, and then copy that rig to all the other animation fbx files that came in with her. What this will do is apply the animations to EllenEnemy's rig.

> Step 22: Create a Humanoid rig. Select EllenEnemy in the Project window. In the Inspector, click the Rig tab and change Animation Type: Humanoid. Importantly, leave Avatar Definition: Create From This Model (Figure 12.16). Click Apply.
>
> Step 23: Create Humanoid Rig and copy Avatar for the remainder of the fbx animations. In the Project window, select pistol idle and shift select down to pistol walk (basically all the fbx files that start with pistol – but not EllenEnemy). In the

FIGURE 12.16 Import settings for the Rig of EllenEnemy.

Inspector, change Animation Type: Humanoid and Avatar Definition: Copy From Other Avatar (Figure 12.17).

Step 24: Assign EllenEnemyAvatar as the Source Avatar. In the Project window, expand EllenEnemy and look for something called EllenEnemyAvatar (towards the bottom of the list). Drag that over to the Source input field of the Inspector (Figure 12.18). Click Apply.

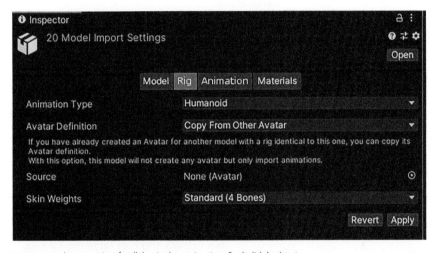

FIGURE 12.17 Import settings for all the pistol xxx animations. Don't click Apply yet.

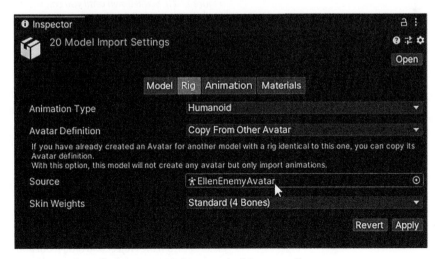

FIGURE 12.18 Assigning EllenEnemyAvatar as the Source avatar for all the animation files.

Why?

This process is a little goofy to set up but has tremendous power. Now, select any of the pistol animations (pistol run arc or instance), and in the Inspector, click the Animation tab. At the bottom of the Inspector, you'll see the EllenEnemy character animated to that animation clip (Figure 12.19). Let's start a simple situation where Ellen stands at idle.

> *Step 25: Create an Animator Controller. Select the NPC folder and use the + button to create an Animator Controller. Rename it "EllenEnemyController".*
>
> *Step 26: In the Hierarchy, select EllenEnemy and drag EllenEnemyController from the Project into the Controller input field of the Animator component (Figure 12.20).*
>
> *Step 27: Double click EllenEnemyController to open the Animator. This can be done in the Project window or the Inspector.*
>
> *Step 28: Make some adjustments to pistol idle and import it into the Animator. In the Project window, select pistol idle. In the Inspector, click on the Animation tab. Rename the animation to "idle_anim" and click on the Loop Time check box. Finally, under Root Transform Rotation, click Bake Into Pose and change Based Upon: Original (Figure 12.21). Scroll down until you can see the Apply button and click it.*

Why?

Lots happening here. All the Mixamo animations come in named "mixamo.com." Useless. Renaming them as we go will make them easier to work with. The idle needs to loop (thus clicking the Loop Time). Baking the Root Transform Rotation using the Original rotation will make sure that the animations are indeed facing forward. We will do similar things to this for every animation before we're done.

> *Step 29: Drag pistol idle into the Animator. Grab pistol idle from the Project and drag it out into the Base Layer area of the Animator. Unity will*

FIGURE 12.19 By having the animations inherit the avatar from EllenEnemy, all the animations now have a rig and geometry to be animated.

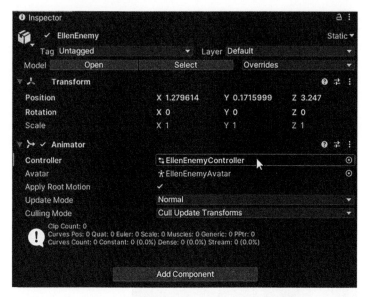

FIGURE 12.20 Assigning the new Animator Controller EllenEnemyController to control EllenEnemy.

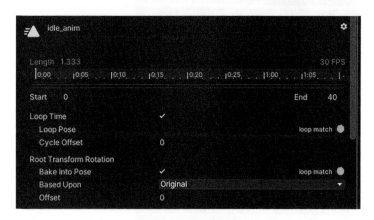

FIGURE 12.21 Preparing pistol idle for use in scene with renaming and looping.

automatically connect this new State to the Entry state (Figure 12.22).

Step 30: Go back to the Scene window and play the Game. Watch the Scene window and EllenEnemy will shift into her idle (Figure 12.23).

Step 31: Unpack the EllenEnemy prefab in the scene. Select EllenEnemy in the Hierarchy. Right click and chose Unpack Prefab.

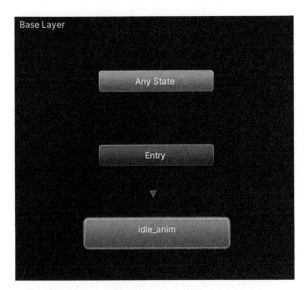

FIGURE 12.22 Importing an animation into the Animator.

FIGURE 12.23 EllenEnemy shifting to her idle animation. Obviously, we need to fix that gun.

Why?

We need to get that gun off her thigh and into her hand. To do this, we'll actually bring in another copy of the gun and hide the one in the holster. The reason for this is that

459

the gun in the holster has a special kind of component called a Skinned Mesh Renderer, which means that the position of the geometry is tied to the position of joints. This means we can't easily just move the gun.

The process will be a quick three steps: hide the gun in the holster, export/import the gun from Maya, and position it as a child of the joints in her hand.

> *Step 32: Hide the holster gun. In the Hierarchy, expand EllenEnemy and select Ellen_gun_geo. In the Inspector, turn it off by clicking the top left-most checkmark (right next to the name Ellen_gun_geo). It will disappear in the Scene window and be grayed out in the Hierarchy.*
> *Step 33: Import Ellen_Gun (from Step 3). Select the NPC folder, right click and choose Import New Asset. The Ellen_Gun is likely on your Desktop. Find it and click Import.*
> *Step 34: Apply the existing Gun_mtl to Ellen_Gun. In the Project window, select the newly imported Ellen_Gun. In the Inspector, click the Materials tab. Drag Gun_mtl from NPC/Materials into the Gun_mtl input field and hit Apply.*
> *Step 35: Position the gun in EllenEnemy's right hand. Drag Ellen_Gun into the Scene view. Maneuver it so that it is sitting roughly in her palm (Figure 12.24).*

FIGURE 12.24 Positioning Ellen_Gun in EllenEnemy's right hand. Exact placement is not important; give it a rough shot.

Step 36: Make Ellen_Gun a child of the right hand joint. In the Hierarchy, expand EllenEnemy. Look for the mixamorig:Hips object (this is the rig mixamo created). Expand it and keep expanding until mixamorig:RightHand becomes visible. Drag Ellen_Gun onto mixamorig:Right hand to make it a child of the hand (Figure 12.25).

Step 37: Play the game and observe the gun in hand (Figure 12.26). If you find it needs to be adjusted, stop the game, adjust, and play again.

Step 38: Create a prefab out of this gun-tottin' Ellen. Drag EllenEnemy from the Hierarchy into the Prefabs folder. Then delete EllenEnemy from the Scene view panel. Not to worry, whenever we need her (and her gun and idle animation) we can just drag her out from the Prefab folder again.

Step 39: Grab a few more animations and get them into Unity. Go back to Mixamo. Search for "Shooting" in the animations. Click on the Shooting clip shown in Figure 12.27.

FIGURE 12.25 Making Ellen_Gun a child of the right hand joint so where the hand goes, the gun goes.

461

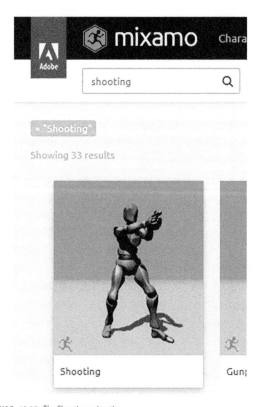

FIGURE 12.26 Gun in hand.

FIGURE 12.27 The Shooting animation.

Why?

The pack we downloaded in the earlier step has a huge collection of movement animations but does not include one of the character actually shooting the gun. For our design, the character is going to stop when they shoot their weapon; so we need to track down an animation that will show this.

> *Step 40: Download Shooting but don't bring the Skin. To do this, click the Download button on the right side of Mixamo's interface. Make sure that Format: FBX for Unity (.fbx) and Skin: Without Skin (Figure 12.28).*
>
> *Step 41: Repeat for "Hit Reaction" and "Death from the Back". Find the animations and download them using the settings in Figure 12.28.*
>
> *Step 42: Shop out any other pistol animations while you're here. Do a search of "pistol" and you'll find a nice alternative Pistol Idle. If you find something you like, click it, and download it. Again, without skin.*
>
> *Step 43: Import the new individual animations into Unity. Back in Unity, right click on the NPC folder and choose Import New Asset. In the Downloads folder of your machine should be EllenEnemy@ Shooting, EllenEnemy@Hit Reaction, EllenEnemy@Death from the Back, and any other animation you picked up. Import them.*
>
> *Step 44: Set the Rig settings to Animation Type: Humanoid, Avatar Definition: Copy From Other Avatar, and Source: EllenEnemyAvatar. A repeat of Steps 23 and 24. Click Apply.*
>
> *Step 45: Not necessary if you only brought in the Shoot animation, but if you downloaded*

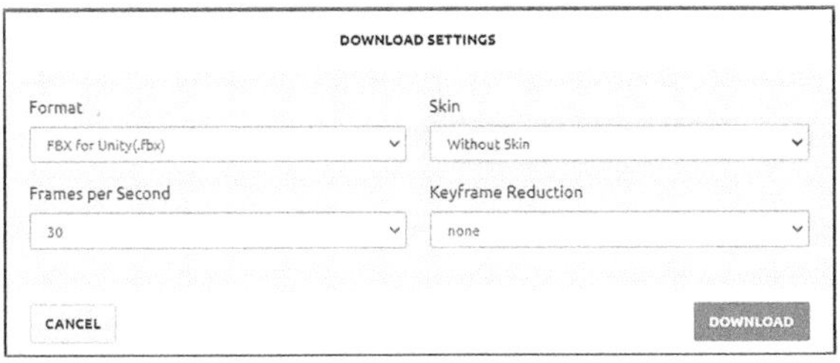

FIGURE 12.28 Exporting just the animation. No need for skin this time (we've already imported that).

an alternate idle, prepare that clip (rename it, set it to Loop Time, and Root Transform Rotation>Bake Into Pose). Then in the EllenEnemyController, delete idle_anim and bring your version in. The Animator will automatically connect it as the default state.

Conclusion

Unfortunately, here is where we need to leave EllenEnemy. No worries though. Later, we'll spend plenty of time teaching her to patrol the level, chase the player, and attack them when they are close enough. But to do that, we first need to learn more about the Animator and how to write some code to control it. We'll start on that in Chapter 14 and then again spend a lot of time on AI in Chapter 17.

For now, let's quickly review what this chapter has covered. Using Mixamo, a model can be auto-rigged, and MoCap animations exported associated with that rig. Inside of Unity, the Mixamo-produced rig can be used to create an Avatar that can then be controlled by Mixamo-produced motion-capture clips. While this might not be the solution for every game, it is a very quick way to get your characters in game and ready to be taught where to go.

If you're an animator you may be yelling, "blasphemy!" And that's OK too; if you'd prefer to animate yourself, be sure you do. Take a look at the upcoming chapters controlling the FPSController and we'll look at how to use keyframed animation there.

For now, it's onto the basics of C#. The fun is just beginning!

CHAPTER 13

Introduction to C#

Finally! We're onto interaction. While creating the art for games is a challenging and fulfilling exercise, until the interaction is scripted, it's simply an environment to walk through, or characters animating in a vacuum. Coding will finally allow us to actually build a game.

In this chapter, we will look at how to make a machine that is blindingly fast and yet blindingly stupid do amazing things. The computing power of your computer – regardless of its specs – is faster than many ever imagined. The number of calculations being made each second on a user's behalf are stunning, even if the user is only browsing the web. The math alone required to draw the geometry we have been working with in the past chapters is calculated at a rate many times faster than the computers that sent men to the moon. And yet, all those calculations are done by a machine that can't figure out the difference between the words "Update" and "update"!

The point here is that coding requires exact syntax. Capital letters (or not), punctuation, and placement of scripts are all critically important to computers. They will always follow your instructions exactly, and if one letter is off, they can't figure out how to get around the roadblock.

With this in mind, we will start out by looking at a few general rules to writing code in Unity. Most of these rules and ideas are general to all coding, but we will focus on a Unity-centric approach.

C#

Ironically, Unity is built in C++ (not C#). However, C++ is a pain to learn and, for most coders, higher level coding languages are a much more approachable way to train a computer to do tasks. C# is the undisputed preferred language of coding for Unity, and it has generally deprecated (abandoned) all other previously used languages, including a variant of JavaScript and a variation of Python called Boo.

C# has some rules and some conventions that will help a script be easier to read, write, and work with. Let's look at a piece of example code (Figure 13.1).

There are several parts called out in the illustration:

> **Libraries** – *This is included at the top of the script as it lets Unity know which libraries of terms and commands we are going to use in the script. If Unity knows which libraries we plan to use, it can then check those libraries for details on how to do the things we write in the code below. By default, Unity includes these libraries; although they aren't the only ones Unity has access to. Later, we will look at adding other libraries to the beginning of scripts so that Unity can go look new terms up when we use them.*

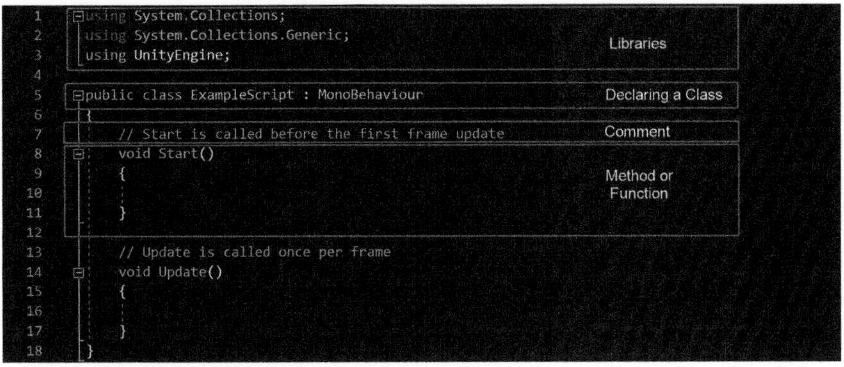

FIGURE 13.1 Example empty script created in Unity and viewed in Visual Studio.

Class Declaration – *A class, in this case, is a script. It's a collection of instructions that will be represented in Unity as a component that is attached to an object (referred to as GameObjects in Unity). In Figure 13.1, we are declaring a script named "ExampleScript" that is public (meaning other scripts can see and talk to it). Further the new script (class) is of type MonoBehaviour. Don't worry about this last part; for us, all of the scripts we will create will be of type MonoBehaviour. Notice that the name of the class, ExampleScript, is capitalized, camel-cased, and has no spaces.*

Comments – *Anytime a line starts with "//" it signals to Unity: Don't worry about this; ignore it. Comments are things coders leave for themselves or other coders. Unity ignores it, but documenting code is considered good practice and can indeed help a coder keep track of what they're doing even if no one else ever reads the code.*

Methods/Functions – *These are events. Basically, a method is a block of code that can be called at various times in the game. For instance, the method highlighted in Figure 13.1 is called Start, which is a special term for Unity. Unity knows to fire the instructions in this method at the start of the game. Sometimes methods are called functions, which is also a good descriptive term as this chunk of code adds functionality to the game.*

There are some very special names of functions that are built into the Unity libraries: Awake, Start, and Update are a few. Update is a function that fires every frame. This means that in every frame, the instructions within the Update function are completed. Other important built-in functions in Unity include things like OnCollisionEnter (do this work when something collides with whatever this script is attached to). However, a function can be named anything you want: MyCoolMethod is a valid name of a function. But such a method will need other instructions on when to fire that method. More on this later.

Before the name of the function will be a word that defines the kind of content the function produces (often called "returning"). So "void Start()" means that this function (called Start) returns nothing (void). Method declarations could also take the form "int Start()" which means, *this method, called Start, is going to spit out an integer when the instructions are completed.*

After the name of a function are ()'s. In these a code can include arguments or chunks of data that the function will need to complete its work. If the function does not require any information to complete its work, the () will be empty.

Importantly, notice that the name of methods/functions are also capitalized and there are never any spaces within the name. "MyCoolFunction" is ok, "My Cool Function" is not.

{} – Curly brackets, braces, squiggly brackets, whatever you call them, they are important. That signify the beginning and ending of a block of code. So, notice that immediately beneath the declaration of the ExampleScript class is an open curly bracket that has a matching close curly bracket at the end of the code. This means that all the code within ExampleScript is contained with these curly brackets. This is the same for functions. Immediately beneath the line "void Start()" is both an open and closed curly bracket indicating the start and end of the function.

Although not required, most coding software assists by creating dashed lines to help the coder see that curly brackets are opened and closed. Further, they are usually

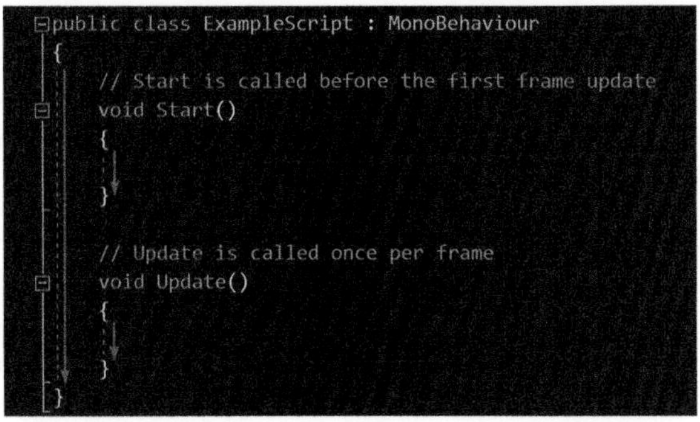

FIGURE 13.2 Brackets indicate the start and end of a function or class. Usually they are vertically aligned, and code contained in the function or class is tabbed one more level in than the curly bracket.

stacked vertically (Figure 13.2). Note that code that is within the two curly brackets is tab-indented one level.

Finally, two more important syntax note:

> **;** – The ";" in code is like the "." in English. It marks the end of a sentence of a thought. Usually within a function will be several lines of code, and each will end with a ";". Forgetting this is the most common mistake for beginning coders.
>
> **Dot Syntax** – When C# is referring to something, it can drill down to components of that thing (or drill up) by using a ".". So, earth.unitedStates. texas.sanAntonio would be an example of how I could use dot syntax to indicate where I'm at. Notice there are no spaces anywhere within a dot syntax string of characters and camel-casing is used to signify different words within. So, for instance if we wanted to get the location of a badguy, a dot syntax statement might look like:

```
badguy.transform.position.x;
```

This is referencing the gameObject "badGuy" and then drilling down to the Transform component (the same Transform seen in the Inspector) and then looking at the Position X attribute.

And with that, let's get busy building code. There are lots more important things to talk about (variables for starters); but let's explore them as we need them.

Much of successful early coding skills come from recognizing patterns. So, watch for the syntax in the examples and be careful to include spaces where the example includes it and leave them out when it does not.

C# in Unity and Visual Studio

As we've discussed earlier, Unity is a form of middle-ware. It assembles assets, including code, that were built elsewhere. Unity will compile code, it will read code, and it will act on code, but it won't allow you to write code. To do this, we need to use some Integrated Development Environment (IDE). IDEs make the work of a programmer easier by combining lots of different aspect of code-building into one package. An IDE will understand the libraries of the code that is being written and provide helpful hints and auto-formatting that greatly speed the rate of authoring code and help the user see when code is correct (or not).

The IDE that most folks use is Visual Studio (presently 2017 or 2019 – either will work). When Unity was first installed on your machine, it should have automatically installed a version of Visual Studio on your machine. By default, Unity installs Visual Studio 2017, although upgrading to 2019 is free (using the free version of Visual Studio (Visual Studio Community) that Unity uses). For the screenshots in this chapter, we will be using Visual Studio 2017 since that's what's installed by default. But if you're running 2019, no worries. Some of the colors might be a little different, but the functionality is the same.

Before we get busy writing code, let's make sure that the installation is complete and that Unity knows where the installation is.

> *Step 1: Ensure that Visual Studio is installed. Click the Windows start menu (the little window icon in the bottom left corner of your screen) and begin typing "Visual Studio". Among the options this pops up will be an app called Visual Studio Installer. Launch this. If a Visual Studio Installer does not pop up among your installed apps, you'll need to install Visual Studio Community (https://visualstudio.microsoft.com/*

FIGURE 13.3 The Visual Studio Installer interface.

vs/community/). However, it should have been
installed so you can move onto the next step.

Step 2: In the resulting interface (Figure 13.3), click
the Modify button.

Step 3: There scroll down to the Mobile & Gaming
section and look for the "Game development
with Unity" module. It should be checked. If it is
not, do so, and then click the Modify button at
the bottom right (Figure 13.4).

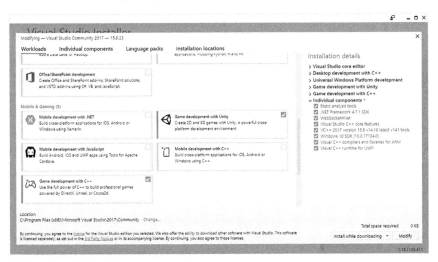

FIGURE 13.4 Ensuring Visual Studio has the Unity libraries installed.

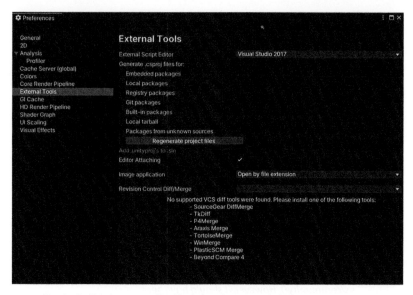

FIGURE 13.5 Ensuring that Unity knows to use Visual Studio for code creation and editing.

Step 4: Make sure Unity knows to use Visual Studio. Launch your project via the Unity Hub and then within Unity choose, Edit>Preferences. In the Preferences window (Figure 13.5), on the left choose External Tools. On the right make sure that External Script Editor: Visual Studio 2017 (or Visual Studio 2017 (Community), or Visual Studio 2019) is selected. The only setting not acceptable is "Open by file extension". If it says that, choose Browse from the drop down menu and map where the Visual Studio is installed (usually C:\Program Files (x86)\Microsoft Visual Studio 14.0\Common7\IDE\devenv).

Alright, now to move onto actually writing some code!

Tutorial 13.1: Hello World!

Step 1: Create a new Scene. File>New Scene.

Why?

We're going to be a doing a lot of testing. This means a lot of playing the game. Currently, MainLevel is a big level and takes a while to start up and play. While we're roughing out code, we don't want to lose all of that time. So a new scene will be lean and mean and let us iterate more quickly.

> *Step 2: Expose the Console. At the very bottom of either the default interface, or the two by three interface we're currently using is a little tiny line that is the Console. The Console is a text tool that Unity can use to provide feedback to the developer. When we're ready to write code, this is really the single most important part of the interface. Select Window>General>Console. This will expose a floating Console. Nest it into the interface by dragging the Console tab to the location you want to pin it to. I prefer pinning it to the bottom of the interface where I can expand it to read all the details it provides (Figure 13.6).*
>
> *Step 3: Create a folder to contain scripts. If there isn't already a folder called Scripts in the Project window, click the + button and choose Folder. Rename the folder Scripts.*
>
> *Step 4: Create a new script called HelloWorldScript. In the Project window, with the Scripts folder selected, again click the + button and choose C# Script. The new script will be created with an invitation to immediately rename it. Enter HelloWorldScript (no spaces) as the name of the script.*

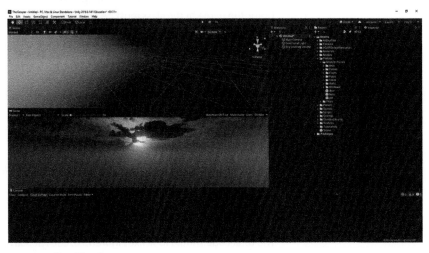

FIGURE 13.6 Pinned Console.

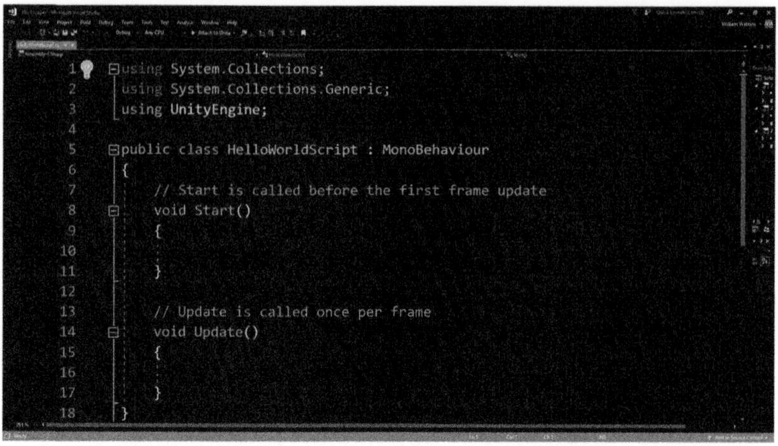

FIGURE 13.7 Newly created HelloWorldScript opened in Visual Studio.

Step 5: Open the script in Visual Studio. Do this by double clicking on the HelloWorldScript. After a brief pause, Visual Studio will open and the script will show up looking like Figure 13.7.

Tips and Tricks

Notice that after the libraries, the name of this class is the same name as the script (HelloWorldScript). This is not only convenient, but necessary. If a script is renamed in Unity, the name of the class must be renamed to match.

Within Visual Studio, the color scheme can be changed using Tools>Options. There, change the Color scheme: Dark. It's much easier on the eyes.

Also within Visual Studio, holding the Ctrl-key down and scrolling up and down on the mouse will make the font appear larger and smaller.

Step 6: Make the script say hello. Within the Start() function build in a line that prints to the Console. The line should read:

```
print("Hello World");
```

The total code should look like Figure 13.8. Use File>Save (Ctrl-S) in Visual Studio and return to Unity.

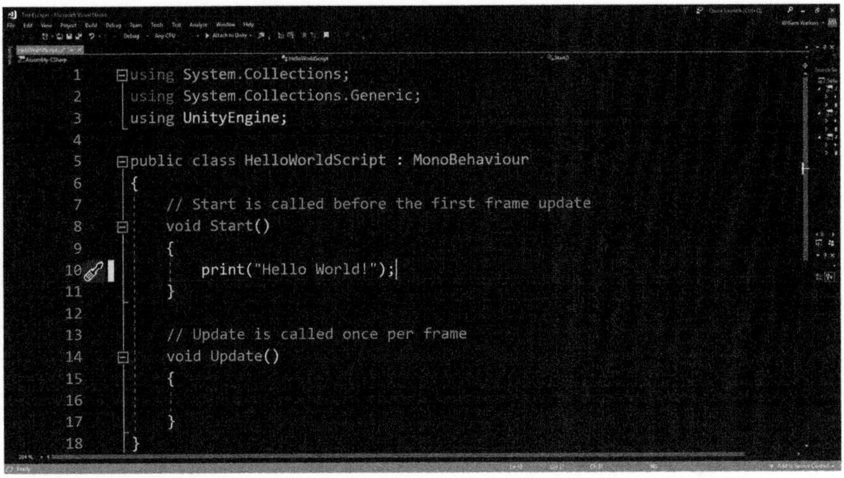

FIGURE 13.8 Code that allows for a simple message (Hello World) to be written to the Console.

Why?

When returning to Unity, the bottom right of the interface might show a little spinning circle. This means that Unity is compiling the code. What's happening here is that Unity is reading the code and trying to see if it understands the instructions. If there are syntax errors, they will pop up on the Console in red. Double clicking that error will open the code again in Visual Studio to point out where the problem might be. If there are no syntax errors and Unity understands all the new instructions not much will happen – and that's a good thing.

What this script does is when the game starts (in the Start() function, see?), the Console will print the string (just a collection of characters) "Hello World!".

> Step 7: Put the code in the game. Create a new empty GameObject (GameObject>Create Empty). Drag the HelloWorldScript onto the empty GameObject in either the Hierarchy or the Inspector. Importantly, the Inspector for the selected empty GameObject should appear like Figure 13.9; a GameObject with a new component.

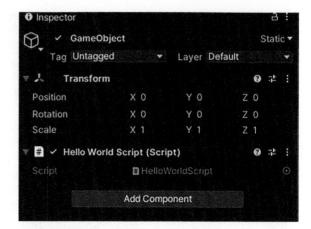

FIGURE 13.9 After properly compiling, a script is added to the scene by dragging it onto the object in the Hierarchy or the Inspector.

Why?

Most scripts do nothing if they just live in the Project window. They need to be in the game to be active. Unity hangs scripts off of GameObject to indicate that they are actually to be executed when the game is played. It's a common mistake for beginning coders to write a script and forget to apply it to their game.

> Step 8: Play the game. Hit Ctrl-P and look at the Console (Figure 13.10). Hit Ctrl-P to stop playing the game.

Why?

Alright, so not terribly exciting so far. But this is an important (and traditional) step to setting up code. The Console writing this string out shows us that the script has

FIGURE 13.10 Hello World!

been seen by Unity, Unity understands the script, and it indeed fires it at the start of the game.

> Step 9: Have game write to the console very frame.
> Double click the HelloWorldScript in the Project window and back in Visual Studio, cut the print line of code from the Start() function and instead paste it into the Update() function (Figure 13.11). Save and return to Unity.
>
> Step 10: Play the game and check the Console (Figure 13.12). Stop playing the game at any time.

```
1    using System.Collections;
2    using System.Collections.Generic;
3    using UnityEngine;
4
5    public class HelloWorldScript : MonoBehaviour
6    {
7        // Start is called before the first frame update
8        void Start()
9        {
10
11       }
12
13       // Update is called once per frame
14       void Update()
15       {
16           print("Hello World!");
17       }
18   }
```

FIGURE 13.11 Moving the print line of code to be fired every frame.

Console

Clear Collapse Clear on Play Clear on Build Error Pause Editor ▾

Hello World!
UnityEngine.MonoBehaviour:print(Object)

Hello World!
UnityEngine.MonoBehaviour:print(Object)

Hello World!
UnityEngine.MonoBehaviour:print(Object)

Hello World!
UnityEngine.MonoBehaviour:print(Object)

Hello World!
UnityEngine.MonoBehaviour:print(Object)

FIGURE 13.12 Moving the print command to Update() means "Hello World!" is printed every frame of the game.

Why?

It's important to understand that functions not only include instructions but have specific times to fire. In Start(), the instructions are carried out when the game starts. In Update(), they fire every frame. Sometimes we need things to fire every frame (like listening for player input), but usually Unity shouldn't be tying up processor cycles every frame.

Tutorial 13.2: Opening Doors

Now that we've looked at how to make a script and attach it, it's time to look at making a script do real work in the game. To do this, we'll start with a script that opens our doors. This script will be constructed in this new empty scene but will be applied to the door prefab and so will work back in the MainLevel too. Before we get started, delete the old GameObject that contained the HelloWorldScript so it is no longer used in the game.

> Step 1: Create a floor. GameObject>3D Object>Plane. In the Inspector, change its Positions X, Y, and Z to 0 to stick it in the middle of the world.
> Step 2: Place the door prefab into the scene on the floor. Remember to grab the prefab door from the Prefabs folder so that the changes we make here will transfer over to the MainLevel. Exact placement is not important (Figure 13.13).
> Step 3: Place the FPSController into the scene. The exact placement is unimportant but grab FPSController from the Project folder (Standard Assets>Characters>FirstPersonCharacter>Prefabs) and place it into the scene. Move it up so that it is standing just above the floor. Be sure to delete Main Camera from the scene so that there is only one camera (the one on FPSController) (Figure 13.14).

Why?

The point of this tutorial is to make the doors slide open as we walk up to them. In order to make this work, there needs to be a way to actually move up to the doors – thus

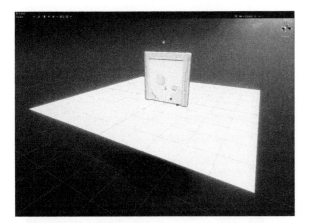

FIGURE 13.13 Placed door prefab.

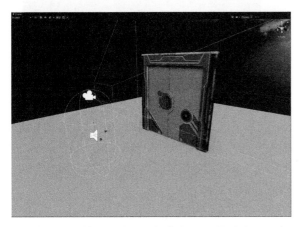

FIGURE 13.14 Placed FPSController. Note that for this screenshot, the Intensity of Directional LIght was reduced considerably to be easier to see.

the FPSController. Note that if the FPSController is selected in the Inspector, there are a lot of components there. Notably, it contains a Character Controller and a Rigidbody component.

> Step 4: Add a Box Collider to the door. In Hierarchy, select door (the parent most object of the door prefab). Then, in the Inspector, click the Add Component button. In the input field that pops up there, start typing "Box Collider" and

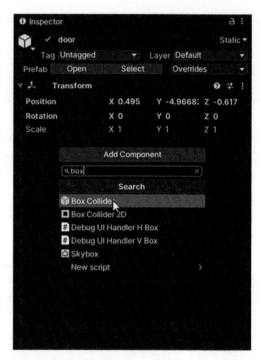

FIGURE 13.15 Adding a Box Collider component.

then select *Box Collider* from the filtered list (Figure 13.15). When done, *Box Collider* will show up as a component in the Inspector, and there will be a little green box in the Scene (Figure 13.16).

Step 5: Resize and place the Box Collider. Figure 13.17 shows the Box Collider component in the Inspector. There is a little button that allows the user to *Edit Collider*. Click that and in the Scene window use the little green dots that appear on each plane of the Box Collider to the adjust the box so that it roughly matches Figure 13.18.

Why?

This collider will become a trigger. It will trigger the doors opening for us. So it needs to be about the size of the doors, but have enough of it in front of the doors so they open before we smack into them, and close behind us once we're through them.

FIGURE 13.16 Poorly placed Box Collider. In Unity, colliders are always color coded in green.

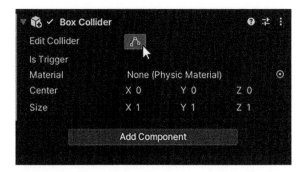

FIGURE 13.17 The Edit Collider button will allow the size and shape of the collider to be adjusted.

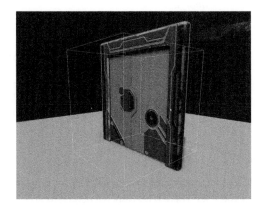

FIGURE 13.18 The adjusted collider. This will act as the trigger to open the doors when we walk up to the door and close them behind us when we move away from it.

Tips and Tricks

The handles to edit the collider are maddeningly small. It's easy to miss them. If you do, just click on door again, and again activate the Edit Collider button. Grab with care.

> *Step 6: Play the game and get stuck. Ctrl-P will allow the player to try and walk up to the doors, but because of the Box Collider we'll be stopped before we ever get to the doors.*
>
> *Step 7: Convert the Box Collider to a Trigger. In the Inspector, the Box Collider has a check box for "Is Trigger". Check this. Play the game and you should be able to walk through the doors again.*

Why?

A Trigger is a sort of box collider that registers when something has intersected with it, but it still allows whatever hit it to pass through. The Trigger will trigger some event that we'll write into script.

> *Step 8: Turn on the Mesh Colliders for door_l and door_r. These were turned off in earlier chapters to allow the player to move through the scene. Now they need to be active again. In the Hierarchy, select door_l and in the Inspector check Mesh Collider on again. Repeat for door_r.*
>
> *Step 9: Create a SlidingDoorScript. In the Project window, select the Scripts folder, and use the + button to create a new C# Script. Immediately rename it to SlidingDoorScript. Double click it to open in Visual Studio.*
>
> *Step 10: Clean up SlidingDoorScript. Select the Start() and Update() functions (including their curly brackets) and delete them (Figure 13.19).*

Why?

This script is going to have a single purpose: open and close the door. There is no work we need it to do every frame or when the game starts. Therefore, there is no need for Start() or Update(). Notice that the curly brackets

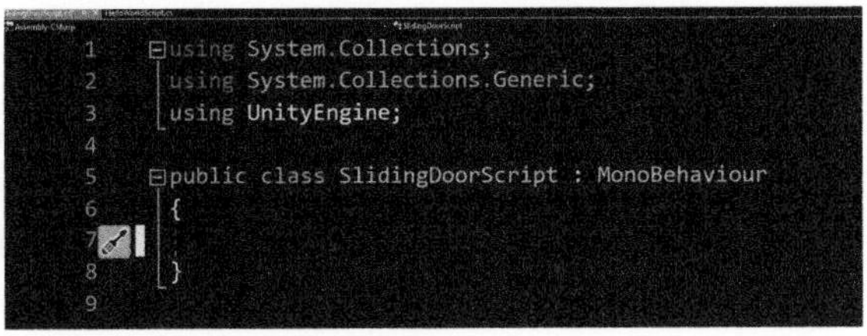

FIGURE 13.19 Deleting unneeded functions.

for those two functions are deleted, but the open curly bracket and closed curly bracket that define the beginning and end of the *class* have remained.

> Step 11: Create a new OnTriggerEnter() function. Within the existing brackets, start typing "OnTriggerEnter" (without the quotes). As this happens, Visual Studio will start suggesting built-in functions that are part of the libraries it is using (Figure 13.20). Either click on, or arrow down to the OnTriggerEnter and hit Enter. Visual Studio will fill out the format for OnTriggerEnter() for you (Figure 13.21).
>
> Step 12: Have the console indicate when the trigger has been tripped. In the OnTriggerEnter() function, add the line:

```
print("I've been triggered");
```

The code should look like Figure 13.22. Save and return to Unity.

FIGURE 13.20 Because Visual Studio and Unity are tied, as a built-in function's name begins to be typed, Visual Studio will suggest some solutions.

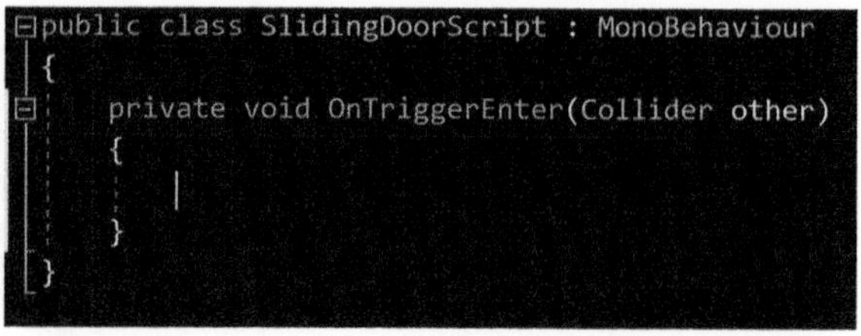

```
public class SlidingDoorScript : MonoBehaviour
{
    private void OnTriggerEnter(Collider other)
    {
        |
    }
}
```

FIGURE 13.21 When one of the hints is clicked, Visual Studio will automatically format the function. Notice it has filled in arguments ((Collider other)) and placed the starting and ending brackets.

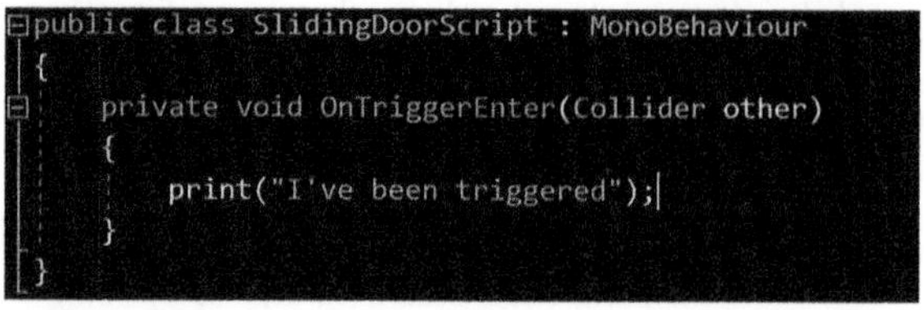

```
public class SlidingDoorScript : MonoBehaviour
{
    private void OnTriggerEnter(Collider other)
    {
        print("I've been triggered");|
    }
}
```

FIGURE 13.22 Code that will let the developer know that the trigger is working.

Why?

This is a typical coding method. Create the trigger, check to see if it actually gets activated. In the movies, its common to see a coder laying down hundreds of lines of code with a triumphant flourish. In reality, coders write a line, see if it works, come back and write the next line, see if it works, etc. Here it's important to make sure that the Trigger is working before adding any other code.

Step 13: Apply *SlidingDoorScript* to the door prefab. After compiling and checking for syntax errors in the Console, drag *SlidingDoorScript* from the Project window onto door in the Hierarchy. When selected, the door's Inspector should appear like Figure 13.23.

Step 14: Play the game and watch the Console. Every time the player gets close to the door and enters the trigger, "I've been triggered" will appear in the Console.

Step 15: Add another function to the script that registers when the player exits the trigger (Figure 13.24). Save and return to Unity to test.

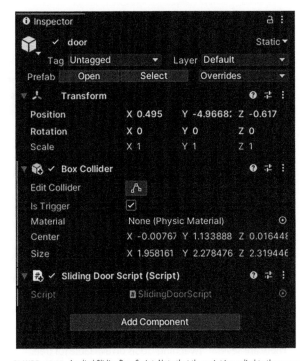

FIGURE 13.23 Applied SlidingDoorScript. Note that the script is applied to the same object that has the Trigger (Box Collider).

```
public class SlidingDoorScript : MonoBehaviour
{
    private void OnTriggerEnter(Collider other)
    {
        print("I've been triggered");
    }

    private void OnTriggerExit(Collider other)
    {
        print("I'm OK now");
    }
}
```

FIGURE 13.24 Adding script to register when the player leaves the trigger. Upon test playing the game, both print commands should be actuated (and show up in the Console) as the player gets close and then moves away from the doors.

DOTween

So now comes the part where the doors actually move. There are many ways to do this: we could animate the doors in Maya and then play that animation in Unity when the player enters the trigger, we could animate the doors in Unity using Unity's animation system and play those animation clips when triggered, we could code it old school by setting a target location and moving a certain amount every frame until we reached the target amount. All of these have their benefits, but we aren't going to any of them here. The animation paths are covered in other chapters in this book, or can easily be found in plenty of YouTube videos. The old school programming is just more than we want to do at this point.

What we *will* do is leverage other code that can be easily and freely implemented. We've already looked at functions that are built into Unity's libraries. For the next steps, additional libraries will be imported and implemented that we can leverage to do advanced things easily.

There are several "tweening" tools on available for free. DOTween and iTween are two of our favorites. For these chapters, the tool of choice will be DOTween, mostly because it continues to be developed (iTween seems to have stagnated as of late). DOTween has a little trickier setup, but performs quickly and will do all the things needed.

> Step 16: Download and install DOTween. In the Asset Store (Window>Asset Store), search for "dotween". DOTween (HOTween v2) is free and should pop as one of the search results. Download and Import. When it is done importing, a window similar to Figure 13.25 will appear. Click on the Open DOTween Utility Panel.
>
> Step 17: Set up DOTween. The DOTween Utility Panel will appear (Figure 13.26 left). Click the Setup DOTween... button. This can take a second as Unity compiles the new scripts DOTween is installing. Finally, it will present an Add/Remove Modules window similar to the right side of Figure 13.26. Click Apply. After that, close the DOTween Utility Panel. There should be a new folder called Demigiant in the Project window.

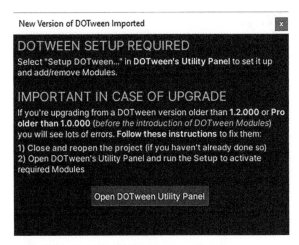

FIGURE 13.25 Starting the setup of DOTween.

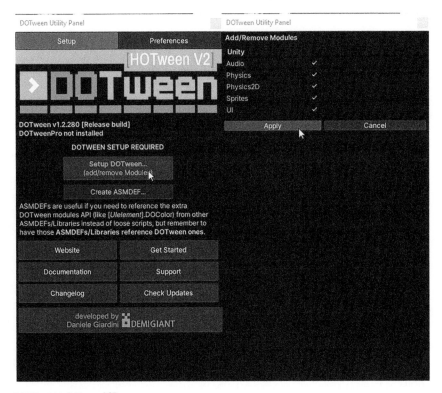

FIGURE 13.26 Setting up DOTween.

Why?

DOTween is just code that someone else has built that, once imported into a project, allows the developer to leverage the thousands of lines of DOTween code into single commands. This is the power of expanding libraries or bringing in other classes. The bounds of the game engine can be nearly infinitely expanded in all directions. But with great power comes great responsibility. In this case, don't move the Demigiant folder. The location of classes like this matter. So treat Demigiant as sacred for now and it will save you hassle later.

> Step 18: Tell SlidingDoorScript to use DOTween. To do this, we'll adjust the library settings at the top (Figure 13.27). It's important to remember that every script that uses DOTween functionality has this added to the libraries.

Tips and Tricks

For now, the documentation might be all Greek to you. But as time goes on, the documentation of any plugin or chunk of code will become very valuable literature. The documentation for DOTween is at: http://dotween. demigiant.com/.

```
1    using System.Collections;
2    using System.Collections.Generic;
3    using UnityEngine;
4    using DG.Tweening;
5
6    public class SlidingDoorScript : MonoBehaviour
7    {
8        private void OnTriggerEnter(Collider other)
9        {
10           print("I've been triggered");
11       }
12
13       private void OnTriggerExit(Collider other)
14       {
15           print("I'm OK now");
16       }
17   }
18
```

FIGURE 13.27 Adding DOTween to the list of libraries (and thus the list of commands that this script knows).

Variables

In C#, variables are buckets of information. A variable can hold gameObjects, integers, numbers with decimals (floats), strings of letters, and/or even things like booleans (true or false). Variables are important for code as they become the easiest way for a script to keep track of any particular object, number, or text string. When the developer populates a variable (puts something in the bucket), the script is able to easily reach out and grab that bucket and access whatever is inside of it without having to do the hard work of going out and finding the object/number/text/whatever each time it needs it.

In C#, variables are defined by first defining if it is public or private. Public variables can be accessed by other scripts; private variables cannot. Next, the declaration defines what type of information the variable will contain (GameObject, int, float, bool, and Transform are a few). Finally, the declaration will list the name of the variable. Variable names are always lowercase, no spaces, and camel-cased. So:

```
public GameObject player;
private float playerSpeed;
private int playerAmmoCount;
```

defines a bucket named "player" to hold a GameObject that every script can access. A bucket that holds numbers with decimal points (float) is named playerSpeed, and this number can only be accessed by this script (since its private). And finally, a who number (integer) will be stored in a private bucket named playerAmmoCount.

Most of programming boils down to putting information in buckets, accessing that information, manipulating it, and then storing it in other buckets. Understanding variables is key to all coding.

> Step 19: Teach SlidingDoorScript which objects to slide open. Create two variables to hold both doors. We want the variables to be accessible for all the code so they will be declared outside any of the functions (Figure 13.28). Save in Visual Studio and return to Unity.

489

```
1   using System.Collections;
2   using System.Collections.Generic;
3   using UnityEngine;
4   using DG.Tweening;
5
6   public class SlidingDoorScript : MonoBehaviour
7   {
8       public GameObject lDoor;
9       public GameObject rDoor;
10
11      private void OnTriggerEnter(Collider other)
12      {
13          print("I've been triggered");
14      }
15
16      private void OnTriggerExit(Collider other)
17      {
18          print("I'm OK now");
19      }
20  }
21
```

FIGURE 13.28 Declaring two variables for lDoor and rDoor. These are public for now.

Why?

When Unity finishes compiling the code, the Sliding Door Script component will look different in the Inspector. Since we've added to public variables, the variables will now be visible inviting the developer to populate them (Figure 13.29).

> Step 20: To populate these public variables, drag the gameObjects from the Hierarchy (door_l to L Door and door_r to R Door) into the Inspector. The Sliding Door Script now knows who the left and right doors are.
>
> Step 21: Find the desired positions of the open and closed doors. Ideally, the axis of each of these doors matches that of the parent so that when selected, the Positions X, Y, and Z are all 0. However, as often happens in production, sometimes the modelers don't prepare the files quite like the coder would like. No sweat

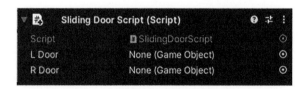

FIGURE 13.29 Public variables show up in the Inspector.

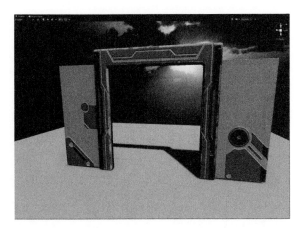

FIGURE 13.30 Moving the doors to an open position and taking note of their Position X values.

> though. Just select door_l and door_r and record what their Position X value is. On ours it is −1.29 (we'll round to −1.3). This is the value the door has when it is closed.

Next, take each door and slide it in one direction to an open position (Figure 13.30). Note the value of the Position X for each. If using the prepared project files from the support site, these are about −0.15 for door_l and −2.4 for door_r. After the values are recorded, move the doors back to closed.

> Step 22: Create the DOTweens to move the doors. In SlidingDoorScript, replace the print commands with lines of code to match Figure 13.31.

Why?

The line:

```
lDoor.transform.DOLocalMoveX(-.15f,
.5f);
```

...says, "go to the object contained in the variable lDoor. Go to its Transform component and use the DOLocalMoveX function to move it. Move it to -.15 in

```
using System.Collections;
using System.Collections.Generic;
using UnityEngine;
using DG.Tweening;

public class SlidingDoorScript : MonoBehaviour
{
    public GameObject lDoor;
    public GameObject rDoor;

    private void OnTriggerEnter(Collider other)
    {
        lDoor.transform.DOLocalMoveX(-.15f, .5f);
        rDoor.transform.DOLocalMoveX(-2.4f, .5f);
    }

    private void OnTriggerExit(Collider other)
    {
        lDoor.transform.DOLocalMoveX(-1.3f, .5f);
        rDoor.transform.DOLocalMoveX(-1.3f, .5f);
    }
}
```

FIGURE 13.31 Using DOTween to animate the doors opening and closing.

local X (meaning in relation to its parent) and do it over .5 seconds" Notice that 0.15 and 0.5 have an "f" behind them to help Unity know that these are floats (as opposed to integers or doubles).

The specifics of DOLocalMoveX comes from the documentation website (Figure 13.32). There it lists the DOLocalMoveX under the Transform category (thus the lDoor.*transform*.DOLocalMove). Further it reveals the arguments the function DOLocalMoveX expects to see: the value of "to" (as a float), the value of "duration" as a float, and whether or not to snap the movement (as a Boolean). Notice that sometimes, as is the case here, an argument can be left off if it's the last one (here the Boolean of whether to snap or not was left off).

FIGURE 13.32 A quick shot of the documentation for DOTween that help us understand what arguments the DOLocalMoveX expects to see.

```
using System.Collections;
using System.Collections.Generic;
using UnityEngine;
using DG.Tweening;

public class SlidingDoorScript : MonoBehaviour
{
    private GameObject lDoor;
    private GameObject rDoor;

    private void Awake()
    {
        lDoor = transform.Find("door_l").gameObject;
        rDoor = transform.Find("door_r").gameObject;
    }
```

FIGURE 13.33 Populating the lDoor and rDoor variables via script. In this case only looking for objects that are children of whatever this script is attached to.

> *Step 23: Populate the doors via script. Change the two variables lDoor and rDoor to private, and then when the game very first starts (Awake()), have the script find among its children the objects door_l and door_r and put them into the lDoor and rDoor variables (Figure 13.33). Save and return to Unity. Test to make sure it still works.*

Why?

In this case, we want to make sure this code will work for every instance of the door we have in the scene. This method means that when the game very first starts, before it does anything else (that's what happens in Awake()), it populates the variables itself by finding objects among its children. When this is all done, all the doors will open automatically as the player walks up to them.

Notice though, that this is finding objects by name. If your doors are named something besides door_l and door_r, be sure to use that in the code. Also, it will be important not to change the name of those objects in the future or it will break the code.

> *Step 24: Tweak and update. If the doors are opening too late, make the Trigger bigger. If the doors are opening too slow or too fast, adjust them in the code (remember it's the second argument*

in the DOLocalMoveX(−0.15f,0.5f) line of code).
Keep testing until the movement and timing
feels right. When it's all good, make sure all
this work is propagated to all the doors by
selecting door and using the Overrides pull-
down menu (on the Prefabs line) and Apply All
(Figure 13.34).

Step 25: Make the floor a bit larger and place a
bunch of door prefabs. Test. Each of the doors
should automatically open as the player
approaches them.

Step 26: Find a sound for the doors opening and
closing. Lots of great resources out there to
choose from. FreeSound.org is one of our
favorites. Although it requires registration,
it's a great community of sound clips shared
for free or with some variation of a Creative
Common License. When a good sound is found.
Download it.

Step 27: In Unity, create a new folder called Audio
and import the sound file. Import it by either
dragging it from the finder into Unity, or right

FIGURE 13.34 Making sure all the instances of this door will open as we approach them.

clicking on the Audio folder and choosing Import New Asset…Unity is pretty tolerant of sound file formats: aiff, wav, and ogg are all good. However, it doesn't like .flac sounds.

Step 28: Add the sound to the door prefab. Select the door in the Hierarchy. In the Inspector, click on Add Component and add an Audio Source component. Expand this new component, and drag the newly imported clip into the AudioClip input field. Still in the Audio Source component, turn off Play on Awake and slide the Spatial Blend slider to 1 (Figure 13.35).

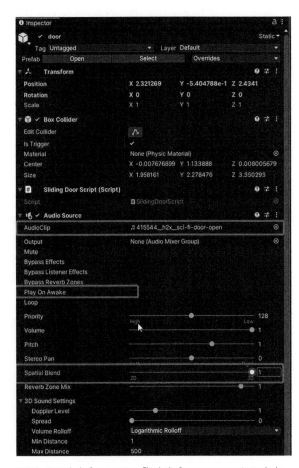

FIGURE 13.35 Audio Source settings. This Audio Source component is attached to the parent door.

Why?

An Audio Source indicates a location that an audio clip will emanate from. The Audio Source component always needs a clip (the actual sound file) to be defined. Turning off Play on Awake makes sure that the sound only plays when the player walks through it (which the script will do in a minute). And finally, adjust the Spatial Blend to 3D means that the player will hear the sound in their left and right headphones when playing the game.

There's lots more cool stuff (reverb zones, fall off, Doppler effects) that can be done with Unity's Audio system. We won't get to most of it here, but if you are interested, take a deeper dive.

> Step 29: Create a variable to store the Audio Source in SlidingDoorScript. Do this by creating a private variable that holds an AudioSource. Add the line shown in Figure 13.36.
>
> Step 30: Allow SlidingDoorScript to find the Audio Source component on its own. In the Awake() function, tell this script to go find the component of type Audio Source that is attached to the same gameobject this script is attached to (Figure 13.37).

```
public class SlidingDoorScript : MonoBehaviour
{
    private GameObject lDoor;
    private GameObject rDoor;
    private AudioSource doorSound;
```

FIGURE 13.36 Adding a variable to hold the Audio Source just created.

```
public class SlidingDoorScript : MonoBehaviour
{
    private GameObject lDoor;
    private GameObject rDoor;
    private AudioSource doorSound;

    private void Awake()
    {
        lDoor = transform.Find("door_l").gameObject;
        rDoor = transform.Find("door_r").gameObject;
        doorSound = GetComponent<AudioSource>();
    }
```

FIGURE 13.37 Allowing the script to populate the doorSound variable with the Audio Source component.

Why?

GetComponent<Type of Component>() is a powerful tool. Any component can be accessed with any script in this way. In the line of code shown in Figure 13.37, we are saying "into the bucket (variable) doorSound, put the AudioSource component that is also attached to this gameObject."

> *Step 31: Play the sound on opening and closing. Now that the script knows where the sound is, it just needs to be told when to play it. In OnTriggerEnter and OnTriggerExit, add the line of code shown in Figure 13.38. Save in Visual Studio and return to Unity.*
> *Step 32: Test. Play the game.*
> *Step 33: If all's well, process the prefab's override. Select door in the Hierarchy, and in the Inspector use Overrides>Apply All.*
> *Step 34: Open MainLevel.*
> *Step 35: Make the door instances not Static. Search for all instances of door. At the top of the Hierarchy, use the Search input field and search for "door". Shift select all of them (door, door(1), door(2), etc.) and in the Inspector check off the Static checkbox in the top right corner.*

Why?

Static objects can't move. The doors are probably marked as Static as they were set that way for light baking. But now, we need them to move.

```
private void OnTriggerEnter(Collider other)
{
    lDoor.transform.DOLocalMoveX(-.15f, 1f);
    rDoor.transform.DOLocalMoveX(-2.4f, 1f);
    doorSound.Play();
}

private void OnTriggerExit(Collider other)
{
    lDoor.transform.DOLocalMoveX(-1.3f, 1f);
    rDoor.transform.DOLocalMoveX(-1.3f, 1f);
    doorSound.Play();
}
```

FIGURE 13.38 Playing the doorSound.

Step 36: Save and test. All the doors in the level should open as the player approaches them, and close as they move away. Further, the sound should play as the player enters and leaves the trigger.

A Final Note: Unity's API

When reading a tutorial like this, or watching a YouTube video, it's sometimes hard to envision where the authors got the information. How does he know how Unity declares a variable? How does he know that SetActive(false) turns something off? The answer is Unity's API. API stands for Application Programming Interface. It's an interface that defines how different software can interact, what commands can be used, etc. Unity doesn't want to keep this secret; on the contrary, it's in their interest that as many people as possible know it and understand it. Unity's API is actually one of the reasons why developers are drawn to Unity over their competitors – the API is better written and easier to decipher.

To get to the API, in Unity, select Help>Scripting Reference. This will fire up the web browser on your machine and welcome you to the "Unity Scripting Reference!". There is a search in the top right corner where an intrepid seeker can enter specific commands or things like "activate object". At first, the API can be daunting and be tough to understand. But there are two main things to get into the habit of looking at and understanding.

The first is the very first few lines of any page (Figure 13.39). This shows the format that a tool actually has. So, in Figure 13.39, we are looking at Instantiate (it means to make an instance in the scene). There are many ways listed there to use this. **Instantiate** (in bold) is the actual class that we can use in script. In each of the lines shown there, the various arguments it expects are listed.

So for instance. The fourth line down reads:

```
public static Object
Instantiate(Object original, Vector3
position, Quaternion rotation);
```

Object.Instantiate

public static Object **Instantiate**(Object **original**);

public static Object **Instantiate**(Object **original**, Transform **parent**);

public static Object **Instantiate**(Object **original**, Transform **parent**, bool **instantiateInWorldSpace**);

public static Object **Instantiate**(Object **original**, Vector3 **position**, Quaternion **rotation**);

public static Object **Instantiate**(Object **original**, Vector3 **position**, Quaternion **rotation**, Transform **parent**);

FIGURE 13.39 The Unity API for Instantiate. Learning to read the API is key to success beyond any tutorial.

The important part is:

```
Instantiate(Object original, Vector3
position, Quaternion rotation);
```

This means that if using Instantiate in this way it expects three things, the original, the position, and the rotation (see them in there separated by commas?). And that the original thing needs to be an Object, the position a Vector3 (a type of information usually representing the Position in X, Y, and Z), and the rotation is represented by a Quaternion (a cool imaginary number you might not remember from high school math). Don't worry about the types right now (Vector3, Quaternion, etc.), but do focus on understanding that the API tells us to use three arguments and that these arguments need to be of a specific type.

Also important in the API (and honestly the way I learned to code in Unity) are the examples (Figure 13.40).

Sometimes the authors of the API show off too much and have a bit of "let me show you what I can do!" in the examples. But often they are the best way of understanding the class in action. Usually, these code snippets are well commented to help understand what is happening in the code. Often, copying and pasting from the example into your own code is a good start to reaching functionality.

Instantiate can be used to create new objects at runtime. Examples include objects used for projectiles, or particle systems for explosion effects.

```
using UnityEngine;

// Instantiate a rigidbody then set the velocity

public class Example : MonoBehaviour
{
    // Assign a Rigidbody component in the inspector to instantiate

    public Rigidbody projectile;

    void Update()
    {
        // Ctrl was pressed, launch a projectile
        if (Input.GetButtonDown("Fire1"))
        {
            // Instantiate the projectile at the position and rotation of this transform
            Rigidbody clone;
            clone = Instantiate(projectile, transform.position, transform.rotation);

            // Give the cloned object an initial velocity along the current
            // object's Z axis
            clone.velocity = transform.TransformDirection(Vector3.forward * 10);
        }
    }
}
```

FIGURE 13.40 An example in the API for Instantiate. These examples are a great way to see something in action.

Every command we look at in this and the following chapters can be found in the API. Don't ever close it down; always have it open and let it be your guide to not just copying code out of a book, but moving towards real understanding.

Conclusion

And with that we'll leave this chapter. Through the course of this chapter, we have created new scripts, attached those scripts to gameObjects (which means they are used in the game). Within those scripts, we've looked at creating and populating variables. Using the variables we have fired code-driven animation and played sounds.

But we're just beginning. There is so very much more to coding. In the next chapter, we'll begin to look at how to use coding to control animations that were completed in Maya and how to start firing weapons.

CHAPTER 14

FPS Animations

In the last chapter, we laid out the basics of coding in C#. We looked at how to create a new script, how to edit the script, and how to apply that script to the game. But opening doors automatically is just the start. In this chapter, we will look at using code along with Unity's Animator system to allow the player to have arms and importantly have those arms play animations.

Before we get started, let's lay out the overall process covered in this chapter. The process is one not dissimilar to one that would take place in a studio where the modelers, texture artists, animators, and coders might all be different people. We will be preparing and cleaning files before they are taken into Unity for final assembly.

1. In Maya, delete unused geometry from the animated scene.
2. In Maya, bake the animation so that constraints and other animation-centric tools are removed from the file.
3. Export the animated (and baked) files from Maya as FBXs.
4. In Substance, export the textures (if you haven't already done so in Chapter 12).
5. In Unity, assemble the animated FBXs, the exported texture files.
6. In Unity, separate the animations in the FBX into Animation Clips.
7. In Unity, using Animator, define what clips to use when using Booleans and triggers.
8. Create the code that flips the boolean and triggers the triggers to make the animation clips play according the user input.

Tutorial 14.1: First Person Animation in Unity

The animations have been prepared (and written about) by Kassandra Arevalo in Chapter 11. If you followed along with that chapter and have your own animations to use, great! Use those. If not, and you are interested in writing code without being an animator, the files that Kassandra animated are on the support website in the support files for this chapter. For the tutorials included here, we will be using Kassandra's animated files.

It's worthwhile to point out that this is different than the process we used (and will use) for the Mixamo-exported MoCap animations. In Chapter 12, we used Mixamo and auto-rigged the NPC and assigned motion-captured animations to it. We will use those in Chapter 17 when we assemble the AI. For now, we are using animations keyframed by an animator. The preparation of the files in Maya and its implementation in Unity will be different from the process we will use in Chapter 17.

Maya Animation Preparation

Step 1: From the Support Files for this chapter, open Ellen_gun_animations.

Why?

No need to set a project for now. The texture files will be separate and assembled in Unity later. All that is needed is the geometry and animation for now. However, it is important to note that the file being animated here already has the UVs complete and the materials applied before the rigging and animation began.

Step 2: Swap to the default persp camera. In the main View Panel, use Panels>Perspective>persp.
Step 3: Ensure that the Outliner is showing by activating it through the UI buttons on the far left (Figure 14.1).
Step 4: Delete unseen geometry. Figure 14.2 shows the geometry included in the rig that the first person will never see. Select it and delete it.

FIGURE 14.1 Activating the Outliner. The Outliner will be one of the easiest ways to select objects, especially if they are hidden.

Baking Keys

When animating, there are lots of tools to help the rig be easy to work with. IK, constraints, etc. all help make the process of animating easier. However, these constraints and other rig-centric tools don't always transition well into game engines. Unless an animator/rigger is using something like stretchy IK (where joints are allowed to stretch), most all animation really is the process of rotating joints. Baking Keys for a rig is the process of setting Rotation Keys (as well as unneeded Translate and Scale keys) every frame. This locks the animation down and makes it harder to edit, but importantly it makes the animation so that it will transition well into a game engine.

Step 5: Bake the keys for Ellen_Rig. Change to Animation mode from the pull-down at the top left of the Maya interface (Figure 14.3). In the Outliner, select Ellen_Rig. Choose Key>Bake Simulation□. In the resulting Bake Simulation

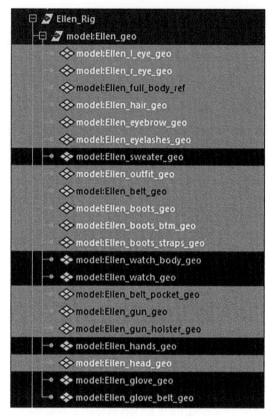

FIGURE 14.2 The geometry that the FPSController will never see. Removing it from the file will keep it streamlined and keep it from showing up in Unity.

FIGURE 14.3 Swapping to Animation mode. This produces new pull-down menus to choose from.

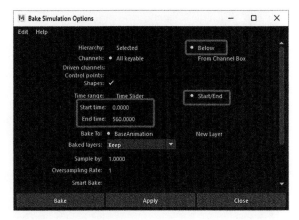

FIGURE 14.4 Bake Simulation Options.

> *Options window, change Hierarchy: Below, Time Range: Start/End, Start time: 0, End time: 560 (Figure 14.4). Hit Bake.*

Why?

Changing Hierarchy to Below means that Maya will bake the keyframe for all the objects below the selected object. For us, this means all the joints for the rig will have their keys baked in. Sliding the Current Time Marker in the time slider would reveal that the first animation begins at frame 0 and ends at frame 560, thus the setting for Start/End and setting the Start Time at 0 and End Time at 560.

The process of Baking the keys can take a while. It's setting an awful lot of keyframes as it goes. The progress can be seen in the time slider at the bottom. Give it time to complete.

> *Step 6: Bake the keys for the Gun_grp and gunClip_ CTRL_group. Same process as Step 5.*

Why?

Gun_grp and gunClip_CTRL_group both have keys on them. Further, Gun_grp's position is being defined by a Parent Constraint. By baking the keys, the constraints are no longer need to define the position of the gun and the clip.

FIGURE 14.5 Now that keys are baked, these constraints are no longer needed.

> *Step 7: Delete the now unnecessary Parent Constraints. Gun_grp and gunClip_CTRL_group both have unnecessary constraints (Figure 14.5). Find them, select them, and delete them.*

Why?

These constraints would likely make no real difference in Unity. But cleaning up assets not needed helps keep the files lean and the game engine running smoothly for longer.

> *Step 8: Delete aim, gun_CTRL, leftHand_locator, rightHand_locator, and gunClip_CTRL_group (Figure 14.6). Again, all great tools while animating, just in the way in the engine.*

Why?

Strictly speaking, there are loads of other things we could actually clean from the file. This rig is powerful and complex, and actually has two joint chains and only one deforms the mesh. However, once this asset is inside Unity, all of that will be buried anyway, and while unnecessary, the developer would never have to mess with it. So it'll stay.

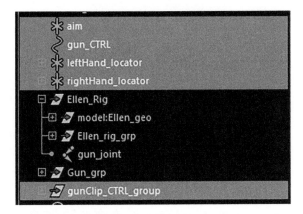

FIGURE 14.6 Deleting a few other things that helped in the animation process but get in the way in the engine.

> *Step 9: Make sure that everything still plays as it should. Do this by dragging the Current Time Marker, or just hitting the play button down in the Timeline. If all is well, the arms, hands, and weapon will still move as they should.*
>
> *Step 10: Save as a new file name. Save as something like "Ellen_gun_animations_BAKED".*

Why?

It is important that the old non-baked version of the animations is not saved over. This baked version is great for the game engine – but nearly impossible to edit. Keep the old unbaked version in case animations need to be adjusted.

> *Step 11: Export as fbx. Choose File>Export All. In the Export All window, make sure File of Type: FBX Export. In the Options…section, under Geometry make sure Smooth Mesh and Triangulate is checked and also make sure Animation is checked this time. Export the file to the Unity project file in the Assets folder and specifically in the Models folder (TheEscaper\Assets\Models).*

Tips and Tricks

There may be some Warnings and Errors that pop up. Most of these might be associated with Constraints

(constraints that don't matter anymore), Animation Curve Tangents (which Unity will take care of), or Unsupported Transform nodes. All of these, in this case, should be fine. Just click the Close button.

> Step 12: Repeat for the baking and culling process for Ellen_grenadeLauncher_animations. Open the file. Bake the keys (Keys>Bake Simulation) from Start Time: 0 to End Time: 567 for Ellen_Rig and Grenade_launcher_grp. Delete aim, leftHand_locator, grenade_group, and the grenade_launcher_grenade_parentConstraint (under Grenade_launcher_grp). Under Ellen_Rig>model:Ellen_geo, delete everything except sweater, watch_body, watch, hands, glove, and glove_belt. Double-check that nothing has been deleted that's still needed by dragging through the timeline. Save as Ellen_grenadeLauncher_animations_BAKED.
>
> Step 13: Export as fbx as Ellen_GrenadeLauncher. Remember to export into the Unity project file (TheEscapers/Assets/Models). Be sure to include Animations in the export options. Again, don't worry about the errors on this one (there will still be some constraints floating around).

Tips and Tricks

These last few steps are pretty technical. And they are very specific to the file. If you're struggling with which assets to delete, just focus on getting rid of the unnecessary geometry (the things under Ellen_geo). As long as that is gone, the exported file will be fine.

If you're still struggling, the support files for this chapter include both the pre-bake and post-baked versions of the animations.

Substance Painter Output

While we're preparing files for Unity, let's go ahead and get the textures out of Substance Painter. You may have already done this in Chapter 12 for the NPCs; if so, skip these Substance Painter steps (jump down to Putting it Together in Unity) as the Unity project will already have the necessary textures. The Substance Painter files used to texture the character and her weapons are huge (and available on the support website in the "Substance Painter Assets" folder). If you don't want to mess with downloading the files just to export them, the exported textures are also available under "Painter Texture Outputs."

> Step 14: Export the textures for the character. Use your own Substance Painter files, or the ones on the support website. Be sure to make the Output Directory you're the Textures folder in the Assets folder of the Unity project (TheEscaper/Assets/Textures). Also remember to change Output Template: Unity HD Render Pipeline (Metallic Standard) with a File Type:targa (Figure 14.7).
>
> Step 15: Repeat for the grenade launcher that is included in the props_texturing Substance Painter asset. This includes the textures for the grenade launcher and the grenade. These may already be in your Unity project (check the Assets/Textures folder for props_Grenade_launcher assets). If they are not there from our earlier exports, open props_texturing from the support files. Export just the grenade launcher assets (Figure 14.8).

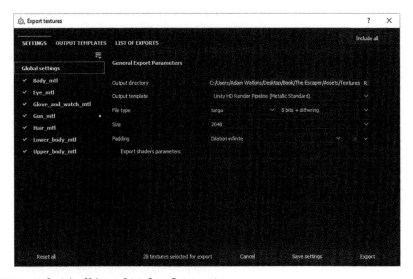

FIGURE 14.7 Reminder of Substance Painter Export Textures settings.

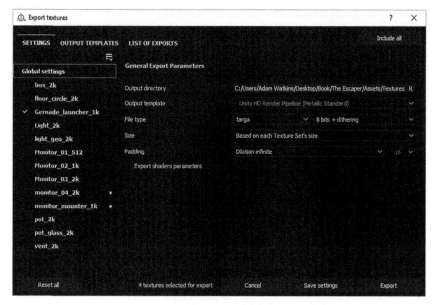

FIGURE 14.8 Exporting the grenade launcher textures from Substance Painter.

Putting It Together in Unity

Now that all the assets have been exported, and exist in the Unity project, it's time to tie them all together. Open the Unity project and we'll get to it.

Step 16: Extract the materials for Ellen_Gun and Ellen_GrenadeLauncher. In the Project window, select Ellen_Gun (the fbx). In the Inpector, select the Materials tab and click the Extract Materials button. Naviagate to the Materials folder in the Unity project file. The materials should show up both in the Inspector (Figure 14.9) and in the Materials folder of the project. Repeat for Ellen_GrenadeLauncher.

Step 17: Bring Ellen_Gun and Ellen_GrenadeLauncher out into the scene for inspection (Figure 14.10). Just drag them from the Project window into the Scene window.

Step 18: Rebuild the materials. In the Materials folder should be Grenade Launcher_1k, Grenade_launcher1k1, and some mode_Body materials. These are the materials for the newly imported assets. Plug the Textures (Base Map, Mask Map,

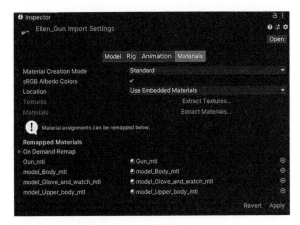

FIGURE 14.9 Extracting the materials for Ellen_Gun.

FIGURE 14.10 In order to see adjustments to materials, bring the two files out into the scene.

and Normal Map (that you've marked as Normal)) into their respective channels. This can take just a little time as some of the Texture files have some long names as output by Substance Painter.

Why?

It is likely that some of these shaders will need to be adjusted once the game is going. If desired, play with the Materials a bit as they are being built. Don't be afraid to experiment (try turning the Metallic slider up for the guns for instance) to get the look more like you'd like. In general though, for now, the output from Substance Painter will be a great baseline.

Step 19: Delete Ellen_Gun and Ellen_GrenadeLauncher from the Hierarchy (importantly: don't delete them from the Project window).

Why?

It was important to see these in the scene with the current lighting scheme; however, as we start building in the mechanics of the coding, this will most effectively happen in a new scene.

Step 20: Create a new scene. Create a floor from a plane. Adjust the Directional Light intensity to around 500 Lux (or to taste).

Step 21: Place FPSController into the scene. Also be sure to delete Main Camera.

Step 22: Drag Ellen_Gun from the Project into the Scene window and make it a child of FirstPersonCharacter (the camera and child of FPSController). Select Ellen_Gun in the Hierarchy and move it around so that the gun is about where it should be for a first-person-shooter game. We settled at X: 0.15 and Y: –1.5 (the Transform Position values in the Inspector). It will still look a bit odd in the Game window (Figure 14.11).

Why?

Exactly where this should appear is up to preference. But we prefer the gun to not take up too much space in the

FIGURE 14.11 Even with an adjusted positioning, there's still something disconcerting about those weird hands.

FIGURE 14.12 The Near Clipping Plane (highlighted) indicates the distance that the Unity camera begins drawing geometry. Any geometry (like the arms) that are close than this are "culled" or left out and not drawn.

game view. Thus we've got it not only slid down, but off to the side.

The weirdness in the hands is because of the Near Clipping Plane of the camera. Figure 14.12 shows the camera (FirstPersonCharacter) selected. Notice the highlighted plane. This represents the Near Clipping Plane. This means Unity will not draw any polygons nearer than that plane.

> *Step 23: Reduce the Near Clipping Plane to allow the player to see the hands. Select FirstPersonCharacter in Hierarchy (this is the camera), and in the Inspector expand the General section and change the Clipping Planes Near: 0.1. Things should look much better in the Game window now.*

Importing and Adjusting Animation Rigs

As covered before, a "rig" is a collection of joints or handles that allows the animator to deform a mesh. In Unity, this will be an important thing to define as it also allows the developer a tool with which to control what

FIGURE 14.13 Creating an Avatar for the imported rig. This avatar will allow us to control the animations.

animations play when. The setup is not hard, but also not intuitive. A few times through, and it will become like second nature.

> *Step 24: Create an Avatar for Ellen_Gun. In the Project window, select the imported fbx of Ellen_Gun. In the Inspector window, click the Rig tab. Change Avatar Definition: Create From This Model. Hit Apply (Figure 14.13).*

Why?

Just by way of explanation, in the Project window, expand Ellen_Gun. There, among the children will be something similar to Figure 14.14. This is the newly created Avatar. There's much more to be done with this as we go.

Animations in Unity

There are several ways to work with Animations in Unity. Each animation can be brought in as a separate asset (which we will do later for the AI), or they can all come in as one file – which is what is happening here. The fbx Ellen_Gun actually has several animations that we need to break up into Animation Clips. Currently, there is just one ("Take 001") that can be seen in Figure 14.14. But with a bit of work in the Import settings, this can be broken down into its constituent animation parts.

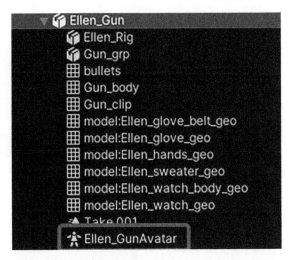

FIGURE 14.14 The newly created Avatar.

Step 25: Create the idle animation clip. Select Ellen_ Gun in the Project window and in the Inspector, click the Animation tab. Rename Take 001 to "idle_anim". Scroll a little ways down and enter Start: 0 and End: 120. Finally, click on the Loop Time check box (Figure 14.15).

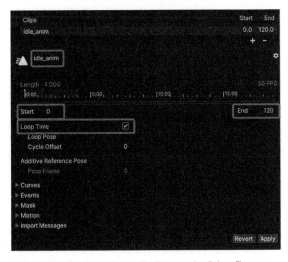

FIGURE 14.15 Defining and Animation Clip. This one is the idle loop. The exact frames came from the animator.

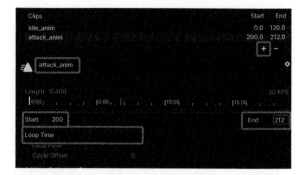

FIGURE 14.16 Creating attack_anim Animation Clip.

Clips	Start	End
idle_anim	0.0	120.0
attack_anim	200.0	212.0
walk_anim	300.0	331.0
got_Caught_anim	400.0	426.0
reload_anim	500.0	564.0
+ –		

FIGURE 14.17 Imported Animation Clips.

Step 26: Add a new attack animation clip. Still in the Inspector, under the Clips area, click the + button to add a new Animation Clip. Rename it "attack_anim", change the range from 200 to 212 (Start: 200, End: 212). Leave Loop Time off on this one as the player will click the mouse each time they plan to fire (Figure 14.16).

Step 27: Add walk, gotCaught, and reload animation clips. "walk_anim" should have a range of frames 300–331 and should be looped. "gotCaught_anim" should have a range of 400–426 and not loop. "reload_anim" should have range of 500–564 and not loop (Figure 14.17). Finally hit Apply.

Controlling Animations

Unity's Animator mechanism is a combination of visual graph-making and coding. The core idea is that we will create an Animator Controller (to control the animations, you see), and then within this controller the developer can establish states (which are really animations) and transitions that define when to move between the states.

A little bit of coding allows the player to trigger the transitions between states.

> Step 28: Create an Animator Controller. In the Project window, click the + button and choose Animator Controller. Rename it "EllenGunController".
>
> Step 29: Plug the Animator Controller into Ellen_Gun's Animator. Then in the Hierarchy, select Ellen_Gun (should be a child of FirstPersonCharacter). From the Project window, drag EllenGunController into the Inspector window into the Controller input field (Figure 14.18).
>
> Step 30: Double click to open the EllenGunController. This can be done by double clicking it in the Project window or in the Inspector. The Animator window will appear (Figure 14.19).

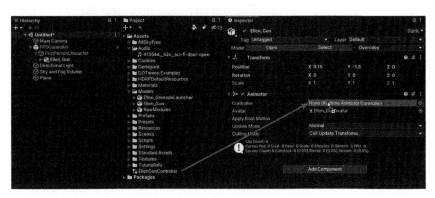

FIGURE 14.18 Plugging in the EllenGunController into the Ellen_Gun Animator.

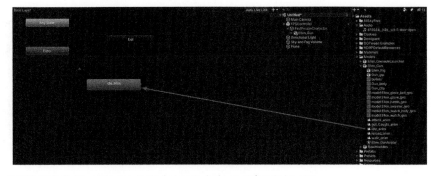

FIGURE 14.19 Placing an animation clip into the Animator by dragging it from the Inspector.

Step 31: Set idle_anim to be the default animation state. First find the animation clips in the Project window. They will be inside the Ellen_Gun fbx (just expand it to expose it). Drag it from the Project window into the Animator to place it.

Why?

A lot happens here all of the sudden. "idle_anim" is represented as a state within the Animator, and since it is the first state a transition (orange arrow) is created between the Entry node and this new idle_anim state. This means, "upon entry (when we first see the thing this Animator is attached to), transition directly to idle_anim (play that animation)." Since idle_anim was marked with Loop Time (back in the Import settings of the Inpector), and since there is no transition *out* of idle_anim, it will keep looping idle_anim.

Play the game and give it a look.

Step 32: Create an attack_anim state and a Trigger to tell it when to fire. First drag attack_anim from the Project window into the Animator window. Then in the far left panel of the Animator, click the Parameters tab. Finally, click the + button in the Parameters window and choose Trigger. Rename the trigger "attack" (Figure 14.20).
Step 33: Create a transition from Any State to attack_anim. Right click on Any State and choose Make Transition. Move the mouse down and click on attack_anim to complete the transition (Figure 14.21).

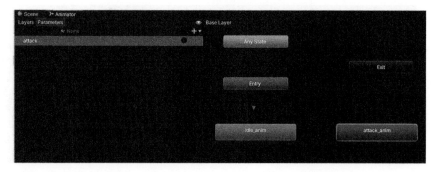

FIGURE 14.20 Bringing in the attack_anim from the Inspector, and then building a trigger named attack.

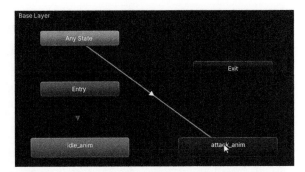

FIGURE 14.21 Creating a transition from Any State to attack_anim.

Why?

Here we are setting up a pathway so that the animator, from any place in the chart we're building, can move into attack_anim. We need to make sure the pathway only happens when the "attack" trigger has been triggered though.

> *Step 34: Establish the parameters that allow the animation to move into attack_anim. Click on the transition arrow between Any State and attack_anim. This transition will appear in the inspector. First, expand Settings and change Transition Duration: 0. Then in Conditions, click the +button (Figure 14.22).*

Why?

Change the Transition Duration to 0 means don't build in any transition from whatever animation its playing and the attack_anim. When the player presses the fire button, the fire animation should play right away.

By clicking the +button in the Conditions area, we are defining what needs to happen to move into this transition. Currently, there is only one parameter (the trigger "attack") so it appears there. When attack is triggered, Animator will move from whatever state it is in to attack_anim (and we'll see it fire the gun).

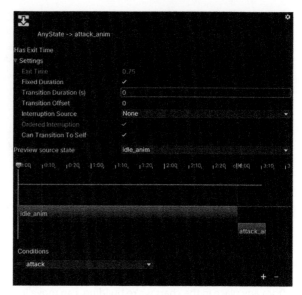

FIGURE 14.22 Defining the transition between Any State and attack_anim.

> *Step 35: Create a transition out of attack_anim back into idle_anim. Right click on attack_anim (Make Transition) and drag to idle_anim.*

Why?

We'll adjust this later, but for now, it means "when attack_anim is done, move on over to idle_anim".

Controlling Animator with Code

The Animator is a component like Transform, and any other script. The way to access the component is with GetComponent<NameOfComponent>(). Once a script is knows who the Animator is, it can swap Booleans or fire triggers. Now we need to start building the script that listens for input from the player, and based on that input changes parameters within the Animator.

> *Step 36: Create a new script called "PlayerControlsScript". Do this in the Scripts folder and then open the script in Visual Studio.*

```
void Update()
{
    if (Input.GetButtonDown("Fire1"))
    {
        print("pew pew");|
    }
}
```

FIGURE 14.23 Having Unity listen (every frame) to see if the player presses the Fire1 button.

> Step 37: Have the script listen for input. In the Update() function, enter the code shown in Figure 14.23. Save and return to Unity.

Why?

In C#, if statements take a particular form. In pseudocode:

```
if(this is true)
{
    Do This Work;
}
```

In this case, the things Unity is check is true is whether or not someone is pushing the button Fire1 down. If this is true, Unity will print "pew pew" to the console.

Input has a few different ways of working. GetButtonDown means that "on the frame that this button is pressed" (as opposed to GetButton (which keeps firing every frame the button is held down), or GetButtonUp (which fires when the button is released)). The name of these buttons (i.e. Fire1) can be found in Edit>Project Settings in the Input Manager (Figure 14.24). Using button names like this means we can write the code once and Fire1 will mean left-mouse button if someone is playing on a PC, but could be right-trigger if they were playing on a console. It's one of the powers of Unity's develop-once-deploy-everywhere strategy. It is important to note that we are listening for buttons by *name*, so Fire1 needs to appear exactly as it does in the Input Manager (capital F, no space, number 1).

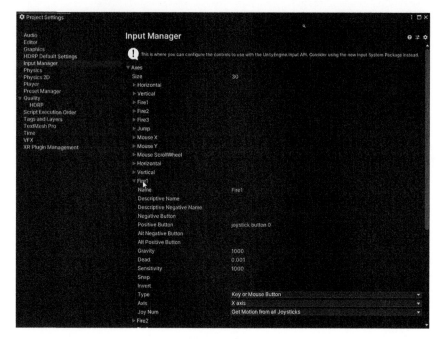

FIGURE 14.24 Input Manager where the button named Fire1 is defined.

Step 38: Test to see if Unity is hearing the input. Drag PlayerControlScript from the project and drop it onto FPSController. Play the game and press the left-mouse button to fire. The Console should show "pew pew" each time you press the left-mouse button (Fire1).

Step 39: Make the PlayerControlScript aware of Ellen_Gun and its Animator. Create a private variable to store ellenGun and another private variable to store the Animator component on ellenGun. Using the Awake() function, populate ellenGun by finding the object named "Ellen_Gun". Then, populate the variable ellenGunAnimator by finding the component on ellenGun that is of type "Animator" (Figure 14.25).

Why?

What this does is create two buckets and fills those buckets with the GameObject Ellen_Gun and its Animator component. From here on out, when we need

```
public class PlayerControlScript : MonoBehaviour
{
    private GameObject ellenGun;
    private Animator ellenGunAnimator;

    private void Awake()
    {
        ellenGun = transform.Find("FirstPersonCharacter/Ellen_Gun").gameObject;
        ellenGunAnimator = ellenGun.GetComponent<Animator>();
    }
}
```

FIGURE 14.25 Creating and populating variables so that PlayerControlScript knows who Ellen_Gun is and where its Animator component is.

```
void Update()
{
    if (Input.GetButtonDown("Fire1"))
    {
        ellenGunAnimator.SetTrigger("attack");
    }
}
```

FIGURE 14.26 Triggering the attack trigger in the Animator attached to Ellen_Gun.

to talk to Ellen_Gun's animator component, we just use ellenGunAnimator and the script knows where it is.

> Step 40: Fire the attack trigger. Replace the print line with that seen in Figure 14.26. Save and return to Unity.

Why?

Triggers fire once and then reset (at least that's what they're supposed to do). So, SetTrigger("attack") will fire the attack trigger in the Animator, which will transition from Any State into the attack_anim state. The Animator is then set so that when the attack_anim is done, it automatically goes back to idle_anim.

> Step 41: Compile and test. Back in Unity, play the game. When the left-mouse button is pressed, the attack animation will play.
> Step 42: Create a Boolean for isWalking. Go back into the EllenGunAnimator (either click on the Animator tab at the top left of the interface or double click the

FIGURE 14.27 Creating an isWalking and isIdling boolean within the Animator.

EllenGunController in the Project or Hierarchy).
In the Parameters area, click the + and add
a boolean. Name it "isWalking" repeat for
"isIdling" (Figure 14.27).

Why?

Booleans will work a bit different than Triggers in
the Animator. While Triggers do just that – they
trigger something to happen – a boolean is keeping
track of a *state of being*. For instance, when the player
fires their weapon, the Animator can then check to
see if the character is idling or moving. If moving, play
the walk animations, if idling, play the idle animation.
In the Animator, these Booleans will be used when to
shift between states. Later, in script, these Booleans
will be turned on and off depending on the player's
inputs.

Step 43: Bring in walk_anim (from Project window
into Animator) and create a transition from both
idle_anim and attack_anim to it (Figure 14.28).
Step 44: Define the transition between idle_anim
and walk_anim. Select the transition arrow and
in the inspector turn off Has Exit Time. Add a
Condition so that isWalking: true (Figure 14.29).

Why?

Has Exit Time means the animation must complete before
transitioning. When moving from idle to walk, we don't
want to wait until the idle completes – when the user
starts moving, we should immediately start playing the

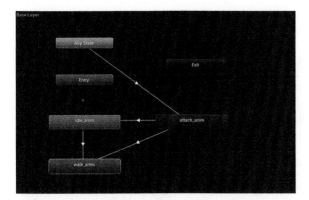

FIGURE 14.28 Creating pathways from attack_anim and idle_anim to get to walk_anim.

FIGURE 14.29 Transition settings from idle_anim to walk_anim. Notice no Exit time and new isWalking condition.

walking animation. Turning Has Exit Time off makes the transition immediate.

Adding the isWalking Boolean to the Conditions means that when isWalking is marked as true then we will activate this transition.

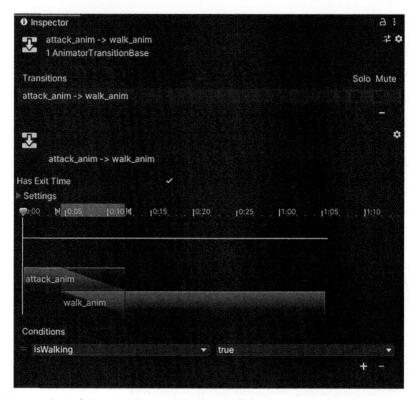

FIGURE 14.30 Settings for the transition between attack_anim and walk_anim.

Step 45: Define transition between attack_anim and walk_anim. Similar to the last, but Has Exit Time needs to remain checked (Figure 14.30).

Why?

In this case, it will be important for the attack animation to complete; thus, Has Exit Time remains checked. It is important to remember to set up the isWalking Boolean set to true as the condition that must be met to move from attack_anim to walk_anim.

Step 46: Define transition between attack_anim and idle anim. Identical to the last step except the condition that must be met is the Boolean isIdling must be true (Figure 14.31).

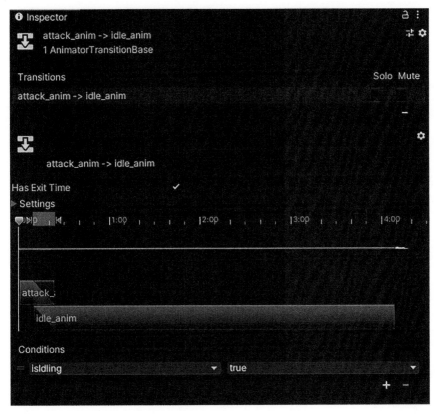

FIGURE 14.31 Defining the situation in which to move from attack_anim to idle_anim.

Step 47: Create and define how to get from walk_
anim, back to idle_anim. Right click on walk_
anim (Make Transition) and drag to idle_anim.
Edit the transition to not have an exit time and
Conditions have isIdling to true (Figure 14.32).

Step 48: Listen for input in the code, and switch
the Booleans accordingly. Within the Update()
function, add the lines highlighted in
Figure 14.33. Save and return to Unity.

Why?

The "||" means "or". Alternatively "&&" means "and". This
code means: "if the player presses (and holds) the buttons
Vertical or Horizontal, then go to the ellenGunAnimator

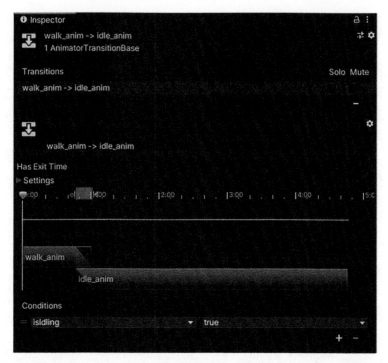

FIGURE 14.32 Transition between walk_anim and idle_anim. No Exit Time and isIdling being true as the Condition that must be met.

```
void Update()
{
    if (Input.GetButtonDown("Fire1"))
    {
        ellenGunAnimator.SetTrigger("attack");
    }

    if (Input.GetButton("Vertical") || Input.GetButton("Horizontal"))
    {
        ellenGunAnimator.SetBool("isWalking", true);
        ellenGunAnimator.SetBool("isIdling", false);
    }
    else
    {
        ellenGunAnimator.SetBool("isWalking", false);
        ellenGunAnimator.SetBool("isIdling", true);
    }
}
```

FIGURE 14.33 Turning Booleans on and off by listening for the buttons "Vertical" and "Horizontal".

and set the isWalking Boolean to true, and set the isIdling
to false. Otherwise (else), if the player is not pressing
Vertical or Horizontal, then set isWalking to false and
isIdling to true."

Step 49: Play and test in Unity.
Step 50: Apply the prefab overrides to FPSController.
    Select it in the Hierarchy and in the Inspector
    apply the overrides (Figure 14.34).
Step 51: Hide Ellen_Gun.
Step 52: Repeat for Ellen_GrenadeLauncher. Yes,
    that's a lot for one step. Figure 14.35 shows the
    animation ranges for Ellen_GrenadeLauncher
    (don't forget to set up the rig). Figure 14.36
    shows the script with the added variables and
    adjustments to include the Grenade Launcher
    content.
Step 53: Before testing, create a weapon swap
    control. On Start(), hide Ellen_GrenadeLauncher
    (Figure 14.37). Then in the Update(), let the user
    swap between weapons by hitting the 1 or 2
    key on their keyboard (Figure 14.38). Be sure to

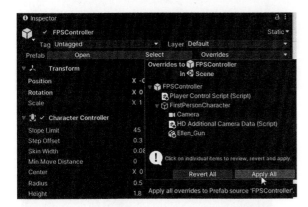

FIGURE 14.34 Applying the changes to FPSController so they will be active
everywhere FPSController is used.

Clips	Start	End
idle_anim	0.0	150.0
attack_anim	200.0	220.0
walk_anim	300.0	340.0
gotCaught_anim	400.0	428.0
reload_anim	500.0	567.0
	+	−

FIGURE 14.35 Animation ranges for Ellen_GrenadeLauncher.

```
public class PlayerControlScript : MonoBehaviour
{
    private GameObject ellenGun;
    private Animator ellenGunAnimator;
    private GameObject ellenGrenade;
    private Animator ellenGrenadeAnimator;

    private void Awake()
    {
        ellenGun = transform.Find("FirstPersonCharacter/Ellen_Gun").gameObject;
        ellenGunAnimator = ellenGun.GetComponent<Animator>();
        ellenGrenade = transform.Find("FirstPersonCharacter/Ellen_GrenadeLauncher").gameObject;
        ellenGrenadeAnimator = ellenGrenade.GetComponent<Animator>();
    }

    void Update()
    {
        if (Input.GetButtonDown("Fire1"))
        {
            ellenGunAnimator.SetTrigger("attack");
            ellenGrenadeAnimator.SetTrigger("attack");
        }

        if (Input.GetButton("Vertical") || Input.GetButton("Horizontal"))
        {
            ellenGunAnimator.SetBool("isWalking", true);
            ellenGunAnimator.SetBool("isIdling", false);

            ellenGrenadeAnimator.SetBool("isWalking", true);
            ellenGrenadeAnimator.SetBool("isIdling", false);
        }
        else
        {
            ellenGunAnimator.SetBool("isWalking", false);
            ellenGunAnimator.SetBool("isIdling", true);

            ellenGrenadeAnimator.SetBool("isWalking", false);
            ellenGrenadeAnimator.SetBool("isIdling", true);
        }
    }
}
```

FIGURE 14.36 Updated script.

```
private void Awake()
{
    ellenGun = transform.Find("FirstPersonCh
    ellenGunAnimator = ellenGun.GetComponent
    ellenGrenade = transform.Find("FirstPers
    ellenGrenadeAnimator = ellenGrenade.GetC
}

private void Start()
{
    ellenGrenade.SetActive(false);
}

void Update()
{
```

FIGURE 14.37 Turning off the Ellen_GrenadeLauncher when the game starts.

```
void Update()
{
    if (Input.GetKeyDown(KeyCode.Alpha1))
    {
        ellenGun.SetActive(true);
        ellenGrenade.SetActive(false);
    }
    if (Input.GetKeyDown(KeyCode.Alpha2))
    {
        ellenGun.SetActive(false);
        ellenGrenade.SetActive(true);
    }
```

FIGURE 14.38 Swapping between the weapons.

> *reactivate Ellen_Gun in the Hierarchy/Inspector*
> *before testing.*
> *Step 53: Don't forget to apply the changes to the*
> *prefab*

Tutorial Conclusion

And with that we've used code to control different animation clips by listening for user input. There's loads more that can be done with these techniques, and in fact, there are multiple animation still unused. But once the core idea of the Animator and firing triggers or flipping Booleans in the Animator with script is understood, any animation can be played when the developer wants it.

We'll be back to work with these weapons much, much more. They still need to actually fire. But for now, we'll leave them along and start to build some hazards in the game. Namely, in the next chapter, we will look at an idea called Raycasting and use it to create cameras that will be on the lookout for the player. If the player is spotted, the game will be over!

CHAPTER 15

Raycasting and Render Textures

In this chapter, we will be covering two areas that are disparate and seemingly unrelated. And, indeed, in coding terms there is not much that ties these two together. However, both will be used in a core mechanic of our game: the security cameras.

As the player attempts to escape the facility, dodging or taking out AI (artificial intelligence) along the way to the boss, she will also need to avoid cameras placed throughout the hallways and rooms. Although the cameras can be shot and taken offline, if they see the player, the game is over. The process of Raytracing is how we will determine if a camera can see a player or not.

To aid the player, the view of the security camera will be visible on several monitors throughout the facility. This will allow the player to plan their path and try to identify where the cameras might be placed. In order for the player to see what the camera sees, we will be using Render Textures to render a camera's view to a texture. Along the way, we'll go back and visit some other shader types that we skipped up to now. So, this chapter will have a bit of something for coders and technical artists.

The process will go like this: first we'll organize the hierarchy for the geometry to aid in movement. Second, we'll get acquainted with Unity's animation system. Then we'll build a Raycasting mechanism into the camera so that it can tell us what it "sees." We'll add a spotlight so the player has a hint as to where the camera is looking. And finally, we'll make sure that monitors in the facility render what these security cameras see.

Tutorial 15.1: Animating the Camera

There are actually several ways to tackle this part. In earlier chapters, we made the doors move using DOTween, and we could do that here as well. However, using Unity's animation tools we can have much more control over the animation, its timing, how it eases in and out of keyframes, and a host of other animation-centric areas. Since we haven't done any animation in Unity yet, we'll tackle this challenge this way.

> Step 1: Organize the hierarchy for the security_cam. In the Project window, track down the security_cam prefab (probably Prefabs>Props). Double click the prefab to open it in the prefab editor. Organize the hierarchy to match Figure 15.1.

Why?

You may have already organized the geometry when modeling it way back in Chapter 1. But the focus back then was on form and topology, not on organizing

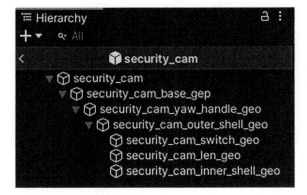

FIGURE 15.1 security_cam organized for animation.

for animation. Since we are animating in Unity, organizing is a simple thing to do. The organization shown in Figure 15.1 shows one in which when the security_cam_yaw_handle_geo is rotated along the Y-Axis it rotates everything except the base. And then security_cam_outer_shell_geo will allow us to control how the camera looks up and down (along its X-axis).

> *Step 2: Create a new level and place the security_cam anywhere in it. The security_cam can also be placed in any of the previous test scenes made for other levels. We just need it in a scene that isn't the MainLevel for quick testing.*
>
> *Step 3: Start creating animation clips. Do this by selecting security_cam in the Hierarchy and choosing Window>Animation>Animation.*
>
> *Step 4: Create an Animator and Animation Clip. In the middle of the Animation window is a hint that says, "To begin animating security_cam, create an Animator and an Animation Clip" with a Create button. Click it (Figure 15.2).*
>
> *Step 5: Save an Animation clip named securityCam180_anim. After hitting the Create button in the Animation window, Unity will ask you where to save the anim file. Create a new folder called "Animations" (which will be in the Assets folder of the Unity project), then name the anim file securityCam_anim and save.*

FIGURE 15.2 Animation window with limited functionality. However, after creating an Animator and Animation Clip, much will become possible.

Why?

Organization is important. Always. Taking a moment to save animations in an Animations folder makes sure there are no assets just floating around the Assets folder.

An anim file is really an animation clip that is generated by Unity. We've brought in animation clips from Maya in the last chapter, and we looked at how to fire them in the Animator. We will do that here as well, but instead of doing the animation in Maya and importing the clip, we'll create the clip within Unity.

Finally, what's up with the name? There will be places in the level where the camera will need to sweep 180 degrees (which is what we're animating here) where a camera is posted on a wall in a hall. However, if a camera were stuck in the corner of a room, it should only rotate 90 degrees. The idea here is that we will create animation clips for both situations, and then attach the one needed for each situation.

> *Step 6: Add an animation Property to rotate the security_cam_yaw_handle_geo. On the left part of the Animation window is a button called Add Property. Click it and then start expanding security_cam_base_geo and then security_cam_yaw_handle_geo. Finally, expand the Transform (that is a child of security_cam_yaw_handle_geo) and click the +button next to Rotation (Figure 15.3). The result is shown in Figure 15.4.*

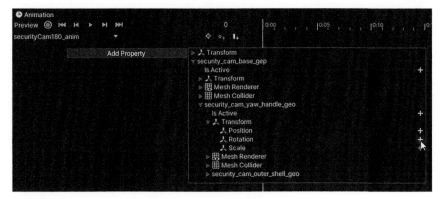

FIGURE 15.3 Adding a Rotation property for security_cam_yaw_handle_geo.

FIGURE 15.4 Results show the Property in the Animation window and a keyframe (little gray diamond) at frames 0:00 and 1:00.

Why?

When Unity creates a property, it creates two keyframe (gray diamonds) as well. Arbitrarily, Unity creates them at 0 seconds and 1 second. Notice that the time unit in Unity is 60fps. So 0:40 is 0 seconds and 40 frames into the animation. 60 frames is 1 second. To make this work, we'll edit the keyframes Unity creates by default and add some more.

> *Step 7: Enable Recording mode to edit keyframes. In the top left corner of the Animation window (Figure 15.5) is the Enable Recording Mode button. When clicking the top of the Animation window, it turns red. The current time marker in Unity is the long white line.*

FIGURE 15.5 Enabling recording mode.

FIGURE 15.6 Using the Go To Next Keyframe button is a quick way to get to the next spot in the timeline that we need to overwrite.

Step 8: Record over the first keyframe with a Rotation Y: −90 value. Leave the current time marker at 0:00 (where there already is a keyframe) and, in the Hierarchy, select security_cam_yaw_handle_ geo. In the Inspector, the Rotations X, Y, and Z should all be highlighted red (the areas we're recording). Enter −90 in the Rotation Y. This will automatically overwrite the keyframe at 0:00.

Step 9: Record over the keyframe at 1:00 with a Rotation Y: 90 value. At the top of the Animation window, click on the Go To Next Keyframe button (Figure 15.6). The current time marker will jump to 1:00. In the Inspector (with security_cam_ yaw_handle_geo still selected), enter Rotation Y: 90. This will overwrite the key at 1:00.

Why?

In the Animation window, hit the Play button at the top left. Unity will play a much-too-fast animation of the camera swinging from −90 to 90 in Y. We're not worried about timing quite yet, just getting the values in.

Step 10: Adjust the timing. In the Animation window, Alt-Right-Click and drag to zoom out in time. This will show more seconds/frames. Click on the keyframe at 1:00 and move it to 8:00. Adjust if you feel it's too fast or slow.

Step 11: Add a keyframe at 9:00 to keep the camera still for a second. Move the current time marker

FIGURE 15.7 Add a Keyframe Button. Adding a keyframe this way later than an extant keyframe will pause the animation.

to 9:00 and click the Add Keyframe button (Figure 15.7). This will create another keyframe a second after the last so that the camera pauses.

Step 12: Add another Rotation Y: −90 keyframe at 17:00. Zoom out to make sure you can see 17:00. Move the current time marker to 17:00 and then (making sure security_cam_yaw_handle_geo is selected in the Hierarchy), in the Inspector enter Rotation Y: −90.

Step 13: Add another keyframe at 18:00. Move the current time marker to 18:00 and click the Add Keyframe button.

Why?

The last two steps are making sure that (1) the animation loops because the first and last keyframe are the same (Rotation Y: −90) and making sure that there is a second's pause as the camera reaches its widest part.

The general pacing can be seen in Figure 15.8. If the movement is too slow or fast, it is easy to grab hold of the keyframes and move them closer together (to make things faster) or further apart from each other (to slow things down). Adjust if desired.

FIGURE 15.8 Final animation for securityCam180_anim.

FIGURE 15.9 Creating a new clip within the Animation window.

> Step 14: Create a new clip: securityCam90_anim. In the Animation window, the top left corner will display the name of the current animation clip. Click on that and from the drop-down menu select Create New Clip… (Figure 15.9). Navigate to your Animations folder and save this new clip as "securityCam90_anim".

Why?

This will be the animation clip that rotates only 90 degrees (for when a camera is placed in a corner). Although we could come back and make this animation clip anytime we needed to, doing it now while we're already in the tool will save time.

> Step 15: Repeat Steps 6–13. Remember: Add Property to security_cam_yaw_handle_geo for Rotation. Make sure keyframe recoding is on. With security_cam_yaw_handle_geo selected in the Hierarchy, use −45 as the first Rotation Y keyframe. Use 45 for the second. Adjust timing (we used 4:00 since it rotates half the distance) and add the extra keyframe to pause the movement. The Animation window should look fairly similar to the previous animation clip, only with slightly different timing. The animation that plays should show the camera moving 90 degrees (from −45 to 45 and back again) (Figure 15.10).

FIGURE 15.10 Finished Animation for securityCam180_anim.

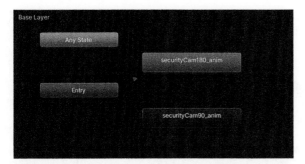

FIGURE 15.11 The current state of security_cam Animator Controller.

FIGURE 15.12 Setting a new default empty state.

> *Step 16: Close the Animation window.*
> *Step 17: Apply the Prefabs Overrides to security_cam.*
> *Step 18: Set up the security_cam Animator Controller. In Hierarchy, select security_cam, and then in the Inspector in the Animator section under Controller double-click security_cam (I know the naming is awkward here by Unity's default). This will open the Animator window (Figure 15.11).*
> *Step 19: Create a new empty default state. In the Base Layer part of the Animator window, right click on any empty space and choose Create State>Empty. Right click on this new New State icon and choose Set As Layer Default State (Figure 15.12).*

Why?

Setting up this empty state and then making it the default eans that there is no default animation that plays. The camera is still by default. This will allow us to place a camera without animation if it helps the game play.

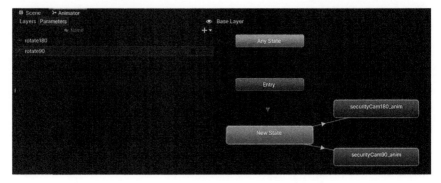

FIGURE 15.13 Setting up transitions from the default (still) New State to the two animation states.

Step 20: Create two Booleans and create transitions that use them for a rotate180 and rotate90 (Figure 15.13). Not shown in the screenshot (but covered in the last chapter) are the steps of selecting each of the transitions and making sure to add Conditions (rotate180 to Tru for the New State>securityCam180_anim transition and rotate90 to True for the New State>securityCam90 transition).

Step 21: Create a CameraAnimationChooserScript. Remember to create this script in the Scripts folder. The script is shown in Figure 15.14. Save and return to Unity.

```
public class CameraAnimationChooserScript : MonoBehaviour
{
    public enum CamAnim {Still, Hallway, Corner}
    public CamAnim camAnim;

    Animator myAnimator;

    private void Awake()
    {
        myAnimator = GetComponent<Animator>();
    }

    void Start()
    {
        if(camAnim == CamAnim.Hallway)
        {
            myAnimator.SetBool("rotate180", true);
        }

        if (camAnim == CamAnim.Corner)
        {
            myAnimator.SetBool("rotate90", true);
        }
    }
}
```

FIGURE 15.14 CameraAnimationChooserScript.

Why?

Much of this script should look pretty familiar. It creates a variable (called myAnimator) that stores the Animator component. In the Awake(), we populate that variable. And then in the Start(), we set the Booleans created in earlier steps.

The new thing is this "enum." Enumerators and enums are more than we want to cover at any great extent here, but for our purposes, that way it is set up will allow for a drop-down menu in the Inspector with Still, Hallway, and Corner as the choices. Then, depending on what is chosen, on Start(), this script will go and flip the appropriate Booleans in the Animator Controller.

> Step 22: Add this script to security_cam. Do this by dragging the script from the Inspector to the security_cam in the Scene window or (if its selected) in the Inspector. When applied, it should look like Figure 15.15.

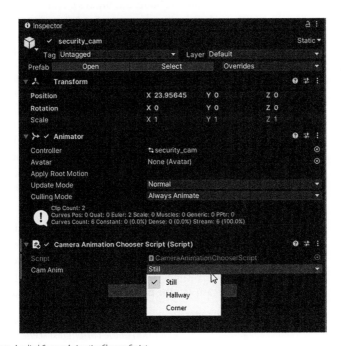

FIGURE 15.15 Applied CameraAnimationChooserScript.

Step 23: Apply the Prefab Overrides. We want every camera we place to have this script, the Animator, and the Animator Controller attached to it.

Tutorial Conclusion

And with that we have a customizable animated camera. It still can't "see" the player, doesn't have a spotlight, and doesn't render to a monitor, but we'll solve that soon.

Tutorial 15.2: Raycasting

Raycasting can be an abstract concept for beginning coders, but it is of immense use. Unity's API describes Physics.Raycast as "Casts a ray, from point *origin*, in direction *direction*, of length *maxDistance*, against all colliders in the Scene." In our vernacular, this means, "Unity shoots an invisible line (ray) out from some point you define. It shoots this ray in a direction you define and for the distance you define." The other thing that is important about Raycasting is that it can store information about what it hits in a thing called a RaycastHit.

This can become useful for supersonic weapons (weapons where the bullet moves faster than the player would see). When the player fires, raycasting would send a ray out of the front of the gun and tell the engine, "I've shot forward until I hit the wall/bad guy/floor/whatever." Then, Unity, depending on what was hit, could make some decisions and put a bullet hole decal on the wall, or take health away from the bad guy. These "smart lines" that are rays can be used to build all sorts of interaction.

In this case, Raycasting will be used to determine if the camera "sees" the player. We will raycast out of the front of the camera and store whatever the ray hits into a RaycastHit variable. The script will check to see if the thing inside of RaycastHit is the player, and if it is, the player loses.

Step 1: Create a scene to test. This can just be an extension of the current test scene, and the specifics are unimportant. Just give the space

*some walls (mine are built from cubes) and a few
other 3D shapes scattered through the space. Be
sure to also put FPSController in there and delete
Main Camera (Figure 15.16).*

Step 2: Create a Raycast source point. *Create a
new empty GameObject (GameObject>Create
Empty). Make it a child of security_cam_outer_
shell_geo and in the Inspector make Positions X,
Y, and Z and Rotations X, Y, and Z all 0. Rename it
"RaycastSource". In Scene window, move it only
along the Z axis so that it sits just in front of the
lens (Figure 15.17).*

FIGURE 15.16 A playground in which to build the Raycasting mechanism.

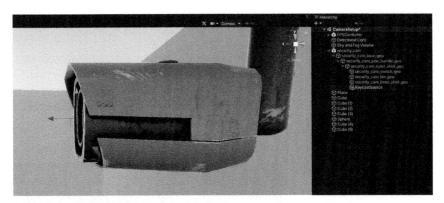

FIGURE 15.17 RaycastSource is a child of the security_cam_outer_shell_geo. Note that in 3D space, RaycastSource is moved just in front of the lens.

Why?

By making this empty GameObject a child of the shell, when the camera rotates, this will rotate with it. By putting it in front of the lens, we ensure that the ray that will be cast from this object doesn't get stopped by the camera itself.

> *Step 3: Create a new script called CameraRaycastingScript. Attach the script to the security_cam in the Hierarchy.*

Why?

This script could be attached to a lot of things and, in fact, would make the code a little easier if it were attached to RaycastSource. However, the idea here to not hide scripts in places that are tough to remember where they are attached. Since security_cam already has the CameraAnimationChooseScript, putting this script on the same object keeps the camera-centric scripts consolidated.

> *Step 4: Create a public variable called "scSrc" that stores a GameObject. Add the code shown in Figure 15.18. For now, also delete the empty Start() and Update() functions. Save and return to Unity.*

Why?

Up to now, we've generally been working with private variables and populating them via script. In this case, we'll make the variable public and define its content in the Unity editor. rcSrc will store the RaycastSource GameObject just created.

```
public class CameraRaycastingScript : MonoBehaviour
{
    public GameObject rcSrc;
```

FIGURE 15.18 Creating a public variable named rcSrc to store a GameObject.

```
private void Update()
{
    RaycastHit thingHit;
    Physics.Raycast(rcSrc.transform.position, rcSrc.transform.TransformDirection(Vector3.forward), out thingHit);
    Debug.DrawLine(rcSrc.transform.position, thingHit.point, Color.yellow);
}
```

FIGURE 15.19 The basic mechanics of a Raycast (plus a little pizzazz with the DrawLine so we can see the ray).

> *Step 5: Populate the new rcSrc variable. In Hierarchy, select security_cam. In the Inspector, the CameraRaycastingScript should have a new public variable called "Rc Src" with an input field next to it. From the Hierarchy, drag the newly created RaycastSource GameObject into the Rc Src input field in the Inspector. From now on, in the code whenever we reference "rcSrc," Unity will know we mean the RaycastSource GameObject.*
>
> *Step 6: Create the basic Raycasting mechanism. Figure 15.19 shows the core mechanics of the Raycasting mechanism within the Update() function. Include this in the code. Save and return to Unity.*

Why?

In this case, every frame needs to be reporting what the camera sees. Therefore, we put it in an Update() function.

The first line:

```
RaycastHit thingHit;
```

...creates a variable (a bucket) called thingHit that stores things of type RaycastHit. This is where the Raycast will report the things it has struck.

The next line:

```
Physics.Raycast(rcSrc.transform.
position, rcSrc.
TransformDirection(Vector3.forward),
out thingHit);
```

...says, "Cast a ray. Have it start from RaycastSource's position (rcSrc.transform.position), in the direction RaycastSource is pointing (rcSrc.TransformDirection(Vector3.

547

forward)), and store what it hits in the thingHit bucket (out thingHit)."

Finally, the last line draws a yellow line (only visible in the Scene view) that starts where the RaycastSource is and ends when the ray hits something.

> Step 7: Play the game. Tada! A yellow line which just shows the path the ray is following (Figure 15.20).
> Step 8: Have the RaycastHit report back on what it's hit. Add the line shown in Figure 15.21. This will output to the Console the GameObjects that the Raycast hits.
> Step 9: Play the game and watch the Console (Figure 15.22).
> Step 10: Customize the camera. Select the security_cam_outer_shell_geo object in the Hierarchy. Rotate it down so that it looks down into the scene (this will rotate all its children as well – including the RaycastSource). Select security_cam, and in the CameraAnimationChooserScript, use the Cam Anim to change to Hallway.

FIGURE 15.20 The LineDraw allows the developer to see the path the Raycast takes. Notice that this line is not visible in the Game window – only the Scene. It is meant only for the developer.

```
private void Update()
{
    RaycastHit thingHit;
    Physics.Raycast(rcSrc.transform.position, rcSrc.transform.TransformDirection(Vector3.forward), out thingHit);
    Debug.DrawLine(rcSrc.transform.position, thingHit.point, Color.yellow);
    Debug.Log(thingHit.collider.gameObject);
}
```

FIGURE 15.21 Adding code that reports back on what the ray casts against.

FIGURE 15.22 The console showing (every frame) what object the RaycastSource is raycasting against.

> Step 11: Play the game and watch the Console. As the camera pans across the room, the Console will change to show the GameObjects the Raycast is casting against (Figure 15.23).
>
> Step 12: Tag FPSController as Player. Select FPSController in the Hierarchy. In the Inspector, look for the Tag pulldown menu. Use it to tag FPSController as Player (Figure 15.24).

Why?

Anything can be assigned a tag. Tags can be used to classify a group of types of objects. So, we could label all the bad guys as "Enemies" so that we don't have to compare names in code but rather tags (or groups of types of objects). "Player" is a built-in tag, but custom tags can be created using Tag>Add Tag…

For now, we'll be telling the script to report back only when it has cast its ray against something tagged as Player (the player).

> Step 13: Streamline the script to only call out when the ray casts against the player. Figure 15.25 shows the altered script that has gotten rid of the original Debug.DrawLine and Debug.

549

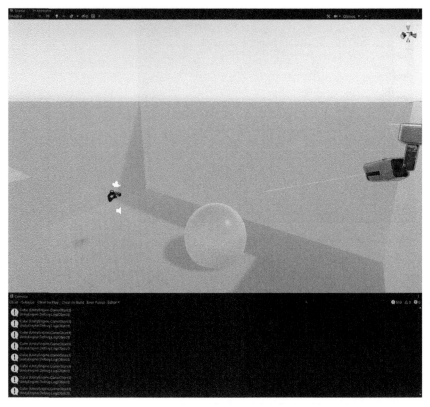

FIGURE 15.23 The animated camera in action with the Console reporting back on the various objects the ray casts against.

FIGURE 15.24 Assigning a Player tag to FPSController.

```
private void Update()
{
    RaycastHit thingHit;
    Physics.Raycast(rcSrc.transform.position, rcSrc.transform.TransformDirection(Vector3.forward), out thingHit);
    Debug.DrawLine(rcSrc.transform.position, thingHit.point, Color.yellow);

    if(thingHit.collider.gameObject.tag == "Player")
    {
        Debug.Log("I've seen the player!");
        Debug.DrawLine(rcSrc.transform.position, thingHit.point, Color.red);
    }
}
```

FIGURE 15.25 Altered script to only holler if the camera has "seen" the player.

FIGURE 15.26 A smart camera that knows when its hit the player. The line renders red and the Console calls out when the thingHit contains an object tagged as "Player".

Log lines and replaced it with a Debug.Log that calls out only if thingHit includes an object tagged as "Player" and added a line that changes the line to red. Save and return to Unity.

Step 14: Play the game and watch the Scene and Console. The line will change to red and the Console will yell every time the camera hits the player (Figure 15.26).

Step 15: Return the camera to a still camera (not animated). Remember do this by selecting security_cam and changing the CameraAnimationChooserScript's Cam Aim to Still.

Step 16: Apply All the Overrides for security_cam (Figure 15.27).

Step 17: Apply Overrides to FPSController. At this point, it just tags FPSController as Player. But this needs to be remembered in all levels.

Tutorial Conclusion

"Now wait a minute!" I hear you saying, "This is hardly a functioning game mechanic." You're right. Currently a script that writes to the Console means little to the player.

FIGURE 15.27 Applying all the changes to security_cam so everywhere it is used in scene will share the functionality. Notice that Cam Anim has been returned to Still.

We have not yet created anything that closely resembles game play. However, the scaffolding for real game play is in place. Later, after we have covered UI and loading levels, plugging in some code where currently we just have Debug.Logs will be a trivial matter. There is an animation for when the character gets caught, a sound could play, UI could show up telling the player, "You've been caught! The adventure is over!," or whatever.

Although we won't be creating these mechanisms in this book, the basics are in place. We *will* be doing a lot more with Raycasting later (when we work with weapons), so this is an introduction to those ideas. However, as you build your version of the game, consider how to leverage the Raycasting happening by the cameras to create new and interesting game play.

The core issue here is that Raycasting is in place and working. What we do with that later, well, that's yet to be seen…

Tutorial 15.3: Camera Extras

In this last tutorial for this chapter, we will add a few bells and whistles to the camera. We'll quickly add a light to the camera so the player knows where the camera's range is. And then we will look at how this "camera" (that currently is only geometry – not a Unity camera that actually "sees" anything) and raycasting can be used as a closed-circuit camera that will render what it sees to another object's texture.

To build these mechanics, stay within the test level created earlier. Later, this finished camera will be placed in the MainLevel, but for now this test level will continue to provide a lightweight sandbox to get things working.

> Step 1: Create a Spotlight. GameObject>Light>Spot Light will create the light. Make it a child of RaycastSource (in the Hierarchy, just drag it onto RaycastSource). Once a child, in the Inspector change Positions X, Y, and Z and Rotations X, Y, and Z all to 0. Add a Cookie (we used Flashlight_Cookie). Finally, adjust the Intensity and Range (we used 20 Ev100 for Intensity and 20 for Range). The results can be seen in Figure 15.28.
> Step 2: Add a camera to the security_cam. Create the camera using GameObject>Camera. Make it a child of RaycastSource and again set its Positions X, Y, and Z and Rotations X, Y, and Z to 0.
> Step 3: Adjust the settings to streamline. Change the Clipping Planes Far: 15. Turn off Audio Listener.

Why?

Adding a lot of cameras to the scene can be expensive. After all, suddenly with extra cameras Unity is drawing things more than once. To help minimize the expense,

553

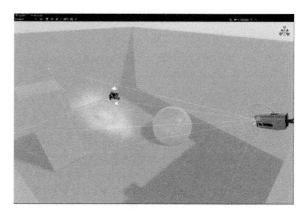

FIGURE 15.28 Adding a Spotlight to give the player a hint about where the camera can see.

making the Far Clipping plan quite small (15 meters in this case) will make sure that the camera isn't drawing too much of the level and is only drawing the walls and props that are within 15 units of it.

This camera shouldn't be listening for anything in game. That should all be happening from the player's viewpoint (the FirstPersonCharacter object is a camera and has an Audio Listener). So, turning off the Audio Listener for this camera will avoid errors.

> *Step 4: Create a Render Texture. In the Project window, create a new folder called "RenderTextures". With that folder selected, choose the + button again and create a Render Texture. Rename it to "DefaultRenderTexture".*

Why?

Render Textures are textures that show what some camera is rendering. The process here will be to make the camera render to this new DefaultRenderTexture, and then apply this DefaultRenderTexture to some material in the scene.

> *Step 5: Bring a monitor prefab into the scene. Monitor_02 is a nice shape, so this is the one we will use.*

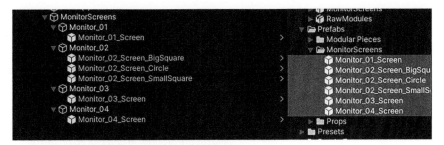

FIGURE 15.29 Extracted monitor screens made into their own prefabs.

Step 6: Import the screens (fbx) in the support files for this chapter. They are called MonitorScreens. The process will be a little bit of a review. Download the fbx from the website and drag it into the Models folder of the Unity project.

Step 7: Create prefabs of the screens. In the Project window, select MonitorScreens and in the Inspector's Material tab Extract the Materials into the Materials folder. Drag MonitorScreens into the scene. Right click it (in Hierarchy) and Unpack Prefab. Drag each of the screens from the Hierarchy to the Prefabs folder to make prefabs out of each screen. Make a new folder in Prefabs called "MonitorScreens" and put these new prefabs in it (Figure 15.29). Finally, delete MonitorScreens from the Hierarchy.

Why?

So we're cheating a little bit here. There are ways to use the current versions of the monitors and have different parts of the shader show different materials (using HDRP Layered Lit shaders). And that is a more efficient way of handling this. However, extracting the geometry of the screens in Maya (which is what the fbx in Step 6 represents) is an easier solution with what we've covered. We've included the Maya files with the screens extracted in the support files if you want to take a closer look. The basic process in Maya was as follows: 1) select the polygons of the screens, (2) edit Mesh>Extract to split the polygons off, 3) remap each screen to its own UV space so it completely filled the UV quadrants, 4) assign a separate default material to each of the screens, and 5) export the fbx.

Now that the scene has the screens as separate prefabs with their own materials, it will be easy to assign a Render Texture to them.

Step 8: Place a screen into place on the monitor chassis. Figure 15.30 shows Monitor_02_Screen_ BigSquare brought in and placed on top of Monitor_02. Remember, vertex snapping is a great way to get it started, although you might need to bring it forward just a little bit.

Step 9: Tie the security_cam camera to the DefaultRenderTexture. Find the Camera object that is the child of RaycastSource (under security_cam). In the Inspector, scroll all the way down to the Output area and expand it. In the Target Texture input field, insert the DefaultRenderTexture from the Project window (Figure 15.31).

Step 10: Use DefaultRenderTexture to define Monitor_02_Screen_BigSquare_Mat. Select the Monitor_02_Screen_BigSquare object in the Hierarchy. In the Inspector, scroll down to the Monitor_02_Screen_BigSquare_Mat section and expand it. Change the shader to HDRP/ Unlit. Finally, drag DefaultRenderTexture from the Project window into the Color slot (of Surface Inputs) for the material. To get really fancy, do the same for Emissive Color. The results should look like Figure 15.32.

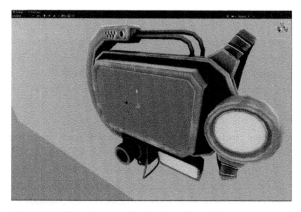

FIGURE 15.30 Placing the screen object in place on the monitor.

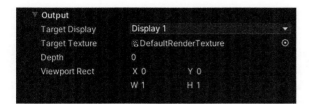

FIGURE 15.31 Making the Camera that is a child of the security_cam geometry so that it renders to the DefaultRenderTexture.

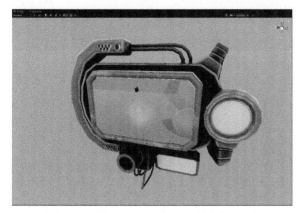

FIGURE 15.32 Using a Render Texture to define the Color attribute of the Unlit material. The screen shows what the camera sees.

Why?

The Unlit shader means that this surface won't be affected by the lights in the scene (as a screen should).

> *Step 11: Change the security_cam to rotate (using the CameraAnimationChooserScript attached to it) and Play the game. In the Scene window, you should see displayed on the monitor the animated version of what the security_cam is seeing. Cool, no?*
>
> *Step 12: Create a script to avoid unnecessary overhead. Create a new C# script and name it "CameraRTSwitchScript". Build the code shown in Figure 15.33. Save and return to Unity.*

```
public class CameraRTSwitchScript : MonoBehaviour
{
    public bool renderToTexture;
    public Camera renderToTextureCamera;

    private void Awake()
    {
        if (renderToTexture != true)
        {
            renderToTextureCamera.targetTexture = null;
            renderToTextureCamera.gameObject.SetActive(false);
        }
    }
}
```

FIGURE 15.33 Code to turn a camera off if it is not being rendered to a monitor in the scene.

Why?

This is an important step. If the game has ten cameras (an arbitrary number at this point), but only three monitors, we want to make sure that only three cameras are doing the work of rendering to a textures. Further, if a camera isn't rendering to a texture, it shouldn't be on at all. What this script does is create a public Boolean (think of this as a switch) that we can choose to turn on or off in the editor. When the game starts, each security_cam (that has this script) will check to see if the renderToTexture Boolean is true; if it is not (!= means "is not equal to"), it clears out the Target Texture attribute of the Camera and shuts it off.

> Step 13: Drag this new CameraRTSwitchScript onto the security_cam in the Hierarchy. Populate the Render To Texture Camera input by dragging the Camera (child of the RaycastSource) into it.
> Step 14: Apply all the Prefab Overrides for security_cam. The final Hierarchy and Inspector should look like Figure 15.34.
> Step 15: Return to MainLevel, place cameras throughout. Be sure to tie some of them (via new Render Textures) to monitors in the scene. Remember to change them to Still, Hallway, or Corner as indicated by their position (Figure 15.35).

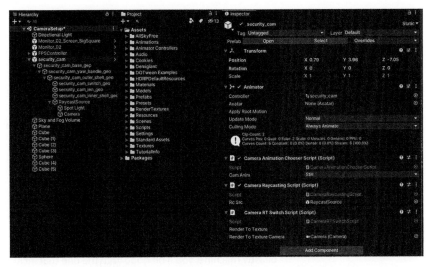

FIGURE 15.34 Final completed security_cam. This prefab is ready to be placed and configured in the scene.

FIGURE 15.35 Some placed cameras in the scene. Place as you'd like, but make sure there is at least one in the armory and none in the first room the game starts at.

> Step 16: Play test. Play the game and make sure that the new camera have not smashed the frame rate on the game. Depending on the power of your machine and video card, you could be bumping up against how much can be drawn.

559

Tips and Tricks

As of this writing, there is a known bug with Render Textures. Hopefully this will be fixed by the time you're using them, but sometimes all will look fine in the Scene view, and when playing the game, the surfaces using the Render Textures suddenly go black. While writing this chapter, sometimes all was well, and sometimes, suddenly poof!, they'd be gone. Such is the nature of bugs.

Luckily, Render Textures is not core to the game play. If it doesn't work, no worries. The game will still work fine. In fact, in the support files there are two versions of the Unity project file: one with Render Textures and one without. The overhead of the second extra cameras rendering take a toll on the frame count. If you've got a beastly machine, you'll be good with the one that includes the Render Textures. If your machine is a mere mortal, use the one without moving forward.

Conclusion

Raycasting is the key concept of this chapter. Render Textures are fun, but if Unity is being persnickety about them, no worries. As you place the cameras throughout the level, you'll likely find the Console firing that you've been caught as you wander through the level to test. This means much of the baseline mechanics are working!

In the next chapter, we will start working with weapons. We'll make the grenade launcher work and the pistol fire. We'll use techniques already covered (Raycasting will make another appearance) and cover new ideas (Instantiate will make its debut).

Weapons

Welcome to Weapons soldier! In this chapter, you will build, test, and fire some of the most intrepid and powerful devices of destruction known to escaping clones trying to escape an orange factory!!

OK, well, actually there are probably more powerful weapons out there. And in fact, creating weapons that are too powerful makes the game too easy and therefore not fun. So while we aren't going to focus on the all-powerful-BFG or any derivative of such a weapons, we will look at how to build the mechanism for the small pistol and the grenade launcher.

Along the way, we will look very carefully at Instantiate and how to use it along with Raycasting so that we can fire a grenade or bullet at the spot that the on-screen reticle identifies. This will require just a bit of UI (don't worry, in the next chapter we'll spend quite a bit more time on it), and a lot of fun new coding. Let's get to it.

Tutorial 16.1: Grenade Launcher

This chapter will focus on the larger of the two weapons. It will largely have much the same mechanics (codewise) as the pistol, but there are a few visual effects that we will introduce with the pistol; so for now, the grenade launcher is easier.

If you want to have real fun, create a new empty Standard Rendering Pipeline project. Go to the Asset Store and search for Unity Particles Pack. Download and import that project and take a look at the cool things that can be done with Unity's particle system…as long as you're using SRP or URP. Unfortunately, we are working in HDRP. While HDRP has some amazing visual fidelity options, much of the visual effects we are enjoying (volumetric light, etc.) are *only* available in HDRP; unfortunately, some things are not quite ready for HDRP as of this writing. The particle pack is one of them. The shaders in Unity's pre-built particle pack are not HDRP compatible. It is possible to reverse-engineer those shaders using Unity's HDRP shader graph (and that's actually what we've done for you), but doing so is well beyond the scope of this book. Hopefully, by the time you are reading this, Unity will have created some HDRP-compatible prefabs that show off their particle system natively. If they do (check out the Asset Store), go ahead and use those. They'll be free and distributed by Unity. We are confident that they will be produced, but currently the content team hasn't quite caught up with the engineering team.

For now, we have created a collection of particle effect prefabs that work in HDRP. They'll be fine for our purposes here. At the support website for this book, you'll find a Unity Package called HDRPParticleEffects in the

Chapter 16 assets. Download this and use Assets>Import Package>Custom Package… to bring the assets into your Unity project.

This HDRP_ParticleEffects folder will include all the things needed to use these particle systems. The particle systems are prefabs that can be dragged into the scene. There are a few there to play with. We won't use them in a tutorial, but look at where things like the GroundFog (Figure 16.1), PressurizedSteam (Figure 16.2), and Steam (Figure 16.3) might be used. There is little performance overhead to these, and they can add some nice movement to the scene.

FIGURE 16.1 Using participle effects to add ground fog.

FIGURE 16.2 Continuing with particle effects to create pressurized steam effects.

FIGURE 16.3 And finally using particle effects for rising steam.

After these particle systems have been explored, played with, and placed in the scene, let's get started on exploring weapons in a separate test scene…

> Step 1: Reopen or create a new Scene with a simple setup. This setup should include a few walls and some random objects. The specifics aren't important; we just need a simple space in which to fire some weapons and see what happens when the projectiles hit things (Figure 16.4).
>
> Step 2: Find, open, and review PlayerControlScript. This script should be on the FPSController. Open it by double clicking on it. The area we are most interested in right now is shown in Figure 16.5 (it should already be in your code).

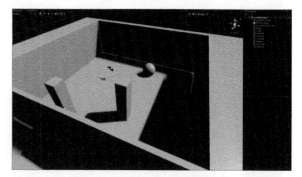

FIGURE 16.4 A simple scene. Make sure the FPSController is in the scene and that any other Main Camera has been deleted.

```
void Update()
{
    if (Input.GetButtonDown("Fire1"))
    {
        ellenGunAnimator.SetTrigger("attack");
    }
```

FIGURE 16.5 Code that listens for the player pressing the Fire1 button. Currently, this just plays an animation through the Animator Controller by turning on the Boolean "attack".

```
public class PlayerControlScript : MonoBehaviour
{
    private GameObject ellenGun;
    private Animator ellenGunAnimator;
    private GameObject ellenGrenade;
    private Animator ellenGrenadeAnimator;
    private string activeWeapon;
```

FIGURE 16.6 Creating a string variable to store activeWeapon.

> Step 3: Create a string that will keep track of
> which gun is active. Up at the top of the script,
> create a string variable called "activeWeapon"
> (Figure 16.6).

Why?

A string is a collection of characters. These can be numbers or letters. It's easiest to think of a string as a word. The word means nothing to Unity, but can be very easy for a user to understand. In this case, we will store which weapon is active by putting in this string variable the words "Gun" or "Grenade".

> Step 4: Start populating the activeWeapon
> string when 1 or 2 is pressed on the keyboard
> (Figure 16.7).

Why?

Notice that these two lines are just added to code already in the script. This just makes sure that the script provides an easy way to check if the weapon is active later. Notice that strings are *always* in quotes.

```
void Update()
{
    if (Input.GetKeyDown(KeyCode.Alpha1))
    {
        ellenGun.SetActive(true);
        ellenGrenade.SetActive(false);
        activeWeapon = "Gun";
    }
    if (Input.GetKeyDown(KeyCode.Alpha2))
    {
        ellenGun.SetActive(false);
        ellenGrenade.SetActive(true);
        activeWeapon = "Grenade";
    }
```

FIGURE 16.7 Make sure the script knows which is the activeWeapon.

> *Step 5: Make sure that when the game starts, the appropriate value is placed in the activeWeapon string (Figure 16.8).*
> *Step 6: Build a mechanism in so that Unity does different work depending on which is the activeWeapon when the Fire1 button is pressed (Figure 16.9).*

```
private void Start()
{
    ellenGrenade.SetActive(false);
    activeWeapon = "Gun";
}
```

FIGURE 16.8 An added line at the Start() when the grenade launcher is put away.

```
if (Input.GetButtonDown("Fire1"))
{
    if (activeWeapon == "Gun")
    {
        ellenGunAnimator.SetTrigger("attack");
        //Fire the gun here
    }

    if (activeWeapon == "Grenade")
    {
        ellenGrenadeAnimator.SetTrigger("attack");
        //Fire the grenade launcher here
    }
}
```

FIGURE 16.9 Reworking the Fire1 area of the code so that different work is done depending on which weapon is active. At this point, the comments just leave us a note of what needs to be done.

FIGURE 16.10 Tracking down the grenade already in the scene.

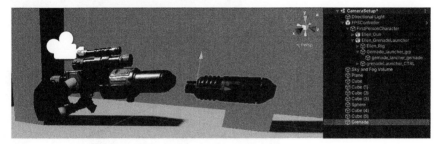

FIGURE 16.11 After duplicating, separating the Grenade from the structure of the FPSController.

Step 7: Extract a grenade to launch. Zoom into the FPSController and select the grenade_launcher_grenade object (Figure 16.10) – this can be done in the Hierarchy or the Scene window. Hit Ctrl-D to duplicate the grenade. Move it out of the FPSController group in the Hierarchy, but drag it down to an empty space in the Hierarchy. Rename it "Grenade" and move it a little ways away from the character. Finally, set its Rotations X, Y, and Z to 0 (Figure 16.11).

Why?

Eventually, we'll engage in a bit of sleight-of-hand. The grenade (grenade_launcher_grenade) is used in things like the reload animation, and so it needs to stay a child of the FPSController. However, when the player presses the Fire1 button, they need to see a grenade go flying out. This new Grenade is going to be the actual thing that is launched, and we'll quickly turn off the one that's still on the end of the gun.

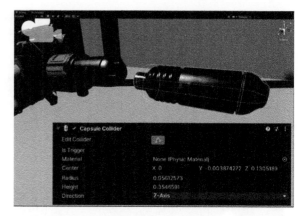

FIGURE 16.12 Adding the Capsule Collider to the Grenade.

FIGURE 16.13 Added Rigidbody component configured for our uses.

> Step 8: Add a capsule collider to Grenade. Select Grenade and, in the Inspector, click Add Component. Start typing "Capsule Collider." Once created, change the Direction: Z-Axis. Then use the Edit Collider button and adjust the Radius and Height so that it roughly fits the Grenade (Figure 16.12).
>
> Step 9: Add a Rigidbody (Add Component) to the Grenade and configure it to match Figure 16.13.

Why?

Eventually it will be important for this Grenade to know when it has actually hit something – when it will explode. We have already used the built in class OnTriggerEnter (remember the doors?). In the coming steps, we'll use a sister class called OnCollisionEnter that fires when

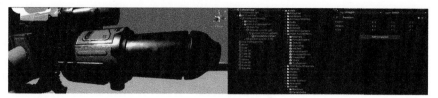

FIGURE 16.14 Creating and positioning the GrenadeLaunchPoint.

something strikes something with a collider. In order for this to work with the Grenade, it needs to have both a Collider (Capsule Collider) and a Rigidbody.

The Rigidbody has a few specific things that need to be adjusted though. First, it shouldn't come out of the gun and just fall to the ground. We will assume the grenade has enough rocket fuel to fly anywhere in the scene; so turning of Use Gravity means it will continue to fly straight. Changing Collision Detection to Continuous Dynamic reduces something called "frame-miss". Frame-miss happens when a collision happens between frames of a game and so the engine doesn't register that the collision has happened.

> Step 10: Create a GrenadeLaunchPoint to define where this Grenade will be launched from. Create an empty GameObject (GameObject>Create Empty). Rename it "GrenadeLaunchPoint" and make it a child of grenade_launcher_grenade. In the Inspector, set Positions X, Y, and Z and Rotations X, Y, and Z all to 0 (Figure 16.14).

Why?

The GrenadeLaunchPoint is going to be the location where we create the new Grenade each time the player fires. By making the launch point be at the same place as the grenade in the gun, we can be sure that the Grenade matches the position of grenade_launcher_grenade.

> Step 11: Make Grenade a prefab. Do this by dragging Grenade from the Hierarchy to the Project window (probably the Prefabs folder). Then delete the Grenade from the Hierarchy window.

569

Why?

We are going to instantiate many of these Grenades, and when the Grenade hits something it will destroy itself. By making Grenade a prefab, we can instantiate it again and again as needed.

Step 12: Make sure PlayerControlScript knows who the GrenadeLaunchPoint and the Grenade prefab are. Add the two lines shown in Figure 16.15 to the top where the variables are being declared. Make sure both are public variables. Save and return to Unity.

Step 13: Populate the two new public variables. Back in Unity, after compiling, drag Grenade from the Project window into the Grenade input field in the Inspector. Then, drag GrenadeLaunchPoint from the Hierarchy into the Grenade Launch Point input field in the Inspector (Figure 16.16).

Step 14: Create code so that when the player presses Fire1, it instantiates Grenade at GrenadeLaunchPoint's location (Figure 16.17). Save and return to Unity.

```
public class PlayerControlScript : MonoBehaviour
{
    private GameObject ellenGun;
    private Animator ellenGunAnimator;
    private GameObject ellenGrenade;
    private Animator ellenGrenadeAnimator;
    private string activeWeapon;

    public Rigidbody grenade;
    public Transform grenadeLaunchPoint;
```

FIGURE 16.15 Adding a variable to track the location of the GrenadeLaunchPoint (its Transform), and the Grenade (specifically that it has a Rigidbody).

▼ ⚙ ✓ Player Control Script (Script)		❷ ⇄ ⋮
Script	⬚ PlayerControlScript	⊙
Grenade	⚙ Grenade (Rigidbody)	⊙
Grenade Launch Point	⚙ GrenadeLaunchPoint (Transform)	⊙

FIGURE 16.16 Populated Grenade and Grenade Launch Point variables.

```
if (activeWeapon == "Grenade")
{
    ellenGrenadeAnimator.SetTrigger("attack");
    Instantiate(grenade, grenadeLaunchPoint.position, grenadeLaunchPoint.rotation);
}
```

FIGURE 16.17 Instantiating the Grenade at the GrenadeLaunchPoint when the player hits Fire1.

Why?

The details for Instantiate can be found in the API (Help>Scripting Reference). Among the things the API will provide is that instantiate basically uses the format Instantiate (thing to instantiate, where to instantiate it, rotation to instantiate it at). So we are instantiating whatever is in the grenade variable, the position of grenadeLaunchPoint, and using the rotation of grenadeLaunchPoint.

> Step 15: Play the game and drop some grenades. When the game is started, hit 2 to swap to the GrenadeLauncher and then start pressing the Fire1 (left-mouse button). Grenades will be left floating in the air – right where we instantiated them (Figure 16.18).
>
> Step 16: Give velocity to Grenades as soon as they are created. Figure 16.19 shows a modification of the Instantiate section of previous steps. Save and return to Unity.

FIGURE 16.18 Creating Grenades is alright, but not quite what we had in mind.

```
if (activeWeapon == "Grenade")
{
    ellenGrenadeAnimator.SetTrigger("attack");
    Rigidbody clonedGrenade;
    clonedGrenade = Instantiate(grenade, grenadeLaunchPoint.position, grenadeLaunchPoint.rotation);
    clonedGrenade.velocity = grenadeLaunchPoint.TransformDirection(Vector3.forward) * 10f;
}
```

FIGURE 16.19 Adjusting the Instantiate section of the code to give velocity to the grenades after they are instantiated.

Why?

What really is happening here is that we are creating a temporary variable (clonedGrenade) into which we instantiate the grenade. Because we instantiate it into this bucket, we can then talk to it and tell it to have velocity (since it's a Rigidbody). Velocity (as per the API) needs a vector, which means we need to give it a direction (grenadeLaunchPoint.TransformDirection(Vector3. forward)), which is the +Z direction of the launch point), and a magnitude (in this case 10).

> *Step 17: Test and fire some fairly slow moving grenades (Figure 16.20).*
> *Step 18: Make the magnitude a changeable variable to allow for easier game tweaking. At the top of the PlayerControlScript, create a variable grenadeSpeed that will store a number that can have decimals (a float (Figure 16.21)). Then plug this variable into the velocity line (Figure 16.22). Save and return to Unity.*

FIGURE 16.20 Firing some grenades that fly away and stop when they hit a surface.

```
public Rigidbody grenade;
public Transform grenadeLaunchPoint;
public float grenadeSpeed;
```

FIGURE 16.21 Creating a float variable that will allow changing the speed to happen in the Unity editor.

```
if (activeWeapon == "Grenade")
{
    ellenGrenadeAnimator.SetTrigger("attack");
    Rigidbody clonedGrenade;
    clonedGrenade = Instantiate(grenade, grenadeLaunchPoint.position, grenadeLaunchPoint.rotation);
    clonedGrenade.velocity = grenadeLaunchPoint.TransformDirection(Vector3.forward) * grenadeSpeed;
}
```

FIGURE 16.22 Using that variable to define the velocity magnitude.

> Step 19: Change the Grenade Speed to a non-zero value. In the Inspector, a new variable "Grenade Speed" will show up. Change that to something like 15. Test the game to make sure Grenades still fire.

Making a "Smart" Grenade

So, "smart" might not be exactly the right word. Sentient might be better. The idea here is that the grenade needs to know when it hits something (collides with a collider). When it does, it needs to instantiate an explosion, and then destroy itself.

> Step 20: Create a new script called GrenadeScript.
> Step 21: Create the code as shown in Figure 16.23. Save and return to Unity.

Tips and Tricks

In Visual Studio, begin typing "OnCollisionEnter" and Visual Studio will fill in the rest. The arguments for built-in classes (the (Collision collision) part) are all built into the libraries that Visual Studio has access to.

```
public class GrenadeScript : MonoBehaviour
{
    public GameObject explosion;

    private void OnCollisionEnter(Collision collision)
    {
        Instantiate(explosion, transform.position, transform.rotation);
        Destroy(gameObject);
    }
}
```

FIGURE 16.23 Creating code for the Grenade so that it instantiates an explosion and then destroys itself when it hits something.

573

Why?

With what we've covered, this should be pretty clear. The new OnCollisionEnter simply defines when the code should fire (when the thing this script is attached to enters a collider). The new thing is the Destroy() command. Destroy can be used to destroy all sorts of things including components, scripts, and, in this case, the GameObject that this script is attached to.

> Step 22: Apply and tie up the new script. Edit the Grenade prefab by double clicking it to open the Prefab Editor. There, drag the new GrenadeScript onto the Grenade. Then drag TinyExplosion from the HDRP_ParticleEffects folder into the Explosion input field. Click back on Scene at the top left of the Prefab Editor.
>
> Step 23: Test and witness the never-ending explosion.
>
> Step 24: Edit TinyExplosion to not loop and self-destroy. In the Project window, select TinyExplosion. In the Inspector, turn off Looping and set Stop Action: Destroy (Figure 16.24).
>
> Step 25: Test and save.
>
> Step 26: Add an AudioSource to the TinyExplosion. Find a short sound of an explosion (likely 2

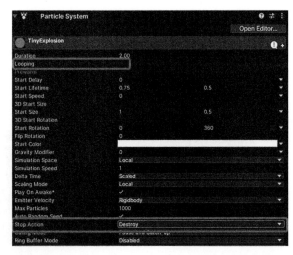

FIGURE 16.24 Setting the TinyExplosion so that it only plays once and then destroys itself when complete.

seconds or less) on some free sounds site (like FreeSound.org). Import it into the Audio folder. Double click TinyExplosion in the Project window. Add an Audio Source component. Drag the downloaded explosion sound into the Audio Clip input field. As a review, still in the Audio Source component, slide Spatial Blend to 1. Make sure Play On Awake is checked this time.

Step 27: Back in Scenes, test and listen for the boom.

Step 28: Add a sound when firing the grenade launcher. Find, download, and import a "rocket launcher" sound. Add an AudioSource component to GrenadeLaunchPoint and populate the AudioClip with this new sound. Turn off Play on Awake and make sure Spatial Blend is set to 1.

Step 29: Add code to play this sound on Fire1. Since PlayerControlScript already knows who GrenadeLaunchPoint is, we just need to tell it to get the AudioSource component on that object and play it (Figure 16.25).

Dummy Grenades and Reloads

Now it's time for some trickier work. Currently, when the player clicks Fire1, a grenade goes shooting off, but there clearly is still a grenade in the front of the launcher. What should happen is that when the player presses Fire1, visually the grenade at the front of the launcher should shoot off, and then the reload sequence should begin.

We'll do this in two steps. First, we'll make sure the dummy grenade (the one sitting on the launcher) turns itself off when we instantiate the new one with velocity. Then we'll build in a timer so the player can't launch another grenade until the animation for reload plays.

Step 30: Make PlayerControlScript keep track of the dummy grenade. Add a variable to store a gameObject called "dummyGrenade" (Figure 16.26).

```
if (activeWeapon == "Grenade")
{
    ellenGrenadeAnimator.SetTrigger("attack");
    Rigidbody clonedGrenade;
    clonedGrenade = Instantiate(grenade, grenadeLaunchPoint.position, grenadeLaunchPoint.rotation);
    clonedGrenade.velocity = grenadeLaunchPoint.TransformDirection(Vector3.forward) * grenadeSpeed;

    grenadeLaunchPoint.GetComponent<AudioSource>().Play();
}
```

FIGURE 16.25 Playing another sound when the layer presses Fire1.

```
public Rigidbody grenade;
public Transform grenadeLaunchPoint;
public float grenadeSpeed;
public GameObject dummyGrenade;
```

FIGURE 16.26 Creating variable for dummyGrenade in PlayerControlScript.

```
if (activeWeapon == "Grenade")
{
    ellenGrenadeAnimator.SetTrigger("attack");
    Rigidbody clonedGrenade;
    clonedGrenade = Instantiate(grenade, grenadeLaunchPoint.position, grenadeLaunchPoint.rotation);
    clonedGrenade.velocity = grenadeLaunchPoint.TransformDirection(Vector3.forward) * grenadeSpeed;

    dummyGrenade.GetComponent<MeshRenderer>().forceRenderingOff = true;

    grenadeLaunchPoint.GetComponent<AudioSource>().Play();
}
```

FIGURE 16.27 Turning off the dummyGrenade on the frame that we instantiate the Grenade with velocity.

> *Step 31: When the grenade is fired, turn the dummyGrenade's renderer off (so it disappears). Add the line shown in Figure 16.27 to the area of PlayerControlScript where we've been handling the Grenade launching. Save and return to Unity.*

Why?

This new line is another illustration of how to get a particular component of a GameObject, and then how to disable the renderer. In this case, we wouldn't want to use dummyGrenade.SetActive(false) as it would turn itself off completely and the GrenadeLaunchPoint beneath it, but we need that GrenadeLaunchPoint to define where to instantiate the new Grenade. So, instead, we'll just turn the renderer off for the dummy grenade and make it invisible.

> *Step 32: Plug grenade_launcher_grenade into the Dummy Grenade input field. Test and see if it disappears when firing.*
> *Step 33: Prevent the player from firing again until the grenade is reloaded. Create a new boolean called "canFireGrenade" at the beginning of the script. Set it to true on Awake() (Figure 16.28).*

```
public Rigidbody grenade;
public Transform grenadeLaunchPoint;
public float grenadeSpeed;
public GameObject dummyGrenade;
bool canFireGrenade;

private void Awake()
{
    ellenGun = transform.Find("FirstPersonCharacter/Ellen_Gun").gameObject;
    ellenGunAnimator = ellenGun.GetComponent<Animator>();
    ellenGrenade = transform.Find("FirstPersonCharacter/Ellen_GrenadeLauncher").gameObject;
    ellenGrenadeAnimator = ellenGrenade.GetComponent<Animator>();

    canFireGrenade = true;
}
```

FIGURE 16.28 Setting up a boolean that will let us turn the ability to fire the Grenade off and on.

Why?

No need for this variable to be public. We'll be controlling it all within script. Sometimes you want a Boolean public to debug; but until then, there's no need for this to be cluttering up the Unity Editor.

> Step 34: Check to see if canFireGrenade is true before firing, and then turn it to false as soon as it's been fired (Figure 16.29). Save and return to Unity.

Why?

We've alluded to && before; but as a review it means "and". So if the active weapon is "Grenade" *AND* canFireGrenade is true, then do the work in the brackets.

```
if (activeWeapon == "Grenade" && canFireGrenade)
{
    ellenGrenadeAnimator.SetTrigger("attack");
    Rigidbody clonedGrenade;
    clonedGrenade = Instantiate(grenade, grenadeLaunchPoint.position, grenadeLaunchPoint.rotation);
    clonedGrenade.velocity = grenadeLaunchPoint.TransformDirection(Vector3.forward) * grenadeSpeed;

    dummyGrenade.GetComponent<MeshRenderer>().forceRenderingOff = true;

    grenadeLaunchPoint.GetComponent<AudioSource>().Play();

    canFireGrenade = false;
}
```

FIGURE 16.29 Checking to see if we can fire the grenade and then turning off the ability to do so.

```
    }  ◄──────  End of Update()

IEnumerator ReloadGrenade()
{
    yield return new WaitForSeconds(1.25f);
    dummyGrenade.GetComponent<MeshRenderer>().forceRenderingOff = false;

    yield return new WaitForSeconds(.5f);
    canFireGrenade = true;
}
}  ◄──────   End of PlayerControlScript.cs
```

FIGURE 16.30 Creating a new IEnumerator, ReloadGrenade(), that turns dummyGrenade back on and flips the canFireGrenade switch back on.

Step 35: Test and witness that the player can only fire one grenade.

Step 36: Create a new Ienumerator called ReloadGrenade() that shows the dummyGrenade again and sets canFIreGrenade back to true with some wait times in between. Figure 16.30 the complete IEnumerator.

Why?

Two important things here: what is an IEnumerator and why do we need it. The IEnumerator cannot be inside another function; so, for instance, it needs to be outside of the Update() function where we have been doing all the work lately. The screenshot shows the end of the Update() function (the last closing bracket) and that's where the new ReloadGrenade() IEnumerator should be built. But notice, that it still needs to be inside the PlayerControlScript class, so it is still before the last bracket for the class.

IEnumerators work much like a regular function, except that they must contain a "yield" statement. Yield in this case means "wait." What this IEnumerator does is wait for 1.25 seconds before turning the dummyGrenade back on, and then waits another 0.5 seconds before allowing the user to fire again. These wait durations might seem a little arbitrary right now, and they were, but with a little testing these were the timings that became apparent once all the animations were tied in together (in a few steps).

```
if (activeWeapon == "Grenade" && canFireGrenade)
{
    ellenGrenadeAnimator.SetTrigger("attack");
    Rigidbody clonedGrenade;
    clonedGrenade = Instantiate(grenade, grenadeLaunchPoint.position, grenadeLaunchPoint.rotation);
    clonedGrenade.velocity = grenadeLaunchPoint.TransformDirection(Vector3.forward) * grenadeSpeed;

    dummyGrenade.GetComponent<MeshRenderer>().forceRenderingOff = true;

    grenadeLaunchPoint.GetComponent<AudioSource>().Play();

    canFireGrenade = false;
    StartCoroutine(ReloadGrenade());
}
```

FIGURE 16.31 Creating the command start the work of the IEnumerator as a coroutine.

> *Step 37: Tell when to start the ReloadGrenade()*
> *IEnumerator. Figure 16.31 shows this line of code.*
> *Save and return to Unity.*

Why?

This work inside the IEnumerator is meant to be firing as the script goes on doing its other work. It's why we are starting it as a "coroutine". In this situation, its actually the only way to fire an IEnumerator.

> *Step 38: Insert reload_anim into*
> *EllenGrenadeController. To do this, find*
> *EllenGrenadeController in the Project window*
> *(should be in the Animator Controllers folder)*
> *and double click it to open the Animator. Track*
> *down the reload_anim animation clip that is*
> *under the Ellen_GrenadeLauncher model in the*
> *Project window as well (should be in the Models*
> *folder). Drag reload_anim into the Animator*
> *window. Select and delete the Transitions from*
> *attack_anim to idle_anim and walk_anim.*
> *Create a new Transition from attack_anim to*
> *reload_anim (Figure 16.32).*
> *Step 39: Adjust the Transition settings to match that*
> *seen in Figure 16.33.*

Why?

It will be important that the attack_anim plays all the way through before moving onto the reload_anim. Therefore, Has Exit Time is checked and Exit Time is set to 1.

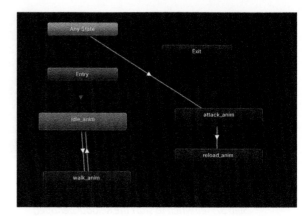

FIGURE 16.32 Rebuilding the EllenGrenadeController to allow for the reload animation to play.

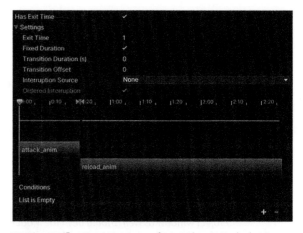

FIGURE 16.33 Transition settings to move from attack_anim to reload_anim.

Further, notice that there are no Conditions for this Transition. It plays automatically.

> Step 40: Create Transitions from reload_anim to idle_anim and walk_anim. Be sure that they are using the conditions isIdling and isWalking, respectively, to determine which state to transition to (Figure 16.34). The Transition for reload_anim->idle_anim is shown in Figure 16.35. The Transition for reload_anim->walk_anim would be just the same but with a different condition.

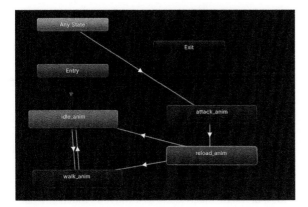

FIGURE 16.34 Final Animator layout. Any State->attack_anim->reload_anim (Transitions automatically) and then Transition from either idle_anim or walk_anim depending on the Booleans.

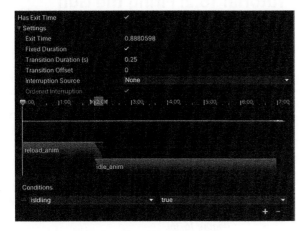

FIGURE 16.35 reload_anim->idle_anim transition settings.

> Step 41: Test. The animations should play, the
> dummyGrenade should pop up at a good time,
> and the player oughtn't be able to fire while the
> launcher is still being reloaded.

Tutorial Conclusion

That's all for the Grenade Launcher for now. Later, it will be important that the sentient Grenade is a little smarter. We'll need it to know when it hits a camera to destroy the camera, but not to destroy a wall if it hits one. We'll need it to do damage by talking to the health of the bad guy's AI later, but not try and talk to the health system of a box (since it won't have one). We will want to create a reticle (via UI) so the player has a better idea of where they are firing. And, of course, currently the player is carrying around an unlimited amount of grenades – there is no ammo count.

But, this is a good start. At this point, the player has one active weapon that convincingly fires a projectile and that projectile explodes when it hits something. The next tutorial will be much faster as it will redo much of what we've talked about here for the small pistol.

Tutorial 16.2: Firing the Gun and Introduction to Ammo

Much of this part will be a review. Most of the mechanics of this gun will be similar to the grenade launcher, so we will move through those steps quickly. However, in this part, we will introduce the idea of a Trail Renderer for a bit of visual pizzazz and give the weapon an arbitrary ten shots before reloading.

> Step 1: Create a GunLaunchPoint. Again, this will be an empty GameObject, although this time placement will be a bit more manual. Make it a child of Gun_grp, but you will need to manually maneuver it so that it is at the tip of the gun (Figure 16.36).

Tips and Tricks

To see the gun easily, hide the Ellen_GrenadeLauncher by selecting it in the Hierarchy and turning off the top check box in the Inspector. Don't forget to turn it back on later.

> Step 2: Create a little GunBullet from a sphere. Create a sphere (GameObject>3D Object>Sphere), name it GunBullet, and make it small enough so it makes sense coming out of the gun.

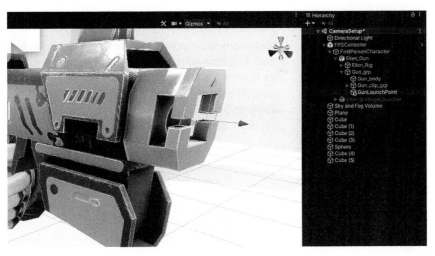

FIGURE 16.36 Creating the GunLaunchPoint, maneuvering it to the correct location manually, and placing it in the appropriate place in the Hierarchy.

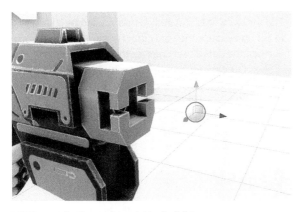

FIGURE 16.37 Creating, naming, and sizing GunBullet.

> *Figure 16.37 shows a sphere with its Scales X, Y, and Z at 0.008 (although this number is arbitrary).*
>
> Step 3: Add necessary Rigidbody. GunBullet will already have a Sphere Collider on it, but add a Rigidbody. Be sure to turn off Use Gravity and set Collision Detection: Continuous Dynamic.

583

Why?

Don't worry too much what this will look like. It will be so small and move so fast the player won't even be able to see it. We will be adding the Trail Renderer to make it a bit more visible in the game. However, getting the Colliders and Rigidbody set up correctly will be important to make this bullet actually do work once it's in the scene.

> *Step 4: Add a Trail Renderer component to GunBullet. Again, with GunBullet selected in the Inspector click the Add Component and start typing "Trail Renderer".*

Why?

Trail Renders are lines that are drawn behind an object as it moves through space. You've likely seen this effect in hack-n-slash games with a fast moving sword. Here, we'll make a small line trail behind the bullet at its fired.

The tricky thing is that Trail Renderers can be a little goofy to set up because they only draw when something moves. Further, the default settings for the Trail Renderer is useless (it's 1 meter wide by default). Try reaching out and moving GunBullet forward a little in the Scene window and you'll see the craziness.

> *Step 5: Tweak the Trail Renderer settings to match that shown in Figure 16.38.*

Why?

Notice that in the Width section the first Key is very, very small (0.015). The second Key was added by right clicking on the red line and choosing Add Key. This second key is moved down to 0 on the Y. These values were found by moving the GunBullet, turning the values down, moving GunBullet again, turning the values down again, and so on.

> *Step 6: Drag GunBullet to a new place and see the bright pink Trail Renderer appear. Tweak the width settings if desired (Figure 16.39).*

FIGURE 16.38 Adjusting the width and length of the trail renderer, and making sure it doesn't cast shadows.

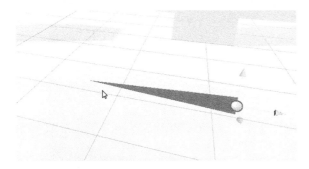

FIGURE 16.39 Dragging GunBullet will show the trail renderer.

Why?

That bright pink in Unity actually always indicates that a material or texture is missing. At this point, the Trail Renderer doesn't have a material yet, so it defaults to that pink to let the user know that one needs to be built and assigned.

Step 7: Create a new material called
BulletTrailRendererMat. Do this in the Project
window by clicking on the + button and choosing
Material. Select the Material and, in the Editor,
set it to Shader: HDRP/Unlit. Change the Color
and Emissive Color to something you like
(Figure 16.40).
Step 8: Apply the new BulletTrailRendererMat to
the Trail Renderer. Select GunBullet and drag
BulletTrailRenderer to the Material input field in
the Trail Renderer.
Step 9: Make GunBullet a prefab, and delete it from
the Hierarchy.
Step 10: In PlayerControlScript, create the
variables we'll need for the bullet mechanism
(Figure 16.41). Save and return to Unity.
Step 11: Fill in the variables (Figure 16.42).

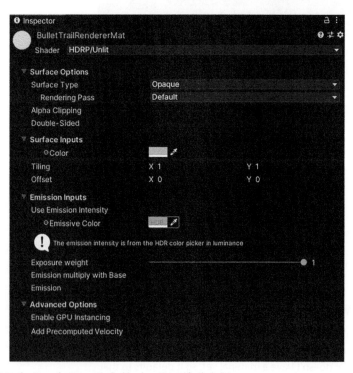

FIGURE 16.40 Creating and setting up the Trail Renderer Material for the bullet.

```
public Rigidbody bullet;
public Transform bulletLaunchPoint;
public float bulletSpeed;
bool canFireBullet;
public int bulletAmmo;
```

FIGURE 16.41 Creating familiar variables for the gun.

FIGURE 16.42 Filling in the variables to get started on the gun mechanism.

Why?

It's fun to just write a lot of code, but it's often helpful to take a second to fill them up in Unity before writing a bunch of new code. It's very common for beginning coders to write a bunch of code and then not be able to run the game as Unity throws an error that the variables are populated.

> Step 12: Turn canFireBullet on in Awake()
> (Figure 16.43) and build (what should look
> like) very familiar code down in the section of
> the script where "Gun" is the active weapon
> (Figure 16.44). Save and return to Unity.
> Step 13: Test. The game should shoot a very small
> projectile with a delicate Trail Renderer behind it.
> Strangely, it will bounce off the walls. If the Trail

```
private void Awake()
{
    ellenGun = transform.Find("FirstPersonCharacter/Ellen_Gun").gameObject;
    ellenGunAnimator = ellenGun.GetComponent<Animator>();
    ellenGrenade = transform.Find("FirstPersonCharacter/Ellen_GrenadeLauncher").gameObject;
    ellenGrenadeAnimator = ellenGrenade.GetComponent<Animator>();


    canFireGrenade = true;
    canFireBullet = true;
}
```

FIGURE 16.43 Turning on the canFireBullet Boolean.

```
if (activeWeapon == "Gun" && canFireBullet)
{
    ellenGunAnimator.SetTrigger("attack");
    Rigidbody clonedBullet;
    clonedBullet = Instantiate(bullet, bulletLaunchPoint.position, bulletLaunchPoint.rotation);
    clonedBullet.velocity = bulletLaunchPoint.TransformDirection(Vector3.forward) * bulletSpeed;
}
```

FIGURE 16.44 Constructing the bullet weapon to work very similar to the grenade.

Renderer is too small for your tastes, or the bullet too slow, make changes to the Trail Renderer settings or the bulletSpeed variable.

Step 14: Make the GunBullet destroy itself when it hits something (Figure 16.45).

Step 15: Prevent Fire1 spamming. Add the code shown in Figure 16.46 where we press Fire1. Then create a new IEnumerator that waits for the 12 frames of the attack_anim (the shooting and recoil animation) before switching the canFireBullet Boolean back on again (Figure 16.47).

Step 16: Start keeping track of ammo. Add the line shown in Figure 16.48. Save and return to Unity.

```
1    using System.Collections;
2    using System.Collections.Generic;
3    using UnityEngine;
4
5    public class BulletScript : MonoBehaviour
6    {
7        private void OnCollisionEnter(Collision collision)
8        {
9            Destroy(gameObject);
10       }
11   }
```

FIGURE 16.45 A simple BulletScript to destroy the bullet when it hits a collider.

```
if (Input.GetButtonDown("Fire1"))
{
    if (activeWeapon == "Gun" && canFireBullet)
    {
        ellenGunAnimator.SetTrigger("attack");
        Rigidbody clonedBullet;
        clonedBullet = Instantiate(bullet, bulletLaunchPoint.position, bulletLaunchPoint.rotation);
        clonedBullet.velocity = bulletLaunchPoint.TransformDirection(Vector3.forward) * bulletSpeed;

        canFireBullet = false;
        StartCoroutine(PauseGun());
    }
}
```

FIGURE 16.46 Temporarily turning off the ability to fire the gun when its fired; but starting the Coroutine that will turn it back on again.

```
IEnumerator PauseGun()
{
    yield return new WaitForSeconds(.2f);
    canFireBullet = true;
}
```

FIGURE 16.47 Waiting for the 12 frames (0.2 seconds) before allowing canFireBullet to be true again.

```
if (Input.GetButtonDown("Fire1"))
{
    if (activeWeapon == "Gun" && canFireBullet)
    {
        ellenGunAnimator.SetTrigger("attack");
        Rigidbody clonedBullet;
        clonedBullet = Instantiate(bullet, bulletLaunchPoint.position, bulletLaunchPoint.rotation);
        clonedBullet.velocity = bulletLaunchPoint.TransformDirection(Vector3.forward) * bulletSpeed;

        canFireBullet = false;
        StartCoroutine(PauseGun());

        bulletAmmo--;
    }
}
```

FIGURE 16.48 Deducting 1 from ammoCount each time Fire1 is pressed when activeWeapon is Gun.

Why?

ammouCount--; is actually short for ammoCount=ammoCount – 1; In other words, "ammoCount is now equal to whatever ammoCount was minus 1".

> Step 17: Select FPSController in the Hierarchy (so that PlayerControlScript is visible in the Inspector). Play the game, fire the gun, and watch the Bullet Ammo variable in the Inspector. It should be dropping by one each time the Fire1 button is pressed, dropping even into negative numbers.
> Step 18: Stop the player from firing when out of ammo so that there is time to reload the weapon (Figure 16.49).
> Step 19: Build BulletReload IEnumerator (Figure 16.50).

Why?

So this IEnumerator triggers some Booleans in the ellenGunAnimator that haven't been created yet. But we should still be able to see what the code is doing: it sets

589

```
if (Input.GetButtonDown("Fire1"))
{
    if (activeWeapon == "Gun" && canFireBullet)
    {
        ellenGunAnimator.SetTrigger("attack");
        Rigidbody clonedBullet;
        clonedBullet = Instantiate(bullet, bulletLaunchPoint.position, bulletLaunchPoint.rotation);
        clonedBullet.velocity = bulletLaunchPoint.TransformDirection(Vector3.forward) * bulletSpeed;

        bulletAmmo--;
        if(bulletAmmo <= 0)
        {
            canFireBullet = false;
            StartCoroutine(BulletReload());
        }
        else
        {
            canFireBullet = false;
            StartCoroutine(PauseGun());
        }
    }
}
```

FIGURE 16.49 Checking to see if there are still bullets. If not, canFireBullet becomes false and BulletReload (an IEnumerator we haven't built yet) will start. Notice that the PauseGun() mechanism is moved down into the else statement.

```
IEnumerator BulletReload()
{
    ellenGunAnimator.SetBool("needReload", true);

    yield return new WaitForSeconds(1.3f);

    ellenGunAnimator.SetBool("needReload", false);
    canFireBullet = true;
    bulletAmmo = 10;
}
```

FIGURE 16.50 BulletReload IEnumerator.

needReload to true, waits for 1.3 seconds (the time it takes to roughly play the attack_anim and the reload_anim), then turns needReload off in the ellenGunAnimator and allows the user to fire the gun again. Finally, because the Animator has played the reload animation, the script resets the ammoCount back to 10.

> *Step 20: Adjust ellenGunController to allow for reloads. In the Inspector, double click on EllenGunController to open the Animator. Find the model Ellen_Gun and drag reload_anim into the Animator. Finally, create a Transition from attack_anim to reload_anim and transitions from reload_anim to idle_anim and walk_anim (Figure 16.51).*

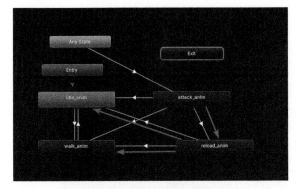

FIGURE 16.51 Setting up the Transitions for reload_anim.

FIGURE 16.52 A new Boolean parameter called needReload that is expected back in code.

> *Step 21: Create a new Parameter boolean called "needReload" (Figure 16.52).*
> *Step 22: Build the Transition attack_anim->reload_anim with a Condition of needReload: true (Figure 16.53).*

Why?

So when the player hits the Fire1 button, the code checks to see if ammo is more than 0. If not, it sets the needReload parameter to true in the Animator. So, the Animator, when it finishes attack_anim, sees that needReload is true and moves onto reload_Anim. Or at least that's what it should do. We need to make sure it doesn't first attempt to head to idle_anim or walk_anim because isWalking or isIdling will also be true.

FIGURE 16.53 The settings for the Transition between attack_anim and reload_anim.

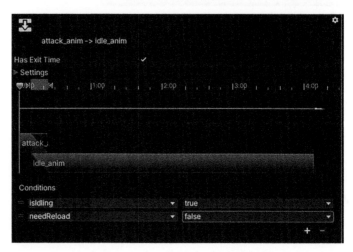

FIGURE 16.54 Ensuring that attack_anim only moves to idle_anim or walk_anim if needReload is false.

Step 23: Add a conditions for the Transitions attack_anim->idle_anim and attack_anim->walk_anim to only move to those states if needReload is false (Figure 16.54).

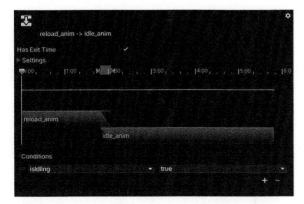

FIGURE 16.55 Providing a way out of reload_anim by checking what other Booleans (isWalking or isIdling) are true.

> *Step 24: Add conditions to the Transitions reload_anim->idle_anim and reload_anim->walk_anim that check to see if isWalking is true or isIdling is true (Figure 16.55).*
> *Step 25: Apply All for the Prefab overrides for FPSController to lock in the changes.*

Tutorial Conclusion

We'll leave the gun here. There is still work to be done. Some you know how to do (and should), like adding a sound when the pistol is fired. Other things like making sure the bullet actually does damage to something will be covered in later chapters.

For now, relish the testing that both weapons work. Tweak the settings that are needed to give the game the feel you find pleasing and then move onto the last tutorial to make sure the weapons are accurate.

Tutorial 16.3: Raycasting for Accuracy

I know, I know. Reticles are for wusses. And yet, so many games have them! If you don't know, reticles are the little crosshairs that most first-person games have that show

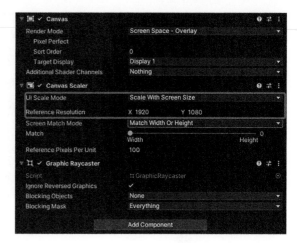

FIGURE 16.56 Changing the Canvas so that if the player's screen gets bigger or smaller, the UI will stay the same size on screen.

the player where they are actually aiming. The problem is that if a reticle is provided for a user, they expect their bullet/grenade to actually fly towards that space. In this tutorial, we will place a reticle in the scene, and then make sure that our projectiles hit the spot the player is aiming at.

> Step 1: Create a UI Image. Go to
> GameObject>UI>Image. This will create three
> things in the scene: 1) Canvas, 2) Child Image,
> and 3) EventSystem. Select the Canvas and
> change the settings as per Figure 16.56.
> Step 2: Rename the Image (UI) to "ReticleUI" and
> center it. Select Image and rename it. Then
> in the Inspector look for the Anchor Presets
> button (at the top left of the Rect Transform
> area (Figure 16.57)). Hold down the Shift and Alt
> buttons and click the icon right in the middle.
> There should now be a pretty ugly white box in
> the middle of the Game Window (Figure 16.58).

Why?

We will talk much more about his later as understanding UI is important to a cohesive game play experience. For now, suffice it to say, by holding the Shift and Alt buttons

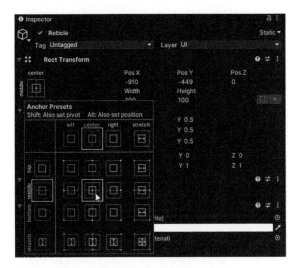

FIGURE 16.57 Placing the ReticleUI in the middle of the screen.

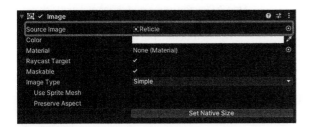

FIGURE 16.58 ReticleUI placed in the middle of the screen. Well, it's not a reticle quite yet. . .

down, we are setting the Anchor (the pivot) of the Reticle in the middle of the image *and* setting the image in the middle of the screen.

> Step 3: Bring in the Reticle texture from the support website. In the Project window, create a new folder called "UIElements". Go to the support website and in the support documents for this chapter is a file Reticle.psd. Import Reticle.psd into the UIElements folder.
>
> Step 4: Adjust the settings for UI. With Reticle selected in the Project change Texture Type: Sprite (2D and UI). Hit the Apply button.

595

Why?

This Reticle.psd file has an alpha channel build in to allow parts of the image to be transparent. By setting the import settings to recognize the file as a Sprite, Unity will automatically find the alpha channel and prepare the file for low-overhead, high-fidelity, UI display.

Step 5: Apply the Reticle texture to the Reticle. In the Hierarchy, select ReticleUI. In the Inspector, look for the Source Image input field. Drag Reticle (the imported texture/Sprite) into that input field (Figure 16.58). The Game window will now show a visible reticle (Figure 16.59).

Step 6: Adjust settings for ReticleUI to not be so big and obtrusive. In the Inspector, look for the Rect Transform section and change Width and Height to 50. If desired, go down to the Image section and double click on the Color swatch where the color (including the Alpha/Transparency) can be shifted (Figure 16.60).

Step 7: Play the game and shoot at a wall (it's easier to see the problem with the Grenade Launcher). Notice that the spot the grenade actually strikes is not where the reticle is pointing at (Figure 16.61).

FIGURE 16.59 Results in the Game window.

FIGURE 16.60 Adjusted ReticleUI.

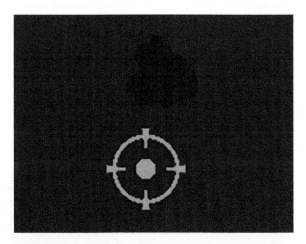

FIGURE 16.61 The current problem with our weapons system; the weapons don't shoot at the reticle's location.

Problem and Solution

Figure 16.62 illustrates the problem. The camera (in white) has a centered reticle (small red circle on the diagram). The sight line of the camera passes through the middle of

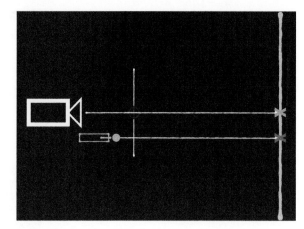

FIGURE 16.62 A diagram of the problem of UI with a centered reticle and a projectile-based weapon.

the reticle on its way to a spot on the green wall. However, the weapon (in blue) is pointing straight and its path is different than that of the camera's line of sight.

Rotating the weapon (or launch point) slightly doesn't solve the problem either. At the sweet spot distance (Figure 16.63), the impact point for the weapon would indeed line up with the reticles indicated point; but as soon as the wall is closer (Figure 16.64), the impact point and reticle would be offset again.

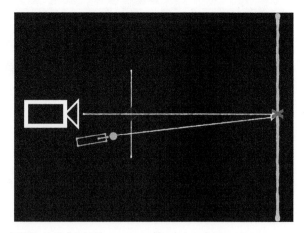

FIGURE 16.63 Rotating the weapon would work at one distance only...

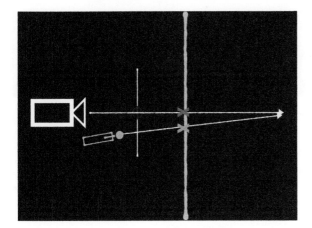

FIGURE 16.64 As soon as the wall was closer (or further), the impact and reticle would no longer line up.

The solution to this is going to be to Raycast from the player camera and store the point at which the ray hits a collider. Then, each of the launch points can be pointing towards that point. Since the launch points define the direction of the velocity of the projectiles (bullet and grenade), this will send the projectiles to the place the reticle is pointed at.

Let's make this happen.

> Step 8: Make PlayerControlScript aware of where the player camera is. We're really only interested in where the camera actually is (as the origin of the Raycast), so the variable declaration should store a Tranform that we'll call "playerCamera". Then, populate the variable on Awake() (Figure 16.65).

```
public int bulletAmmo;

Transform playerCamera;

private void Awake()
{
    playerCamera = transform.Find("FirstPersonCharacter");

    ellenGun = transform.Find("FirstPersonCharacter/Ellen_Gun").gameObject;
```

FIGURE 16.65 Creating a variable to store the Transform of the FirstPersonCharacter (actually the camera for the FPSController) and then filling it with code on Awake().

```
if (Input.GetButtonDown("Fire1"))
{
    RaycastHit thingHit;
    Physics.Raycast(playerCamera.position, playerCamera.TransformDirection(Vector3.forward), out thingHit);

    grenadeLaunchPoint.transform.LookAt(thingHit.point);
    bulletLaunchPoint.transform.LookAt(thingHit.point);

    if (activeWeapon == "Gun" && canFireBullet)
```

FIGURE 16.66 Raycasting and then pointing the launch points at the place the ray is casting against.

Step 9: Create the Raycasting mechanism and then make sure the launch points are pointing in the correct direction. Figure 16.66 shows code placed just inside the Fire1 input area (before it worries about which is the active weapon). Save and Return to Unity.

Why?

The only real new idea here is the LookAt() command. Look at takes the positive Z axis of an object and points it towards a location. In this case, it's the thingHit.point. Remember that thingHit is the Raycast hit created a couple of lines earlier.

This work is done inside the Fire1 area. Why not earlier in the Update() function? The way this is working is that on the single frame that the player presses Fire1, a single ray is shot out, where it strikes is stored, and the launch points point at it. Then, later in the same frames a projectile is sent in that direction. If this were outside the if (Input. GetButtonDown("Fire1")) section, it would be doing all that work every frame. That's a lot of work to do 60 times a second when it could be done once the player pushes the button.

Step 10: Test, and both weapons should be shooting projectiles that hit right where the reticle shows they should (Figure 16.67).
Step 11: Apply Prefab Overrides to FPSController and save the Scene. We'll be back here later for more adventures.

FIGURE 16.67 Raycasting and projectile weapons working together for good.

Conclusion

For now we'll leave weapons behind…but not for long! Still to come are UI elements that help the player know how much ammo they actually have. Still to come is the ability for the grenades and bullets to actually do something in the game (destroy a camera, or shoot a bad guy, etc.). There's much to still do, so keep reading to find out more!

CHAPTER 17

AI

AI. This is a term that in recent years is uttered with reverence. The power of a computer to make its own decisions, to grow, and to learn has made great strides. It is at the cutting edge of computer science today. And luckily for us, it has very little to do with what "AI" refers to in game engines!

This actually takes a lot of the weight off of us as coders. We aren't building constructs of high-end computing here but rather simple decision trees that non-playable characters (NPCs) are able to use to decide how to behave in game. In this chapter, we will be building such a tree and specifically looking at how to allow an AI character to idle at their post, detect the player in the simplest way (by measuring distance), chase the player, and eventually attack the player.

Along the way, we will explore a lot of the tools Unity has in place to facilitate such efforts: Navigation Mesh, Navigation Mesh Agents, Vector3.Distance(), Animator, and Animation Events. When this chapter is complete, ol' multiple versions of EllenEnemy will be guarding the facility on high alert to take the player out.

To do this, we will need to start and stop the game often. So while building this section, work off of a test scene (the one in the support files is called AITest). It should be a fairly simple setup that has a few walls and other barriers to work with (Figure 17.1). Notice that it has FPSController (from the Standard Assets folder) placed in the scene and Main Camera has been deleted. A few adjustments to the Exposure on the Sky and Fog Volume and the Intensity on Direction Light have been made. The blue material on the walls is arbitrary and made just to make the screenshots easier to see.

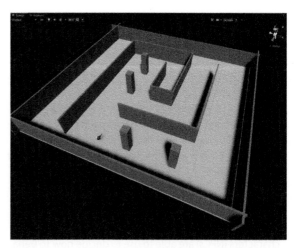

FIGURE 17.1 A sample AITest scene. No specific rules here, just a simple scene to develop code in.

Tutorial 17.1: Creating an AI-Based "Tic-Tac"

To get started, we will do a mini-tutorial that creates a simple form (in this case, a capsule) that will guard the scene and then eventually chase us. Once we understand the specifics of how Unity decides where and AI can move, we can begin layering on details like the animations we brought in from Mixamo.

Before we do that, there are a couple of ideas that are important to touch on. First, Unity's AI mechanism works on the idea of a Navigation Mesh (NavMesh). A NavMesh is literally a polygonal form that Unity creates on top of existing geometry that is visible to no one but objects that have a component called a NavMeshAgent. Technically, NavMeshAgents don't "see" walls, but rather see that there is no NavMesh where the wall is at, and therefore they can't walk through there. The effect is that NavMeshAgents walk around walls and avoid gaps, furniture, and other obstacles. NavMeshes can be complex devices. They can go up and down ramps and stairs. They can even indicate areas where there is a leap possible, where the NavMeshAgent can jump across a gap. However, we'll avoid that for these exercises. What we will do is create a NavMesh, and then create an object with a NavMeshAgent on it that will be able to wander around upon the NavMesh.

> *Step 1: Decide which objects are to be part of the NavMesh. Select all the geometry in the scene (not the FPSController, Directional Light, or Sky and Fog Volume). In the Inspector, check the Static button (top right corner).*

Why?

"Wait, I thought we weren't doing lighting here," you may be seeing. And you're right. The Static checkbox actually is a drop-down menu that if clicked will show there are a lot of flavors of "Static." We used this to mark things that were to be baked in the lighting scheme. However, by using the

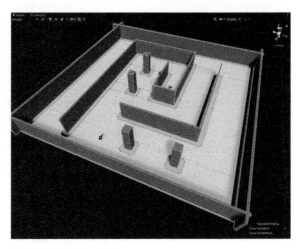

FIGURE 17.2 Baked NavMesh.

generic Static checkbox, objects are also marked as being eligible to be included in other sorts of baking, like baking NavMeshes.

> *Step 2: Create a NavMesh. Select Window>AI>Navigation. Where the Inspector is will now have a new tab: Navigation. Click on the Bake tab within it and click the Bake button (you may need to save the scene if you have not done so already). Very quickly, the NavMesh will be computed and visible in the Scene (Figure 17.2).*

Tips and Tricks

This NavMesh is only visible when the Navigation window is visible. If Inspector is clicked, the NavMesh will go away. Usually it's in the developers interest to not have it visible, but sometimes it's critical to see it.

Why?

So what are we seeing here? The cyan-colored NavMesh will leave holes for walls and pillars. This NavMesh is where a NavMeshAgent can move. If the NavMeshAgent needs to move closer to the walls, this can be adjusted in the Navigation window under the Bake tab by adjusting the Agent Radius. Smaller radius means that an agent will have less clearance around obstacles.

Notice that in the Bake tab there are settings for Max Slope and Step Height. The Max Slope determines how steep an incline needs to be for the NavMesh to decide if the NavMeshAgent can walk up it, and when it ceases to be a slope and becomes a cliff. Similarly, Step Height determines how tall a step can be before it's no longer a step and a ledge that the NavMeshAgent can't walk up. In most cases, the default settings work just fine for Agent Radius, Max Slope, and Step Height; but if the model has very steep stairs, or really narrow doorways, these sometimes need to be adjusted.

> Step 3: Create a capsule for AI and give it a
> NavMeshAgent component. The capsule shown
> in Figure 17.3 was created using GameObject>3D
> Object>Capsule and renamed "AI". It has a
> simple red material created and dropped in it for
> clarity. NavMeshAgent is a component, so select
> the capsule and, in the Inspector, click the Add
> Component and search for "NavMeshAgent"
> and add it.

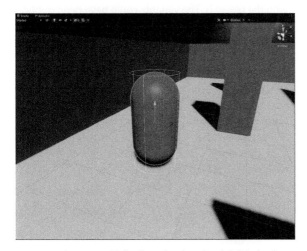

FIGURE 17.3 Our cinnamon Tic-Tac. Notice that it has a Capsule Collider, but the green cylinder around it is the visual representation of the NavMeshAgent component (that can be seen in the Inspector too).

```
using System.Collections;
using System.Collections.Generic;
using UnityEngine;

public class EllenEnemyAIScript : MonoBehaviour
{
    GameObject player;

    private void Awake()
    {
        player = GameObject.FindGameObjectWithTag("Player");
    }
}
```

FIGURE 17.4 Laying the groundwork to chase the player by making sure the script knows who the player is.

Step 4: Create a new script called "EllenEnemyAIScript" (even though this isn't EllenEnemy, it will be eventually). Open it.

Step 5: Make EllenEnemyAIScript aware of who the player is. Create a variable called "player" that will store a GameObject. On Awake(), go out and find a GameObject with the tag "Player" (Figure 17.4).

Why?

There are lots of ways to make sure the script knows who the player is. The variable could have been public, and then we could have dropped FPSController into the variable. But that would have meant that this script would have only worked in *this* scene with *this* instance of FPSController. But we want to build so that the script is reusable; so having the script self-populate the player is a better long-term strategy. We could have also used GameObject.Find("FPSController") instead, which finds an object by name. But this can be a little brittle as well if we end up with a different controller sometime. Since we have a Player tag set up for the doors already, we'll leverage that mechanism here.

Step 6: Add UnityEngine.AI to the inherited libraries (Figure 17.5).

Step 7: Define the NavMeshAgent and tell it to move to the position of the player (Figure 17.6). Save and return to Unity.

```
using System.Collections;
using System.Collections.Generic;
using UnityEngine;
using UnityEngine.AI;
```

FIGURE 17.5 Adding UnityEngine. AI will allow this script to understand when we start talking about NavMesh and NavMeshAgents.

```
public class EllenEnemyAIScript : MonoBehaviour
{
    GameObject player;
    NavMeshAgent myAgent;

    private void Awake()
    {
        player = GameObject.FindGameObjectWithTag("Player");
        myAgent = GetComponent<NavMeshAgent>();
    }

    private void Update()
    {
        myAgent.SetDestination(player.transform.position);
    }
}
```

FIGURE 17.6 Defining the NavMeshAgent, and telling it to set its destination to wherever the player is.

Why?

So notice that there are three steps here. First, creating a variable (called myAgent) to hold a NavMeshAgent. Then in the Awake() function, this myAgent variable is filled by getting the NavMeshAgent component that is attached to whatever GameObject this script is attached to. And finally, every frame (by using the Update() funtion), we use the SetDestination class (that is part of NavMeshAgent component) to define where the AI is supposed to go; in this case, wherever the position of the player is.

> Step 8: Apply the EllenEnemyAIScript to the capsule and play/test. The capsule should doggedly chase the player wherever they run. Notice that the capsule "knows" where walls and other barriers are in the scene.
>
> Step 9: Have the EllenEnemyAIScript measure how far it is from the player and only chase the player if the capsule is less than ten units from it (Figure 17.7).

```
GameObject player;
NavMeshAgent myAgent;
float distanceToPlayer;

private void Awake()
{
    player = GameObject.FindGameObjectWithTag("Player");
    myAgent = GetComponent<NavMeshAgent>();
}

private void Update()
{
    distanceToPlayer = Vector3.Distance(transform.position, player.transform.position);
    if(distanceToPlayer < 10f)
    {
        myAgent.SetDestination(player.transform.position);
    }
    else
    {
        myAgent.ResetPath();
    }
}
```

FIGURE 17.7 Making a variable to store the distance to the player. Then, every frame, measuring the distance and chasing the player if that distance is less than 10.

Why?

The API reports that distance can be measured using Vector3.Distance(object a's position, object b's position). So, the code here first creates a variable called distanceToPlayer to store a number. Then, every frame, that variable is filled by the measurement between object a (the GameObject this script is attached to (transform. position)) and object b (player's position).

Once the script has that number, it can see if it is less than 10. If it is, then it sets the NavMeshAgent's destination to that of the player's. If not, it gives up (ResetPath()).

> Step 10: Change the 10f value to a variable so it can be changed without reediting code (Figure 17.8). Save and return to Unity. There, in the Inspector, change Chase Distance to 10.
> Step 11: Visualize that distance using OnDrawGizmosSelected(). Add the script shown in Figure 17.9 to the end of the script (outside of Update(), but still inside the class). Save and return to Unity.

```
GameObject player;
NavMeshAgent myAgent;
float distanceToPlayer;
public float chaseDistance;

private void Awake()
{
    player = GameObject.FindGameObjectWithTag("Player");
    myAgent = GetComponent<NavMeshAgent>();
}

private void Update()
{
    distanceToPlayer = Vector3.Distance(transform.position, player.transform.position);
    if(distanceToPlayer < chaseDistance)
    {
        myAgent.SetDestination(player.transform.position);
```

FIGURE 17.8 Speeding up development time by making the chase distance an editable variable.

```
private void OnDrawGizmosSelected()
{
    Gizmos.color = Color.green;
    Gizmos.DrawWireSphere(transform.position, chaseDistance);
}
```

FIGURE 17.9 Using OnDrawGizmosSelected() and Gizmos.DrawWireSphere().

Why?

OnDrawGizmosSelected() means "draw some gizmos when this GameObject is selected." Within that function we're defining the color, and then using Gizmos. DrawWireSphere(center of sphere, radius of sphere), we draw a wire sphere. The sphere is centered on the GameObject this script is attached to (transform. position) and the radius is the chaseDistance. Back in Unity, when the capsule is selected it should look like Figure 17.10.

> Step 12: Build a new distance to check for: attackDistance. This is done by adding a new variable called attackDistance and then adding mechanics in the Update() function to only chase if distanceToPlayer is smaller than chaseDistance and greater than attackDistance. But, if distanceToPlayer is less than or equal to (<=) attack distance, stop (and later fire) (Figure 17.11).
> Step 13: If the player gets beyond the chaseDistance again, give up (Figure 17.12).

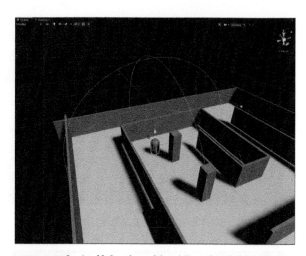

FIGURE 17.10 Results of OnDrawGizmosSelected. Notice this only draws when the capsule is selected.

```
GameObject player;
NavMeshAgent myAgent;
float distanceToPlayer;
public float chaseDistance;
public float attackDistance;

private void Awake()
{
    player = GameObject.FindGameObjectWithTag("Player");
    myAgent = GetComponent<NavMeshAgent>();
}

private void Update()
{
    distanceToPlayer = Vector3.Distance(transform.position, player.transform.position);
    if(distanceToPlayer < chaseDistance && distanceToPlayer > attackDistance)
    {
        myAgent.SetDestination(player.transform.position);
    }
    if(distanceToPlayer <= attackDistance)
    {
        myAgent.ResetPath();
        //Attack stuff here
    }
}
```

FIGURE 17.11 Making the player stop when they are close enough so attack. Later here, the AI will actually attack and fire their pistol.

```
private void Update()
{
    distanceToPlayer = Vector3.Distance(transform.position, player.transform.position);
    if(distanceToPlayer < chaseDistance && distanceToPlayer > attackDistance)
    {
        myAgent.SetDestination(player.transform.position);
    }
    if(distanceToPlayer <= attackDistance)
    {
        myAgent.ResetPath();
        //Attack stuff here
    }
    if(distanceToPlayer > chaseDistance)
    {
        myAgent.ResetPath();
    }
}
```

FIGURE 17.12 Allowing the AI to give up if the player gets away.

Step 14: Visualize the attackDistance by adjusting
OnDrawGizmosSelected(). Change the color, and
draw another DrawWireSphere (Figure 17.13).
Save and return to Unity.

Step 15: Select the capsule and in the Inspector make
sure that Chase Distance is 10, Attack Distance
is 5. The Scene will show the two wire spheres
(Figure 17.14).

Step 16: Test and play. The AI should sit still until the
player gets within the green sphere. Then, it will
chase the player until it reaches a point where
the player is within the red sphere, where the AI
will stop.

Step 17: Adjust to refine game play. This is the
simplest of player detection (distance), but is
a great way to start AI. However, our arbitrary
values of 10 for Chase and 5 for Attack may not
be the best. Remember that EllenEnemy has
animations for shooting her pistol, and would
likely shoot her pistol before she was only 5
meters from the player. So play with the values,

```
private void OnDrawGizmosSelected()
{
    Gizmos.color = Color.green;
    Gizmos.DrawWireSphere(transform.position, chaseDistance);

    Gizmos.color = Color.red;
    Gizmos.DrawWireSphere(transform.position, attackDistance);
}
```

FIGURE 17.13 Changing the color and drawing another wire sphere to show the attackDistance.

613

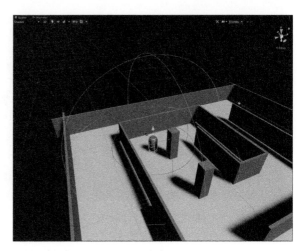

FIGURE 17.14 Wire spheres showing both the chase and attack distances.

and find what makes the most sense. Just remember that Chase Distance needs to be larger than Attack Distance. Remember also that the NavMeshAgent has a Speed setting; so, tweaking that can radically change the overall gameplay as well.

Tutorial Conclusion

Roughing out basic mechanics with a simple capsule is a great way to begin to understand how the game would play. There are lots of other things that could be done here. Could you make the capsule patrol between developer-defined waypoints? Could you make the waypoints random? Could you change the speed from a walk during waypoint patrol to run when chasing? These are all possibilities, and things you may consider as you look at advancing what you know.

For now, we will move on to swap the cinnamon Tic-Tac out for EllenEnemy and her built-in animations. This will change how some of the game works as we will allow her animations to define things like how fast she moves when chasing the player. But the overall effect will be powerful.

Tutorial 17.2: Using Animations (Animator) with NavMesh

Being chased by a red capsule is frightening, but not as interesting as a pistol wielding clone. Later, it will be even more exciting when there is an mob of clones in the space all on the lookout for you, the player. In this tutorial, we will look at leveraging the AI we have already built, and expanding it so that it uses the Mixamo-created animations that we imported in Chapter 12.

Before we get started then with this tutorial, it is important that the work in Chapter 12 has been completed. Your project should have an EllenEnemy prefab. She needs to have an Animator component that has an Animator Controller (EllenEnemyController) and an Avatar (EllenEnemyAvatar). If you do not have these, be sure to download the Unity project from the support website, or go back and hit Chapter 12 so that you're ready to plug her into the mechanics here.

> Step 1: Bring EllenEnemy into the scene. This should be the prefab version of Ellen that includes her Controller and Avatar. She can be placed anywhere as long as she's on the ground.
> Step 2: Add a NavMeshAgent to EllenEnemy. By default, this NavMeshAgent will likely be too big (Figure 17.15).
> Step 3: In her NavMeshAgent, adjust the Radius and Height of her Obstacle Avoidance to more closely resemble her frame. Radius: 0.25 and Height 1.6 seem to work well (Figure 17.16).

Why?

These particular measurements will most assuredly be wrong in the long run. These measurements aren't really the size of the character, but rather the size of the calculation that allows the AI to avoid things (Obstacle Avoidance). Later, as the game takes shape, it's likely that this will need to get a little bigger or smaller as we see how EllenEnemy actually works around obstacles, but

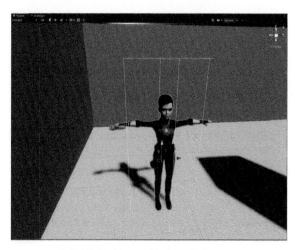

FIGURE 17.15 Default NavMeshAgent on EllenEnemy. Too big!

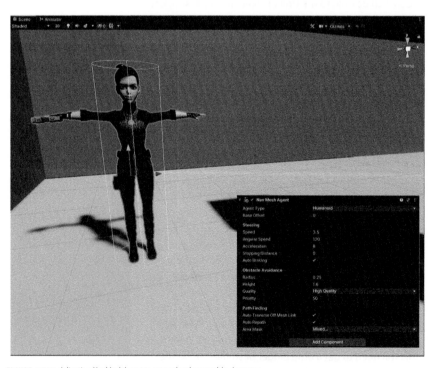

FIGURE 17.16 Adjusting NavMeshAgent to more closely resemble character.

FIGURE 17.17 Magically floating EllenEnemy.

roughly approximating the character's physical frame is a good place to start.

> *Step 4: Play the game and watch her float. She won't chase you now (the AI script we've written hasn't been applied to her yet); but play the game and look closely at her feet. She levitates (Figure 17.17).*

Why?

What's actually happening here is that the NavMesh is not right on top of the meshes it is representing. In other words, in this case, the NavMesh is not on the floor. This can be seen if the Navigation tab is activated (over by the Inspector, remember). To compensate for this, we will move the character a bit lower in relationship to the NavMeshAgent.

> *Step 5: Adjust the Base Offset to adjust EllenEnemy downward within the NavMeshAgent. Base Offset is an attribute of the NavMeshAgent, change it there. −0.095 is a good value to get those feet closer to the floor (Figure 17.18).*

FIGURE 17.18 Adjusting the Base Offset to get the character closer to the floor.

Tips and Tricks

Remember seeing how the NavMeshAgent interacts with the NavMesh can only happen when the game is playing. To find the best value for things like the Base Offset, you must first play the game. Adjustments can be made to most settings in Components while the game is played; however, remember that most changes will revert once the game has stopped. So in this case, play the game, adjust the Base Offset value to get the character positioned correctly, then jot down that value. Then stop the game, and enter the value into the relevant input field again.

> Step 6: Get EllenEnemy to chase the player (sort of). Add EllenEnemyAIScript to EllenEnemy. Adjust her Chase Distance: 10 and Attack Distance: 5 (or whatever you settled on earlier). Play the game and try it out.

FIGURE 17.19 Creating a boolean to keep track of whether the character is chasing or idling, and triggers to set off attack, got hit, and dying animations.

Why?

Yes, yes, it's not right now. She does indeed chase the player, but she chases stuck in the idle pose we set up in Chapter 12. Luckily, we have a plethora of other animations to choose from, including runs and attacks. We just need to get them plugged into the Animator, and fire those animations via the script.

> *Step 7: Set up Parameters in EllenEnemyController.
> Double click EllenEnemyController in the
> Inspector (it might be in your NPC folder or
> organized elsewhere). When the Animator
> opens, create a boolean called "isChasing"
> and three triggers: "attack", "gotHit", and "die"
> (Figure 17.19).*

Why?

In this case, the character is going to be idling, chasing, attacking, getting hit, or dying. The triggers for attack, gotHit, and die should be able to be fired at any time – therefore, they will be triggers. But when the AI is not being triggered by one of those events, it will either be chasing (isChasing) or it won't (isIdling). So we only need one Boolean to keep track of these two animation states.

Preparing FBX Animation Files

There are quite a few animations that will be needed in the next few steps. Let's take a minute to prepare all of

FIGURE 17.20 Import settings for pistol run and EllenEnemy@Shooting.

them, and then we can start tying them together in the Animator.

> Step 8: Prepare the EllenEnemy@Shooting and pistol run. These fbx files should be in your NPC folder. They will need to be adjusted in the Inspector, under the Animation tab individually, but will share the same settings. Select one and, in the Inspector, go to the Animation tab. There, click on Loop Time. In Root Transform Rotation, click Bake Into Pose and Based Upon: Original. For pistol run, be sure to rename the animation (not the FBX) from "mixamo.com" to run_anim. There is no need to rename Shooting (it's descriptive enough). Click Apply (Figure 17.20).

Why?

The looping should be pretty obvious; we want this animation to continue to loop until we move onto something else. The Root Transform Rotation is a little trickier. Without it checked, if the animation is played (down at the bottom of the Inspector window is a little preview window with a play button), the animation runs (or shoots) slightly to the side. By baking the rotation based upon the Original, the animation will be reoriented so that it runs/shoots right along the positive Z axis. This will be important because the character's orientation is being defined by the NavMeshAgent, so the animation should always be facing straight forward.

FIGURE 17.21 Import Settings for non-looped animations for getting hit and dying.

Step 9: Prepare EllenEnemy@HitReaction and EllenEnemy@Death From The Back. These will need to be adjusted one at a time, but will have the same settings in the Inspector under the Animation tab. Do not check Loop Time. But under Root Transform Rotation, click Bake Into Pose and Based Upon: Original. Click Apply (Figure 17.21).

Placing Animations in the Animator

Now that the animation clips have been prepared, they can be imported into the Animator as states. As we did in earlier chapters, just grab the FBX files from the Project window and drag them into the Animator.

Step 10: Place pistol run, EllenEnemy@Death From the Back, EllenEnemy@Hit Reaction, and EllenEnemy@Shooting into the Animator. Their absolute positions aren't terribly important, but the Animator should look something like Figure 17.22.

Step 11: Create Transitions from Any State to Death From the Back, Hit Reaction, and Shooting (Figure 17.23).

Step 12: Adjust the Transition settings for each. Remember to do this, select the transition arrow in the Animator, and then in the Inspector the Transition can be edited. For Any State->Death From The Back and Any State->Hit Reaction, make sure that Has Exit Time is not checked.

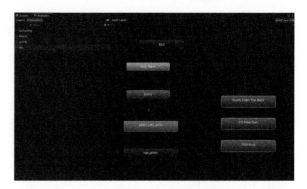

FIGURE 17.22 Animation FBXs placed into the Animator as states.

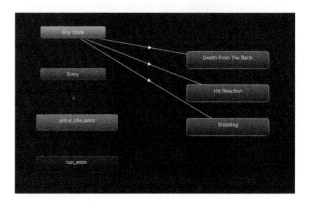

FIGURE 17.23 Transitions from Any State to out three triggered states.

Alternatively, be sure that it is checked for Any State->Shooting. Scroll down to the Conditions area and hit the + button. For Any State->Death From the Back, add a Condition for "die". For Any State->Hit Reaction, add a Condition for "gotHit". And for Any State->Shooting, add a Condition for "attack" (Figure 17.24).

Step 13: Create a Transition from pistol_idle_anim to run_anim (Figure 17.25).

Step 14: Edit the pistol_idle_anim->run_anim to match Figure 17.26. This means turning off Has Exit Time and setting Conditions of isChasing:true.

Step 15: Create a transition from run_anim to pistol_idle_anim and set its transition to match Figure 17.27. Again, turn off Has Exit Time, but this time set the Condition of isChasing:false.

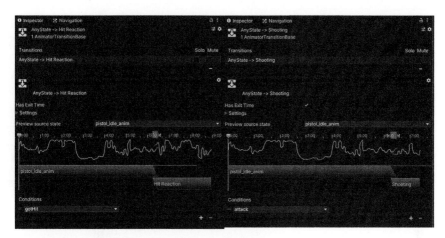

FIGURE 17.24 Transition setting for Any State->Shooting using the trigger attack.

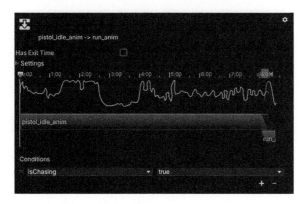

FIGURE 17.25 Providing a way to move from idling to running.

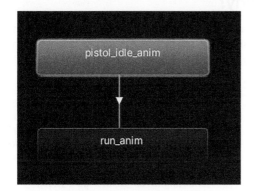

FIGURE 17.26 The transition from idling to running.

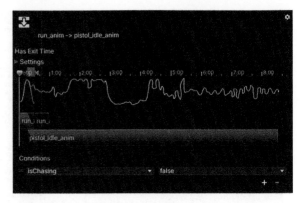

FIGURE 17.27 Transition moving from run_anim to pistol_idle_anim.

Why?

In moving between idle and running, this uses a single Boolean: isChasing. If it's true, we're running, if it's not, we're idling.

> *Step 16: Create Transitions from Hit Reaction, and Shooting to pistol_idle_anim (Figure 17.28).*
> *Step 17: Adjust the Transition for both of these to match Figure 17.29. The key idea here to make sure Has Exit Time is checked. The Condition should be isChasing:false.*
> *Step 18: Create Transitions from Hit Reaction and Shooting to run_anim (Figure 17.30).*

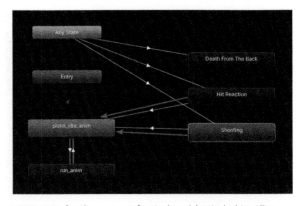

FIGURE 17.28 Providing a way out of getting hit and shooting back into idling.

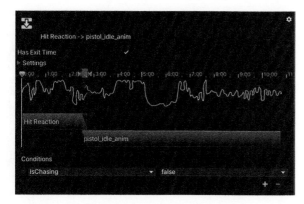

FIGURE 17.29 Transitioning from being hit or shooting back to idle.

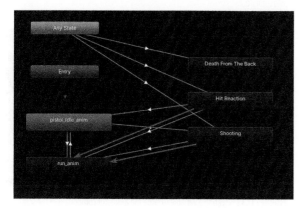

FIGURE 17.30 Creating transitions out of shooting and getting hit back to running.

> *Step 19: Adjust both transitions to match Figure 17.31. Again, make sure the Has Exit Time is checked and isChasing:true.*

Tips and Tricks

While editing any of the Transitions in the Inspector, the transition can be viewed by clicking the play button down in the Preview window. Notice that for simplicity's sake the character stops her run when she gets hit, or shoots. However, you may choose later to come in and build a more complex mechanism that allows here to shoot on the run, or find an animation where she takes a hit while she's running.

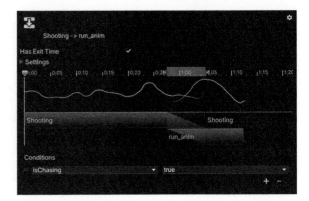

FIGURE 17.31 Setting the conditions for moving from getting hit and shooting back into running.

```
public class EllenEnemyAIScript : MonoBehaviour
{
    GameObject player;
    NavMeshAgent myAgent;
    float distanceToPlayer;
    public float chaseDistance;
    public float attackDistance;
    Animator myAnimator;

    private void Awake()
    {
        player = GameObject.FindGameObjectWithTag("Player");
        myAgent = GetComponent<NavMeshAgent>();
        myAnimator = GetComponent<Animator>();
    }
}
```

FIGURE 17.32 Creating a variable to store the Animator component in the script.

Changing the Triggers and Booleans Via Script

Step 20: Open EllenEnemyAIScript.
Step 21: Make sure the script knows who the Animator component is. Do this by creating a variable called myAnimator and then populating it on Awake (Figure 17.32).

Why?

Just as a quick review, from now on in this script when we need to manipulate the Animator component that is attached to EllenEnemy we just use myAnimator.

```
private void Start()
{
    myAgent.updatePosition = false;
}
```

FIGURE 17.33 Making the animations be the determining factor in how quickly the character moves (not the Move Speed in the NavMeshAgent).

> Step 22: Allow the animations to determine the speed of movement. Add the important line shown in Figure 17.33.

Why?

Remember in earlier tests, EllenEnemy would glide along the ground in idle pose? This was because the NavMeshAgent was defining the speed at which she moved. However, now we have plugged in animations that have their own displacement. In order to get the feet to stay still when they plant for each step, the animations need to determine the speed. This line, myAgent.updatePosition=false; means that the NavMeshAgent isn't in charge of moving the character any longer.

This is an important line that young coders often forget when using Animator and NavMeshAgent. Be sure it's part of your toolbox.

> Step 23: Make sure that the NavMeshAgent doesn't leave the character behind. Copy the lines shown in Figure 17.34 into the bottom of the Update() function.

```
Vector3 worldDeltaPosition = myAgent.nextPosition - transform.position;
if (worldDeltaPosition.magnitude>myAgent.radius)
{
    myAgent.nextPosition = transform.position + .5f * worldDeltaPosition;
}
```

FIGURE 17.34 Keeping the NavMeshAgent and animated character close together.

Why?

The new lines shown in Figure 17.34 come from Unity's API ("Coupling Animation and Navigation"). It's mostly beyond what we want to cover in this volume, but what it does is make sure that if the NavMeshAgent (which is striving to get to the Player when chasing) gets further away from the character than the character radius, to then snap back towards the character. Remember this weird little chunk of code when we see this all in action. The NavMeshAgent (when selected) will look weird, but the functionality will be solid.

Step 24: Ensure the NavMeshAgent and Animator don't separate while in movement. Add a new function as indicated in Figure 17.35. Remember this is a new function, so it can't be inside any other functions, but still needs to be inside the curly brackets for the class.

Step 25: Decide when the isChasing Boolean should be flipped. It should be true when the AI is chasing the player, and off when the player is beyond the chaseDistance (Figure 17.36).

Step 26: Trigger the attack when player is within attack range. Figure 17.37 deletes our comments and adds the actual work of playing the attack animation. Note that it also makes sure that when attacking the NavMeshAgent (which controls the rotation) is focused on the player. Save and return to Unity.

Step 27: Test and play. EllenEnemy should stand there idling until the player gets within her chase range. She'll then speed after the player until she gets close enough for a good shot and then she'll shoot (Figure 17.38).

Step 28: Adjust the rotation of the Shooting animation to be more on target. Do this by selecting EllenEnemy@Shooting in the NPC folder

```
private void OnAnimatorMove()
{
    Vector3 position = myAnimator.rootPosition;
    position.y = myAgent.nextPosition.y;
    transform.position = position;
}
```

FIGURE 17.35 Aligning the NavMeshAgent and Animator in Y while in motion.

```
private void Update()
{
    distanceToPlayer = Vector3.Distance(transform.position, player.transform.position);
    if(distanceToPlayer < chaseDistance && distanceToPlayer > attackDistance)
    {
        myAgent.SetDestination(player.transform.position);
        myAnimator.SetBool("isChasing", true);
    }
    if(distanceToPlayer <= attackDistance)
    {
        myAgent.ResetPath();
        //Attack stuff here
    }
    if(distanceToPlayer > chaseDistance)
    {
        myAgent.ResetPath();
        myAnimator.SetBool("isChasing", false);
    }
}
```

FIGURE 17.36 Flipping the isChasing Boolean on and off in the animator depending on the player's distance from the AI.

```
private void Update()
{
    distanceToPlayer = Vector3.Distance(transform.position, player.transform.position);
    if(distanceToPlayer < chaseDistance && distanceToPlayer > attackDistance)
    {
        myAgent.SetDestination(player.transform.position);
        myAnimator.SetBool("isChasing", true);
    }
    if(distanceToPlayer <= attackDistance)
    {
        myAgent.SetDestination(player.transform.position);
        myAnimator.SetTrigger("attack");
    }
    if(distanceToPlayer > chaseDistance)
    {
        myAgent.ResetPath();
        myAnimator.SetBool("isChasing", false);
    }
}
```

FIGURE 17.37 Triggering the attack animation.

(this is the Shooting state in the Animator). In the Inspector, scroll down to the Preview area and rotate the view by right-dragging until on top of the Ellen avatar. Figure 17.39 (left) shows how she is currently offset and pointing to her right (the player's left). In the Root Transform Rotation area, adjust the Offset to around 11. Scroll down and hit Apply. Figure 17.39 (right) shows her adjusted baked rotation.

Step 29: Test and adjust. Take a look to see if she's more on target when shooting. If need be, adjust the gun in her hand, or rotate her a little further (Figure 17.40).

FIGURE 17.38 Things should be working great now. . .except, she appears to be a terrible shot (always firing a little to the player's left).

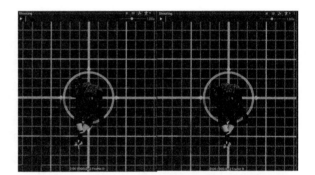

FIGURE 17.39 Using the Root Transform Rotation to offset the character so she is facing forward.

FIGURE 17.40 Adjusted and on-target shooting.

Tutorial Conclusion

This is a good place to pause, save the scene, and apply the prefab Overrides to EllenEnemy. The core of her AI is now complete; but she currently isn't firing anything out of that gun. She also isn't taking damage and her gun won't deliver damage, but those are issues for another upcoming chapter.

Tutorial 17.3: Animation Events and a Working Weapon

In this tutorial, we will make the gun a functioning weapon. Well, a functioning weapon that doesn't do any damage, but one that shoots anyway. To do this, we will leverage concepts covered in past chapters like instantiating bullets. And we will introduce some new ideas, specifically the idea of an Animation Event.

An Animation Event is a marker that is placed within an animation. When that animation is played, the Animation Event can trigger a chunk of code. So, in our case, the idea will be to make an Animation Event in the shooting animation when the bullet would actually exit the gun. That event will trigger the code that instantiates a bullet flying towards the player.

So, the plan for this tutorial will be to first, set up the basic mechanics needed for firing the gun (duplicating and editing a bullet and creating a launch point for EllenEnemy's gun). Then, we'll set up a script to control EllenEnemy's weapon, and then create an AnimationEvent that tells that script when to fire.

> *Step 1: Duplicate GunBullet. This should be in the Prefabs folder. Select GunBullet and hit Ctrl-D. Rename the new GunBullet 1 to "GunBullet_EllenEnemy".*
> *Step 2: Adjust the trail renderer of GunBullet_EllenEnemy with a new material. In the demo files, the material for the original bullet is called BulletTrailRendererMat. A quick shortcut would be to duplicate this material, rename to BulletTrailRendererMat_EllenEnemy, and*

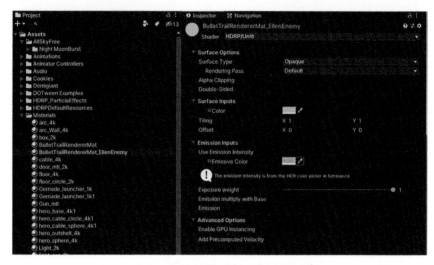

FIGURE 17.41 New material settings for the trail renderer that will follow EllenEnemy's bullet.

then change the Color and Emissive Color to something else (just so the bullets flying around have a different visual style (Figure 17.41)). Alternatively, create a new HDRP/Unlit material and adjust as desired.

Step 3: Assign the new BulletTrailRendererMat_ EllenEnemy to the Trail Renderer component of GunBullet_EllenEnemy. Quick review: select GunBullet_EllenEnemy in the Hierarchy and then in the Inspector scroll down to the Trail Renderer component. Drag the new material into its material input field.

Step 4: Create a gunLaunchPoint and make it a child of EllenEnemy's gun. Create a new empty GameObject and rename it "EllenEnemyGunLaunchPoint". Maneuver it so that it is sitting out at the end of EllenEnemy's pistol. Finally, in the Hierarchy drag it onto Ellen_Gun (the one that is the child of the mixamorig:RightHand joint) to make it a child (Figure 17.42).

Creating the Function to Fire

We now have all the elements we need to fire the gun. We now need to create the mechanics to do so with script. We could put this inside the EnemyEnemyAIScript, but that

FIGURE 17.42 The exact rotation doesn't matter (we'll control that with script), but the launch point out at the end of the gun will give us a good place to instantiate the bullet from.

script is getting fairly long. So instead we'll create it in a separate script to keep all the weapon stuff in one place.

> *Step 5: Create a new C# script and call it "EllenEnemyWeaponScript".*
> *Step 6: Open it and create the same code we did when building the mechanics of the player's pistol (Figure 17.43). The difference is that this time, instead of putting the instructions to fire inside Update() (where we were previously waiting for player input), this time, put it in a public function called "ShootPistol()".*
> *Step 7: Make EllenEnemy a better shot. Add the lines to have the code point the launchPoint at the player's position…and then fire (Figure 17.44). Save and return to Unity.*
> *Step 8: Apply this new script to EllenEnemy. Drag it from the Inspector onto the EllenEnemy instance in the Scene.*

```
public class EllenEnemyWeaponScript : MonoBehaviour
{
    public Transform launchPoint;
    public Rigidbody bullet;

    public void ShootPistol()
    {
        Rigidbody clonedBullet;
        clonedBullet = Instantiate(bullet, launchPoint.position, launchPoint.rotation);
        clonedBullet.velocity = launchPoint.TransformDirection(Vector3.forward * 45f);
    }
}
```

FIGURE 17.43 Creating the function that will fire the gun. Now we just need to decide when to fire this function.

```
public class EllenEnemyWeaponScript : MonoBehaviour
{
    public Transform launchPoint;
    public Rigidbody bullet;

    Transform playerPosition;

    public void Awake()
    {
        playerPosition = GameObject.FindGameObjectWithTag("Player").transform;
    }

    public void ShootPistol()
    {
        launchPoint.LookAt(playerPosition.position);

        Rigidbody clonedBullet;
        clonedBullet = Instantiate(bullet, launchPoint.position, launchPoint.rotation);
        clonedBullet.velocity = launchPoint.TransformDirection(Vector3.forward * 45f);
    }
}
```

FIGURE 17.44 Making the launchPoint look at the player when it comes time to launch a bullet. EllenEnemy's a deadeye!

Why?

Why put it there? Why not on the gun? In actuality, it doesn't matter where it's put as all the things it controls are stored in variables. In this case, we're putting it on the EllenEnemy because that's where the EllenEnemyAiScript is at. This keeps all the scripts involved in the AI control in one place, *and* puts the script on the same gameObject that the Animator is on.

This is critical. The Animation Event we are about to create will be trying to find the function ShootPistol() on the same GameObject as the Animator. So that's where we'll put the script.

> *Step 9: Populate the public variables Launch Point and Bullet. Remember Launch Point will be the EllenEnemyGunLaunchPoint empty gameObject in the scene. Bullet will be GunBullet_EllenEnemy in the Project window.*

Animation Events

It is finally time for the star of the tutorial: Animation Events. These are useful tools that allow a marker to

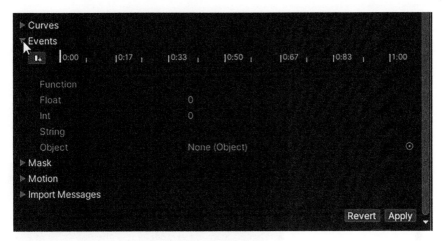

FIGURE 17.45 The Events section of the Animation tab for an animation fbx.

be set within the timeline of an animation. When the animation is played and this marker is hit, it can play a public function that is attached to the same object. Some potential uses of this is a grunt sound that is played when a character throws a punch, or a visual effect that plays as a character strikes the ground, or (in our case) firing the gun at the frame right before the animation recoils.

While Animation Events are powerful and fairly intuitive to use, when used with the Animator, they can be a little hard to find (and then remember where to find them). Follow along in the next few steps and we'll dive down to track them down.

> Step 10: In the Inspector, find EllenEnemy@Shooting (the fbx of the animation we are using to have EllenEnemy shoot).
>
> Step 11: Open the Events section in the Inspector under the Animation tab. This is way down at the bottom, so keep on scrolling down (Figure 17.45).

Awkward Implementation

While Animation Events are easy to understand, the implementation down here is a little tricky. Figure 17.45 shows the Events timeline, you can't actually drag the current-time marker contained there. Instead, you must click-drag the current time marker below that in the preview area (Figure 17.46). Strange, but that's how it works.

> Step 12: In the Preview area for the animation, scrub the current time marker to the point in the animation, just before she recoils from the shot (Figure 17.47). This is at about frame 0:06.

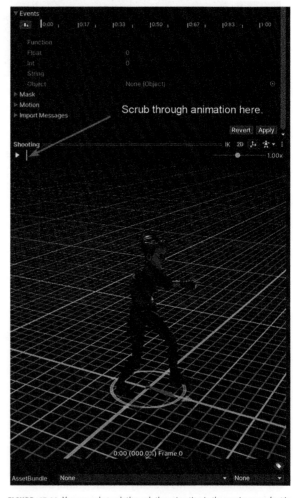

FIGURE 17.46 You can only scrub through the animation in the preview area (not in the events area).

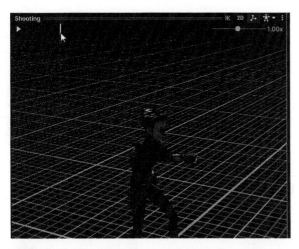

FIGURE 17.47 Scrubbing to fine the frame just before the recoil.

FIGURE 17.48 Add Events button.

> *Step 13: Add an Animation Event. Up the Events section, click the Add Events button (Figure 17.48).*
> *Step 14: Tell the event to fire the ShootPistol() function. In the Function input field, enter "ShootPistol" the name of the function in EllenEnemyWeaponScript. Hit Apply (Figure 17.49).*

Why?

Notice that there are some other input fields there: Float, Int, String, Object. Those are all there in case the function fired needs an input value. Our ShootPistol() requires none, so these can all be left as is.

FIGURE 17.49 Telling this event to fire a function called ShootPistol.

FIGURE 17.50 The bullet firing at the right time.

Step 15: Test and play. EllenEnemy should run up to the player and start firing. The bullet should fly out right on cue (Figure 17.50).

Step 16: Save the scene and apply the Prefab Overrides to EllenEnemy.

Tutorial Conclusion

And that's it for Animation Events. There's still lots of refinement that we could add to this script that you already know how to do…play a sound when she fires, cause her to reload after she's fired a certain amount of bullets, even add a muzzle flash. But we'll leave that up to you. For now, let's start to put everything together in the MainLevel.

Tutorial 17.4: Assembling it all in MainLevel

We've done the test work and now we can put things together in the MainLevel to see how it feels in game. In this mini-tutorial, we will repeat some simple steps to make sure the level will work with our AI (it needs a NavMesh to start with), and then we can use our Prefabs to quickly populate the level with multiple EllenEnemies.

Step 1: Open MainLevel.
Step 2: Ensure that everything is marked as Static, except the doors. A quick way to do this would be to select each of the groups and check that Static is checked. Then, in the Hierarchy, in the search input field, type "door". All the object with "door" in the name will appear. Select door, door (1), door (2), and so on. Then in the Inspector turn off Static.

Why?

The doors can be marked as Static for baking lighting, but they need to be checked off as static elements when 1) we want them to move with script and 2) when we want the AI to be able to walk through them. If the doors were to remain marked as Static, the NavMesh would be built with them as barriers, and the NavMeshAgents would never be able to cross their threshold.

Step 3: Bake the NavMesh. Click the Navigation tab (over near the Inspector). Click the Bake tab within, and click the Bake button. Fairly quickly the NavMesh should show up (Figure 17.51).
Step 4: Inspect the NavMesh throughout. While the Navigation tab is still active, in the Scene view move through the level and make sure that the cyan NavMesh is where it should be. So, for instance in Figure 17.51, the NavMesh definitely goes through the door (as it should). And in Figure 17.52, the NavMesh is shown to even go up the stairs (so EllenEnemy can chase the player across vertical spaces). However, Figure 17.53 shows a narrow hallway, and there are spaces where the NavMesh is dangerously thin.

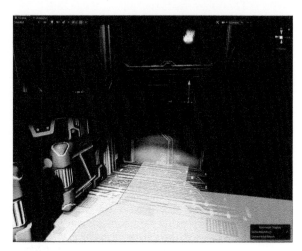

FIGURE 17.51 Baked NavMesh.

FIGURE 17.52 The NavMesh working nicely up the stairs.

Why?

So as long as the NavMesh doesn't disappear completely in a hallway, it will probably be alright. However, if it ever disappears completely, that needs to be adjusted. Otherwise, it will create a strange invisible forcefield for the EllenEnemys NavMeshAgent that won't be able to overcome.

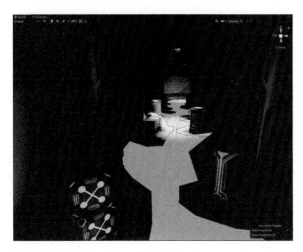

FIGURE 17.53 Potential problems as the NavMesh gets very narrow in a narrow hallway with lots of obstacles.

The roughest way to do this is to go to the Navigation window, the Bake Tab, and adjust Agent Radius to something smaller and Bake again. This will also make the NavMesh get closer to all the walls and barriers though, and sometimes this can cause problems with the NavMeshAgent clipping corners as it navigates around them; so it's usually best to leave a bit of space between the NavMesh and walls. The other way to fix this problem is to move or delete some of the obstacles in a narrow hall like that and rebake.

Ultimately, it's pretty tough to know exactly how a NavMeshAgent will work within a space until you see it in action, so....

> Step 5: Place EllenEnemy throughout the level. Near doors, at stairs, everywhere there might be a guard. Generally for our planned game play, she won't be in the room we start out in, and you may choose to not put her in the CameraRoom or Armory; but for now it doesn't matter. She can be placed anywhere. Be sure you place her near the ground though.

Tips and Tricks

If you place EllenEnemy and she is entirely black, even when she should be in light, you likely have a baked lighting setting not quite right. Go back to Windows>Rendering>Lighting Settings. Make sure that in Mixed Lighting that Lighting Mode: Baked Indirect. You make need to rebake (click the Generate Lighting button).

> *Step 6: Play the game and test. She ought to be able to chase you all over the map. Up the stairs, in and out of rooms, etc. And she should shoot at you when she gets close.*

Conclusion

And there it is. She walks or runs, and tries to kill you when she sees you. This is made possible by the AI methods of a NavMesh and a NavMeshAgent that is able to move about upon it. We've looked at how to allow the animation to define the speed of the NavMeshAgent and how to place Animation Events within the animations. Finally, we've looked at how to trigger different animation states for the AI character so that she knows when to do what.

However, with all of this great AI, we still don't have a game. The player can fire weapons, the AI can fire weapons, but none of the weapons do any damage. In the next chapter, we will look at how to control health systems and inventory. When there are real stakes (we could get shot), the game suddenly begins to get closer to having win and lose states.

CHAPTER 18

Health and Inventory

At the end of the day, health and ammo (or any inventory) is simply a number; usually, it's a whole number, an integer, and usually, it's a positive integer. Keeping track of health and ammo then, is simply a matter of counting—moving up and down in whole numbers.

Scripts to keep track of health usually are fairly simple. They keep track of an integer (called health or healthValue), and then when a bullet hits a character, it calls out to the health script and says, "Hey! Take 10 from whatever your health value is." The health script does it, and then checks if its new health value is at or below 0. If it is, it registers "yer dead!"

In this chapter, we will be creating a health script for both the player and EllenEnemy. After that, we'll expand the ideas of health to ammo (which is also just a matter of counting). Building health is actually one of the easier things to do in coding once the basic mechanics are established.

To build this, we'll start with one of our test scenes to allow for quick starting and stopping. If you saved the test scene from the last chapter that includes EllenEnemy, we can continue on with that (TestAI is the name if you are using the downloaded project files from the support site). If not, then go ahead and make a simple scene with a floor. Make sure that FPSController is in the scene and that Main Camera has been deleted.

Tutorial 18.1: Player Health Script

Step 1: Create a new script called "PlayerHealthScript". Attach it to FPSController (where we're string PlayerControlScript).

Step 2: Build the basic structure of the PlayerHealthScript. This includes a public variable called "health" to store a variable, and then a function to actually subtract health when the player hits or is hit by something that should do damage (Figure 18.1). Save and return to Unity.

```
public class PlayerHealthScript : MonoBehaviour
{
    public int health = 100;

    public void DoDamage(int damageAmount)
    {
        health = health - damageAmount;
        if (health <= 0)
        {
            print("yer dead!");
        }
    }
}
```

FIGURE 18.1 Basic Health Script.

Why?

This script does a few things we haven't done before. The first is that after creating a variable to hold the health value (called health), this script gives it an initial value of 100. After this code is compiled, it won't default to 0; it will default to 100. Notice that this method only works if the code has never been compiled before.

Additionally, this is the first time that we are creating a custom function (DoDamage()) that requires an input: an integer called damageAmount. What this means is that every time any script in the game wants to call out to this DoDamage() function, it must take the form DoDamage(some number); So DoDamage(10), would mean that the script should fire the function DoDamage, and will use 10 any place the function uses the damageAmount variable. So, the line health = health – damageAmount means "the new value of health is equal to 100 minus 10." So, the bullet prefab might carry a value of doing 10 damage, but the grenade launcher might do 30 damage. Using this method, we can vary how much damage is done depending on the situation.

> Step 3: Create a damage box. This will just be a simple object that will do damage to the player when they walk over it. Do this by creating a cube (you can give it a new material (or not)), and in the Box Collider component, check the Is Trigger check box (Figure 18.2).
> Step 4: Create a DamageBoxScript and have it match Figure 18.3. Save and return to Unity.

Why?

This is a pretty simple script, but it's worth breaking some of it down. By default, OnTriggerEnter() requires an input. The input is of type collider and named "other"; basically, this means this function will store the collider of the thing that triggered it in a bucket called "other".

Because the script knows who triggered it, it can check if that thing's gameObject has a tag of "Player". And if it does, go to the thing that triggered it and get a

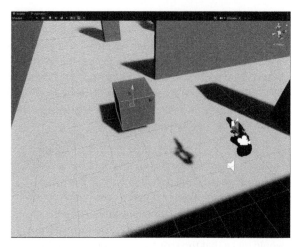

FIGURE 18.2 The "damage box" for testing purposes.

```
public class DamageBoxScript : MonoBehaviour
{
    private void OnTriggerEnter(Collider other)
    {
        if(other.gameObject.tag == "Player")
        {
            other.gameObject.GetComponent<PlayerHealthScript>().DoDamage(5);
        }
    }
}
```

FIGURE 18.3 DamageBoxScript that does damage to whatever runs into its trigger.

component on it called PlayerHealthScript. Then, in that script, fire a function called DoDamage() and pass a value of 5 to it.

We want to make sure that we check the tag of everything that enters so we don't break the game. Pretend, for instance, that this is set where steam is coming out of the ground (so the player takes damage if they run through the steam). Without checking for the tag, the steam would be trying to do damage to every bullet that passed through it, or every EllenEnemy. Further if the bullet or EllenEnemy didn't have a script called "PlayerHealthScript" (which they won't), the game would break as Unity would be unable to fulfill that command.

Step 5: Apply this script to the red cube.

Step 6: Test. Select FPSController so that you can see the PlayerHealthScript in the Inspector. You'll want to watch this during game play. Play the game and have the player walk in and out of the red damage cube. Each time the player enters the cube, the Health variable (on PlayerHealthScript) should drop by 5 (Figure 18.4).

Step 7: Expand this idea to the bullets. In the Project window, find and select GunBullet. It should have on it a script we wrote earlier called "BulletScript" that destroys itself when it hits something. Edit BulletScript to use the idea just created. The script, when complete, should look like Figure 18.5. Save and return to Unity.

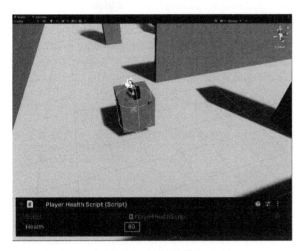

FIGURE 18.4 Entering the damage box should be calling out to the PlayerHealthScript and doing five points worth of damage every time the player enters the box.

```
public class BulletScript : MonoBehaviour
{
    private void OnCollisionEnter(Collision collision)
    {
        if (collision.gameObject.tag == "Player")
        {
            collision.gameObject.GetComponent<PlayerHealthScript>().DoDamage(10);
        }

        Destroy(gameObject);
    }
}
```

FIGURE 18.5 Adjusted BulletScript.

647

Why?

There are a few subtle differences between how we did this in the DamageBoxScript, but they are worth pointing out. Most importantly is that this script is using OnCollisionEnter(). OnCollisionEnter() requires a different input (a variable of type Collision called "collision") than we saw in OnTriggerEnter() (which required a variable of type Collider). But the basic concept is still the same...When whatever this script is attached to collides with something, it will check if that something (stored in the collision bucket) has a tag of "Player". If it does, it will talk to PlayerHealthScript and DoDamage(), passing a value of 10 to that function.

Finally, notice that the Destroy(gameObject) line was there before. It's important that that line is the last as once that line fires, this gameObject is gone (as is the script attached to it); so, no commands will come from this script after that.

Step 8: Test. Since this script is already attached to GunBullet and GunBullet_EllenEnemy, no need to reattach. But when the game is played, make sure the FPSController is selected so you can see the Inspector and the PlayerHealthScript's Health value. Get close enough to EllenEnemy that she starts shooting. As she does, the player's health will decrease by 10 every time a bullet hits them.

Step 9: Adjust the PlayerHealthScript to allow for healing. This should look very familiar to code we've written before. What it does is add to the health value instead of taking it away (Figure 18.6).

Step 10: Import the HealthPack Unity package from the support files. This is a Unity package with some simple code-defined animation and a hologram shader. Once downloaded, use Asset>Import Package>Custom Package... to import it. This will bring in all the textures, shaders, materials, and geometry needed.

```
public void DoHealing(int healingAmount)
{
    health = health + healingAmount;
}
```

FIGURE 18.6 Adding a DoHealing() function to the PlayerHealthScript.

Tips and Tricks

If you are building using URP or the SRP, this package won't work for you (at least the shaders). No big deal though, just assign some other shader to it. The rest of the functionality should be fine.

If you are using HDRP, the shaders here were originally designed by Brackeys (take a look on YouTube for his excellent tutorials). These in particular came from: https://www.youtube.com/watch?v=KGGB5LFEejg.

> Step 11: Place the HealthPack prefab into the scene (Figure 18.7). This should be in the Prefabs folder.
> Step 12: Create a HealthPackScript. It should look like Figure 18.8, which should again be strikingly familiar by this point. Save and return to Unity.
> Step 13: Apply the Script to the HealthPack prefab and test. Make sure you can see FPSController and the PlayerHealthScript's Health value.

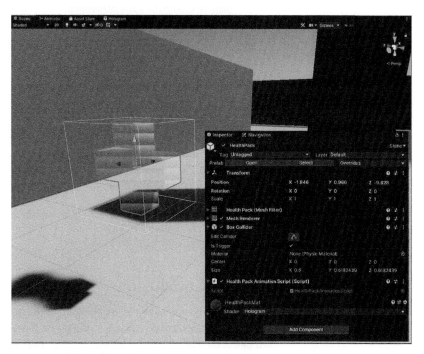

FIGURE 18.7 HealthPack prefab placed in the scene. Notice that it has an animation script (HealthPackAnimationScript) and a Box Collider. Note that the Box Collider has Is Trigger checked.

```
public class HealthPackScript : MonoBehaviour
{
    private void OnTriggerEnter(Collider other)
    {
        if(other.gameObject.tag == "Player")
        {
            other.GetComponent<PlayerHealthScript>().DoHealing(25);
            Destroy(gameObject);
        }
    }
}
```

FIGURE 18.8 HealthPackScript.

```
public void DoHealing(int healingAmount)
{
    health = health + healingAmount;
    health = Mathf.Clamp(health, 0, 100);
}
```

FIGURE 18.9 Clamping the health value so that it doesn't go over 100.

Take some damage and then run over the HealthPack and see that Health value jump back up.

Step 14: Clamp the value of Health so that it can't go over 100. This is done in the PlayerHealthScript by adding the line seen in Figure 18.9.

Why?

This step isn't purely necessary if the designed game play allows the player to supercharge their health. But in most cases you can't get more than 100% healthy. So, clamping the value between 0 and 100 will ensure that the player never gets over 100 health if they've taken just a little damage and pick up a health pack.

Step 15: Apply the Prefab Overrides for HealthPack and FPSController. This will make the scripts just written usable in MainLevel as well.

Tutorial Conclusion

So there 'tis. A complete health system built for the player. Anything that needs to do damage to the player can now just talk to the PlayerHealthScript and fire its DoDamage() function. And health packs or health zones, or however you wish to heal the character, is now in place as well.

It's still a little goofy though. For one thing, we always have to have the FPSController visible to actually see the health as it drops or raises. In the next chapter, UI will be covered and there we can provide the player some visual feedback on what their health really is.

Tutorial 18.2: Building the AI Health System

This will not be a far leap. The EllenEnemy health system will very similar. However, there are a few things that need to be set up before this can work. Specifically, EllenEnemy has a NavMeshAgent, but no collider. Without a collider, we can't use OnCollisionEnter() or OnTrigggerEnter(). So a bit of component adding first, and then we'll quickly build the health system.

> Step 1: Make sure the prefab EllenEnemy is in the scene. If she isn't already, drag her from the Prefabs folder into the scene.
> Step 2: Add a capsule collider and scale to fit. Select EllenEnemy in the Scene window. In the Inspector, Add Component>Capsule Collider. Change the Capsule Collider settings to match Figure 18.10.

Why?

We happen to know that Ellen is 1.6 units tall. So while we could use the Edit Collider button to eyeball the collider in, a Height: 1.6 and Center Y: 0.8 are pretty easy to get exact. The Radius: 0.2 is preference. Too small, and she gets pretty hard to hit, too big and the game gets too easy.

> Step 3: Tag EllenEnemy as Enemy. With EllenEnemy selected, in the Inspector click on the Tag drop-down menu and select Add Tag… (Figure 18.11).
> Step 4: In the Tags & Layers window, under the Tags section click the + button and enter "Enemy" as the name of the new tag (Figure 18.12).
> Step 5: Select EllenEnemy in the Hierarchy again, and again go to the Inspector. There change Tag:Enemy.

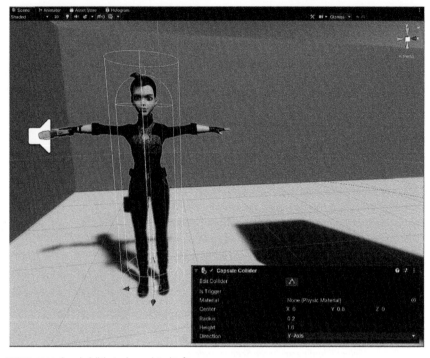

FIGURE 18.10 Capsule Collider in place and sized to fit.

FIGURE 18.11 Creating a new tag.

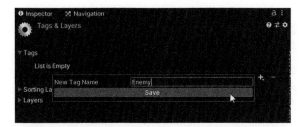

FIGURE 18.12 Creating a new Tag named "Enemy". Note that creating it doesn't automatically apply it to EllenEnemy.

Why?

I know, it seems like we've been here before. The problem is that when we use the Add Tag… method, it creates the tag, but doesn't add it to the object we started on. So after creating the tag, you must come back and still add it to the desired object.

> *Step 6: Create a new script called EllenEnemyHealthScript and attach it to EllenEnemy.*
>
> *Step 7: Build the basics of the health script for EllenEnemy. She won't heal and will only take damage. So we only need a DoDamage() function. Notice that we're giving her half the health to start with (Figure 18.13).*
>
> *Step 8: Edit BulletScript to also do damage to EllenEnemy (or more specifically to the object tagged as "Enemy"). This script already exists, and the edited version should appear like Figure 18.14. Save and return to Unity.*
>
> *Step 9: Test. This time, when playing the game, be sure that EllenEnemy is selected so that her*

```
public class EllenEnemyHealthScript : MonoBehaviour
{
    public int health = 50;

    public void DoDamage(int damageAmount)
    {
        health = health - damageAmount;
    }
}
```

FIGURE 18.13 Basics of the EllenEnemyHealthScript. Been here before…

```
public class BulletScript : MonoBehaviour
{
    private void OnCollisionEnter(Collision collision)
    {
        if (collision.gameObject.tag == "Player")
        {
            collision.gameObject.GetComponent<PlayerHealthScript>().DoDamage(10);
        }

        if(collision.gameObject.tag == "Enemy")
        {
            collision.gameObject.GetComponent<EllenEnemyHealthScript>().DoDamage(10);
        }

        Destroy(gameObject);
    }
}
```

FIGURE 18.14 Edited BulletScript to also damage Enemy-tagged objects.

EllenEnemyHealthScript is visible and the Health value can be seen. Even without a reticle (if you don't have one), the player should be able to shoot at EllenEnemy and, in the Inspector, the Health value should drop.

Step 10: Allow the EllenEnemyHealthScript to trigger the Animator to play the Hit Reaction state. Do this by making sure this script knows who the Animator is, and then firing the gotHit trigger each time it takes damage (Figure 18.15). Save and return to Unity.

```
public class EllenEnemyHealthScript : MonoBehaviour
{
    public int health = 50;
    Animator myAnimator;

    private void Awake()
    {
        myAnimator = GetComponent<Animator>();
    }

    public void DoDamage(int damageAmount)
    {
        health = health - damageAmount;
        myAnimator.SetTrigger("gotHit");
    }
}
```

FIGURE 18.15 Allowing the EllenEnemyHealthScript to fire the Hit Reaction animation state in the Animator.

Why?

We're leveraging a bunch of work we did last chapter. As a review, in the last chapter we edited the Animator to include the Hit Reaction animation and the Death from the Back animation. In addition, gotHit and die were created as Trigger Parameters. Finally, transitions were built from Any State into both Hit Reaction and Death From The Back. Because all those animation states are already in place, with transitions built that can be triggered, we just need to tie into them with the code. For a quick review, the EllenEnemyController should look like Figure 18.16.

> Step 11: Test. Run up to EllenEnemy and shoot with the pistol. Each time she's hit, she should play the Hit Reaction animation.
>
> Step 12: Play the dramatic death animation. Do this in the EllenEnemyHealthScript by checking to see the value of health each time we fire DoDamage(). If it gets below 0, fire the die trigger in the Animator (Figure 18.17). Note that the gotHit trigger is fired only if it does not fire the die trigger. Save and return to Unity.
>
> Step 13: Play and notice some strange happenings. She likely lifts off the ground as she dies, and

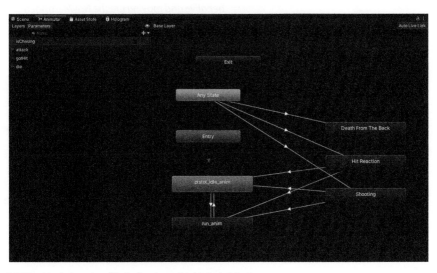

FIGURE 18.16 Just a review of the hard work completed in the last chapter.

```
public void DoDamage(int damageAmount)
{
    health = health - damageAmount;
    if(health <= 0)
    {
        myAnimator.SetTrigger("die");
    }
    else
    {
        myAnimator.SetTrigger("gotHit");
    }
}
```

FIGURE 18.17 Checking health and playing the death animation if it gets below 0.

then suddenly jumps back up and keeps shooting (Figure 18.18).

Step 14: Find EllenEnemy@Death From The Back in the NPC folder and bake its Root Transform Position (Y). Do this by selecting EllenEnemy@ Death From The Back, and then in the Inspector, click on the Animation tab and scroll down to Root Transform Position (Y). Click on Bake Into Pose and then click Apply (Figure 18.19).

Step 15: Test. EllenEnemy should at least fall to the ground, although she also hops right back up.

Step 16: Delete some components so that EllenEnemy knows she's done. The things that are keeping her alive and moving are the NavMeshAgent and EllenEnemyAIScript. When her health is below 0, delete the unused Components (Figure 18.20). Save and return to Unity.

FIGURE 18.18 Strange happenings in our animator.

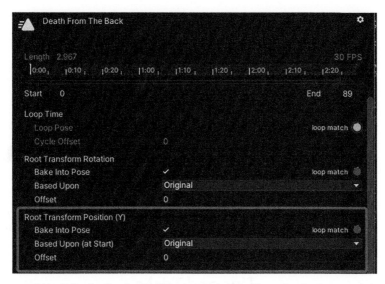

FIGURE 18.19 Baking the Root Transform Position (Y) into the animation. This will cause the animation to control where it sits in Y when it falls (and not the NavMeshAgent).

```
public void DoDamage(int damageAmount)
{
    health = health - damageAmount;
    if(health <= 0)
    {
        myAnimator.SetTrigger("die");
        myAnimator.ResetTrigger("attack");

        Destroy(GetComponent<EllenEnemyAIScript>());
        Destroy(GetComponent<EllenEnemyWeaponScript>());
        Destroy(GetComponent<CapsuleCollider>());
        Destroy(GetComponent<NavMeshAgent>());
    }
    else
    {
        myAnimator.SetTrigger("gotHit");
    }
}
```

FIGURE 18.20 Deleting components and resetting triggers that are no longer needed once she plays her death animation. This gets rid of more than needed, but it will keep unnecessary work from being done by components that aren't needed any longer.

FIGURE 18.21 EllenEnemy, when out of health stays down.

> *Step 17: Test. Once EllenEnemy is out of health, she'll collapse properly and will remain there (Figure 18.21).*

Tips and Tricks

Remember that to be able to talk to (including Destroy) NavMeshAgent, we need to add:

```
using UnityEngine.AI;
```

to the top list of libraries.

> *Step 18: Finally, make sure that the grenade is a one-shot-one-kill weapon. Open GrenadeScript and edit it to mimic Figure 18.22.*
> *Step 19: Apply the Prefab Overrides for EllenEnemy. Save the scene.*

```
public class GrenadeScript : MonoBehaviour
{
    public GameObject explosion;

    private void OnCollisionEnter(Collision collision)
    {
        if (collision.gameObject.tag == "Enemy")
        {
            collision.gameObject.GetComponent<EllenEnemyHealthScript>().DoDamage(50);
        }
        Instantiate(explosion, transform.position, transform.rotation);
        Destroy(gameObject);
    }
}
```

FIGURE 18.22 Using what we know to make the grenade to 50 damage.

Step 20: Just for fun, go back to MainLevel and give it a try. All the instances of EllenEnemy that were placed in the last chapter should now come after the player. And importantly, the player should be able to shoot at and frag EllenEnemy.

Tutorial Conclusion

Health systems really are not terribly difficult. Remember that health is a number, and create mechanics to change it (DoDamage() or DoHealing()), and then decide who can talk to those functions and you're done.

Since the player's interface currently doesn't show that they are hit, it's a little unfulfilling. But in the next chapter we'll provide UI the clue about the player as to whether they're in trouble or not.

Tutorial 18.3: Ammo

Ammo is like a health script for bullets. As long as we can track the number of bullets, we can then subtract when the player fires or add when they pick up an ammo pack.

The trickiest part of this tutorial is just making sure to place the new code in places that makes sense. EllenEnemy will have unlimited ammo, so no need to worry about her. But the player needs to have an ammo count. Currently, the game is tracking the mechanics of the player's weapons in PlayerControlScript. This is really the best place to keep track of ammo. And in fact, if you have been following the tutorials, the variables for grenadeAmmo and bulletAmmo are already created (Figure 18.23).

The task then is making sure we know how to subtract from these ammo counts (when the player pressed Fire1) and how to add to them (when the player runs over an Ammo Pack in the game).

Before we get into that, we can decide how the game is going to play. For simplicity's sake, let us assume that the player will begin the game with both the pistol and the

```
public class PlayerControlScript : MonoBehaviour
{
    private GameObject ellenGun;
    private Animator ellenGunAnimator;
    private GameObject ellenGrenade;
    private Animator ellenGrenadeAnimator;
    private string activeWeapon;

    public Rigidbody grenade;
    public Transform grenadeLaunchPoint;
    public float grenadeSpeed;
    public GameObject dummyGrenade;
    bool canFireGrenade;
    public int grenadeAmmo;

    public Rigidbody bullet;
    public Transform bulletLaunchPoint;
    public float bulletSpeed;
    bool canFireBullet;
    public int bulletAmmo;

    Transform playerCamera;
```

FIGURE 18.23 The variables bulletAmmo and grenadeAmmo have already been created in PlayerControlScript (or they should have anyway). If they aren't in yours, be sure to create them.

grenade launcher and that both have their ammo clips full. Let us also arbitrarily decide that the player can hold three grenades at a time and can fire 12 bullets before having to reload. However, the player can carry up to 36 bullets at a time.

Step 1: Create a new variable of type int called "bulletsInClip". Although it doesn't need to be in this exact place, Figure 18.24 shows it declared right after the bulletAmmo variable.
Step 2: Load the character up when the game starts. Assume that the character has started with weapons that are fully loaded. So they have

```
bool canFireBullet;
public int bulletAmmo;
public int bulletsInClip;
```

FIGURE 18.24 Creating a new variable to keep track of how many bullets are left in the clip. This will allow us to track how many bullets can be fired before reload is needed.

660

```
private void Start()
{
    ellenGrenade.SetActive(false);
    activeWeapon = "Gun";

    bulletAmmo = 36;
    bulletsInClip = 12;
    grenadeAmmo = 3;
}
```

FIGURE 18.25 Creating via script the ammo counts.

> 3 grenades, 12 bullets in their clip, and another
> 24 rounds (36 bullets). In Start(), assign values
> (Figure 18.25).

Why?

This will overwrite some values we've entered for Grenade
Ammo and Bullet Ammo out in the Unity Editor, but that's
alright. Eventually, these variables will be made private
anyway (once we have UI).

> Step 3: Subtract one from the grenadeAmmo count
> each time the player presses Fire1 and the
> activeWeapon = "Grenade" (Figure 18.26).
> Step 4: Prohibit the player from actually firing a
> grenade if they are out of ammo. Do this by
> placing another if statement that checks for the

```
if (activeWeapon == "Grenade" && canFireGrenade)
{
    grenadeAmmo--;
    ellenGrenadeAnimator.SetTrigger("attack");
    Rigidbody clonedGrenade;
    clonedGrenade = Instantiate(grenade, grenadeLaunchPoint.position, grenadeLaunchPoint.rotation);
    clonedGrenade.velocity = grenadeLaunchPoint.TransformDirection(Vector3.forward) * grenadeSpeed;

    dummyGrenade.GetComponent<MeshRenderer>().forceRenderingOff = true;

    grenadeLaunchPoint.GetComponent<AudioSource>().Play();

    canFireGrenade = false;
    StartCoroutine(ReloadGrenade());
}
```

FIGURE 18.26 Subtracting one from grenadeAmmo each time the player presses Fire1 and the grenade launcher is active.

ammo count (Figure 18.27) and putting all the script that fires the grenade within that group (Figure 18.27).

Step 5: Rearrange the Gun section to work the same way (Figure 18.28). However, we need to keep track of both our total ammo count and the rounds in the clip. Notice that there is an adjustment before the reloading section that is checking for bulletsInClip (instead of what used to be bulletAmmo).

```
if (activeWeapon == "Grenade" && canFireGrenade)
{
    if(grenadeAmmo > 0)
    {
        grenadeAmmo--;
        ellenGrenadeAnimator.SetTrigger("attack");
        Rigidbody clonedGrenade;
        clonedGrenade = Instantiate(grenade, grenadeLaunchPoint.position, grenadeLaunchPoint.rotation);
        clonedGrenade.velocity = grenadeLaunchPoint.TransformDirection(Vector3.forward) * grenadeSpeed;

        dummyGrenade.GetComponent<MeshRenderer>().forceRenderingOff = true;

        grenadeLaunchPoint.GetComponent<AudioSource>().Play();

        canFireGrenade = false;
        StartCoroutine(ReloadGrenade());
    }
    else
    {
        //Play some clicking sound....
    }
}
```

FIGURE 18.27 Checking to see if there are still grenades available before firing.

```
if (activeWeapon == "Gun" && canFireBullet)
{
    if(bulletAmmo > 0)
    {
        bulletAmmo--;
        bulletsInClip--;

        ellenGunAnimator.SetTrigger("attack");
        Rigidbody clonedBullet;
        clonedBullet = Instantiate(bullet, bulletLaunchPoint.position, bulletLaunchPoint.rotation);
        clonedBullet.velocity = bulletLaunchPoint.TransformDirection(Vector3.forward) * bulletSpeed;

        bulletLaunchPoint.GetComponent<AudioSource>().Play();

        if (bulletsInClip <= 0)
        {
            canFireBullet = false;
            StartCoroutine(BulletReload());
        }
        else
        {
            canFireBullet = false;
            StartCoroutine(PauseGun());
        }
    }
}
```

FIGURE 18.28 Adjustments to the script to reduce both bulletAmmo and bulletsInClip when pressing Fire1.

Step 6: Adjust the IEnumerator BulletReload()
to utilize our new bulletsInClip paradigm
(Figure 18.29). Note that this replaces the line
that used to be there that reset the bulletAmmo.
Save and return to Unity.

Step 7: Test. The pistol should work very well,
reloading every 12 bullets until all 36 are
expended. Then when Fire1 is clicked, nothing
happens. However, the grenade launcher
won't work quite as well. Likely, when the
player finished firing three grenades, even
though they won't be able to fire a fourth, the
animation that reloads the grenade launcher
will still play. This give us a chance to review
the Animator.

Step 8: Open the EllenGrenadeController.
Hopefully this is easily found in the Animator
Controllers folder of the Inspector. But if
not expand FPSController>FirstPersonChar
acter>Ellen_GrenadeLauncher and double
click it from the Animator component there
(Figure 18.30).

Step 9: Create a new Boolean parameter called
"needsReload".

Step 10: Adjust the attack_anim->reload_anim
Transition so that it only occurs when
needReload is true (Figure 18.31).

```
if (activeWeapon == "Gun" && canFireBullet)
{
    if(bulletAmmo > 0)
    {
        bulletAmmo--;
        bulletsInClip--;

        ellenGunAnimator.SetTrigger("attack");
        Rigidbody clonedBullet;
        clonedBullet = Instantiate(bullet, bulletLaunchPoint.position, bulletLaunchPoint.rotation);
        clonedBullet.velocity = bulletLaunchPoint.TransformDirection(Vector3.forward) * bulletSpeed;

        bulletLaunchPoint.GetComponent<AudioSource>().Play();

        if (bulletsInClip <= 0 && bulletAmmo > 0)
        {
            canFireBullet = false;
            StartCoroutine(BulletReload());
        }
        else
        {
            canFireBullet = false;
            StartCoroutine(PauseGun());
        }
    }
}
```

FIGURE 18.29 Making the BulletReload() work reset the bullets in the clip (but not the players overall bullet count).

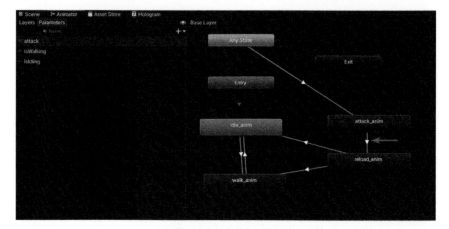

FIGURE 18.30 The EllenGrenadeController from our earlier efforts. Hint: the problem is in the transition highlighted with the red arrow.

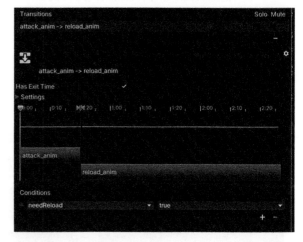

FIGURE 18.31 After creating a needReload parameter, the transition from attack_anim to reload_anim can have a new Condition created.

Why?

It's important to notice that this Transition had not conditions before. This meant that every time attack_anim was done playing, it automatically shifted to reload_anim. This was why, even though the player couldn't fire another grenade, the animation was still playing showing the reload anim. By placing this condition there (which the pistol has, by the way), we can make sure and check to see if the Boolean is true before playing the animation.

> Step 11: Check to see if there are still grenades available before turning the needReload boolean on for the EllenGrenadeController. This has two parts. First adjust the code to match Figure 18.32 so that it only fires the ReloadGrenade() IEnumberator if grenadeAmmo > 0. Otherwise, turn needReload off (because there are no grenades available).
> Step 12: Add the line of code shown in Figure 18.33 to the ReloadGrenade() IEnumerator. Save and return to Unity.
> Step 13: Test. The grenade launcher should now fire three grenades, but not reload a fourth because it hasn't one.

```
if(grenadeAmmo > 0)
{
    grenadeAmmo--;
    ellenGrenadeAnimator.SetTrigger("attack");
    Rigidbody clonedGrenade;
    clonedGrenade = Instantiate(grenade, grenadeLaunchPoint.position, grenadeLaunchPoint.rotation);
    clonedGrenade.velocity = grenadeLaunchPoint.TransformDirection(Vector3.forward) * grenadeSpeed;

    dummyGrenade.GetComponent<MeshRenderer>().forceRenderingOff = true;

    grenadeLaunchPoint.GetComponent<AudioSource>().Play();

    canFireGrenade = false;
    if (grenadeAmmo > 0)
    {
        StartCoroutine(ReloadGrenade());
    }
    else
    {
        ellenGrenadeAnimator.SetBool("needReload", false);
    }
}
```

FIGURE 18.32 Checking to see if there are still grenades left before deciding what animations to play.

```
IEnumerator ReloadGrenade()
{
    ellenGrenadeAnimator.SetBool("needReload", true);

    yield return new WaitForSeconds(1.25f);
    dummyGrenade.GetComponent<MeshRenderer>().forceRenderingOff = false;

    yield return new WaitForSeconds(.5f);
    canFireGrenade = true;
}
```

FIGURE 18.33 Flipping on the needReload Boolean.

665

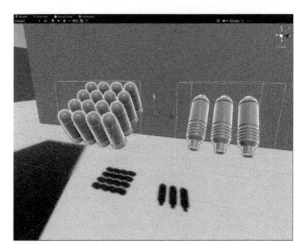

FIGURE 18.34 Two prepared ammo packs.

Reloading Ammo

Believe it or not, we've just completed the hardest part. Reloading the ammo will be piece of cake. The basic idea is we will create two new scripts (one for a bulletPack and one for a grenadePack) that, when the player runs over them, will reach out to this PlayerControlScript and reset the numbers for the respective ammo count.

> Step 14: Bring in AmmoPacks from the support files on the website. After downloading them from the website, use Asset>Import Package>Custom Package…and go grab it. This will place two prefabs into the Prefabs folder: BulletsPack and GrenadePack. Drag them out into the scene (Figure 18.34).

Why?

There is nothing particularly special about these assets. They have a custom shader on them with a Fresnel effect for visual pizzazz. However it is important to notice that both of the prefabs have a Box Collider that has Is Trigger checked. I bet you can see where we're going with this…

```
public void ResetGrenadeAmmo()
{
    grenadeAmmo = 3;
    dummyGrenade.GetComponent<MeshRenderer>().forceRenderingOff = false;
    canFireGrenade = true;
}

public void ResetBulletAmmo()
{
    bulletAmmo = 36;
    bulletsInClip = 12;
    canFireBullet = true;
}
```

FIGURE 18.35 Creating public functions that reset the weaponry.

> Step 15: Inside of PlayerControlScript, create a couple of functions that do the work of resetting the guns back to full ammo, turning the appropriate Booleans on, and making the dummyGrenade visible again (Figure 18.35).

Why?

This script already knows all the variables for the ammo numbers. It knows who the dummyGrenade is. And it knows the Booleans necessary to allow the guns to be fired again. Therefore, it's best to do all the resetting in functions in this script.

However, just because the functions are in this script doesn't mean other things can fire these functions…

> Step 16: Create a new script called BulletReloadScript (Figure 18.36). Save.

```
public class BulletReloadScript : MonoBehaviour
{
    private void OnTriggerEnter(Collider other)
    {
        if(other.gameObject.tag == "Player")
        {
            other.gameObject.GetComponent<PlayerControlScript>().ResetBulletAmmo();
            Destroy(gameObject);
        }
    }
}
```

FIGURE 18.36 BulletReloadScript.

Why?

So this is doing things we've seen before with one new addition. We know what OnTriggerEnter does, and we've seen the process of checking if the thing that entered the trigger is tagged "Player". We've even seen the process of getting a script on the thing that entered the trigger. This is very similar to our DoDamage() methods of earlier. Only here, we're firing a public function that resets everything needed for the bullet ammos.

Step 17: Create a new script called GrenadeReloadScript (Figure 18.37). Save and return to Unity.

Step 18: Apply BulletReloadScript to the BulletsPack and the GrenadeReloadScript to the GrenadePack.

Step 19: Test. Fire all the ammo for the grenade launcher, and then run over the GrenadePack. The dummyGrenade should appear on the end and the player should be able to fire again.

Step 20: Apply the Prefab Overrides to BulletsPack, GrenadePack, and HealthPack (if not done already).

Step 21: Save the test level.

Step 22: Open MainLevel and populate it with strategic ammo and health packs throughout (Figure 18.38).

```
public class GrenadeReloadScript : MonoBehaviour
{
    private void OnTriggerEnter(Collider other)
    {
        if (other.gameObject.tag == "Player")
        {
            other.GetComponent<PlayerControlScript>().ResetGrenadeAmmo();
            Destroy(gameObject);
        }
    }
}
```

FIGURE 18.37 GrenadeReloadScript.

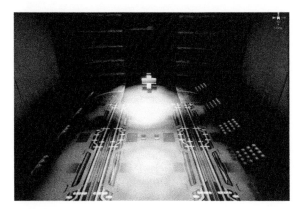

FIGURE 18.38 Placed health and ammo packs. Particularly look at getting them in the armory, and just before you enter to meet the boss.

Conclusion

Only one chapter to go. At this point, we have most of the mechanics in place. But even though the player's health is counting down, there's currently nothing telling the player that they've lost if their health reaches 0. This is also the case for their ammo count. To solve these problems, we need to provide a User Interface (UI) for the player to provide visual feedback.

We've touched on it briefly for the reticle, but in the next chapter we will dive into more robust uses of Unity's UI system to inform the player of how to play the game, how they're doing in the game, and whether they've won or lost.

CHAPTER 19

UI

Untill now, we have been doing a lot of work behind the scenes. There are hundreds of lines of code that are doing all sorts of work, but from the player's perspective, the current game consists of walking around a darkly lit space with AI coming out of the shadows to shoot, but not do any damage.

It's time now to start to build feedback for the player so that they know what the game is about, what their goal is, how to win, and what their health and ammo is. This is usually done through some form of User Interface (UI), sometimes called Graphical User Interface (GUI).

Unity's approach to this has been a shifting one. The approach they have settled on most recently is graphically based; the developer can actually lay things out visually. But there is still a perspective shift that needs to happen. Up to now, working in Unity has been largely in a 3D space. The user views this 3D space through a virtual camera that draws the objects, textures, lightings, and animations the developer has placed there. For UI, we need to start adjusting to thinking in "screen space."

Screen Space

Consider the two screenshots show in Figures 19.1 and 19.2. Both of these are the same scene. In both, a Canvas has been created for the UI. In Figure 19.1, there are three things to note. First, the little red circle is actually the entire 3D scene (itty, bitty, tiny). The big white square in that scene represents the Canvas in which the UI will be built. Notice that the shape of the big white square in the Scene window is the same *shape* as the Game window. This can be seen in Figure 19.2. As the Game window is resized so that it's wide and short, the Canvas in the Scene view does the same thing.

This is similar to how games work. The game a developer builds could end up being played on a wide variety of different screens of varying sizes, shapes, and resolutions.

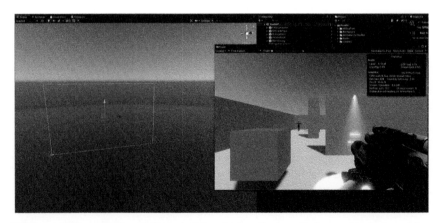

FIGURE 19.1 A UI Canvas. Note the entire 3D scene inside the red circle, and the shape of the Canvas matches the Game window.

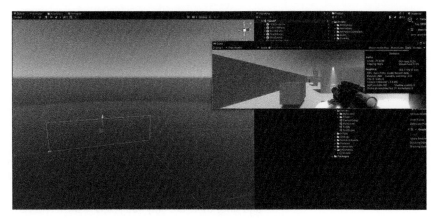

FIGURE 19.2 Notice that the Game window is resized, and the Canvas is resized as well.

The goal then in UI is to create a system that is flexible in a variety of screen situations. Roughly, each pixel of the screen is translated into the 3D space as a unit. That is why the Canvas appears so huge in relationship to the 3D space.

So the goal is to make sure that interface experience is relatively consistent for players on a variety of machines. Unity does this in two ways:

1. The Canvas includes a component called Canvas Scaler. What this will do is rescale the canvas – and importantly, all the elements within it – to match the resolution of the player's screen. By default, this is set to a Constant Pixel Size, which is useless and should almost always be changed to Scale with Screen Size.
2. Unity allows for two important ideas: a pivot and an anchor. The pivot is similar to the pivot in 3D. If the pivot of an element is in the center, it will rotate around that center; but if the pivot is on the bottom left corner (for instance) of the element, it will rotate the entire object around that corner. The anchor is where Unity pins the element to within the Canvas. So an image with its pivot on the bottom left, that is anchored to the bottom left of the Canvas, will always show on the bottom left of every user's screen.

673

An element with a pivot in the middle that is anchored to the middle of the canvas will always appear in the middle of the screen. However, if a developer is working with a screen that is 1920×1080 and has a UI element that is 200×200 and sets the pivot to the center and the anchor to the center, and then *moves* the element to the bottom left (which means she moved it 760 pixels to the left, and then 340 pixels down), Unity will record its location as X=−760 and Y=−340 from its anchor. The problem is that if a player then opens this file on a screen that is 800×600, Unity would move it 760 pixels to the left from the middle – and since there are only 400 pixels to the left of center on that screen, the UI element is completely missing from this player's experience. If something is meant to be on the bottom left, top right, bottom middle, etc. Be sure to be thinking of setting both the Pivot and the Anchor to that location.

We will be doing this in action in the course of these tutorials, but talking through the ideas ahead of time will help make the process reasons make more sense.

Tutorial 19.1: Reticle, Ammo, and Health UI

In this tutorial, we will import and assemble the UI elements for game play. This will include the reticle so the player knows where they are firing, ammo indicators for the gun and grenade, and a health indictor to show what the player's health is.

We'll build this right within MainLevel as these sorts of changes don't transfer between levels quite as easily as prefabs.

> *Step 1: Open MainLevel.*
> *Step 2: Create a Canvas for UI. Select*
> *GameObject>UI>Canvas. Two objects*
> *will appear in the Hierarchy: Canvas and*
> *EventSystem (Figure 19.3).*

FIGURE 19.3 Establishing a UI system in Unity always consists of at least a Canvas and an EventSystem.

Why?

Don't delete either of these objects. The EventSystem contains the mechanics that allow things like buttons to work. With students, it's very common to have them ask about a non-working UI system and, after a long time looking at code, the instructor finally asks, "Did you delete the EventSystem?" "Yeah," they respond, "I didn't put it there and didn't know what it was for so I got rid of it." Remember, *you need this object*. Don't delete it.

The Canvas will hold the UI elements that are tied to Screen Space. There are other ways to work with Canvas (and we will in a bit); but for the main UI (reticle, health, and ammo indicators), these will all be tied to this Canvas.

> Step 3: Configure the Canvas. Select Canvas in the Hierarchy, then in the Inspector set UI Scale Mode: Scale With Screen Size and in Reference Resolution X: 1920 Y: 1080 (Figure 19.4).

Why?

As discussed in the introduction, this will make sure that the elements within this canvas get bigger or smaller in accordance with the resolution of the player's screen resolution. 1920×1080 is 1080p and the resolution of most folks' monitors these days, and so it is a good place

FIGURE 19.4 Canvas Scaler settings.

to start with. The value could be other things, 800×600 for instance; just as long as it's not changed after its set and UI elements are built.

> Step 4: Import the UI texture files. On the support website is a folder called "UI Elements". In this folder, are several PSD and PNG files that we'll use for the rest of this tutorial. You may have already imported Recticle into the UIElements folder in the Unity project (check the Project window); if you have, don't import that, but bring in the rest of the images by dragging them from the finder into the UIElements folder in Unity, or right click on UIElements and choose Import New Assets...
>
> Step 5: Set Ammo_BG, Ammo_Bullet_FG, Ammo_Grenade_FG, Ammo_Magazine_FG, and Health_FG to be imported as Sprites. Select all the new assets just imported in the UIElements folder, and in the Inspector change Texture Type: Sprite (2D and UI). Hit Apply.

Why?

This will see the alpha channels for all the textures and prepare them for a lightweight implementation into Unity.

Note that they are all a very boring gray. This is by design. In Unity, 50% gray means that we can change the color however we desire. Pure white or pure black images are tough to get just right, and moving an image that is (for example) blue to red is even worse. A 50% gray image will let us change the color to anything we want.

> Step 6: Create the Reticle. Select Canvas and then select GameObject>UI>Image. Rename it Reticle. In the Inspector, look for the Rect Transform and click the button in the top left (Figure 19.5) to set the Pivot and Anchor. As a review, hold the Alt and the Shift buttons down and click the Center/Middle button.
>
> Step 7: Resize Reticle to 70×70. Still in the Inspector, change the Width/Height to both read 50.
>
> Step 8: Plug the Recticle Sprite into the Reticle UI Element. Drag Reticle from the UIElements folder into the Image>Source Image input field in the Inspector. Adjust the Color/Opacity as desired.

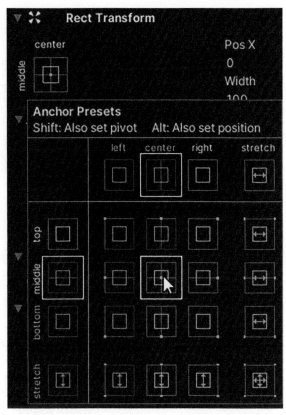

FIGURE 19.5 Setting the Pivot of the Reticle to the center of the image and anchoring it to the center of the Canvas.

Step 9: Create the Ammo backgrounds. Create a new UI Image (GameObject>UI>Image) and rename it "BulletAmmo_BG". Then set its pivot and anchor to the bottom left (Figure 19.6); remember do this in the Rect Transform using the Anchor Presets button and holding down the Alt and Shift buttons when clicking the bottom left button.

Step 10: Set BulletAmmo_BG so that its Width and Height are 150.

Step 11: Assign the sprite Ammo_BG from the UIElements in the Project window to the Source Image input field in the Inspector. Adjust the color as desired (Figure 19.7).

Step 12: Create GrenadeAmmo_BG. Do this quickly by duplicating BulletAmmo_BG (this will also

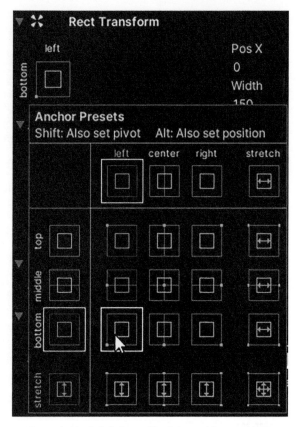

FIGURE 19.6 Locking the BulletAmmo_BG to the bottom left corner of the UI.

FIGURE 19.7 BulletAmmo_BG placed in scene with assigned sprite and color adjustments.

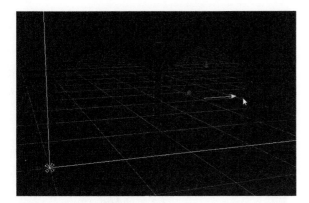

FIGURE 19.8 Offsetting GrenadeAmmo_BG.

duplicate its Pivot and Anchor) and rename it to "GrenadeAmmo_BG".

Step 13: Position GrenadeAmmo_BG to be a little to the right of BulletAmmo_BG. This can be done numerically or visually. Let's do it visually by selecting GrenadeAmmo_BG in the Hierarchy and hitting F to frame it in the Scene window. Swap to the Move tool (W) and slide it in X (red handle) so that it's offset from BulletAmmo_BG (Figure 19.8).

Why?

It's important to see that both of these backgrounds have the same pivot and anchor. Because of this, the screen size could change and these two elements would remain at the same distance from each other. However, their distance from the Reticle (which has a different Pivot/Anchor) would change.

Step 14: Create Health_FG. Do this by duplicating GrenadeAmmo_BG and renaming it "Health_FG". Then move it to approximate Figure 19.9. Finally, plug Health_FG from the UIElements folder into the Source Image input field.

Step 15: Create the grenade indicators. Start with a fresh UI Image (GameObject>UI>Image). Rename it "GrenadeIndicator1". Make it a child of GrenadeAmmo_BG. Use the Anchor Presets to set the Anchor and Pivot to the Center/Middle.

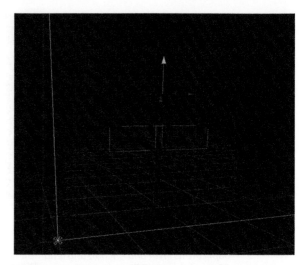

FIGURE 19.9 Creating the Health_FG UI element.

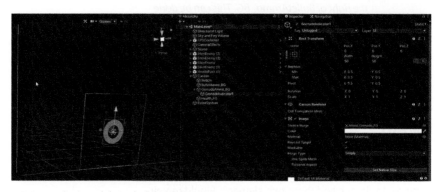

FIGURE 19.10 Creating and placing the GrenadeIndicator1.

Set the Width/Height settings to 50. Finally, use the sprite Ammo_Grenade_FG to define the source image (Figure 19.10).

Why?

Wait a minute...didn't we just say it was important for the UI elements down here in the left corner to all share the same Anchor/Pivot? We did, but by making this GrenadeIndicator1 a child of GrenadeAmmo_BG, the Anchor/Pivot will set a relationship to the parent

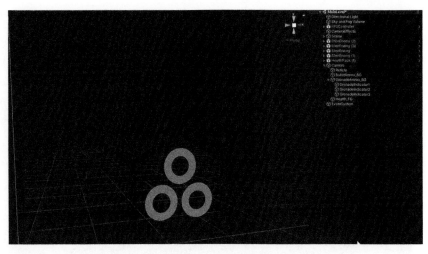

FIGURE 19.11 Duplicating, renaming, and positioning the other GrenadeIndicators. Adjust color if desired.

(not the Canvas). Centering this indicator and the two indicators to come at Center/Middle will make sure that they maintain their relative position and size to the BG.

> *Step 16: Duplicate and position two more GrenadeIndicator2 and GrenadeIndicator3 to roughly match Figure 19.11. All that needs to happen is to duplicate, rename, and position.*
>
> *Step 17: Create 12 BulletIndicators. These were done in the same way as Step 16 except (of course) these indicators are children of BulletAmmo_BG and use Ammo_Bullet_FG as the sprite. The exact placement isn't important; however, we will need space below them for a number to indicate how many clips remain (Figure 19.12).*
>
> *Step 18: Create two BulletClipIndicators. Again, these should be children (and centered on) BulletAmmo_BG. The look should roughly approximate Figure 19.13.*

Health Indicator

The UI plan here is to make a bar that sits behind the Health_FG that will get smaller as the player's health decreases. There are some coding tricks we're going to do later that will scale that UI element. But to make the math easier, we're going to create a UI Panel and give it some

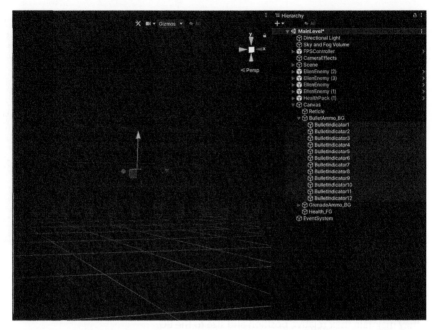

FIGURE 19.12 Bullet Indicators.

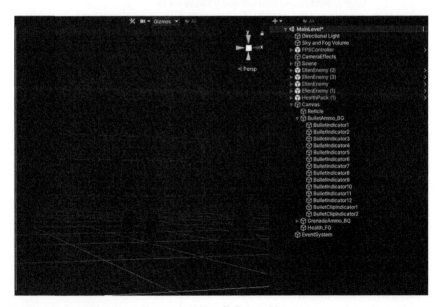

FIGURE 19.13 Creating clip indicators. These are also children of BulletAmmoBG.

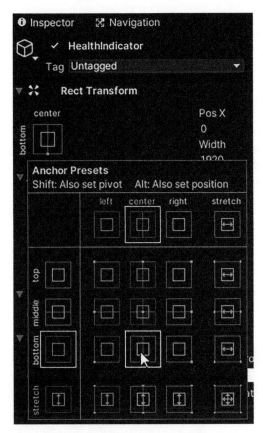

FIGURE 19.14 Setting pivot and anchor for HealthIndicator to bottom left.

specific measurements that will be easier to adjust later. This also mean that the setup is a little strange, but the benefits will become more clear later.

> Step 19: Create a UI Panel. GameObject>UI>Panel. Rename to "HealthIndicator".
> Step 20: Use the Anchor Presets button and set HealthIndicator's Anchor and Pivot (hold Shift and Alt down) to the bottom left (Figure 19.14).

Why?

This is *not* going to be a child of the Health_FG…if it was, it would be in front (and we need it to be behind).

As a result, its anchor needs to coordinate with the Health_FG so they stay locked together if the screen is resized by a player.

Step 21: Change Width: 50, Height: 100.

Why?

This seems arbitrary, but that Height: 100 is carefully planned. Height = 100, Health = 100...see the idea? Later when the health goes down, we'll adjust the Height value to match.

Step 22: Use the Move Tool to move HealthIndicator so the bottom of the panel is at the bottom of the character outline's feet (Figure 19.15). Don't worry for now if it's as tall at her head.

Step 23: Use the Scale Tool to scale HealthIndicator to cover the outline. Hit R to activate scale and scale HealthIndicator so that it completely covers the outline (Figure 19.16).

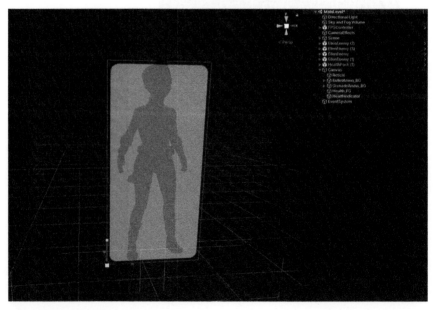

FIGURE 19.15 Aligning (by moving) the HealthIndicator so the bottom aligns with the bottom of the feet of the character outline.

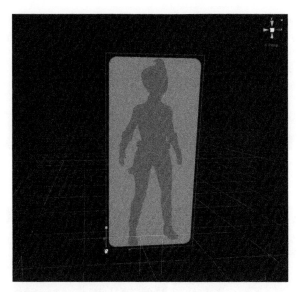

FIGURE 19.16 Using Scale to make HealthIndicator the desired size without changing Width and Height settings.

Why?

Notice that when scaling, the Width and Height settings remain at 50 and 100, respectively. This means that our Height=100 is still intact and we can use it later to tie it easily to the Health value.

> Step 24: Put the HealthIndicator behind the Health_FG by changing the order it appears in the Canvas. It should appear before Health_FG (and thus be drawn first) and can be moved by selecting it in the Hierarchy and moving it above Health_FG (Figure 19.17).
> Step 25: Adjust HealthIndicator color to taste (Figure 19.18).

Tutorial Conclusion

And with that, the UI elements are in place. The don't do anything yet, that is still to come in code. But the pieces are ready to take instructions. Feel free to adjust colors as desired, even change the overall size.

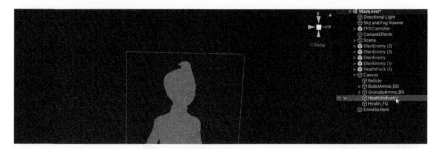

FIGURE 19.17 Changing the order in the Hierarchy changes which UI element is drawn first and which are drawn later (and thus on top of earlier ones).

FIGURE 19.18 Adjusted color on HealthIndicator.

Tutorial 19.2: Using Code to Effect UI Elements

In this tutorial, we will write code that changes the UI. In some cases, we'll just turn elements on and off and, in others, we will change the size. In all cases, we will use code we've already started to effect the UI elements we built in the last tutorial.

Step 1: Open PlayerControlScript.
Step 2: Make sure PlayerControlScript knows the library UnityEngine. Add the line shown in Figure 19.19 to the top with the other Libraries.
Step 3: Create public variables of type Image for all of the bullet indicators (Figure 19.20) so that the script will know these UI Images.
Step 4: Repeat for the bullet clip indicators and grenade indicators (Figure 19.21). Save and return to Unity.

```
using System.Collections;
using System.Collections.Generic;
using UnityEngine;
using UnityEngine.UI;
```

FIGURE 19.19 Making sure this script will know how to talk to UI objects.

```
public class PlayerControlScript : MonoBehaviour
{
    public Image bulletIndicator1;
    public Image bulletIndicator2;
    public Image bulletIndicator3;
    public Image bulletIndicator4;
    public Image bulletIndicator5;
    public Image bulletIndicator6;
    public Image bulletIndicator7;
    public Image bulletIndicator8;
    public Image bulletIndicator9;
    public Image bulletIndicator10;
    public Image bulletIndicator11;
    public Image bulletIndicator12;
```

FIGURE 19.20 Creating variables to store all of the indicators for the bullets. The names are arbitrary.

```
    public Image bulletClipIndicator1;
    public Image bulletClipIndicator2;

    public Image grenadeIndicator1;
    public Image grenadeIndicator2;
    public Image grenadeIndicator3;
```

FIGURE 19.21 Creating variables to store the bullet clip indicators and grenade indicators. The names are arbitrary.

> *Step 5: Back in Unity, populate all the new public variables. This can take a while, but make sure they are all filled in with the actual objects from the Hierarchy (Figure 19.22).*

Tips and Tricks

If this were not in a book, this would usually be done with script (i.e. bulletIndicator1 = GameObject. Find("BulletIndicator1").GetComponent<Image>();). But the script is getting too long to indicate easily in the screenshots, so we will be using a public variable method like this for now.

FIGURE 19.22 Filled in variables.

Additionally, there are some great ways to organize a list of variables that are a bit beyond the scope of this book (Headers, etc.), but take a look at the API as your code gets larger and more complex.

Case Switches or Switch Statements

These can be thought of as variants of *if* statements. The general form of these is to create a switch, and then depending on what is in the switch to change the action. So, in the case the ammo is equal to 11, turn off bulletIndicator1. In case the ammo is equal to 10, turn off bulletIndicator2, and so on."

> *Step 6: Create a new function to handle the UI for the bullet indicators. It should look something like Figure 19.23.*

```
void UpdateBulletUI()
{
    switch (bulletsInClip)
    {
        case 11:
            bulletIndicator12.enabled = false;
            break;
        case 10:
            bulletIndicator11.enabled = false;
            break;
        case 9:
            bulletIndicator10.enabled = false;
            break;

        case 1:
            bulletIndicator2.enabled = false;
            break;
        case 0:
            bulletIndicator1.enabled = false;
            break;
        default:
            break;
    }
}
```

FIGURE 19.23 Function using a Switch Statement to turn UI off depending on how many bullets are left in the clip. Notice the break part way down (it's a long function), but the pattern should be clear.

Why?

Notice that the last chunk of code there is:

```
default:
        break;
```

That's actually pretty important and required to make sure the game doesn't crash if something goes wrong. It's an easy part of a Switch statement to forget...but don't.

> Step 7: Tell PlayerControlScript when to fire this new function. When the bulletsInClip count is changed (up where the player hits Fire1 and it checks for the active weapon), the script needs to fire the new UpdateBulletUI() function (Figure 19.24). Save and return to Unity.
> Step 8: Test. Play the game and fire the pistol. As the player fires, the UI should update with individual shell icons switching off (Figure 19.25).

```
if (activeWeapon == "Gun" && canFireBullet)
{
    if(bulletAmmo > 0)
    {
        bulletAmmo--;
        bulletsInClip--;

        UpdateBulletUI();

        ellenGunAnimator.SetTrigger("attack");
        Rigidbody clonedBullet;
```

FIGURE 19.24 Telling the script to fire the UpdateBulletUI() function when the bulletsInClip amount changes.

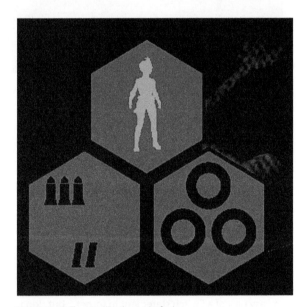

FIGURE 19.25 Changing UI as the pistol is fired.

Step 9: Turn the bullet indicators back on after reload. The script already contains an IEnumerator BulletReload() that resets the bulletsInClip to 12. Here is the natural place to flip all the indicators back on. Save and return to Unity (Figure 19.26).

Step 10: Test. Back in Unity, fire until the pistol needs to reload. After it has done so, the UI elements should turn back on.

```
IEnumerator BulletReload()
{
    ellenGunAnimator.SetBool("needReload", true);

    yield return new WaitForSeconds(1.3f);

    ellenGunAnimator.SetBool("needReload", false);
    canFireBullet = true;
    bulletsInClip = 12;
    bulletIndicator1.enabled = true;
    bulletIndicator2.enabled = true;
    bulletIndicator3.enabled = true;
    bulletIndicator4.enabled = true;
    bulletIndicator5.enabled = true;
    bulletIndicator6.enabled = true;
    bulletIndicator7.enabled = true;
    bulletIndicator8.enabled = true;
    bulletIndicator9.enabled = true;
    bulletIndicator10.enabled = true;
    bulletIndicator11.enabled = true;
    bulletIndicator12.enabled = true;
}
```

FIGURE 19.26 Turning the bullet indicators back on after reload.

> Step 11: Expand BulletReload so that when the player reloads from a clip, it turns off one of the clipIndicators. The code shown in Figure 19.27 is at the bottom of BulletReload().
>
> Step 12: Turn the clip indicators back on when the character picks up an ammopack. ResetBulletAmmo() is the function where the bulletAmmo is reset, so this is a natural place to turn the clip indicators back on (Figure 19.28). Save, return to Unity, and test.
>
> Step 13: Create function with Switch statement to turn off grenade indicators (Figure 19.29).

```
if(bulletAmmo == 24)
{
    bulletClipIndicator1.enabled = false;
}
if(bulletAmmo == 12)
{
    bulletClipIndicator2.enabled = false;
}
```

FIGURE 19.27 Checking to see how many bullets are left, and based on that number, turning off the resulting clip UI.

```
public void ResetBulletAmmo()
{
    bulletAmmo = 36;
    bulletsInClip = 12;
    canFireBullet = true;

    bulletIndicator1.enabled = true;
    bulletIndicator2.enabled = true;
    bulletIndicator3.enabled = true;
    bulletIndicator4.enabled = true;
    bulletIndicator5.enabled = true;
    bulletIndicator6.enabled = true;
    bulletIndicator7.enabled = true;
    bulletIndicator8.enabled = true;
    bulletIndicator9.enabled = true;
    bulletIndicator10.enabled = true;
    bulletIndicator11.enabled = true;
    bulletIndicator12.enabled = true;

    bulletClipIndicator1.enabled = true;
    bulletClipIndicator2.enabled = true;
}
```

FIGURE 19.28 Turning the clip indicators back on when the character has loaded up on ammo.

```
void UpdateGrenadeUI()
{
    switch(grenadeAmmo)
    {
        case 2:
            grenadeIndicator1.enabled = false;
            break;
        case 1:
            grenadeIndicator2.enabled = false;
            break;
        case 0:
            grenadeIndicator3.enabled = false;
            break;
        default:
            break;
    }
}
```

FIGURE 19.29 Updating the grenade indicators.

```
if (activeWeapon == "Grenade" && canFireGrenade)
{
    if(grenadeAmmo > 0)
    {
        grenadeAmmo--;
        UpdateGrenadeUI();
        ellenGrenadeAnimator.SetTrigger("attack");
        Rigidbody clonedGrenade;
```

FIGURE 19.30 Updating the grenade indicator UI whenever the number of grenades change.

```
public void ResetGrenadeAmmo()
{
    grenadeAmmo = 3;
    dummyGrenade.GetComponent<MeshRenderer>().forceRenderingOff = false;
    canFireGrenade = true;

    grenadeIndicator1.enabled = true;
    grenadeIndicator2.enabled = true;
    grenadeIndicator3.enabled = true;
}
```

FIGURE 19.31 When new grenades are picked up, the UI indicates it.

> *Step 14: Fire the UpdateGrenadeUI() function*
> *whenever the number of grenades change*
> *(Figure 19.30). Just find where grenade--; is, and*
> *that's the place to update the code.*
> *Step 15: Turn the grenade indicators back*
> *on when the player picks up new ammo.*
> *This is done currently in the script in the*
> *ResetGrenadeAmmo() function (Figure 19.31).*
> *Save and return to Unity.*
> *Step 16: Test. At this point, all of the ammo UI should*
> *be working.*

Health UI

Thus far in this tutorial, the process has been switching
UI images on and off by enabling/disabling the Image
component. But UI can be manipulated in many more
ways. Although we won't deal with it here, UI can have
its material adjusted, it can be animated, and it can have
animated masks (just to name a few of the things it
can do).

```
using System.Collections;
using System.Collections.Generic;
using UnityEngine;
using UnityEngine.UI;

public class PlayerHealthScript : MonoBehaviour
{
    public int health = 100;
    public RectTransform healthIndicator;

    public void DoDamage(int damageAmount)
```

FIGURE 19.32 Storing the RectTransform that will be adjusted when the health changes.

For now, we'll look at adjusting the size of an element – the HealthIndicator as the layer's health value changes. To do this, we will work with something called RectTransform.sizeDelta. RectTransform = Rectangle Transform, and it is the 2D paradigm that the sprites of UI work within.

Step 17: Open PlayerHealthScript.
Step 18: Add UnityEngine.UI; to its libraries.
Step 19: Create a new variable called healthIndicator that will store a RectTransform (Figure 19.32). Save and return to Unity.

Why?

Yes, we could be storing healthIndicator as a GameObject, or as an Image, or as a host of other things. But by storing it as a RectTransform, we can save quite a few keystrokes later when using RectTransform.sizeDelta.

Step 20: Plug in the HealthIndicator object into the Health Indicator input field in Player Health Script.
Step 21: Make health equal the sizeDelta (Height) of healthIndicator. Do this back in PlayerHealthScript. Add the line shown in Figure 19.33.
Step 22: Add the same line to the DoHealing() function since the health value changes there as well and the UI should change to show it (Figure 19.34). Save and return to Unity.
Step 23: Test and pick a fight with an EllenEnemy. As her bullet hits the player, the UI for the Health indicator should decrease (Figure 19.35).

```
public void DoDamage(int damageAmount)
{
    health = health - damageAmount;
    healthIndicator.sizeDelta = new Vector2(50, health);

    if (health <= 0)
    {
        print("yer dead!");
    }
}
```

FIGURE 19.33 Using RectTransform.sizeDelta to tie the Height of the HealthIndicator to the actual value of health. Remember that the size of the health indicator was 50 wide and 100 tall.

```
public void DoHealing(int healingAmount)
{
    health = health + healingAmount;
    health = Mathf.Clamp(health, 0, 100);
    healthIndicator.sizeDelta = new Vector2(50, health);
}
```

FIGURE 19.34 Updating the Height of the HealthIndicator when health goes back up as well.

FIGURE 19.35 On the losing side of a fight with EllenEnemy. As health goes down in the script, the UI changes to alert the player.

Tutorial Conclusion

That's it. Once the UI has been set up, tying things together so that numbers actually affect the UI is not difficult, if the developer can just track down when the numbers change. Once that's understood, the UI can be changed (in our case) by turning things on and off and changing the size.

But that's not all. Coming up, we'll start to use UI to create buttons and move between levels.

Tutorial 19.3: Buttons and Moving between Scenes

This tutorial will focus on interactivity of UI elements. We will also use it to show how to move between scenes so we can have an intro scene, the game scene (our current MainLevel), and a Game Over scene.

Step 1: Create a new scene (File>New Scene). Immediately save the Scenes folder as "IntroScene".

Step 2: Populate for beauty. Figure 19.36 is one solution. Just some quick notes: after creating the new level, to get the scene completely black we changed the Main Camera's Volume Layer Mask: Nothing, Probe Layer Mask: Nothing. Then the Directional Light and Sky and Fog Volume were deleted. Assets from the prefab folder were assembled and some new lights put into position. Build as you'd like. However, buttons will run down the left side of the screen in this example, so an offset composition can be useful.

Step 3: Import button UI elements. In the support files for this chapter are four button images in a folder called ButtonAssets. Import all those assets (or the entire folder) into the UIElement folder of the Project.

FIGURE 19.36 IntroLevel using prefabs already in the project.

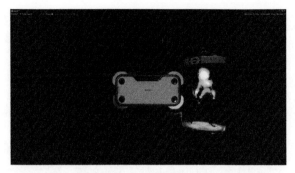

FIGURE 19.37 Using an imported image to define the regular state of a button.

Step 4: Change the Texture Type (import settings) to Sprite (2D and UI) for all four.

Step 5: Create a UI Canvas (GameObject>UI>Canvas). In the Inspector, change its Canvas Scaler to UI Scale Mode: Scale with Screen Size and Reference Resolution X: 1920, Y: 1080.

Step 6: Create a UI Button (GameObject>UI>Button). Rename it "StartButton".

Step 7: Set the Anchor and Pivot to the Center/ Middle. This will stick the button right in the middle of the screen.

Step 8: Use button_normal as the Source Image. With StartButton selected in the Hierarchy, drag button_normal from the UIElements/ ButtonAssets folder into the Image>Source Image input field. Still in the Image section, click the Set Native Size button (Figure 19.37).

Step 9: Use Sprite Swap. Still in the Inspector, scroll down to the Button component. Change Transition: Sprite Swap.

Why?

The default mode for Transition is Color Tint. This can work fine as it will change the color of the button as the mouse moves over the button, or the player clicks it. But we have prepared other versions of the button to control these states. These will allow for a more sophisticated visual effect.

Step 10: Test. Play the game and click that button to see how the sprite states work.

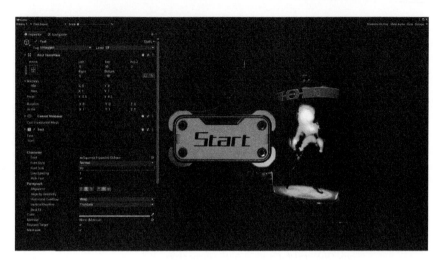

FIGURE 19.38 Changed UI Text using a new font.

Step 11: Download and import a custom font. Unity works well with TrueTypeFonts (.ttf). There are thousands of free.ttfs online (1001freefonts.com, and others). Just Google "free ttf," and loads of options will present themselves. When the font it downloaded, it will likely be in a.zip archive. Unzip before import. Import is easiest here by dragging the fonts from the Finder into the Project window. And of course, fonts are small, so grab multiple fonts while looking for the right one.

Step 12: Change the text to "Start" and use a new font. Expand the StartButton and see that there is a child UI Text object there. The text can be changed in the Inspector. There, the font, the font size, the alignment, and color can easily be changed (Figure 19.38).

Tips and Tricks

The Text UI can be a little tricky. There is a temptation to put text in and then just scale the text up using the Scale tool, but this always results in crummy looking fonts. The correct thing to do is increase the Font Size setting in the Inspector. In fact, sometimes the best thing to fix crummy fonts is making the Font Size much, much bigger, and then scaling the object down. This will provide sharp fonts.

The other things that's tricky about the UI Text is that sometimes as the font size gets big, the text just disappears. The reason for this is that the text has grown larger than the Rect built to hold it (the text box). Figure 19.39 shows the Rect Tool active, and the little blue dots (highlighted in red) show the bounds of the Rect. Dragging those blue handles will increase the size of the Rect (text box), and it can become big enough to show the text again.

> *Step 13: Move StartButton over to the left. Do this with the Move Tool (Figure 19.40).*
>
> *Step 14: Duplicate StartButton, rename it QuitButton, and adjust font and position to match Figure 19.41.*
>
> *Step 15: Create a new UI Text. GameObject>UI>Text. It might be hard to see (small and dark gray), but for now rename it "Title" and use the Anchor Presets to set it to Middle/Center.*
>
> *Step 16: Change Title's Font and Color. Use a white color for now.*
>
> *Step 17: Use the Rect Tool to move the Title up to a location above the buttons. Change the font to something much bigger (Figure 19.42 is using a Font Size: 180). Remember the Rect Tool may be*

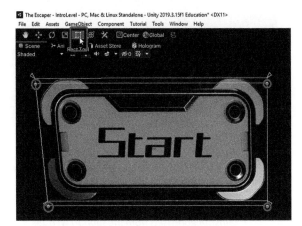

FIGURE 19.39 Rect Tool and the handles created to adjust the text box.

FIGURE 19.40 Moving the StartButton over to allow for other text.

FIGURE 19.41 Duplicated button to create QuitButton.

FIGURE 19.42 Title in place.

needed to scale the Rect (text box) big enough to contain the larger text.

Step 18: Use InstructionAssets to create instructions for the player. This is all review: import InstructionAssets from the support website. Set all to Sprite (2D and UI). Use UI Images

FIGURE 19.43 Providing instructions on how to play for the player. Adjust to taste.

> *(Pivot/Anchor on Middle/Center). Arrange and label with UI Text (Figure 19.43).*
> *Step 19: Save, and let's make some script!*

Interactive Buttons

Up to now, we have been leveraging the built-in components of the UI Button. There are two parts to each by default: the graphical element, and the Text overlaid on that button. The text can be deleted altogether if desired. The graphical part of the button has several components built in. We've already looked at the Image section, and have interacted a bit the Button part (Figure 19.44) – this is where we defined the various states of the Sprite Swap. However, the important thing now is at the bottom of the Button component: On Click().

OnClick() does what you would guess: when the player clicks on this button, what should happen? This can be a rich environment full of complex interactions, but for this book the focus will be on firing a particular function on a particular object. In this situation, the particular functions the buttons will fire will either move us onto the game or quit it altogether.

> *Step 20: Create a new empty GameObject and call it "ScriptHolder". It's location is unimportant in the scene.*
> *Step 21: Create a new C# script called "MenuInteractionScript" and apply it to ScriptHolder. Open MenuInteractionScript.*

```
using System.Collections;
using System.Collections.Generic;
using UnityEngine;
using UnityEngine.SceneManagement;
```

FIGURE 19.44 In order to load different levels/scenes in Unity, we must use the SceneManagement library.

```
public class MenuInteractionScript : MonoBehaviour
{
    public void LoadMainLevel()
    {
        SceneManager.LoadScene("MainLevel", LoadSceneMode.Single);
    }
```

FIGURE 19.45 Creating the mechanism to load the MainLevel scene.

```
public void QuitGame()
{
    Application.Quit();
}
```

FIGURE 19.46 Function to quit the game.

Step 22: Add a new library to allow for the management of scenes in Unity (Figure 19.44).

Step 23: Create a new function: LoadMainLevel() and match Figure 19.45.

Step 24: Create another function that quits the game (Figure 19.46). Save and return to Unity.

Step 25: Tie the buttons to these new functions. First, select StartButton in the Hierarchy. In the Inspector, scroll down to the Button component and click the + button. Drag ScriptHolder from the Hierarchy into the input field that reads None (Object). Finally, click on the No Function pulldown menu and choose MenuInteractionScript>Load MainLevel() (Figure 19.47).

Step 26: Repeat for QuitButton; only make sure it uses MenuInteractionScript>QuitGame().

Why?

In both of these situations, this only works if the functions are public (which both LoadMainLevel() and QuitGame() are).

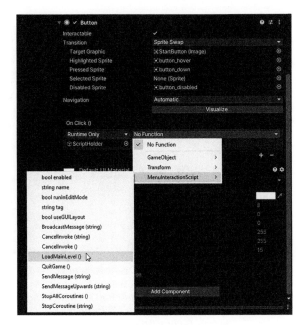

FIGURE 19.47 Making the StartButton fire the LoadMainLevel function in the MenuInteractionScript when it is clicked.

> *Step 27: Set up Build Settings so the SceneManager can do its work. Select File>Build Settings. In the Build Settings window, drag (from the Inspector) IntroLevel and MainLevel into the Scenes In Build Section (Figure 19.48). Close the Build Settings window.*

Why?

In Unity's vernacular, a "Build" is the actual game that a player would play. It will contain the executable and all other needed files to run the game. The Build Settings window allows developers to decide which platform to build to (bottom left) and which Scenes to actually include. If this isn't filled out to include MainLevel, then the LoadMainLevel() function would not work.

> *Step 28: Test the Start button. Save IntroLevel (File>Save) and then play the game. When the Start button is clicked, after a brief pause, the MainLevel should show and the game is on!*

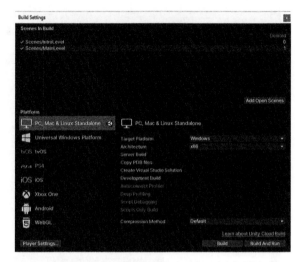

FIGURE 19.48 Assigning the levels created that should be included in the build.

> *Step 29: Make a build to test the Quit button. Again, open File>Build Settings. Click on the Build button. Unity will then ask where to place the build. DO NOT build this in the Project folder. Instead, go to the Desktop; create a new Folder (give it a name) and click Select Folder. Unity will then start the process of assembling all the necessary assets (Figure 19.49).*

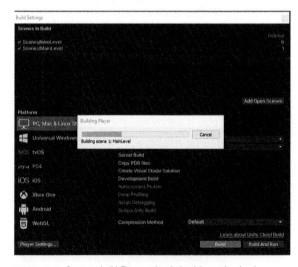

FIGURE 19.49 Creating a build. This can take a little while, so take a break.

Why?

Application.Quit() can only be tested on a build. So in order to make sure that Quit button works, a build has to be output.

Even though Unity suggests that the build be put in the Unity Project folder; it's usually best to build elsewhere. Builds are only distributed to players, and it will be important to just have the important stuff included. Building to a new folder on the desktop is an easy way to make sure all the necessary assets (and nothing else) are in one location.

> *Step 30: When the build is done, launch it (The Escaper), and try the Quit button.*

Tying Up Some Loose Ends

We now know some things that will be important for other aspects of the game. We need a You Lose screen and a You Win screen. We can quickly create those by duplicating and adjusting this IntroLevel. But we also need to start making sure that the game knows when to show these levels. In the following steps, we'll tie up all those issues to make sure that when the players health <= 0, the LooseLevel will launch and when the player hits Escape, the game will quit.

One thing that we'll leave undone is the WinLevel. In the next and last chapter, we will create the final boss battle, and the WinLevel will be brought up then when the boss has been defeated.

> *Step 31: Duplicate IntroLevel twice. Name one "LoseLevel" and the other "WinLevel".*
> *Step 32: Open each and adjust (Figures 19.50 and 19.51). Delete things not needed, rearrange buttons, etc. Notice that the StartButton remains the same, but the text has been changed to "Try Again?". But since trying again just means launching MainLevel, no code needs to be changed.*

FIGURE 19.50 The LoseLevel. No new coding needed here, just a rearrangement of UI pieces.

FIGURE 19.51 The WinLevel. No new coding need here, just a rearrangement of UI pieces.

Step 33: Add both to the Build Settings. File>Build Settings. It doesn't matter which order they are in, but IntroLevel needs to be first (Figure 19.52).

Step 34: Open MainLevel. And open PlayerHealthScript.

Step 35: Adjust PlayerHealthScript to include the SceneManagement library, and the command to load the LoseLevel when health is less than 0 (Figure 19.53). Save and return to Unity.

Step 36: Test and get shot. Pick a fight with EllenEnemy and lose it. When health is 0, LoseLevel should pop up, and importantly, the Play Again? Button will start the game again.

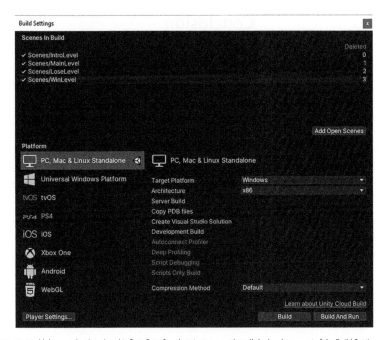

FIGURE 19.52 Make sure that IntroLevel is first. But after that, just ensure that all the levels are part of the Build Settings.

```
using System.Collections;
using System.Collections.Generic;
using UnityEngine;
using UnityEngine.UI;
using UnityEngine.SceneManagement;

public class PlayerHealthScript : MonoBehaviour
{
    public int health = 100;
    public RectTransform healthIndicator;

    public void DoDamage(int damageAmount)
    {
        health = health - damageAmount;
        healthIndicator.sizeDelta = new Vector2(50, health);

        if (health <= 0)
        {
            SceneManager.LoadScene("LoseLevel", LoadSceneMode.Single);
        }
    }
}
```

FIGURE 19.53 Adjustments to make sure the game is over when health drops below 0.

Conclusion

And suddenly we have a game! Almost. Currently, there is a lose state, but no way to win. In the next chapter, we will build the final boss battle and make sure that the security cameras work so the player has a way to win.

In this chapter, a new UI was built that clued the player into their health and ammo levels. New levels to start the game, replay when the player loses, and replay when the player wins have been established. UI layout has been covered, and the ability to make buttons actually do work has been illustrated.

UI can do a lot more than this; in fact, in the next chapter we will look at one more way to use it other than overlaying it on the screen. But with the current tools covered here, UI is now in your toolbox.

CHAPTER 20

Boss Battle

It's time for the *rumbling timpani's, lightning, lens flares* FINAL BATTLE!! In this chapter, we'll quickly build the basis of the boss battle and see how to win the game. Now this brings up an important issue of game play that we haven't touched: balance.

Balance is the idea that the game is fun to pick up and difficult to master. This is an idea in the early days of Pong and later Atari that Nolan Bushnell put forward. It was the reason why everyone wanted to lay their quarters at the altar of a video game cabinet.

Today, balance is as important as ever. An overpowered player, or weapon, or mechanic, or boss can take all the fun out of a game. AAA developers spend a long time working through the details of how balanced a game is. Is it too hard? Is it too easy? Where is the balance?

Unfortunately, in the confines of a book, it is difficult to effectively analyze, let alone build and test balance. This will be up to you. Instead, we will focus on the mechanics of the weapon and the boss. That means this final battle might turn out to be too easy (or too hard), and it will be up to you so adjust the speed, etc. to make it fun.

But enough with the caveats. Let's get to building game play.

Tutorial 20.1: Final Boss

In this tutorial, we will look at using a multitude of skills we've built up over this book. There will be a sort of simplistic AI of the boss looking at the player (with a bit of a delay). We will use IEnumerators to build in a sort of timer so that the boss fires a rocket every 3 seconds. We will use Instantiate to create new clones to come after the player, new health and new ammo packs to revitalize the player. We will expand what we know about UI to create a health bar that is locked in 3D space to the boss. And finally, when it's all done and the player has triumphed, the game will be over and the player congratulated on their win.

Step 1: Open MainLevel and maneuver to the FinalBoss Room.
Step 2: Adjust the hierarchy of the hero prefab. In the Project window, find the hero prefab (not the imported fbx). It will likely be in the Prefabs/Modular Pieces folder. Double-click it to open it in the Prefab Editor (Figure 20.1).

Why?

Ideally, all the geometry comes from the modeler all set up for animation, or coding. But usually the modeler doesn't know the final use of the model, and it's really beyond their concern. So, it is not unusual to receive

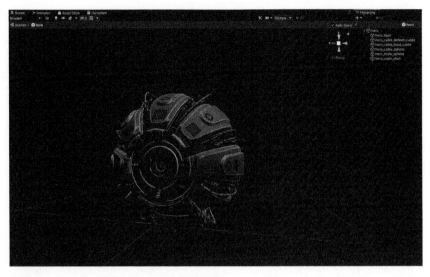

FIGURE 20.1 Prefab editor for hero.

an asset similar to this where all the parts are separate meshes, but not organized in a way to allow for the movement we would want. But by editing the prefab, we can organize the geometry in its hierarchy so that we can animate the boss as needed.

The play is to make the boss' upper sphere part rotate within the base. The base, of course, should remain still.

> Step 3: In the Hierarchy, make hero_middle_sphere, hero_outer_shell, and hero_cable_front_cable children of hero_cable_sphere. Do this by dragging each onto hero_cable_sphere (Figure 20.2).

Why?

Why the hero_cable_sphere? At the top of the Unity interface is the ability to change whether Unity is showing the axis of a selected object at its Pivot or Geometric Center (Figure 20.3). We have looked at this briefly before, but here it is especially important. This needs to read Pivot (click it if it reads Center). Regardless of where Unity shows the pivot (in the case of showing the handle at the Center),

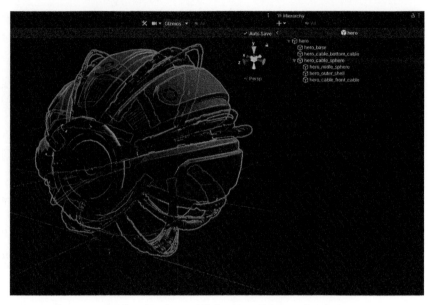

FIGURE 20.2 Creating a simple rig by making objects a child of an object with the axis in the right place.

FIGURE 20.3 There are times when showing the gizmo at the geometric center is useful, but when trying to find its actual rotation point, make sure the gizmos are set to show the actual Pivot.

the actual pivot of the object (and the point around which Unity rotates an object) does not change. If the gizmo is displayed at the actual pivot, you can see where script would actually rotate the object.

With the gizmo showing the actual pivot of objects, move through the different parts of the hero. Most of the objects have their pivot in a spot that isn't centered at the middle of the bigger sphere shape. The one that does is hero_cable_sphere. So, quickly making everything a child of that object makes sure that all of the top part of hero rotates around an appropriate pivot.

By the way, if there isn't an object with a good pivot, another option here would be to create a new empty gameObject, place it at the desired pivot of rotation, and make the desired objects a child of this gameObject. Then, in code, we would rotate the gameObject and all would rotate around the axis desired.

Step 4: Return to MainLevel. Click the Scenes button at the top left of the Prefab Editor window.

```
public class FinalBossScript : MonoBehaviour
{
    Transform player;
    public float followSpeed = 3f;
    Transform rotationPoint;

    private void Awake()
    {
        player = GameObject.FindGameObjectWithTag("Player").transform;
        rotationPoint = transform.Find("hero_cable_sphere").transform;
    }

    private void FixedUpdate()
    {
        Vector3 relativePos = player.position - rotationPoint.transform.position;
        Quaternion toRotation = Quaternion.LookRotation(relativePos);
        rotationPoint.transform.rotation =
            Quaternion.Lerp(rotationPoint.transform.rotation, toRotation, followSpeed * Time.deltaTime);
    }
}
```

FIGURE 20.4 The start of FinalBossScript.

> *Step 5: Move the FPSController into the FinalBossRoom. This will allow for testing the final boss battle without having to play all the way through the game to get there. Save and return to Unity.*
> *Step 6: Create a new C# called "FinalBossScript". Create the code shown in Figure 20.4.*

Why?

The first part of the script should look familiar. It creates three variables, the first to store who the player is (that we populate in the Awake() function), the second to store a number (a float) called followSpeed that we give an initial value of 3 to (although this could be changed later), and the last to store where the rotation should happen from. Then in the Awake, we populate the player variable and the rotationPoint.

After that, lots of new things happen. First, notice that we have a function called FixedUpdate(). FixedUpdate() happens every frame, but happens after Unity has calculated all the commands that are part of Update() in this or other scripts. By using a FixedUpdate() method, we can be sure that this code is being sure to know where the player is before starting to calculate where to work.

The first two lines in this function are some vector math that we don't want to get into in this volume, but the line

```
Vector3 relativePos = player.position - transform.position;
```

is defining a new Vector3 (position) by subtracting the boss' vector3 from the player's.

The line after that

```
Quaternion toRotation = Quaternion.LookRotation(relativePos);
```

is calculating a new rotation value (as a Quaternion) that is derived using LookRotation to define where the object should rotate towards (where it should "look at").

And then, finally, a crazy line that uses something called "Lerp." Lerp is actually a contraction for "linear interpolation." In this case, it means that it will change the rotation over time (linearly interpolate between two values) from its current position (rotationPoint.transform. rotation) to a new rotation value (toRotation). It gets its speed from followSpeed, and Time.deltaTime makes sure the speed is the same on a supercomputer and your grandma's computer as it measures the speed by time (not by frames). Notice that this line is actually one line of code (check out where the ";" is), but for screenshot purposes it is broken into two lines (which will still work).

We've already used LookAt(), and that could work here as well. But LookAt() updates every frame, and this would mean that the boss was locked onto the player every frame (and it would be difficult for the boss to miss). By creating a Lerp function, there is a little delay that will visually make the boss move like a bigger piece of machinery and give the player a fighting chance.

> *Step 7: Apply FinalBossScript to hero. And test (Figure 20.5).*
> *Step 8: Add a GrenadeLaunchPoint to hero. Open the hero prefab in the Prefab Editor by double-clicking hero in the Project window. Create a new*

FIGURE 20.5 With the new FinalBossScript, hero should rotate to follow the player.

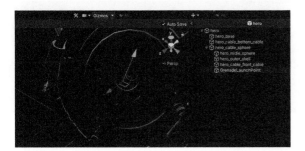

FIGURE 20.6 Creating a new grenade launch point and ensuring it is appropriate in the Hierarchy.

empty GameObject and place it just in front of the front barrel of the hero (Figure 20.6). Rename it "GrenadeLaunchPoint" and make it a child of hero_cable_sphere. Return to Scenes.

Why?

Although we could make the grenade script ignore the collider of the hero, it's easier to reuse the same script, and simply make sure that the grenade (that we're about to instantiate) is created outside the sphere to begin with.

Step 9: Edit FinalBossScript. Create the variables to store the grenade, grenade speed, and the launch point. Populate the launch point with script for now (Figure 20.7).
Step 10: Create an IEnumerator called "FireWithDelay()" (Figure 20.8).

```
Transform rotationPoint;

Transform grenadeLaunchPoint;
public Rigidbody grenade;
public float grenadeSpeed = 30f;

private void Awake()
{
    player = GameObject.FindGameObjectWithTag("Player").transform;
    rotationPoint = transform.Find("hero cable sphere").transform;
    grenadeLaunchPoint = transform.Find("hero_cable_sphere/GrenadeLaunchPoint");
}
```

FIGURE 20.7 Creating necessary variables for the grenade launching process.

```
IEnumerator FireWithDelay()
{
    while (gameObject)
    {
        Rigidbody clonedGrenade;
        clonedGrenade = Instantiate(grenade, grenadeLaunchPoint.position, grenadeLaunchPoint.rotation);
        clonedGrenade.velocity = grenadeLaunchPoint.TransformDirection(Vector3.forward) * grenadeSpeed;

        yield return new WaitForSeconds(3f);
    }
}
```

FIGURE 20.8 Creating a loop that fires a grenade every 3 seconds.

Why?

While loops perform work as long as a condition is met. In this case, while(gameObject) means: "While this gameObject exists, keep doing the work in my curly brackets." The work contained in those curly brackets should look familiar as it was copied/pasted from the player's grenade launcher mechanism. Then, the line to wait 3 seconds is added as the last part of the work to do.

Step 11: For now, tell this coroutine to get going when the game starts (Figure 20.9). Save and return to Unity.
Step 12: Test and play. Be sure to plug in the Grenade prefab, but then the boss should be following the player and firing a grenade every 3 seconds.

```
private void Start()
{
    StartCoroutine(FireWithDelay());
}
```

FIGURE 20.9 Temporarily allowing the Boss to fire grenades right way.

```
public void StartFiring()
{
    StartCoroutine(FireWithDelay());
}
```

FIGURE 20.10 Creating a public function that will actually start the boss firing rockets.

Tips and Tricks

Depending on the lighting scheme you are currently working with, that grenade could be a little tough to see. Consider opening the Grenade prefab and adding a light (or two) on the back of the grenade. Generally, make sure these are cheap (don't turn on shadows, etc.). Small things like this can help make the visual effect more interesting and let the player know when the grenade is on its way.

> Step 13: Rework FinalBossScript so that the FireWithDelay() IEnumerator only gets started when a new function (StartFiring()) is triggered (Figure 20.10). This is easily done by changing Start to StartFiring and making the new function public.

Why?

For testing, having the boss firing grenades at the start of the game works fine. However, when this game really starts, the boss shouldn't be firing rockets every 3 seconds at the player when they are on the other side of the facility. This should only happen when the player walks into the FinalBossRoom.

> Step 14: Create a new Box Collider (trigger) that makes the boss start firing only when the player enters the FinalBossRoom. Do this by creating a new empty GameObject, placing it just inside the door to the FinalBossRoom, and adding a Box Collider component to it. Be sure to mark Is Trigger to on (Figure 20.11).
> Step 15: Create a new script "FinalBossRoomTrigger". Figure 20.12 shows what this script should do. Save and return to Unity.
> Step 16: Add FinalBossRoomTrigger to the BossTrigger object. Plug in the Boss variable with hero.

717

FIGURE 20.11 Trigger at the entrance to the FinalBossRoom that will start the boss firing.

```
public class FinalBossRoomTrigger : MonoBehaviour
{
    public GameObject boss;

    private void OnTriggerEnter(Collider other)
    {
        if(other.gameObject.tag == "Player")
        {
            boss.GetComponent<FinalBossScript>().StartFiring();
            Destroy(gameObject);
        }
    }
}
```

FIGURE 20.12 Creating a trigger script so that when the player enters the room, the boss gets busy and starts firing.

> Step 17: Test by starting with FPSController out in the hallway (the boss should not be firing grenades), and then walking into the room (when the boss should start firing every 3 seconds).

Why?

Probably you've noticed by now that even if the boss is firing grenades at the player, the player currently takes no damage. This is because up to now, only the player could fire a grenade, and the grenade doesn't know how to do damage to the player yet. This will be fixed in a second, but first let's build a health script for the boss.

FIGURE 20.13 Added Sphere Collider to the hero.

> *Step 18: Add a Sphere Collider to hero (Figure 20.13). Notice this is the parent-most object (hero) that doesn't have any collider. Also notice that this will likely break the boss for a bit as the GrenadeLaunchPoint is likely inside of this collider (and thus would cause any grenades to explode).*

Why?

Without a collider, this boss won't know when it's been hit by the player's grenades or bullets.

> *Step 19: Create a new C# script called "FinalBossHealthScript". Have it mimic the other health scripts we have previously constructed (Figure 20.14). Save and return to Unity.*
> *Step 20: Apply FinalBossHealthScript to hero.*
> *Step 21: Create a new tag of Boss and apply it to the hero. Remember that this is actually a two-step process. First, using the Tag pull down menu (on hero), use Add Tag…to create the new tag, and then come back to assign this new tag to hero (Figure 20.15).*
> *Step 22: Make the grenade to damage to both the boss and player. This is done by editing the GrenadeScript (creating in past tutorials).*

```
public class FinalBossHealthScript : MonoBehaviour
{
    public int health = 300;

    public void DoDamage(int damageAmount)
    {
        health = health - damageAmount;

        if (health <=0)
        {
            print("I'm the boss and I'm dead");
            //Instantiate broken version of boss
            //Wait for a bit, and then end the game
        }
    }
}
```

FIGURE 20.14 Creating the start of FinalBossHealthScript. Notice that the comments are leaving notes on what this will do in the future.

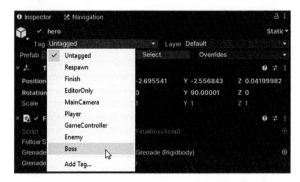

FIGURE 20.15 Creating and then assigning a tag of Boss to hero.

> Just add the two sections to check for Boss and Player (Figure 20.16).
> Step 23: Repeat for BulletScript (although this will only need the lines to affect objects tagged as Boss) (Figure 20.17).

Why?

Couldn't this be done more elegantly? Heck yes. If the enemy, boss, and player shared the same healthscript, it wouldn't take quite so many lines of code here. However, in a learning situation where we are layering one idea on top of another, this sort of clumsy approach here is necessary. Later, as you build your own games, you will find efficiencies we have not taken advantage of here.

```
public class GrenadeScript : MonoBehaviour
{
    public GameObject explosion;

    private void OnCollisionEnter(Collision collision)
    {
        if (collision.gameObject.tag == "Enemy")
        {
            collision.gameObject.GetComponent<EllenEnemyHealthScript>().DoDamage(50);
        }

        if (collision.gameObject.tag == "Boss")
        {
            collision.gameObject.GetComponent<FinalBossHealthScript>().DoDamage(50);
        }

        if (collision.gameObject.tag == "Player")
        {
            collision.gameObject.GetComponent<PlayerHealthScript>().DoDamage(50);
        }
        Instantiate(explosion, transform.position, transform.rotation);
        Destroy(gameObject);
    }
}
```

FIGURE 20.16 Adding the ability to do damage to both the Boss and Player.

```
public class BulletScript : MonoBehaviour
{
    private void OnCollisionEnter(Collision collision)
    {
        if (collision.gameObject.tag == "Player")
        {
            collision.gameObject.GetComponent<PlayerHealthScript>().DoDamage(10);
        }

        if(collision.gameObject.tag == "Enemy")
        {
            collision.gameObject.GetComponent<EllenEnemyHealthScript>().DoDamage(10);
        }

        if (collision.gameObject.tag == "Boss")
        {
            collision.gameObject.GetComponent<FinalBossHealthScript>().DoDamage(10);
        }

        Destroy(gameObject);
    }
}
```

FIGURE 20.17 Adjusting BulletScript to do damage to the boss.

Tips and Tricks

In the process of creating a new collider around hero, you may discover that suddenly the grenades explode in the face of the boss. This is because the grenades are instantiating inside the new sphere collider, and when they hit the collider, they explode. Coincidentally, they are also doing damage to the boss. If this is happening in your game, be sure and move GrenadeLaunchPoint outside the Sphere Collider of hero.

> *Step 24: Test and see if the player can lose and the boss take damage. At this point, the grenades launched from the boss should explode when they hit the player and do damage. Pretty quickly, the player should lose the game. Similarly, select the hero so that the FinalBossHealthScript can be seen in the Inspector. As the player hits the boss with bullets or grenades, the health value should go down.*

Boss Health Bar

A health bar isn't a new idea; we created one for the player earlier. However, that health bar is in screen space. In this part, we will look at a different way to work with UI that locks a piece of UI to geometry in the scene. Specifically, we'll put the health bar on the boss so that the player can see how healthy the boss is.

> *Step 25: Create a new UI Canvas (GameObject>UI>Canvas). Rename it "FinalBossUI_Canvas".*
> *Step 26: Configure the Canvas to Render Mode: World Space with the FirstPersonCharacter as the Event Camera. Remember FirstPersonCharacter is a child of FPSController (in the Hierarchy) and is actually the camera (Figure 20.18).*

Why?

A Render Mode of World Space means that this UI isn't locked into the screen space but rather exists in the 3D space of the game. This means it can (and needs to be) moved and scaled into place as it will remain locked to a location in 3D space.

> *Step 27: Add a Panel UI to the FinalBossUI_Canvas. Select FinalBossUI_Canvas and choose GameObject>UI>Panel. Change the new panel*

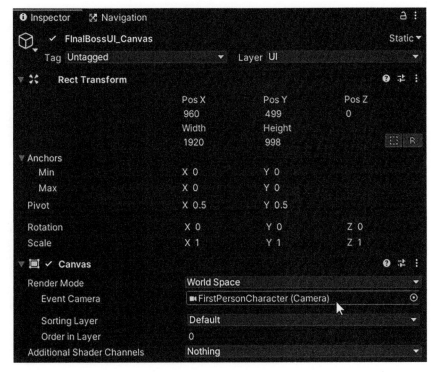

FIGURE 20.18 Setting the new Canvas to exist in World Space (not screen space).

> *to be green and probably no alpha (opaque). Hit F to frame it (it'll be huge).*
> *Step 28: Resize FinalBossUI_Canvas so that Width: 300 and Height: 30. Select FinalBossUI_Canvas and then make these adjustments in the Inspector (Figure 20.19).*

Why?

You can probably guess why we're doing this, but the idea here is to make sure that the Width value is the same as the health value of the boss. This will make resizing the bar a simple matter. Notice that we are leaving the Anchor/Pivot at middle. This will make the progress bar scale from the middle (not an end).

> *Step 29: Move and scale FinalBossUI_Canvas into place in from of the boss. Remember, this time use the Move (W), Scale (R), and Rotate (E) tools*

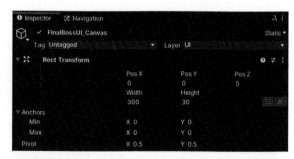

FIGURE 20.19 Setting up some easy-to-manipulate Width and Height settings for the FinalBossUI_Canvas.

FIGURE 20.20 Moving the FinalBossUI_Canvas into place.

to get it where it needs to be (Figure 20.20). Do not change the Width and Height settings.

Tips and Tricks

Remember that, by default, the Canvas is HUGE. It will need to be scaled, way, way down to get it small enough to fit the scene again. A helpful tip is to make FinalBossUI_Canvas a child of hero. Then select it and in the Inspector change Left, Top, Pos Z all to 0. Hit F to frame it and then scale and it should scale down centered on the hero. Be sure to move it so it is not the child of hero when it is set up as it should be.

Step 30: Create a new material and call it HeroHealthBar_Mat. Assign this material to the Material input field of the Panel (that is a child of

FIGURE 20.21 Adjustments to the UI Panel to give a bit o' glow to the Panel.

```
using UnityEngine;
using UnityEngine.UI;

public class FinalBossHealthScript : MonoBehaviour
{
    public int health = 300;
    public RectTransform healthBar;

    public void DoDamage(int damageAmount)
    {
        health = health - damageAmount;
        healthBar.sizeDelta = new Vector2(health, 30f);

        if (health <=0)
```

FIGURE 20.22 Tying the Width of FinalBossUI_Canvas to the health of the boss.

the FinalBossUI_Canvas). Play with the material
(try HDRP/Unlit with some emissions) until
satisfied (Figure 20.21).

Step 31: Tie the boss' health to the FinalBossUI_
Canvas. Reopen FinalBossHealthScript and make
the changes highlighted in Figure 20.22. Save
and return to Unity.

Step 32: Test. As the player shoots anything and hits
the boss, the health bar should shrink.

Final Theatrics

At this point, the game knows what to do when the
player's health is 0 or less (it shows LoseLevel). Now we
need to build in the ability to win the game – which will
happen when the boss' health is 0 or less. To add some
excitement to this, we'll make the boss break up with
some explosive force.

There are some fantastic shatter plugins available on the
Unity Asset Store. However, they can be a little expensive.

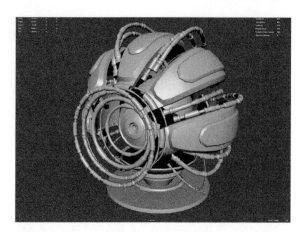

FIGURE 20.23 The deconstructed version of the hero in Maya.

So to work around this, Figure 20.23 shows some work done back in Maya. Although we won't do it here as a tutorial, the file is included in the support files (BossHeroDecontructed.mb). The inner-most sphere was split apart using Maya's Shatter (FX|Effects>Shatter) to split it into a few different parts. Shatter in Maya is pretty old and notorious for crashing (pretty tough to work with actually); so, if shattering forms is important to your game, it would be worthwhile looking at some of the many other shatter scripts available online for Maya, or buying one of the solutions on the Unity Asset Store.

Other than the inner sphere, the hero asset has been separated into its separate shapes and moved so that they aren't overlapping. This will keep errors from happening when we apply physics to all these shapes. Feel free to take a look at the file from the support files if interested.

The plan is that when the hero's health is 0 (or less), we will swap out this version of the hero with all its separated parts. We'll give a bit of explosive force and watch all the parts fly off.

> *Step 33: Download and import DestructedHero. fbx from the support website. Alternatively, you could download the Maya file and export it manually; but the export is the FBX. Import it into the Models folder of the project.*

Step 34: Use current materials for the model. In Unity, select the imported FBX DestructedHero. In the Inspector, click the Materials Tab. Now use the same materials used on the non-destructed hero for this version of hero. These materials will likely be in the Materials folder. If you're in a fancy mood, create a new material for the shatterInterior (maybe with some red glow) and use that for the shatterInteriorSI material (Figure 20.24). Click Apply.

Step 35: Add colliders and rigidbodies to all the parts. Drag DestructedHero out into the Scene (doesn't really matter where). In Hierarchy, expand DestructedHero and select all of the parts beneath it. In the Inspector, add a Mesh Collider and a Rigidbody component to all of them at the same time. Make sure Mesh Collider has Convex checked (Figure 20.25).

Step 36: Make a prefab out of DestructedHero. Remember do this by dragging the edited version from the Hierarchy into the Prefabs folder of the Project. Delete DestructedHero from the scene.

Step 37: Adjust FinalBossScript to make the switch (Figure 20.26).

Step 38: Test (Figure 20.27). Play the game and win… hit the boss so that it's health drops below 0 and see it fall apart as the destructed version (with its colliders and rigidbodies) comes into existence.

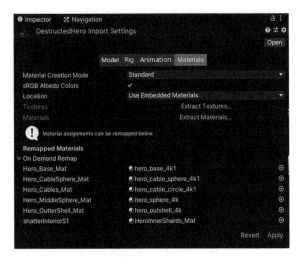

FIGURE 20.24 Mapping existing materials on the newly imported FBX.

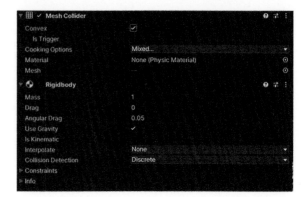

FIGURE 20.25 Setting up the parts of DestructedHero to all have Mesh Colliders and Rigidbodies.

```
public void DoDamage(int damageAmount)
{
    health = health - damageAmount;
    healthBar.sizeDelta = new Vector2(health, 30f);

    if (health <=0)
    {
        Instantiate(destructedHero, transform.position, transform.rotation);
        Destroy(gameObject);
    }
}
```

FIGURE 20.26 Swapping out the destructed version of the hero when its health is 0 or less.

FIGURE 20.27 Destructed version falling apart.

Step 39: Create a "ScriptHolder" gameObject (an empty GameObject).
Step 40: Create a new script called GameOverScript (Figure 20.28).

```
using System.Collections;
using System.Collections.Generic;
using UnityEngine;
using UnityEngine.SceneManagement;

public class GameOverScript : MonoBehaviour
{
    public void GameOver()
    {
        StartCoroutine(EndGame());
    }

    IEnumerator EndGame()
    {
        yield return new WaitForSeconds(3);
        SceneManager.LoadScene("WinLevel", LoadSceneMode.Single);
    }
}
```

FIGURE 20.28 GameOverScript.

```
if (health <=0)
{
    Instantiate(destructedHero, transform.position, transform.rotation);
    GameObject.Find("ScriptHolder").GetComponent<GameOverScript>().GameOver();
    Destroy(gameObject);
}
```

FIGURE 20.29 Allowing the BossHealthScript to fire the GameOver function in GameOverScript.

Step 41: Let FinalBossScript fire the GameOverScripts'
GameOver() function (Figure 20.29).

Why?

We haven't used GameObject.Find("Name of Object") very often. It can be expensive to have the game search the entire level for an object by name. So we'd never (for instance) have this in an Update() function. But in this case, since it's only going to happen once, it makes things pretty speedy to write this sort of code.

However, it will be important that the name of the script holder is *exactly* "ScriptHolder".

We've made this separate ScriptHolder gameObject because the FinalBossHealthScript destroys itself (actually destroys the gameObject that the script is attached to) and so wouldn't be around to let the player see the destruction they have wrought. But having the FinalBossHealthScript call out to another object

```
using System.Collections;
using System.Collections.Generic;
using UnityEngine;
using UnityEngine.SceneManagement;
using DG.Tweening;

public class GameOverScript : MonoBehaviour
{
    public CanvasGroup whiteOut;
    public Camera playerCam;

    public void GameOver()
    {
        StartCoroutine(EndGame());
    }

    IEnumerator EndGame()
    {
        playerCam.DOShakePosition(1f, 1, 10, 90f, true);
        yield return new WaitForSeconds(3);

        whiteOut.DOFade(1f, 3f);
        yield return new WaitForSeconds(3.5f);

        SceneManager.LoadScene("WinLevel", LoadSceneMode.Single);
    }
}
```

FIGURE 20.30 Some adjustments to the GameOver script (just as an example of how it could be expanded).

(that won't be destroyed) means that script (GameOver) can take care of business after FinalBossHealthScript is gone.

> *Step 42: Test.*
> *Step 43: Create a Build. See if the WinLevel and LoseLevels work. You should notice a problem that when WinLevel or LoseLevels launch, there is no mouse/cursor.*
> *Step 44: Adjust MouseInteractScript to include the Start() function shown in Figure 20.30.*

Why?

The FPSController hides and locks the mouse. Without unlocking and showing it when the Game Over screens appear, it remains hidden and the player is unable to click any of the buttons.

> *Step 45: Move FPSController back to the beginning point of the game, and play through it, making notes of needed balance adjustments.*

```
public class MenuInteractionScript : MonoBehaviour
{
    public void Start()
    {
        Cursor.lockState = CursorLockMode.None;
        Cursor.visible = true;
    }

    public void LoadMainLevel()
```

FIGURE 20.31 Unlocking and showing the cursor for the GameOver scenes.

Conclusion

Of course, there are lots of other things that can be done to help make this final scene more climatic. Figure 20.31 shows an adjusted version of the GameOver script that includes shaking the camera, and a whiteout.

There are lots of other things that could be done with what you know now. There should be a sound cue of an explosion when the boss falls apart. Maybe the boss spawns new EllenEnemy's every 5 seconds. Maybe boss only takes damage if it is hit right in the red eye. Could there be spawn points around boss that provide health and ammo for the player if the battle becomes longer? Could parts of the floor fall away through battle that would lead to death if the player stepped on them? Maybe the boss' version of the grenades does splash damage if it lands near the player. The list goes on and on.

At this point, all of the above suggestions are possible with your current knowledge level. It now boils down to your ambition, and how the game should be balanced.

The game is now complete. It can be adjusted (and should), but it has health systems all around, a win state, and a lose state. Take what you know and build on to make a sophisticated experience for the player.

A version of the game with a few adjustments is included on the support website. Grab hold of that and pick apart things that you want to include in your version. Reverse-engineering is a powerful way to learn new coding tricks, and breaking apart someone else code can yield treasures you wouldn't have stumbled upon otherwise.

Index

Note: *Italic* page numbers refer to figures.

Advanced Skeleton and Rapid Rigs 410
AI
    animation events and working weapon
        631–638
    assembling MainLevel 639–642, *639*, *640*
    creating AI-based "tic-tac" 605–614
    game engines 603
    tools 604
    using animations (animator) with NavMesh
        615–631
AI-based wayfinding
    adding UnityEngine 608, *609*
    allowing AI *613*
    awake() function 609
    baked NavMesh 606, *606*
    capsule 607, *607*
    changing color and drawing 613, *613*
    defining NavMeshAgent 608, *609*
    laying groundwork 608, *608*
    long-term strategy 608
    making a variable 609, *611*
    NavMeshAgent 605
    results of OnDrawGizmosSelected 611,
        611, *612*
    speeding up development time 610, *611*
    using OnDrawGizmosSelected() and
        Gizmos.DrawWireSphere() 611, *611*
    wire spheres shown 613, *613*
AI health system
    allowing EllenEnemyHealthScript 653, *654*
    baking root transform position (Y) 656, *657*
    capsule collider settings 651, *652*
    checking health and playing, death
        animation 655, *656*
    creating new tag 651, *652*, *653*
    damage Enemy-tagged objects 653, *654*
    deleting components and resetting
        triggers 656, *657*
    edited BulletScript 653, *654*
    health stays down 658, *658*
    review of hard work completed 655, *655*
    strange happenings our animator 655, *656*

    trigger parameters 655
AITest 604, *604*
alphas usage 108, *110*
Ambient Occlusion 98
ammo; *see also* trail renderer
    adjustments 662, *662*
    after creating needReload parameter
        663, *664*
    checking grenades, before firing 662, *662*
    creating script, counts 661, *661*
    EllenGrenadeController 663, *664*
    flipping needReload boolean 665, *665*
    health script, bullets 659
    making BulletReload() 663, *663*
    mechanics 659
    reloading 666–668, *666–668*
    subtracting one from grenadeAmmo
        661, *661*
    variables 659, *660*, *660*
anchor points 104, 105, *105*
animating camera
    adding rotation property 536, *537*
    CameraAnimationChooserScript 542, *542*,
        543, *543*
    creating new clip 540, *540*
    current state 541, *541*
    enabling recording mode 537, *538*
    enumerators 543
    final animation 539, *539*
    finished animation 540, *540*
    keyframes 537, *537*, 538, *538*, *539*
    limited functionality 535, *536*
    organization 534, 535, *535*
    pacing 539
    setting new default empty state 541, *542*
    setting up transitions 542, *542*
animation 420–421
    pipeline 442
animation events/working weapon
    awkward implementation 635–638,
        636–638
    concepts 631

animation events/working weapon (*cont.*)
creating function to fire *633, 634,* 632–634
launch point 632, *633*
new material settings 632, *632*
tools 634
application programming interface (API)
defined 498
instantiation 498–499, *499, 500*
scripting reference 498
area light 215, *215,* 229, *229*
arm controls set up
rigging 400–402, *400–402*
arm joints creation 376, *376,* 377, *378*
asset movement process 148
atlas 74
attack animation 431–433, *432, 433*
Autodesk Maya 1
automatic UV 89
auto rigging
adjusting base map color tints 453, *453*
Mixamo 443–449
placed scene with cheater light 451, *451*
plugged textures to create materials
451, *452*
setting up animator 454–464
setting up subsurface scattering, skin
shader 451, *452*
substance painter output 449–450, *450*
subsurface scattering effects *452,* 453, *453*

baked mesh data 101
Bake pivot 366
baking 93, 97–98
camera adjustments and postprocessing
236–241, *236–240*
character texturing 322, *322,* 323
error 322
expensive calculations 233
hallway prebaked and postbaked 235, *236*
lightmap information 233
quick settings 234, *235*
setting lights in each prefab 233, *234*
baking animation keys
constraints 505, 506, *506*
culling process 508
deletion 506, *507*
game engine 507
rig-centric tools 503
setting rotation keys 503
simulation options 505, *505*

swapping to animation mode 503, *504*
warnings and errors 507
balance 709
balance skin variation 327, *328*
base color, PBR 99
base floor creation 44–54, *45–47, 49–54*
belt, character modeling 287, *288*
belts, straps, pockets, holster, and boots
353–354, *353, 354*
bevel command 288, *289*
bevel tool 9, *10*
binary system 43
binding joints 400
bind skin 391, *392*
blending mode, definition 101
blendshape 296
body, character modeling 268–273, *268–273*
body adjustment, character modeling 292, *293*
Boo 466
boots, character modeling 287, *288, 289*
boss battle
added sphere collider 719, *719*
adjusting BulletScript 720, *721*
assigning and creating tag 719, *720*
creating loop 715, *716*
creating simple rig 711, *712*
creating variables 715, *716*
final boss 710–722
FinalBossScript 713, *713,* 714, *715,* 719, *720*
final theatrics 725–730
FixedUpdate() 713
grenade launch point 715–716, *715*
health bar 722–725
multitude skills 710
pivot/geometric center 712, *712*
prefab editor 710, *711*
public function 717, *717*
temporarily allowing boss 716, *716*
trigger 717, *718*
unlocking and showing cursor 731, *731*
box modeling 7, 245
bridge tool 25
brush, short cuts to tweak 103–104
built-in functions 467–468, 483, *483*

C#
addding script to scene, after compiling
475, *476*
API 498–500
class declaration 467

comments 467
DOTween 486–488
empty script example 466, *466*
HelloWorldScript creation 474, *474*
libraries 466
methods/functions 467–468, *469*
pinned console 473, *473*
print command to Update() 477, *477*
print line of code, fired every frame 477, *477*
syntax 469–470
undisputed preferred language 466
Unity and visual studio 470–472
variables 489–498
cables base material 121, *121*, 123
camera configuration *418–421*, 418–419
camera extras
    adding spotlight 553, *554*
    build the code 557, *558*
    closed-circuit 553
    color attribute 556, *557*
    DefaultRenderTexture 556, *557*
    extracted monitor screens 554–555, *555*
    mechanics 553
    placed cameras 558, *559*
    placing screen object 556, *556*
    prefab, placed and configured 558, *559*
    process, Maya 555–556
    rendering 554
Canvas Scaler 673, *675*
carbon fiber 124, *125*
Center Pivot 40
Change Pivot 40–41
Channel Box 8, *8*, *9*, 27, 389
    input stack of 15, *17*
Channel Box editor 424, 434
character, gaming 243
character modeling 243, 297, *297*
    belt 287, *288*
    body 268–273, *268–273*
    body adjustment 292, *293*
    boots 287, 288, *288*, 289, *289*, 290
    clean up 295, *295*, 296, *296*
    concept art 244, *244*
    ear 264–265, *264–265*
    eyeball 247–249, *247–249*
    eyelids creation 249–253, *250–252*, 253
    eye socket creation 253, 254, *254*, 255
    forehead 257, *257*
    gloves 289, 290, *291*
    hairs 281–284, *281–284*

hands 274–281, *274–281*
head 262–264, *262–264*
image plane setup in Maya 245–247, *246*
internal structures 267, *267*
mouth 261, *261*
neck 265, *266*
nose 256, *256*, *257*, 258, *258–259*, 260, *260*
outer garment base 285, *286*
polycount 245
preview materials 286, *287*
style sheet 244
sweater 284, 285, *285*, *286*
watch 290, *292*
watchband 292, *293*
weapon 292–294, *293*, *294*
workflow 245
character rig 414–415
characters making 243
character texturing 321–323
    baking 322, *322*
        error 322
    belts, straps, pockets, holster, and boots
        353–354, *353*, *354*
    chest logo 363, *364*
    export 322–323
    Export Textures 365–367, *366*, *367*
    eye 333–340, *335–341*
    gloves 354–360, *355–360*
    gun 363, *364*
    hair 331–333, *331–333*
    import the model 322
    leather material 353, *353*, *354*
    metal bolts 365, *365*
    pants 348–352, *349–352*
    skin texturing 323–329, *324–329*
    upper body 340–347, *342–348*
    watch 361–362, *362*
character UV mapping 300
    body 302–308, *303–308*
    cleanup process 302
    eye 308–309, *309*
    garment 312–319, *313–317*
    hair 309–311, *310*, *311*
    mesh inspection 300–302, *301*, *302*
Checker Map 318
checker texture 58, *59*, *60*
chest logo, character texturing 363, *362*
chest weighting 394, *395*
Circularize Components 21
class declaration 467

clavicle and body controls 406–409, *406–409*
clavicle and shoulder joint 377, *377*
cleaning up odd jitters 428
cleanup process
    character modeling 295, *295*, 296, *296*
    character UV mapping 302
click-dragging 422
clipping planes 553
color distribution 323, 324–325, *325–326*
color setting 117
color variation 327, *328*
Combine and Separate 33–34, *33*
Combine command 33–34
comments 467
Component Editor 395, *397*
concept art 244, *244*
constrains 402
controlling animations
    creating transition 518, *519*
    defining transition 520, *519*
    placing an animation clip *517*, 518
    plugging Animator Controller 517, *517*
    visual graph-making and coding 516
controlling animator with code
    animation ranges 529, *529*
    applying changes to FPSController 529, *529*
    creating and populating variables 522, *523*
    creating boolean 524, *524*
    creating pathways 524, *525*
    defining situation 526, *527*
    Input Manager 521, *522*
    pseudocode 521
    script listen (every frame) 520, *521*
    swapping 529, *531*
    transition settings 524, *525*, 525, *526*
    triggering 523, *523*
    turning booleans on and off 526, 527, *528*
    updated script 529, *530*
Control Vertices (CV) 34, *34*
cookies
    adjusted emissive color 230–231, *232*
    applying changes, instances of prefab
        227, *228*
    directional light 232, *232*
    emissive shaders 231, *232*
    first pass at area lights 229, *229*
    IES 224
    images 224
    import settings 225–226, *226*
    increasing Texture Atlas 224–225, *225*

overrides 228, *228*
placed area light 229, 229
prefab editor 231, *231*
shadow casting effect 223
spot light 227, *227*
copying, skin weighting 397–400
Create Cables or Pipes 34–36, *34–36*
curvature generator 120, *120*
curve tool 51–52
cutting process
    UV mapping
        hide the seams 316
        stretching 316
        texel density 316
cut UV 62, *62*
CV *see* Control Vertices (CV)

dark metal material 97, *100*, 102
decimal system 43
default blending mode 101
Delete Edge command 27, 30
deployment strategies 135
directional light 183, 212–213, *213*, 232, *232*
Display Layer Editor 415
display layers 415–418, *416–417*
dot syntax 469
DOTween
    adding libraries 488, *488*
    documentation 488
    setting up 486, *487*
    starting setup 486, *487*
    tweening tools 486
driver joint chain 400
Duplicate Faces command 16
Duplicate Special 39, *39*
Duplicate with Transform 38–39, *38–39*

ease-in's and ease-out's 429, *431*, *432*, 434
edge 4
    flow 257
    ring 10
    variation 344, *345*, *346*
edgewear effect 108, 112, *112*
Ellen_full_body_ref 392, 397–398
Ellen_sweater_geo 398
emission intensity 183–184
emissive channel 129, 131
exhale moment
    idle animation 427, 428
Export Textures 365–367

move the gun to origin 366–367, *367*
    testing 366–367, *366*
Extract Faces 33
extrude along a curve 37, *37*, *38*, 52
extrude tool 11, *11*, 13, *13*, 14, *15*
eye, UV mapping 308–309, *309*
eyeball, character modeling 247–249, *247–249*
eye-catching visual 1
eyelids creation, character modeling 249–253,
    250–252, *253*
eye socket creation, character modeling 253,
    254, *254*, 255

face 4–5
facial expression rig 296
fill layer 103
final theatrics
    adjustments to GameOver script 730, *730*
    allowing BossHealthScript 729, *729*
    deconstructed version 726, *726*
    destructed version falling apart 727, *728*
    explosive force 725
    FPSController 730
    GameOverScript 728, *729*
    mapping existing materials, imported FBX
        726, *727*
    setting up parts 727, *728*
    shatter plugins 725
    swapping out destructed version 727, *728*
finger controls 405, *406*
finger joints 379, 380, *380*, 381, *382*
fingers duplication 380, 381, *381*
first-person shooter (FPS) animation 413–414
    attack animation 431–433, *432*
    camera configuration *418–421*, 418–420
    character rig 414–415
    cleaning and preparing files 502
    cleaning up odd jitters 428
    display layers 415–418, *416–417*
    ease-in's and ease-out's 429, *431*
    frame rate 427, *427*
    game animations 420–421
    "Got Caught" animation 434–438, *436*, *437*
    Graph Editor 429–431, *430*
    idle animation *427*, 427–428
    Kassandra's animated files 502
    pose creation 421–422
    preparation (*see* Maya animation
        preparation)
    reload animation 438–439, *439*

save files 415
two-handed weapon setup 424–427, *426*
walk animation 433–434, *436*
weapon movement 422–424, *423*, *425*
FK *see* forward kinematics (FK)
FK arm setup 402
flipped faces 300
floor scratches 100, *101*
foot controller 390
foot hierarchy setup 390–391
foot roll rig 387–390, *389*, *390*
forehead, character modeling 257, *257*
forward kinematics (FK) 424
4096 × 4096 (4k) textures 96
4k (4096 × 4096) texture 74
FPS animation *see* first-person shooter (FPS)
    animation
FPS_Cam viewport 418, 419, *419*, 424
Fragment Shader 2
frame-miss 569
frame rate 427, *427*
Freeze Transformation 30
full-body joint skin weighting 396, *398*

game animations 420–421
game engines 128, 133–134
garment, UV mapping 312–319, *313–315*, *317*
generators 100, *101–123*, *102*, *104*, *105–121*
geometry errors 42–43
gizmos 3
glass materials 126, *126*, 127, *128*
gloves
    character modeling 289, 290, *291*
    character texturing 354–360, *355–361*
"gobo" 223
"Got Caught" animation 434–438, *436*, *437*
Grab and Smooth sculpting 263
grab tool 281
Graph Editor 429–431, *430*, 438
graphical user interface (GUI) *see* user
        interface (UI)
Graphic API 2
grenade launcher
    activeWeapon 565, *566*
    adding Capsule Collider 567–568, *568*
    adding variable 570, *570*
    Animator Controller 564, *565*
    creating and positioning,
        GrenadeLaunchPoint 569, *569*
    creating string variable 565, *565*

grenade launcher (*cont.*)
    float variable 571, *571*
    FPSController 564, *564*
    HDRP 562
    instantiation 570, *570*, 571, *571*
    line at Start() 566, *566*
    populated variables 570, *570*
    pressurized steam effects 563, *563*
    reworking 566, *566*
    Rigidbody component 568, *568*
    rising steam 563, *564*
    separating, structure of FPSController
        567, *567*
    smart 573–581
    tracking down 567, *567*
    using participle effects 563, *563*
    velocity magnitude 571, *573*
grenade launcher and pipe 440
grid 44, *44*
Grow Selection 32–33
Grunge Leak Dirty 99
gun
    character texturing 363, *364*
    joint 410

hairs
    character modeling 281–284, *281–284*
    character texturing 331–333, *332–333*
    UV mapping 309–310, *310–312*
hands, character modeling 274–281, *274–281*
HDRP *see* High-Definition Render
    Pipeline (HDRP)
head, character modeling 262–264,
    262–264
head skin weighting 393, *393*, 394, *395*
health bar 722–725, *723–725*
health indicator
    adjusted color 685, *686*
    aligning/moving 684, *684*
    changing the order 685, *686*
    desired size, using scale 684, *685*
    measurements 683
    setting pivot and anchor 683, *683*
healthValue 643
heel controller 390
height map, PBR 99, 111
hero assets 54
Hide Model 41
hide the seams, UV mapping 316

high-definition render pipeline (HDRP) 92–93,
    135–136
high dynamic range images (HDRI) 217

IDE *see* integrated development
    environment (IDE)
idle animation 420, 427–428, *428*
IK *see* inverse kinematics (IK)
IK arm setup 403–406, *403*, *404*, *405*
IK handle 385, 386, 387, *388*, 403
Illuminating Engineering Society (IES) 224
image plane setup in Maya 245–247, *246*
inhale moment, idle animation 427, 428, 429
instance 39
integrated development
    environment (IDE) 470
internal structures, character modeling
    267, *267*
inverse kinematics (IK) 383, 385, 386, 424

joint behavior *370*, 370–371
joint chain creation
    rigging 371–374
        neck 373, *374*
        root and spine joints 372, *373*
joint orient 376, 380
joint placement 371
    left arm 374–382, *375–382*
joint setup
    legs 383–387, *384–387*
    right arm 382–383, *383*

kitbashing
    building out extended floor 188, *189*
    building up walls 186, *186*
    built platform with stairs 192, *192*
    catwalks and stairs 196, *197*
    combinations of modules 194, *195*
    complicated module collection 193, *193*
    creating roof 196, *196*
    creating small armory 194, *194*
    dressed hallways 188, *188*
    dressed out CameraRoom 193, *193*
    dressedStorageHangar 197, *198*
    duplicating hall module 187, *187*
    filling in ceiling with floor prefabs 186, *187*
    finishing out room 191, *191*
    hallway module 185, *186*
    leveraging effective grouping 190, *190*

placed monitor *192*, 193
pre-built curved wall modules 188, *189*
process 185
putting ceilings 188, *189*
roughed out CameraRoom 191, *191*
StorageHangarEntry 194, *195*
StorageHangar floor mapped out 194, *195*
utilization 193, *194*
variations 190, *190*

labor-filled process 135
Lamina faces 43
layers, Substance Painter UI 97
layout
    adding extra visual interest 176, *177*
    adding trim 176, *178*
    creating ceiling 182, *182*
    defined 171
    door frames 181, *181*
    dressed set 184, *184*
    duplicated and snapped prefabs 175, *175*
    ensuring glass prefabs 182, *182*
    filling in corners 179, *180*
    geometric center of objects 178
    kitbashing 185–198
    level flow 172
    light streaming 183, *183*
    project settings 173, *174*
    roughing out door and windows 180, *180*
    snapping 176, *177*
    volumes 174
    wall placement 179, *179*
leather material, character texturing 353, *353*
left arm joint structure 374–382, *375–382*,
      405, *405*
left clavicle skin weighting 396, *399*
left foot controller setup 390, *390*
left foot rig setup hierarchy 390, *391*
leftHand_locator 435
left leg joint structure 385
legs joint setup 383–387, *384–387*, 388
lerp 714
levels, texturing 122–129, *123–129*
libraries 466
light direction 97–98
lighting
    area 215, *215*
    artistic functions 205
    baked 210–211

camera exposure 218, *219*
challenge 241, *242*
cookies 223–232
cubemap asset 217, *218*
description 209
directional 212–213, *213*
dirty volumetric and big rings 221
hardware-driven 210
HDRI-based skies 217, *217*
high-end software rendering solutions 210
mixed 211
physical-based rendering techniques 136
point 213–214, *214*
postprocessing effects 216
power of prefabs 219–223, *220–224*
real time 210
rendering calculations 210
spot *214*, 214–215, 221, *221*, 223, *224*
lighting probes 241–242
light intensities 165
linear interpolation 714
Locatorleftparent 1 435
locators 419

manipulation tools, translation 3–4
Map Size section 72
Mari 61
marking menu 4, 8, 26
Mask Editor 101
material adjustment
    adding finished lights to hallway 168, *169*
    adjusted shader 168, *169*
    adjusting camera 159, *160*
    adjusting intensity of point light 165, *165*
    auto exposure 159
    changing transparent shader 166, *167*
    duplicating floor to make ceiling 162, *164*
    emissive surfaces 159
    hallway created by duplicating section
      164, *165*
    measuring light intensities 166
    move/translate tool and snapping 162, *163*
    moving duplicated floor 161, *161*
    rotating placed wall module 162, *163*
    tracking down glass material 166, *166*
    transparency inputs 166, *167*
    unconvincing light 168, *168*
    vertex snap method 161, *162*
    virtual environments 159

material assignments, UV mapping 318, 320
material distribution, UV mapping 319, *319*
Maya animation preparation
    activating outliner 503, *503*
    adjusted positioning 512, *512*
    baking keys 503–508
    controlling animations 516–520
    controlling animator with code 520–531
    creating attack_anim animation clip
        516, *516*
    delete unseen geometry 503, *504*
    extracting materials 510, *511*
    idle animation clip, defining 515, *515*
    imported clips 516, *516*
    importing and adjusting rigs 514, *514*
    materials adjustment 510, *511*
    near clipping plane 513, *513*
    newly created Avatar 514, *515*
    substance painter output 508–510,
        509, *510*
Maya modeling
    anatomy
        edge 4
        face 4
        normal 5
        object mode 5
        vertex 4
    assignments 41–42, *42*
    base floor creation 44–54, *45–47*, *49–54*
    commands
        Center Pivot 40
        Change Pivot 40–41
        Combine and Separate 33–34, *33*
        Create Cables or Pipes 34–37, *34–36*
        Duplicate, Duplicate with Transform
            38–39, *38–39*
        Duplicate Special 39, *40*
        Extract Faces 33
        Extrude Along a Curve 37–38, *37–38*
        Grow and Shrink Selection 32–33
        Hide Model 41
        mirror 39, 40
        Snapping 41
        View Control 41
    geometry errors 42–43
    grid 44, *44*
    modular set pieces 43
    navigation 1–2, *2*
    normal 5, *6*
    rendering 2–3

rules
    polycount 6
    size and proportion 7
    topology 6, *6*
security camera modelling 7–32, *8–13*,
    15–29, *31*
3D model 3
translation 3–4
user interface 2, *2*
maya/substance painter, exporting asset
    asset movement process 148
    extracting materials 150, *151*
    geometry imported 146, *146*
    marquee select geometry freeze
        transformations 145, *145*
    normal maps 149, *150*
    NormalTexture 149
    shaders 147
    static meshes 144
    templates 148
    textures 147, *148*
mesh inspection, character UV mapping
    300–302, *301*, *302*
metal bolts, character texturing 364, 365, *365*
metallic, PBR 99
Metallic Grate Wide 99
metallic roughness 92
methods/functions 467–468, *467*
middle line problem 302, *302*
mirror 39, 40
mirroring, skin weighting 397, *399*
mirror joints 382–383, *383*
mirror plane, position 108
Mixamo
    defined 443
    download settings for Unity 448, *449*
    extract materials 449
    facial animation tools 443
    FBX 2013 444, *445*
    grab FBX files 448, *449*
    gun exporting 445
    imported version of character 445, *446*
    login and use Characters link 445, *446*
    motion-capture clips 464
    pistol/handgun locomotion pack 447, *447*
    placing markers 447, *447*
    sending EllenEnemyfbx 445, *446*
    UVed version of Ellen 443, *444*
Mixamo-exported MoCap animations 502
Modeling Toolkit 21, *22*

models arrangement 94, *95*
modular pieces, texturing 94
  export models 94, 95
  import to Substance Painter 95–96
  models arrangement 94, *95*
modular set pieces 43, 52, 53, *53*, *54*
motion capture (MoCap) 442, 443–449,
      444–447, *449*; *see also* auto rigging
motion trail 436, 437, *437*, 440
mouth, character modeling 261, *261*, 267, *267*
move tool 13, 14, *15*
Multi-Cut tool 21, 22, 260, 268, 269, 274, 278,
      279, 290, 301
multiple texturing files 95
multiply blending mode 101, 102

navigation 1–2, *2*, 97
navigation mesh (NavMesh)
  adjusting base offset 617, *618*
  adjustingNavMeshAgent 615, *616*
  AI mechanism 605
  Animator Controller 615
  changing triggers and Booleans 626–630,
      626, *627–630*
  creating boolean 619, *619*
  default NavMeshAgent 615, *616*
  magically floating 617, *617*
  measurements 615, 617
  mechanics 614
  placing animations in animator 621–626,
      622–626
  preparing FBX animation files 619–620,
      620, *621*
NavMeshAgent 605
neck
  character modeling 265, *266*
  joint chain 373, *374*, *375*
neck skin weighting 393, 394, *394*
N-gon 20, *20*, *21*, 43
  mesh inspection 300–301, *301*
non-manifold geometry 42
non-playable characters (NPCs) 603
normal detailing 109, *111*
normal map, PBR 99, 111–112, *112*
nose, character modeling 256, *256*, *257*, 258,
      258–259, 260, *260*
nostrils internals, character modeling 267, *267*
NURBS 34, 35, *35*, *36*, 37, 388, 416, *417*, 425

Object Mode 5, 31

one-man-army approach 108
opacity channel 126, 127, *127*
opening doors
  adding Box Collider component
      479–480, *480*
  adjusted collider 480, *481*
  creating a floor 478
  deleting unneeded functions 482, *483*
  placed Box Collider 480, *481*
  placed door prefab 478, *479*
  placed FPSController 478, *479*
  size and shape of collider 480, *481*
  trigger 480
Optimize command, body UV 305, *306*
orange panels 118
orient constraint 402
orient UV 64, *65*, 65
origin 2
outer garment base, character modeling
      285, *286*
outer shell 16, *17*
Outliner 31, 418, 423, 426
overlapping faces 301, *301*
overshoot pose 436

painted approach 115–116, *114*
painter texture outputs 450, 509
painting skin weights 391–396, *393–396*
panel, Substance Painter UI 97
pants, character texturing 348–352, *349–352*
parenting 31, 32
perspective view, image planes 246
Per Vertex Algorithm 356, *356*
photogrammetry 207, *207*
physically based camera systems 136
Physically-Based Rendering (PBR) 92–93
  material channels 98–100, *100*, *101*
pipe material 125, *126*
pivot positioning 45
pixels 65
planar projection 63
player health script
  adjusted BulletScript 647, *647*
  basic structure 644, *644*
  clamping health value 650, *650*
  collision 648
  damage box, testing purposes 645, *646*
  DamageBoxScript 645, *646*, 648
  DoDamage() function 645, *646*
  DoHealing() function 648, *648*

player health script (*cont.*)
   HealthPack prefab 649, *649*
   HealthPackScript 649, *650*
pod model, UV 74–89, *75–89*
point light 164, *165*, 203, *203*, 213–214, *214*
pole 247
polycount 6, 27, 245
   reduction methods 27, *28*, 29, *29*
polygon 2 334
Polygon Fill tool 116, 117
post script
   daytime lighting 206, *206*
   lighting schemes 205
   photogrammetry 206, *207*
   terrain 206, *207*
power of prefabs 219–223, *220–224*
Prevent Negative Scale setting 25
preview materials, character modeling 286, *287*
primitive polygons 14
procedural texturing 102, 334
proportion, 3D modeling 7

quad 3, *6*
Quad Draw Tool 250
   boots pattern and belt 287, 289
   eyebrow 284
   eyelids creation 249, *250*
   gun holster 294
   hair 282
   outer garment base 285

RaycastHit 544
raycasting 531, 571
   accuracy 593–600
   adjusted ReticleUI 596, *597*
   altered script 549, *551*
   animated camera in action 548, *550*
   applying changes 551, *552*
   assigning FPSController 549, *550*
   build, playground *545*
   concept 544–545
   console (every frame) 548, *549*
   creating UI image 594, *594*
   creating variable 599, *599*
   diagram, centered reticle and projectile-
      based weapon 596, *597*
   LineDraw 548, *548*
   mechanics 547, *547*
   placing ReticleUI in screen 594, *595*
   pointing launch points 600, *600*

problem, weapons system 596, *597*
projectile weapons 600, *601*
public variable 546, *546*
RaycastSource 545, *545*
reports back 548, *548*
results in game window 596, *596*
rotating weapon 598, *598*
smart camera 551, *551*
supersonic weapons 544
raytracing
   animating the camera 534–544
   description 533–534
referencing character rigs 414–415
referencing process 372
refine hand topology 278, *279*
refraction model 166, *167*
reload animation 438–439, *439*
Reload Reference 414
renderer 2
rendering process 2, 6, 20
reticle 419, 420, *420*
   assigned sprite and color adjustments
      677, *678*
   bullet indicators 681, *682*
   Canvas Scaler settings 675, *675*
   creating and placing GrenadeIndicator 1
      679, *680*
   creating clip indicators 681, *682*
   creating Health_FG UI element 679, *680*
   duplicating, renaming and positioning
      681, *681*
   establishing, Canvas and EventSystem
      674, *675*
   locking 677, *678*
   offsetting 679, *679*
   setting pivot 676, *677*
re-topologizing tool 250, 251; *see also* Quad
      Draw Tool
retopology 281, 285
returning 468
reverse-engineering 731
rigging 244, 369, 410, 411
   arm controls set up 400–402, *400–402*
   clavicle and body controls 406–409,
      407–409
   constrains 402
   final hierarchy 410, *411*
   finger controls 405–406
   foot hierarchy setup 390
   foot roll rig 387–390, *390*

gun joint 410
IK arm setup 403–405, *403–405*
joint behavior *370*, 370–371
joint chain creation 371–374
    neck 373, *374*
    root and spine joints 372, *373*
joint placement 371
    left arm 374–382, *375–382*
joint setup
    legs 383–387, *384–387*
    right arm 382–383, *383*
skin weights 391, *392*
    copying 397–400
    mirroring 397, *399*
    painting 392–396, *393–398*
right arm joint setup 382–383, *383*
root and spine joints 372, *373*
root_motion joint 391
root transform rotation 620, 628, *630*
rotate tool 18
roughness, PBR 99, 100

scale or snapping 48
scale tool 11, 13, 14, *15*, 79
screen space 672–674, *672*, *673*
scriptable rendering pipelines 135
sculpting software 93
sculpting tool 268, 281, 282
seam artifact 66
security camera, UV 66, *68*, 69, *70*, 70
security cameras 533
    modelling *7–29*, 7–32, *31*
Separate command 33–34
setting up animator
    assigning animator controller
        EllenEnemyController 456, *458*
    assigning EllenEnemyAvatar as Source
        avatar 455, *455*
    exporting animation 463, *463*
    gun in hand 461, *462*
    importing animation into animator 458, *459*
    import settings for pistol animations
        454–455, *455*
    import settings for rig 454, *454*
    inherit avatar from EllenEnemy 456, *457*
    making Ellen_Gun, child of right hand joint
        460–461, *461*
    positioning 460, *460*
    preparing pistol idle, renaming and
        looping 456, *458*

shifting to idle animation 458, *459*
shooting animation 461, *462*
Shaded viewing mode 303
shader 92–93, 126, 128, 129, *130*, 131
shape
    Maya model 22, 24
shape evolving 292, 293, *293*
Shift-click trick 346, 359
Shirk Selection 32–33
size, 3D modeling 7
skinned mesh renderer 460
skin texturing 323–330, *324–330*
skin weighting
    rigging 391, *392*
        copying 397–400
        mirroring 397, *399*
        painting 392–396, *393–398*
smart grenade
    creating code 573, *573*
    creating variable 575, *576*
    Destroy() command 574
    final animator layout 580, *581*
    IEnumerator 578, *578*, 579, *579*
    playing sound 575, *575*
    rebuilding 579, *580*
    self-destroy 574, *574*
    setting TinyExplosion 574
    setting up boolean 576, *577*
    transition settings 579, *580*, 580, *581*
    turning off 576, *576*
smart material 102–103
smoothness remapping 181
snapping 172–173
Snapping 41
"Snap to Projected Center" 379, *379*
Soften Edge command 10, *11*, 13, 14, 253
sourceimages folder 94
spacing 431
spot light *214*, 214–215, 220, *221*, *222*, 223,
    224, *227*
Standard Assets 199, 200
status bar, Substance Painter UI 96
Steel Gun Painted 124–125, *126*
Steel Painted Scraped Dirty 103, 104, 105,
    112, 113
straight lines drawing method 106
straps layer 122–123, *123*, *124*
stretching, UV mapping 316
style sheet 244
Subdivision Axis 27

Substance Painter 92, 93, 118, 322, 356, 363
    UI *96*, 96–97
substance painter output 450, *450*,
        508–510, *509*
sweater, character modeling 284, 285, *285*, *286*
symmetry 12, *12*
syntax 469

Target Weld Tool 28
tessellated NURBS 35, *36*
Tessellation section 35, 43
texel density 71–73, 80
    for other models *81–86*
    UV mapping 316
Texture Set List 97
texturing 91–92, 132
    Ambient Occlusion 98
    baking 93
    generators 100, 101–122, *102*, *104–107*,
            109–121
    levels 122–129, *123–129*
    light direction 97–98
    modular pieces 94
        export models 94, 95
        import to Substance Painter 96–97
        models arrangement 94, *95*
    navigation 97
    PBR 92–93
        material channels 98–100, *100*, *101*
    with photoshop 316
    rest of models 129, *130*, 131, *131*
    result of 129, *130–131*
    in Substance Painter 316
    Substance Painter UI *96*, 96–97
texturing software 61
3D Cut and Sew UV Tool 303
    arms and hands cutting 305
    ear cutting 303
    eyeball UV mapping 308
    hair 309
    sweater cutting 315
3D model 3
3D viewport, navigation 97
3D Cut and Sew UV tool 67
thumb and tip topology 274, *274*, *275*
Time Slider 422, 427, 428, *428*
timing 431
toggle symmetry 105, *106*
Toolbox 24
tools bar, Substance Painter UI 96

topology 6, *7*, 260, 263, 282
    error 302
trail renderer
    adjusting width and length 584, *585*
    BulletReload IEnumerator 589, *590*
    construction 587, *588*
    creating, naming and sizing GunBullet
            582, *583*
    creating and setting up material 586, *586*
    creating GunLaunchPoint 582, *583*
    creating variables 586, *587*
    deducting 1 from ammoCount 588, *589*
    destroy 588, *588*
    dragging 584, *585*
    ensuring 592, *592*
    filling variables 586, *587*
    hack-n-slash games 584
    new boolean parameter 591, *591*
    providing way out 593, *593*
    setting up transitions 590, *591*
    temporarily turning off 588, *588*
    turning on canFireBullet boolean 587, *587*
    waiting for 12 frames 588, *589*
transform, Maya model 22–24
translation 3–4
tri-planar projection 323
tube model 37
tweaked topology 269, *270*
2D viewport, navigation 97
256 × 256 floor piece 57, *58*
two-handed weapon setup 424–427, *426*

UI elements
    case switches/switch statements 688–693,
            689–693
    creating variables 686–687, *687*
    filled in variables 687, *688*
    health 693–695, *695*
    interactivity 696
UI panel 97
uneven UV distribution 310
Unity asset creation
    bit about Unity UI 140–143
    colliders 156–159, *157*
    creating empty HDRP project 139, *139*
    creating prefabs 155–159, *156*
    efficient layout 140, *140*
    exporting asset from Maya and substance
            painter 144–155
    game engines 133–134

levels of power 134
material adjustment 159–169
modules installation 137, *138*
optimizing layout 140, *140*
rebuilding materials 150–154, *152–154*
rendering pipelines 135
Unity Hub 136–137, *138*
Unity asset store 726
Unity-centric approach 466
Unity Hub 136–137, *138*
Unity level creation
    exit Prefab editor 205, *205*
    importing package 200, *201*
    layout 171–198
    long view 173
    organizing and prefab-manipulation
        techniques 172
    placed FPSController 200, *205*
    play button 204, *205*
    post script 206–207
    settings for point light 203–204, *203*
    snapping 172–173
    walking through 199–205
Unity UI
    game 141
    hierarchy 142
    inspector 142
    organized Unity project 143, *143*
    project 142
    scene 141
    streamlined project 143, *143*
universal render pipeline (URP) 135
unparenting 32
upper body, character texturing 340–344,
    341–348
upper shell hole 19, *19*
user interface (UI)
    buttons and moving between scenes
        696–707
    changed UI text 698, *698*
    defined 671
    duplicated button 699, *700*
    elements effect 686–696
    imported image 697, *697*
    interactive buttons 701–705, *702–704*
    Maya modeling 2, *2*
    moving StartButton 699, *700*
    providing instructions 701, *701*
    rect tool 699, *699*
    reticle, ammo and health 674–685

screen space 672–674, *672, 673*
title in place 699, *700*
tying up loose ends 705–707, *706–707*
visual effect 697
UV
    the floor 63–71, *63–71*
    for other models *81–89*
    pod model 74–89, *75–89*
UV Editor 57, *58,* 58, *59*
UV mapping 57, 297, 299–300, 319–320
    body UV 302–308, *303–308*
    character UV mapping 300
        mesh inspection and cleanup 300–302,
            301, 302
    cutting process
        hide the seams 316
        stretching 316
        texel density 316
    eye UV 308–309, *309*
    garment UV 312–319, *313–315, 317–319*
    hair UV 309–311, *310–312*
    materials arrangement 318, 319, *319*
UV points 59–60, *60*
UV random color 123
UV shell 64, 75, *76*
UV tiles 60–61, *60, 61*

variables, C#
    Audio Source component 496, *496*
    Audio Source settings 495, *495*
    declaration 489, *490*
    DOLocalMoveX function 491–492, *492*
    hold Audio Source 496, *496*
    information buckets 489
    instances 494, *494*
    moving the doors to open position
        490, *491*
    playing doorSound 497, *497*
    populating script 493, *493*
    private 489
    public 489, *490,* 490
    tweak and update 493
    using DOTween 491, *492*
Vertex 4
vertex snap method 161, *162*
video cards 210
View Control 41
viewport, Substance Painter UI 96
Viewport 2.0. 2
virtual environments 159

visual appearance 244
visual studio
    adding script 484, *485*
    applied SlidingDoorScript 484, *485*
    built-in function's 483, *483*
    code creation and editing 472, *472*
    coding, trigger 483, *484*
    color scheme 474
    format the function 483, *484*
    IDE 470
    installation 470
    interface 471, *471*
    libraries 471, *471*
    opening doors 478–485
    simple message coding 474, *475*
volumetric lighting artifacts 185

walk animation 433–434, *435*
wall models 118
watch
    character modeling 290, *292*
    character texturing 361, *362, 363*
watchband, character modeling 292, *293*
weapons
    character modeling 292–294, *293, 294*
    firing gun and ammo 582–593
    grenade launcher 562–582
    movement 422–424, *423, 425*
    raycasting 593–600
workflow, character modeling 245

ZBrush 61, 93, 245, 251, 282, 297
zero length edge 43

Printed and bound by CPI Group (UK) Ltd, Croydon, CR0 4YY

24/10/2024

01778301-0001